MACRO/MICRO
A BRIEF INTRODUCTION TO SOCIOLOGY

Lorne Tepperman
University of Toronto

Michael Rosenberg
Dawson College

With the assistance of Sandra Badin

Prentice-Hall Canada Inc.

Canadian Cataloguing in Publication Data

Tepperman, Lorne, 1943-
  Macro/micro: a brief introduction to sociology
ISBN 0-13-541723-6
1. Sociology.   I. Rosenberg, M. Michael.   II. Title.
HM51.T46 1991   301   C90-094675-X

© 1991 Prentice-Hall Canada Inc., Scarborough, Ontario

Credits are listed throughout the book and at the back of the book. Every reasonable effort has been made to find copyright holders. The publishers would be pleased to have any errors or omissions brought to their attention.

Prentice-Hall, Inc., Englewood Cliffs, New Jersey
Prentice-Hall International, Inc., London
Prentice-Hall of Australia, Pty., Ltd., Sydney
Prentice-Hall of India Pvt., Ltd., New Delhi
Prentice-Hall of Japan, Inc., Tokyo
Prentice-Hall of Southeast Asia (Pte.) Ltd., Singapore
Editora Prentice-Hall do Brasil Ltda., Rio de Janeiro
Prentice-Hall Hispanoamericana, S.A., Mexico

ISBN 0-13-541723-6

Copy Editor: Kat Mototsune
Coordinating Editor: Kelly Dickson
Production Coordinator: Anna Orodi
Cover Design: Dianna Little
Typesetting: Southam Business Information and Communications Group Inc.

    4   AGI   94 93

Printed and bound in the USA by Arcata Graphics Inc.

TABLE OF CONTENTS

Preface   i

Acknowledgements   iii

Chapter 1   **Sociology: The Study of Society**   2
- Personal Troubles, Public Issues   3
- Varieties of Science   6
- Sociology as a Social Science   11
- The Sociological Tradition   15
- Three Social Paradigms   17
- Sociology in Everyday Life   28
- Closing Remarks   30

Chapter 2   **Culture**   36
- Culture is Uniquely Human   37
- Culture Shapes Behaviour   43
- Language   49
- Cultural Integration   50
- Cultural Variation   52
- How Cultures Change   58
- Canadian Culture   59
- Closing Remarks   64

Chapter 3   **Socialization**   68
- Socialization is a Lifelong Process   69
- Becoming Social: Nature Versus Nurture   70
- Acquiring Social Knowledge   73
- Gender Socialization   82
- Agents of Socialization   84
- Socialization Over the Lifecycle   90
- Is There Anyone You Cannot Be?   94
- Closing Remarks   95

Chapter 4   **Deviance and Control**   100
- Deviance and Social Control   101
- Causes of Crime and Deviance   108
- Kinds of Deviant Behaviour   110

Participation in Deviant Activities 113
Class and Juvenile Delinquency 120
Responses to Crime and Deviance 123
Closing Remarks 128

Chapter 5 Social Inequality and Stratification 132
The Reality of Inequality 133
Types of Social Inequality 133
Patterns of Domination and Submission 134
Class 138
Status and Symbolic Resources 143
Social Mobility: Movement Within Stratification 146
Elite Domination 150
Poverty in Canada 156
Closing Remarks 159

Chapter 6 Ethnic and Race Relations 164
Canada's Ethnic Mosaic 165
The Concepts of Ethnicity and Race 167
Ethnic and Racial Groups in Canada 168
Patterns of Ethnic and Race Relations 176
Ethnic Boundary Maintenance and Survival 182
Prejudice and Discrimination 187
Racism 195
Closing Remarks 196

Chapter 7 The Family 202
The Family as a Context for Social Life 203
Perspectives on the Family 204
The Family: A Preliminary View 206
Analyzing Family Patterns 208
Marriage and Family in Canada 217
Problems of the Modern Family 222
The Future of the Family 231
Closing Remarks 233

Chapter 8 Work and the Economic Order 238
The Economic Order 239
The Industrial Revolution 240

Industrial Society 245

Max Weber and the Theory of Bureaucracy 249

Types of Work 256

Problems of Industrial Work: Anomie and Alienation 259

Closing Remarks 267

Chapter 9 Population 272

Population and Human Survival 273

Population Growth and Change 275

Fertility in Canada 282

Morality in Canada's Population 286

Patterns of Migration 290

Closing Remarks 296

Chapter 10 Social Movements and Social Change 302

Understanding Social Change 303

The Sociology of Social Change 304

Publics and Public Opinion 308

Social Movements 309

Types of Social Movements 311

Other Sources of Social Change 316

Global Change 326

Closing Remarks 330

Chapter 11 Methods of Research 334

Scientific Research is Rigorous and Objective 335

Basic Ideas of Social Research 336

Designing a Study 341

Measurement 348

Sampling 352

Data Collection Strategies 355

Closing Remarks 359

Visual Credits 364

Name Index 365

Subject Index 368

PREFACE

This book will introduce you to sociology, taking a multi-paradigm approach. We are going to move among paradigms, or sociological approaches, as smoothly as possible, to show the best of what all the major paradigms contribute to our understanding of social life. In this respect, we are going to be "foxes," not "hedgehogs."

OUR APPROACH: FOXLIKE SOCIOLOGY

Greek philosopher Archilochus remarked, "The fox knows many things but the hedgehog knows one big thing." The philosopher Isaiah Berlin (1978: 22) has expanded this thought to point to "one of the deepest differences which divide writers and thinkers and, it may be, human beings in general", that is, the difference between foxes and hedgehogs. Hedgehogs relate everything they learn to a single central vision or major organizing principle. Foxes "seize upon the essence of a vast variety of experiences for what they are in themselves, without . . . seeking to fit them into . . . any one unchanging, all-embracing . . . unitary inner vision" (Berlin, 1978: 22).

We have all had teachers who are foxes and teachers who are hedgehogs. Moreover, we have all read books by foxes and other books by hedgehogs, though we may not have realized it at the time. The difference between them is striking.

What's more, the gulf in thinking between foxes and hedgehogs is so great that it may produce unfortunate results. People who are foxes may consider people who are hedgehogs boring or simple-minded. People who are hedgehogs may think the people who are foxes are scatter-brained and careless. Each may view the other as an unsuccessful attempt to be like him- or herself: the fox as a second-rate hedgehog, the hedgehog as a failed fox.

One great merit of Berlin's analysis is that it includes a long list of eminent writers and thinkers who belonged to one or the other camp. By Berlin's reckoning, the hedgehogs have included such notable writers as Dante, Plato, Dostoevsky, Ibsen, Proust; the foxes have included Shakespeare, Aristotle, Montaigne, Goethe, Balzac, and Joyce.

We could probably make long lists of famous musicians, writers, actors, etc. who are hedgehogs, and other famous musicians, writers, actors, etc. who are foxes. For example: Bette Midler always plays Bette Midler in the movies (similarly, Barbra Streisand, Burt Reynolds, Jack Nicholson, and Bill Murray always play themselves). Some people call them lousy actors; others say they have "star quality." By our reckoning, they are hedgehogs—always trying to fit the details of their character into a single set of elements.

On the other hand, Meryl Streep *never* plays Meryl Streep—she is different in every movie role she plays. So are Robert deNiro, Paul Newman, Glenn Close, and Ellen Barkin. Some people say that proves they have no "star quality"; others say it proves they are better actors. We would say it proves they are foxes, not hedgehogs.

This may simplify what Isaiah Berlin meant but it does not miss his main point, which is that foxes and hedgehogs are, and will always be, different. Woe to the fox who longs to be a hedgehog, says Berlin; or the hedgehog who yearns for foxhood; and we agree. Success lies in doing well what you do best.

This book approaches sociology in a subtle, foxlike way. It revels in alternative explanations, in the counterpoint of powerful thinkers at odds, in the (as yet) open-endedness of most sociological enquiry. Our ground rules are simple:

- discuss the concepts that sociologists actually find useful;
- report findings that the data support and ignore the rest;
- answer questions that matter in people's lives;
- show how large and small processes – personal troubles and public issues – fit together; and
- never worry that we may have stepped out of one paradigm and into another.

Note that we have placed our chapter on research methods at the end of the book – not right after the introductory chapter, as many authors do. This is because we want to pull lots of rabbits out of hats – interest you in the issues and findings of sociology – before we tell you how sociologists do it. This final chapter will be particularly interesting to students who plan to take another sociology course or perhaps even carry out a research project themselves.

We do not expect our book to turn you all into sociologists, or even convert hedgehog-thinkers into foxes, but that does not matter. Simply, we want to give you our vision of the sociological enterprise and stimulate your own sociological imagination. If we succeed, you may want to go on and learn more about this fascinating field of ours, with its big questions and big answers. Enjoy!

ACKNOWLEDGMENTS

We would like to thank the people who helped us write this book.

First in line for thanks are our two research assistants, Sandra Badin and Andrew Tepperman. They spent the summer of 1989 digging material out of the University of Toronto library and putting it in a form that was useful. Sandra, then a second year undergraduate, and Andrew, a high school junior, performed like true professionals and made writing the book infinitely easier.

The Prentice-Hall Canada organization got things going and kept them going. Pat Ferrier, Acquisitions Editor, introduced the co-authors to one another and helped us plan the book in its broad outline. Jean Ferrier, Project Editor, took over responsibility for the project from Pat and always provided useful advice about the book content. Kelly Dickson, Production Editor, gave us creative assistance in many areas, especially around photographs and inserts. Together, Kelly and Jean kept the project moving for the roughly 16 months it took from start to finish.

Kat Mototsune did a beautiful job of editing the text, offering deft suggestions for improvement throughout the book. Maura Brown created our index in her usual, professional way.

Many colleagues were kind enough to review our chapters at various stages of completion. Thanks to Bill Adcock, Sheridan College; Tom Callaghan, St. Clair College; M. Arthur Clarke, Sir Sandford Fleming College; Larry Comeau, Sheridan College; Dorothy Hewat, Confederation College; and John Steckley, Humber College who looked at some or all of the book as it evolved from proposal to sample to first draft to final manuscript. Our friends Jack Richardson (McMaster); Dennis Magill, Lorna Marsden, Steve Riggins and Ed Thompson (Toronto); and Ann-Marie Ambert (York) read one or more chapters and gave us their thoughts about them. In the end, Jim Curtis (Waterloo) skimmed the whole book and suggested extremely sensible final cuts.

We are indebted to all of these people who helped directly in the publication of this book. We are also grateful to our families for putting up with our psychic absence from "real life" while writing this book. It's nice to be back.

MACRO/MICRO
A BRIEF INTRODUCTION TO SOCIOLOGY

Lorne Tepperman
University of Toronto

Michael Rosenberg
Dawson College

CHAPTER 1

All sociologists watch everyday life. The more closely we watch it, the more complex the patterns of relationships we can see.

SOCIOLOGY: THE STUDY OF SOCIETY

No one is born with plans to become a sociologist. Young children realize that they will have some job when they grow up, but most likely they think of becoming fire fighters, police officers, teachers, doctors, nurses, or rock stars – not sociologists. If someone explained to them what sociologists do, they probably would not think it interesting or important.

Yet all of us are sociologists of a kind by the time we grow up: not in the sense of engaging in formal scientific teaching or research, but in the sense that all of us try to understand our own lives and the lives of people around us. That level of understanding – which is usually called common sense – provides us with a set of explanations about people, their behaviour, and the society we live in. Most of the time, for most of what we do, this common-sense sort of knowledge is sufficient.

We will consider the strengths and weaknesses of common-sense knowledge later in this chapter, but you probably already realize that there are many questions that common sense cannot answer adequately or at all: Why is there such a high divorce rate lately? Why is the murder rate in the United States so much higher than in Canada? Why are some people rich and others poor? Why do so few people take the trains when they travel nowadays? Why do the native peoples have such a high suicide rate? Why do so many people get upset about the arrival of a few illegal immigrants? Why is the "democracy" movement successful in some communist countries while it is unsuccessful in others?

Some of these questions may intrigue you, others may not. But even when it comes to your personal life there will be many questions for which common sense has no answer: Why doesn't John seem to feel the same way about me as I do about him? Why should I keep going to school? When am I going to learn something that will help me get a job? Why do I have to put up with so many stupid rules everywhere I go? Why can't I have a great car like that kid Frank, and how come his father has so much money anyway? Why are my parents always saying that television and rock music are junk?

Like everyone else, sociologists have thought about all of these questions, and many others. Sociologists, however, seek to replace common-sense understanding with scientific explanation: they study people's lives and relationships in an attempt to understand how people are affected by the society in which they live. That means that sociologists are fascinated by big "public issues" such as poverty, race, or the impact of technology. But sociologists recognize that there is another side to these public issues, a personal side. They know that your "personal" problems are similar to many other people's problems. Often, these are problems our society ought to try to solve, because individuals cannot solve them. In that sense, many of your problems and questions are really the personal side of public issues.

Sociologists know that understanding and finding solutions for both public issues and personal problems requires clear thinking and careful research. Common sense and personal experience are just not enough to help you understand how the world works, and how your own life fits in. Instead of depending upon common sense, sociologists have developed a variety of concepts, theories, and scientific research methods, many of which we will discuss in this book.

Our starting point is the connection sociologists make between personal problems and public issues. In terms of concepts and research, it is a connection between what sociologists call **macrosociology** and **microsociology**

MACROsociology/ MICROsociology

Now it is time for a formal definition of sociology, the subject of this book. Scholars have defined it in a great many ways, but most sociologists think of **sociology** as the scientific study of human society and social behaviour. Human beings are social beings in the sense that almost everything we do or try to achieve is done together with other people or in the company of others. Sociologists take as their primary subject matter the social **groups** we create when we get together with others, ranging from small groups—as few as two people—to large entities like corporations, and even whole societies. When looking at social groups, sociologists study such things as the various ways in which participation in groups affects the behaviour and experiences of individual people.

This is an enormous area of study, but most of what sociologists look at falls into one of two related but distinct subfields: macrosociology and microsociology.

Macrosociology is the study of social institutions (for example, the Roman Catholic Church, the Canadian economy, or the government of Britain) and large-scale social groups (for example, ethnic minorities or college students). It also includes the study of social processes and patterns that characterize whole societies (for example, social control, social change), and of the system of social arrangements that makes up a society. In short, macrosociology deals with large patterns formed by large groups of people over long periods of time.

The other side of sociology is **microsociology**. Microsociology is the study of small-scale groups (for example, a rock band, a street gang, your classroom, your friend's family). It is also the study of processes and patterns of social interaction, such as face-to-face interaction, that take place among people within these groups. In this sense, microsociology examines the actual practices of interaction, negotiation, and everyday domination, which produce the stable and enduring patterns studied by macrosociologists.

The contrast with macrosociology is obvious. Where macrosociology takes a broad view of society and a long view of social change—often in terms of decades, centuries, or even millenia— microsociology studies what may happen in the course of a conversation, a party, a classroom lecture, or a love affair.

These differences in perspective play themselves out in a variety of ways. For example, macrosociologists are likely to emphasize how slowly things change, how remarkably persistent a social pattern is as it imprints itself on one generation after another. On the other hand, microsociologists are likely to emphasize how rapidly and subtly things change. They see people, in the course of their relationships, constantly creating and refining the social order.

To the new student of sociology, these differences may sound like impossible barriers between the two subfields, but they are not. Using what the great American sociologist C. Wright Mills called the **sociological imagination,** we can see how these two approaches to sociology reflect different aspects of the social world that are equally real. The trick is to understand how the large and the small, the macro and micro, fit together. Indeed, that is the purpose of this book and the purpose of sociology in general.

To give an example of the approach we are using, consider how combining macro and micro approaches can enhance our understanding of a common social phenomenon: racial discrimination in the workplace. Racial "stratification" in the labour force—a large-scale social process—only exists because (some) people generalize skin colour and other racially specific physical features to mental and moral qualities. They see some racial groups as superior or inferior to others, as more or less intelligent, as lazier or more diligent, and so on.

In part, it is this subjective (micro) aspect of assigning meanings and values to physical features that underlies the structural (macro) problem of discrimination. Microsociologists might study why and how certain physical features came to have those meanings, or they might study how people act out those meanings by engaging in discrimination in a particular workplace. Macrosociologists might study why and how face-to-face discrimination provides on-going economic advantages for the racial majority.

C. Wright Mills (1959) wrote that the **sociological imagination** is the ability to see connections between large and small, changing and unchanging, portions of social life. It requires an awareness of the relation between individuals and the wider society. It helps us to look at our own personal experiences, at what we want out of life and what we are getting. It forces us to ask how our lives are shaped by the larger social context in which we find ourselves. It finally leads us to see the larger social context as the result of millions of people working out their own personal lives.

Imagine sociology as the study of a complex woven tapestry we call "society." Each strand is a single human life. Sociology studies the laws by which these strands combine and come apart, to come together again in a new, never-to-be-repeated pattern. It is sociology's concern with discovering the laws of social life that, ultimately, makes sociology a science.

EXHIBIT 1.1

SEX AND THE ASSEMBLY LINE

In any society, cultural values in one area of life often affect behaviour in another. That is because society is an interlinked system of thoughts and actions.

For example, sociologist Philip Slater writes that " 'the sexual revolution' has been contaminated by male preoccupations with competition and achievement. Most American men aren't really interested in pleasurable stimulation—they want ego-boosting and tension release." How could it be otherwise in a society that places the highest value on power, is competitive and stressful, and forces us to schedule all our activities so we can get the most of everything in the least time? Slater continues:

> Most sex manuals give the impression that the partners in lovemaking are performing some sort of task; by dint of a great cooperative effort and technical skill (primarily the man's) an orgasm (primarily the woman's) is ultimately produced. The bigger the orgasm, the more 'successful' the performance.
>
> This thought pattern owes much to the masculine preoccupation with technical mastery. Women in popular sexual literature become manipulable mechanical objects—like pianos ("it's amazing what sounds he can get out of that instrument") or objects of earthmoving equipment ("he can excavate a swimming pool in just four minutes"). Even more pronounced is the competitve note . . . [which] often makes it seem as if lovemaking were a game in which the first person to reach a climax loses. . . .
>
> Discussions of the sexual act in our society are thus overwhelmingly concerned with how it *ends*. Leisurely pleasure seeking is brushed aside, as all acts and all thoughts are directed toward the creation of a "successful" finale. The better (i.e., the bigger) the climax, the more enjoyable the whole encounter is retrospectively defined as having been. . . . In such a system you can only find out how much you're enjoying yourself after it's all over (just as many Americans travelling abroad don't know what they've experienced until they've had their film developed).
>
> The preoccupation in Western sexual literature with orgasm seems to be a natural extension of the Protestant work ethic in which nothing is to enjoyed for its own sake except striving.

Source: Philip Slater, "Sex in America" chapter 1 in *Footholds: Understanding the Shifting Family and Sexual Tensions in Our Culture.* Toronto: Clarke Irwin, 1977, pp. 7-8

VARIETIES OF SCIENCE

What is science?

We have mentioned several times now that sociology is a science. Before we continue, perhaps we had better clarify what is meant by science and in what sense sociology can be considered a science.

All of us are able to remember our experiences and draw lessons from them. Last week, the veal at Mike's supermarket was great but the vegetables were terrible, so tomorrow I will get the steak I need at Mike's store and buy my vegetables at Frank's corner grocery. We do not need scientific study to make these kinds of ordinary, everyday decisions. As we noted earlier, by and large, experience and common sense work just fine for our everyday needs.

In fact, common sense and remembered experience build up over a long time into something people call folk wisdom. This folk wisdom contains many "rules of thumb" – rules of behaviour that people have found useful over the course of time. Rules of thumb often become pieces of popular advice; for example, "Don't go swimming right after eating a heavy meal." Here are a few examples from a collection by Tom Parker (1983) called **Rules of Thumb**:

- Thinly cut cheese tastes more flavourful than thickly cut cheese.
- Expect to lose one sock every time you do the laundry.
- In editing something you have written, when in doubt, cross it out.
- Patients who are terminally ill are more likely to die after a holiday than before it.

We would not consider any of these to be scientific statements, even if they make sense to us and seem true. The difference between common sense and science is that the former is not tested with data, while the latter is.

Science is the discovery, explanation, and prediction of events in the world we experience, and of the relations between these events. Science requires research, while common sense does not. By **research**, we mean the application of logical, systematic methods to verifiable evidence. The scientific method consists of a systematic, organized series of steps that ensures as much objectivity as possible in researching a problem. It involves constructing theories, collecting evidence, testing predictions against careful observations, and accurately recording the findings. If the predictions we test fail, we must modify or reject our original theory.

To give a better idea of the difference between science and common sense, let's follow up one of the rules of thumb mentioned earlier, that patients who are terminally ill are more likely to die after a holiday than before it. Many people assert this bit of common-sense knowledge without really knowing whether or not it is true.

Suppose you were a scientist assigned the task of determining whether this observation were true or not. You would start to think about how to test if it were true. What's more, as a scientist you would also want to know, if it *is* true, *why* it happens. Why should people be more likely to die after holidays? What theories about human beings would help us understand this event or set of events?

For example, do terminally ill people tend to die after holidays because the care they receive during holidays is worse than usual? Is it because of the exhaustion and stress that often accompany holiday celebrations? Or is it because they are highly motivated to survive until the holiday, after which they no longer have as great a will to live? How can we decide which of these possible explanations – called *hypotheses* – is the best of many that are possible? And what are the theoretical implications of our finding? If we were to conclude from evidence that the last hypothesis is the best one, how does that affect our larger theories about why people live or die? Finally, what are the practical implications, if we want to help people live longer?

These are the thoughts that go through a scientist's mind after someone has asked an interesting question. This brief example has suggested some of the special features of scientific method and thinking.

First, science tries to be objective, not subjective. **Objectivity** is a method of interpreting events, or the relations among them, by using reason and the best evidence possible. To do this means avoiding personal bias, prejudice, or preconception. **Subjectivity** is a tendency to interpret reality from a viewpoint shaped by our own experiences, emotions, opinions, values, and beliefs. Scientists recognize that, in their own everyday lives, subjectivity is bound to creep in. As human beings, we all run the risk of jumping to conclusions without enough regard for evidence or reason. Being scientific in all aspects of our everyday life is simply too difficult and denies the part of us that is—and ought to be—intuitive and emotional. Nevertheless, if science is to be more than a collection of personal prejudices and beliefs, the scientist must strive to be as objective as possible.

The difference between objectivity and subjectivity can be clarified by an example. Dutch sociologist Ruut Veenhoven (1984) has noted that many people criticize life in modern societies. Often they say that life is less satisfying today than it was when they were younger or in pioneer days, or perhaps even than it is in small pre-industrial villages scattered around the world. This personal view of modern society is subjective because it states a personal opinion, shaped by personal experience. It does not use data other people have collected in reliable ways to make a careful comparison of our own society with other ones.

For his part, Veenhoven uses data from hundreds of studies carried out around the world to show that the average person's satisfaction with life is just as high in our own society as it is in any society surveyed. Indeed, measures of health care, life expectancy, and standard of living all suggest that our society may be better than most. On these objective grounds, we are not likely to conclude that life is better, or more satisfying in another kind of society.

This is not to say that Veenhoven is right—that life really *is* better in our own society than anywhere else. However, it means that if we are able to debate this issue objectively we must carefully define what we mean by "better" and collect relevant information to defend our position.

Another characteristic of science is the concern with developing and testing theories. A **theory** is an explanation of the causal relationship between various phenomena or events. An effective theory will not only have explanatory power; it will also enable the scientist to predict future events. In that sense, explanation and prediction are two sides of the same coin.

A well-reasoned theory provides hypotheses that will allow us to test the theory. A **hypothesis** formulates a research problem in such a way that it may be tested empirically, with data. It takes the form of a tentative proposition or prediction about the relation between two or more events. When we formulate hypotheses, we predict the future; when we collect data, we find out if the data support our prediction. If the data do not support it, our theoretical explanation is thrown into doubt: we need to revise the theory.

Let's see how this works on our previous example. Let's look at two of the possible explanations for the death-after-holidays phenomenon. One is that care for the terminally ill is sloppy during the holidays. The other is that terminally ill patients make a greater than usual effort to survive, to enjoy the holiday. We can imagine (if not try) an experiment that would tell us which is the better explanation. We start with two nursing homes of the same quality, housing the same kinds of terminally ill patients. Each has had roughly the same number of deaths for each of the last six months.

In Nursing Home A, we are going to double the nursing staff over the Christmas period. Even if the staff works half as hard, the patients will get the same level of care as they always do. If insufficient care is the real reason for deaths increasing after Christmas, then in January we will see no rise in deaths in Nursing Home A.

In Nursing Home B, we are going to test a different theory. We are going to give patients something to look forward to—and struggle towards—after Christmas. In Nursing Home B, the nursing staff will stay at the same level during Christmas as before (and after) it. However, we are going to play down the significance of Christmas this year and make elaborate plans for the future: a festive Hawaiian-cruise dinner in January; a Mardi Gras costume party (complete with celebrity guests) in March; and a fireworks display and visit by the Prime Minister on July 1.

At the end of January, we can look at the number of deaths occurring in each nursing home in the preceding 30 days and the data—our empirical findings—will give us the evidence to support one hypothesis rather than another. If the number of deaths is down significantly (compared with past years) only in Nursing Home B, we can attribute the reduction to the fact that the patients have something to look forward to after Christmas. If the number of deaths is down significantly only in Nursing Home A, we can attribute the reduction to better care during the holidays. But if the death rates increase after Christmas in both nursing homes, neither hypothesis is valid. We need to look for another explanation.

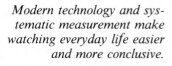

Modern technology and systematic measurement make watching everyday life easier and more conclusive.

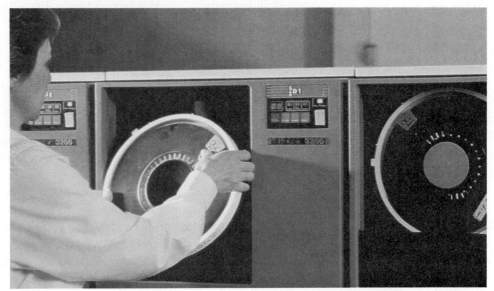

Is sociology scientific?

Perhaps you are wondering if sociology can be scientific. The popular image we have of science is fashioned after physics and chemistry: when we hear the word "science" we often imagine someone wearing a white coat in a laboratory, surrounded by expensive equipment; maybe we imagine rows of computers churning out columns of figures and interesting diagrams with Greek symbols on them. In fact, what we are imagining is not science, but the artifacts of a particular science at a particular time and place. (**Artifacts** are elements of material culture created by human workers.) Sociological research, like any scientific research, works by the collection, organization, and interpretation of data, for the purposes of testing a hypothesis, or of discovering new relations among phenomena.

It is true, however, that sociologists are sometimes limited in the particular methods they can use when doing their research. In the example above, we considered doing an experiment on nursing-home patients to test two competing theories. In practice, we could never do this: even if the findings might be very helpful, our society (like most others) severely limits experimenting on people.

Consider another example. Suppose we wanted to explain why, unlike many South American countries, Canada has never been ruled by a military dictator. As sociologists, we can think about this question in objective ways and even formulate theories, but there is no experiment we can perform that will tell us the answer. What's more, Canadian history will never repeat itself, so an experiment would be irrelevant to predicting the future even if it helped us understand the past.

Fortunately, the scientific method does not require experimentation: there are other ways to carry out research that is scientific. Some fields that study human behaviour—for example, psychology—use experiments almost exclusively. Other fields that study human behaviour—for example, history, economics, and anthropology—do not use experiments at all. We shall have a great deal more to say about how sociologists go about doing research in Chapter Eleven.

There remains a second major problem facing sociology as a science, the problem of objectivity. Physicists, chemists, or astronomers study phenomena which may be very important, but seem to have little impact on ordinary people's everyday lives. In contrast, sociologists often study problems they know about at first hand and which may have an impact on their own lives. A sociologist studying divorce may be personally going through a divorce, for example. As human beings, sociologists are bound to be prejudiced, emotional, and irrational at times. Perhaps you wonder if a science of social behaviour is even possible. We think that it is, if sociologists do their best to ensure that their work is *value free*.

Value-free research is research that excludes all ideological or unscientific assumptions, as well as all personal judgments or biases. The problem of achieving value freedom faces all of the social sciences because the things that we study often include subjects of political debate, religious teaching, or personal commitment. We have to avoid setting up the research problem in a way that protects our own political, religious, or personal principles.

Let's consider a very important example of this. Our society is dominated by males, and males define what is valuable in our society. As a result, up until about ten years ago, no one had done any serious research on housework. Yet housework is a job that has historically occupied more people than any other job in our society. It is because men do not do housework that the topic went unstudied for so long. In fact, women sociologists have led the way in doing research on this activity.

Even in areas in which research has been done, there are many cases in which sociologists have formulated a research problem inadequately because of a narrow way of seeing the world. This is why some sociologists have argued that you need female researchers to give a female perspective on society. Similarly, people belonging to racial minorities or growing up in poverty have claimed the need for their own groups to study society from their own perspective.

If sociology has fallen far short of value-free research in the past, this does not prove that value-free research is impossible. Even if it is impossible now, our failure to date does not mean that we should stop trying to do value-free research. Value freedom in sociology may be impossible, but it is—and should be—the continuing goal of all sociologists, whatever their background. This view has implications for sociology students as well as for sociologists. It means that whenever you are studying sociology, you must be alert to the hidden assumptions that are shaping an argument. Doing so is even more important to good research than carefully collected facts and powerful statistical testing of the results.

The need for value freedom is most important when you are applying social research to real-life circumstances, but this problem of value freedom in "applied" sociological research is not unique to sociology. On the contrary, it affects all applied research. So even in this respect, sociological research is no less scientific than research in psychology, biology, or physics. Good science is always possible in sociology, but the personal limitations of the researcher and the preconceptions of those who are funding the research always threaten value freedom.

Sociology is a science, then—like physics or biology; but as a science, sociology is more like the other fields called *social sciences* than it is like physics or biology.

SOCIOLOGY AS A SOCIAL SCIENCE

What are the social sciences?

There is some disagreement as to precisely what fields the social sciences include. Some fields, like history or geography, have one foot in the camp of social science and another foot in the humanities. So do some other recently established fields that cross disciplinary boundaries: women's studies, Canadian studies, environmental studies. Traditionally, the **social sciences** have included sociology, anthropology, economics, political science, and psychology.

Anthropology is the study of whole human societies. Traditionally, anthropology has included four main subfields: (1) archaeology studies the material remains of people, typically those who lived in the past; (2) physical anthropology studies humans from a biological perspective, focusing on evolution; (3) linguistic anthropology focuses on human language—its description, history, and social use; and (4) cultural anthropology, sociology's closest relative, describes and explains human behaviour in a social context. In the past, sociology concentrated on Western societies, while cultural anthropology focused on non-Western societies. Today, both groups cross this once-rigid boundary: more sociologists conduct research on non-Western societies; and anthropologists often study Western subcultures (such as corporate elites, neighbourhoods, ethnic groups, and gangs).

Economics studies the production, distribution, and consumption of goods and services in society. It is usually considered the most advanced of the social sciences because it is older than the others and because its subject matter is easier to measure with numbers. Economists can answer economic questions by the use of sophisticated mathematical tools largely unknown to the other social sciences. Economics asks questions like these: How do changing interest rates affect business investment? What economic factors cause unemployment? How do taxes affect consumer spending?

Political science is the study of actual forms of government, and decision-making processes in government and elsewhere. The central concerns of political science are power and authority: what they are, how people use them and with what consequences. Here we find a particularly strong overlap with sociology. Like political science, the sociology of politics also deals with political institutions, but does so in relation to the rest of society. It asks questions like these: In what social, cultural, and economic conditions is democracy likely to flourish? Why are some groups or organizations more democratic than others? Sociology studies the social aspects of group decision-making, the informal manipulation of power, and the factors that influence who votes for whom. Thus, sociologists have been particularly active in political polling, and we will discuss this later in this chapter.

Psychology is the study of human mental processes such as emotion, thought, memory, perception, intelligence, voluntary behaviour, and the perception of the self. More than any other social science, psychology focuses on individual behaviour. A subfield called social psychology examines the relations between individual and group behaviour. Both sociologists and psychologists carry out research in the subfield of social psychology.

One of sociology's founders, Emile Durkheim, distinguished sociology from psychology by saying that sociology is the study of "social facts," not of individual people acting freely. By **social facts**, Durkheim meant real forces operating outside us that influence or limit our actions. These social facts are often revealed to us through a study of societal rates.

So, for example, when Durkheim studied suicide he ignored the reasons people gave (in notes) to explain their own behaviour, or the reasons other people gave for the suicides of friends or family members. On the other hand, suicide *rates* offered him a believable explanation of suicidal behaviour. He found that people were more likely to kill themselves during periods of rapid social change or if they were socially isolated (among other things). Both rapid change and social isolation are often outside the individual's control, are real (or objective) forces—not merely imagined—and they push people to act in certain ways: thus, they are social facts. There are many kinds of social facts

EXHIBIT 1.2

HOW SOCIOLOGY IS DIFFERENT

Sociologist Kenneth Westhues points out that sociology is different from other disciplines in the following ways:

(1) Holism

Holism distinguishes sociology from economics and political science. Sociology is not concerned with only one aspect of social life—for example, the economy or government; it is concerned with all of society and how the parts fit together.

(2) Theory Building

Theory building distinguishes sociology from journalism and history. Sociology is not mainly concerned with telling a story; it is concerned with testing a theory that explains the story.

(3) Intellectual Primacy

Intellectual primacy distinguishes sociology from social work, law, and urban plannng. Sociology is not mainly concerned with bringing about social change; it is mainly concerned with understanding and explaining the character of everyday experience.

(4) Sense Evidence

The use of sense (or empirical) evidence distinguishes sociology from philosophy and religion. Sociology is not only concerned with the logic of its theories; it is also concerned about whether these theories are supported by empirical data.

(5) Social Focus

A social focus distinguishes sociology from psychology. Sociology is not concerned with the thoughts and actions of isolated individuals; it is mainly concerned with the ways people interact and create social life together.

Source: Westhues, Kenneth *First Sociology*. New York: McGraw-Hill Ryerson, 1982

and most sociological research begins by examining the most relevant ones.

The social sciences, then, are a related group of disciplines that study some aspect of human behaviour. Historically, researchers in each of these fields have learned from, and referred to, work done in other social sciences. Sociology has been particularly likely to borrow from all of the other social sciences, a tendency that is natural and healthy.

How sociology is different

So far we have taken great pains to argue that sociology is just as scientific as all the other sciences. Sociologists carry out scientific research that is most like research in the applied or historical sciences. In this way, sociology is a lot like the other nonexperimental social sciences—especially anthropology, political science, and economics—from which it also borrows a great deal. Yet sociology is also quite distinct from other disciplines—even from the other social sciences.

Sociology is characterized as a distinctive discipline by its subject matter, by the perspectives it applies to this subject matter, and by its basic concepts. The most crucial difference between sociology and the other social sciences is its subject matter, which is usually described as the relation between individual and society; between social structure and the socialized member of society.

Social structure is any enduring, predictable pattern of social relations among elements of society. These elements may be people, roles, groups, or whole institutions. The key words here are "enduring," "predictable," "pattern," and "people."

Like sociologists, astronomers study enduring, predictable patterns of relations—but these are relations among stars and planets. Like sociologists, psychologists study enduring, predictable patterns of relations—the relations among attitudes, behaviours, and personality traits *within* individuals. Sociologists study enduring patterns of relations—which are predictable because they are enduring—*across* individuals. They study patterns of behaviour that cut across individuals because they grow out of relationships between people.

In the abstract, these ideas may sound difficult, but in practice they are familiar and simple. Consider a common, well-known example—the relationship between a doctor and a patient—that was the topic of a classic analysis by the sociologist Talcott Parsons (1951).

When you visit a doctor for a check-up, you take along very specific expectations. Even if you have never visited that doctor before, you expect the doctor to act in a serious, concerned, and knowledgeable manner. The doctor also expects certain behaviours from you as a patient. For example, the doctor expects you to show concern for your health, pay attention to his or her diagnosis, and defer to the professional judgment you receive.

How do we know that people really have such expectations and these expectations are enduring and predictable? If we violate any of these expectations, both participants—doctor and patient alike—will feel uncomfortable, perhaps even upset or disoriented. If the doctor comes in dressed like a rock star or starts talking to you like an intimate friend, this will confuse and disturb you. If you laugh at the news of a serious health problem or refuse to acknowledge the doctor's expertise, or if you refuse to take the medicine prescribed, the doctor will be puzzled. The interaction will stop flowing smoothly. Both doctor and patient will start wondering what to say and do next.

There are many reasons that social relationships, from the dyad all the way up through a complete society, are enduring and stable. We learn to value stable relationships. Often, we lack the knowledge or courage to change relationships. Sometimes we develop a strong investment in the way things are and stand to lose something if they change. People with the most to lose urge us to meet other people's expectations. These reasons, and many others we shall discuss, help to maintain the social structure of the society in which we live.

Sociologists have found that what we learn about one social structure—for example, a doctor-patient relationship—can help us understand another quite different social relationship. Sociology, then, is in large part the study of social structures—whether the social structure of the medical profession, a business enterprise, a marriage, a political party, or a total society. Sociologists readily apply sociological concepts across a wide range of different social relationships. The willingness to generalize is one of sociology's most characteristic features.

THE SOCIOLOGICAL TRADITION

Sociology developed as a scientific discipline in the late 19th and early 20th centuries, as European thinkers tried to understand the dramatic changes accompanying modernization. For most of human history, change was very slow and few people wondered much about their society. Things were as they always had been (or so it seemed), and those who wondered why were most likely to look to God, to fate, or to the supernatural as an explanation. This attitude began to change in the face of the rapid technological, political, and religious changes which accompanied industrialization and modernization. People began to try to understand their society and to wonder if these dramatic changes could be understood and their future course predicted.

Three individuals are credited with being the founders of sociology as a scientific discipline: Karl Marx, Emile Durkheim, and Max Weber.

Karl Marx (1818-1883) was not, strictly speaking, a sociologist. Nevertheless, sociology derived many of its key concepts—such as the term "class"—from the work of Marx; the questions he asked and the solutions he developed remain important in contemporary sociological thought.

In his work, Marx (for example, see Marx, 1936, 1955, 1969) developed a theory of society and of social change that does not fall within the boundaries of any one modern social science discipline. Marx assumed that economic processes, what he called *modes of production*, were the most fundamental processes in society and helped to explain a great deal about how society is organized. A mode of production such as hunting, for example, will result in a very different set of social relationships among people than will industrial production. In a hunting society, there will be no private property because the animals which are hunted do not belong to anyone; they are outside the boundaries of the society and are hunted for the benefit of all. In contrast, a factory may have an owner and this puts owners and workers in very different social categories or *classes*. Also, since everyone benefits more or less equally in a hunting society, there will be little social conflict among people, although there may be personal conflict. In an industrial society, owners and workers have different interests, and this results in class conflict. However much an owner and a worker may admire one another as individuals, owners and workers as groups are in a state of class conflict.

Marx's work was noteworthy for a number of reasons. His was the first attempt to uncover objective, scientific laws with which to understand society. His was the first significant attempt to make use of history in order to predict the future course of economic and social change. His questions about how society works remain relevant today, even for those who reject his answers.

One of those who rejected Marx's answers was the French sociologist Emile Durkheim (1858-1917). In fact, Durkheim rejected any explanation of society—whether economic, biological, psychological, or philosophical—that he did not deem sufficiently sociological. Durkheim was one of the first European academics to describe himself as a sociologist, and he devoted much of his career to establishing sociology as a distinct and respectable discipline of social science.

The starting point of Durkheim's sociology was the predominance of society over the individual. Society, Durkheim insisted, determines the individual. All of our values, beliefs, attitudes, even our ways of thinking, are derived from society. As an example, Durkheim (1951) took the case of suicide. He showed that suicide is not only an individual act but is also a social act: suicide rates change in accordance with social factors such as place of residence, religion, marital status, age, gender, and so on. More importantly, Durkheim asserted that suicide might be an indication of personal problems, but it is also a manifestation of social problems. For example, because of the rapid pace of social change, modern society is characterized by **anomie**, a state in which people's desires and aspirations are no longer effectively regulated by society. When people find themselves in such a state they become profoundly depressed and are more likely to try to kill themselves. This depression is social rather than individual in origin. People need not have failed to live up to their expectations to be depressed; they may have exceeded them. So, for example, someone who wins a lottery could come to feel as dissatisfied with their life as someone who is fired from their job.

This example illustrates Durkheim's profound use of the sociological imagination. Depression—a personal problem—is shown by Durkheim to be the outcome of broader social forces. His consistent ability to link such phenomena as crime, suicide, or religion to broader social processes has served as a source of inspiration to later generations of sociologists. Moreover, sociologists have also admired Durkheim's (1938) attempts to develop rigorous and consistent sociological research methods, such as his use of suicide rates to uncover the link between suicide and social factors. Although many of Durkheim's assumptions and findings are rejected today, his image of sociology continues to inspire many sociologists.

Like Durkheim, Max Weber (1864-1920) rejected much of the approach used by Karl Marx, but for quite different reasons. Weber rejected the idea that any one factor or set of factors determines either society or the individual. Weber saw society as an extraordinarily complex set of social relationships, which can never be completely explained and whose course can never be completely predicted. All we can do is seek to understand some of the more important factors and identify the impact these factors have had in history. For this reason Weber looks not only to economic factors to explain society but to such other factors as religion, urbanization, the law, science and technology, and political organization (see, for example, Weber, 1961).

In many ways, Weber's sociology is really a sociology of domination and power. In that respect, Weber is typical of German intellectuals at the turn of the century. Where he stands out is in his remarkable historical and technical knowledge, and in his ability to link together extraordinarily diverse social processes. For example, Weber (1974) linked the rise of capitalism to religious doctrine, especially the so-called *Protestant ethic* of hard work. (See Chapter Two for a fuller discussion.) But he also linked the rise of capitalism to many other factors, such as the tendency of European monarchs during the middle ages to ally themselves with large cities in order to gain political control over the independent feudal nobility. In return for their support, the monarchs granted the cities many rights and freedoms which made them free of feudal obligations and allowed their citizens to experiment with alternative forms of production, such as factories.

Weber's impact upon contemporary sociology is immense. Many of the key areas of sociological research, such as stratification and bureaucratic organization, are heavily indebted to his pioneering work (Weber, 1958a). Perhaps his most enduring legacy, however, is his lesson to sociologists never to be satisfied with an easy answer and to avoid all forms of determinism, whether sociological or other (Weber, 1958b).

Today, sociologists still differ in what they consider to be the key concepts and approaches to the study of society. In fact, most sociologists fall into one of three main groups which embrace different sociological paradigms. A **paradigm** is a perspective, or general way of seeing the world. It embodies broad assumptions about the nature of society and social behaviour. A paradigm suggests which questions to ask, and how to interpret answers obtained by research.

THREE SOCIOLOGICAL PARADIGMS

Structural Functionalism

One of the three paradigms in common use is structural functionalism, sometimes simply called *functionalism*. Inspired in part by Emile Durkheim, **structural functionalism** emphasizes the way a society is structured in order that the different parts that make it up function to fulfil the needs of the society as a whole. This perspective looks at society as a social system – a set of components or structures that are interrelated and organized in an orderly way and integrated to form a whole. The term *whole* is important here and, as you can probably guess, functionalists are typically concerned with macrosociological issues.

The main assumptions of structural functionalism are as follows:

- Each social system has certain basic needs that must be met if it is going to continue to survive.
- The various interdependent structures in a social system exist in order to fulfil one or more of these needs.
- Under normal conditions, the social system has a tendency to be in "equilibrium," a state of balance, stability, harmony, and consensus.
- Because all the structures are interrelated and integrated, changes in one will provoke changes in others, so that a new equilibrium is reached.
- Among all the members of society, there is widespread agreement or consensus on what values should be upheld, on what is functional and dysfunctional in society, and on the preference of stability over change.

The image of society presented by structural functionalists is one that is rational, orderly, and stable. Society is rational, functionalists suggest, because it works to meet the needs of the social system as a whole, rather than the personal, irrational, or subjective needs of particular individuals. If the social system *is* rational, then change is more likely to disrupt society than to provide benefits, and functionalists emphasize order over change. They ask a basic question: How does x—some institution, social relationship, or set of practices—help to maintain the social system? Furthermore, functionalists argue that x exists or occurs because it helps to maintain the social order. The explanation they offer for some phenomenon, then, focuses on how it contributes to preserving the social system.

To illustrate these somewhat complex thoughts, let us return to the doctor-patient relationship discussed earlier. Suppose we want to argue in favour of doctors' rights to bill extra fees over and above what public health insurance permits. A structural functionalist might support extra billing in the following way:

> Extra billing helps society to survive by helping to ensure good health. It encourages doctors to give better service. It also encourages patients to take their doctors' advice more seriously, since they are paying for it directly. People in our society value good health very highly: that is why doctors are so highly respected and highly paid. If doctors could not bill their patients extra, this would disturb a traditional part of the doctor-patient relationship. The doctor would become like any other public servant, paid directly from the public purse. It would be more difficult to maintain the rest of the doctor-patient relationship, which calls for trust, discretion, and mutual respect. Once patients lost their respect for the relationship, they would stop taking the good advice doctors offered them.

This example illustrates the basic features of a functionalist explanation; but we need to refine it. Otherwise, the structural functionalist position sounds more complacent and simple-minded than it really is. After all, much of what goes on in society seems neither rational nor to contribute to order and stability. In fact, much of what does go on in our society—and even more of what goes on in societies other than our own—seems to many of us to be simply senseless.

One solution developed by structural functionalists to explain the seeming senselessness of social behaviour is to distinguish between *manifest* and *latent* functions (Merton, 1957). To uncover the functions of a given structure, sociologists look at what its actual consequences are, not at what its purposes are popularly supposed to be. When we do so, we often discover that any social element may have consequences other than those that were intended.

Manifest functions are those functions that are obvious and intended. For example, the manifest functions of a school system are to educate the young and teach them to be responsible citizens. **Latent functions** are unintended and often unrecognized, but will have significant social effects nonetheless. For example, the latent function of schooling may be to provide free baby-sitting services, which helps working parents, and to teach obedience and conformity to rules, which helps future employers when the students join the work force. This means that institutions or behaviours whose manifest functions have lost all meaning or sense may be perpetuated if their latent functions continue to contribute to social order. Functionalists insist that in this way much that seems senseless or disorderly actually works to benefit society.

To repeat, the structural functionalist looks at the consequences—the functions and dysfunctions—of a behaviour or relationship to explain why it endures. Equally, however, the structural functionalist recognizes that a behaviour or relationship can have *unintended consequences* that are dysfunctional for the system. These consequences may even undo what people had intended. Compulsory education, for example, was designed to promote social mobility by giving everyone, including a lower class child, a standard minimum set of qualifications for middle-class occupations. Once most people obtain a high-school diploma, however, it no longer confers any real advantage in the competition for jobs. But not having a high-school diploma confers a real disadvantage because it is now the minimum qualification for a good job.

Structural functionalists argue that, because society is a system of interrelated structures, changes in one part of society always produce changes—often unintended—in another part. Society is constantly reacting and readjusting to new inputs, even when people do not intend the changes that occur.

This observation carries important implications for sociology and also for social planning. Unless we are very clear on what all the likely consequences of a planned change are—the latent as well as the manifest functions, and the dysfunctions as well as the functions—we are very likely to end up with changes we did not want. One sociologist (Sieber, 1981) has called attempts at social planning that fail to think through the consequences "fatal remedies." In the end, they do more unintended harm than they do good.

Conflict theory

Many sociologists find the structural-functional emphasis on order, harmony, and stability misleading and unhelpful. They believe it offers a false picture of how society actually works. One alternate approach many adopt is **conflict theory**.

Conflict theory is a theoretical perspective that emphasizes conflict and change as basic features of social life. For conflict theorists, change is the only constant in society. Conflict and change are inevitable because various groups in society differ in power, status, or influence and are always trying to maintain or improve their respective positions.

From a conflict theorist's perspective, there is one basic sociological question: Who benefits from the existing social organization and who suffers? Like structural functionalists, conflict theorists pay attention to the consequences of behaviours or relationships. However, the conflict theorist does not suppose any behaviour or relationship will benefit the whole society, and does not look for such a benefit. Instead, the conflict theorist looks for particular groups that will benefit most and have the power to gain this benefit.

Although they reject the functionalist emphasis on the social "whole," most conflict theorists engage in macrosociological theory and research. The conflict perspective does not assume that people are innately antagonistic, or that conflict takes place on the level of individuals. Rather, conflict theorists explain that different groups in society come into conflict because the things that people value highly and desire (for example, wealth, prestige, and power) are scarce. To gain control of these valued things means denying them to others. Conflict develops between groups whose goals differ or even oppose each other—for example, the rich and the poor, men and women, workers and management. These categories of opposing people differ in at least one social characteristic: respectively, the amount of wealth they have, their gender, their relationship to power at work. It is the key difference that sets the conflict in motion.

Conflict may also arise out of different conceptions of what is valuable, desirable, or good. Groups may struggle with one another over the right to define good and bad, valuable and worthless. For example, conflicts over the legalization of marijuana or the abolition of the death penalty reflect such differing conceptions of good and bad.

Conflict theorists do not consider conflict to be a destructive force; rather they believe it focuses attention on social problems and brings people together to solve these problems. Indeed, conflict is the source of social movements like the women's movement, civil rights movements, or trade unionism. In this way, conflict serves as the vehicle of positive social change.

The conflict outlook on social life leads in certain very particular directions. For example, it focuses attention away from shared values and towards ideologies and "false consciousness." **Ideology** is a coherent set of interrelated beliefs about the nature of the world and of people. It guides a person's interpretation of, and reaction to, external events. For example, in our society many people believe they are responsible for their own success or failure in life. They think, "I am free to choose the path I will take; if my choice turns out badly, I have only myself to blame." This thinking is part of what is called the "liberal ideology."

The liberal ideology affects the way people behave in a wide variety of situations. On the macrosociological side, it influences which political party they will vote for and whether they will support welfare benefits for the poor, or capital gains taxes for the rich, for example. On the microsociological side, it influences how they will react if they are thrown out of work, battered by a spouse, or mistreated by the government. In both cases, this ideology leads people to "blame the victim" and support the status quo.

In conflict theory, the *dominant ideology* is the ideology of the dominant group. It serves to justify the position, power, and wealth of this group. The rest of us do not rebel because we have learned and come to believe in the dominant ideology. Conflict theorists argue that students are taught this ideology in the schools and through the media.

Marxist theorists, who embrace a particular version of conflict theory, also claim that the dominant ideology promotes false consciousness. **False consciousness**, a term derived from the work of Karl Marx, is a perception of a situation that is not in accord with objective reality. For example, some of us blame the shortcomings of people, not the way society is organized, for causing them such problems as poverty, unemployment, and bad health. The victims are held responsible for their own fate. Conflict theorists believe that such a viewpoint demonstrates false consciousness. Strange to say, even the victims of the system—for example, the chronically unemployed—often display this false consciousness and subscribe to the dominant ideology (see Schlozman and Verba, 1979): they blame themselves.

Conflict theorists vary in what they consider to be the central conflicts in society that shape order and change. Some believe that a wide variety of antagonisms—based on wealth, gender, position at work, ethnicity, race, region—produce conflict in Canadian society. Others, especially Marxist theorists, see these conflicts as secondary to, and connected with, one central conflict in capitalist society: class conflict.

In Marxist terms, a **class** is a set of people with the same relation to the means of production. People who control the means of production—the organizations that hire workers and own the capital that finances these organizations—control the lives of everyone else in society. These capitalists are the ruling class, and the views they form about how the world works serve to justify their position. These views also influence huge social institutions that perpetuate the capitalists' position at the expense of others. Class, then, is important because it gives rise to different life chances—different chances of gaining wealth, prestige, and power, or even good health and a steady job. It does so because one class—the capitalists—controls everyone else.

Although the influence of Marx and his work is evident in conflict theory, the work of Max Weber also inspired some of those who make use of the conflict paradigm. Weber (1958a) argued that conflict arises as much over such intangibles as values, status, and a sense of personal honour as over tangibles such as money or good health. From Weber's point of view, even modern corporations that no longer have any identifiable "owner" still generate conflict, because the bureaucratic management of the corporation comes to think of itself as a status group and acts to further group interests. That is why, Weberian conflict theorists argue, conflict can be found in the socialist Soviet Union just as it can in capitalist North America.

These three scholars were among sociology's most sophisticated people-watchers. In his own way, each set the stage for the work all sociologists do today. Pictured from left to right are Max Weber, Emile Durkheim, and Karl Marx.

  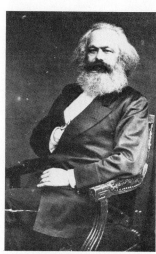

Symbolic interactionism

A little while ago, we considered how a structural functionalist would interpret the relationship between a doctor and patient, and the question of extra billing. A conflict theorist would view the same relationship in terms of competing interests (see, for example, Friedson, 1975; Johnson, 1972). The conflict theorist would argue that since doctors have a monopoly on scarce resources—medical knowledge and the right to apply it—they try to use their advantage to obtain as much deference and the largest payment possible while helping the patient. The patient's goal is to gain as much help as possible for the least money and deference.

Both outlines of the doctor-patient relationship—structural functionalist and conflict theorist—may be partly right. However, each misses the subtlety of the actual interactions between patients and doctors. Since structural functionalism and conflict theory are primarily macrosociological approaches, they pay little attention to the ways people interact with each other in everyday life. Neither explains how the doctor lays a claim to expertise or threatens an uncooperative patient, for example. We must turn to symbolic interactionism, a third paradigm in sociology, for a richer sense of the way in which people work out, or negotiate, an interaction and its outcome.

Symbolic interactionism is a theoretical perspective that sees society as a product of continuous face-to-face interaction among individuals in different settings. To understand this approach, let us consider the words that make up its name: "symbol" and "interaction."

Put in simple terms, a **symbol** is something that meaningfully represents something else. It can be a written or spoken word, a gesture, or a sign (such as a raised fist). **Interaction** refers to the ways two or more people act and respond to one another when they meet. Most interaction among human beings is symbolic, in the sense that words and actions all have meanings beyond themselves. A frown, a kiss, a smile, a word of greeting—all have meanings which are learned, shared, and changed through interaction. Some even have hidden meanings and double meanings.

Symbolic interactionism, then, focuses on the process by which people interpret and respond to the actions of others. Symbolic interactionism studies the way structures, as patterns of behaviour, arise out of these processes. In some ways this is like studying the way that waves, by bringing new grains of sand and taking away old ones, create a beach.

The main assumption of this approach is that people do not respond to the world directly. They respond to interpretations of the world. These interpretations rest on meanings that people attach to the various events, gestures, words, and actions around them. The meanings are social because people create them when interacting, share them, learn them, and sometimes even pass them down from one generation to the next.

Symbolic interactionists do not focus on the major structures of society, such as the economy or government. Rather they study personal everyday life in close detail. This is because they believe that major structures only come into being through day-to-day processes of change and renewal—just like a beach.

EXHIBIT 1.3

SOCIOLOGY AND REAL LIVES

Research often begins with sociologists trying to make sense of the changing lives of people they know. Recently, three sociologists analyzed the rapidly changing lives of Canadian women, after noting enormous changes among their female students. Do you recognize yourself (or some of your classmates) among these fictionalized accounts of ordinary lives?

SUZY: age 18, just out of high school, a straight-A student, who does not yet know what she wants to study but feels confident she will make the right decision and do well

BRENDA: age 18, also just out of high school, a B-student who is taking easy courses and waiting until she gets married to someone she expects to meet at college

DIANA: age 22, who is graduating this year and does not know what she wants to do. She's scared stiff by everything sociology has taught her about job discrimination against women and the probabilities of marriage breakdown.

CARLA: age 25, who has done brilliantly in her studies, but is having trouble deciding whether to work towards a university degree, move to the west coast with her husband, have a baby, or just take a job and relax for a while

GAIL: age 27, who did very well in past university studies, took time off to work but then found there were so many BAs out there that she needed another kind of training in order to get a "reasonable" job. She's back at school.

ANNA: age 33, who dropped out of college over a decade ago to follow her man across the continent. Now she's on her own again, back after doing a variety of jobs (among them, driving a bus, delivering mail, doing rough carpentry) to finally get a diploma.

ROSA: age 37, a graduate scientist, divorced with two children, who was a housewife for almost a decade. Now she is trying to get trained for para-legal work and achieve economic independence.

MARGARET: age 50, a public-school teacher who is taking one or two courses a year towards a college certificate, but finds it tough going. Her husband and daughter will not help out with household chores and other family responsibilities. When her old aunt broke a hip, Margaret was late getting in all her class assignments.

Adapted from Jones, C. L., L. Marsden, and L. Tepperman *Lives of Their Own: The Individualization of Women's Lives*. Toronto: Oxford University Press (Canada), 1990, pp. 1-2.

However, in important ways society is *not* like a beach and social relations are *not* like grains of sand depositing on the beach. Unlike grains of sand, people have consciousness and will. To a large degree, ordinary people make the waves that build up the beach we call social structure. So, to understand social structure we have to understand what is in the minds of the people—powerful and less powerful—making these social waves.

The German sociologist Max Weber said that sociologists must practice **verstehen**, a German word meaning "understanding" or "insight." In sociology, we take this to mean that sociologists must take into account the emotions, thoughts, beliefs, and attitudes of all acting individuals. We must know their intentions—their reasons for the behaviour we observe. *Verstehen* consists of placing ourselves in the position of the actors and seeing the world from their point of view; it is empathetic understanding. According to Weber, it is not enough for a sociologist to explain a social phenomenon only by referring to large social forces. We must also try to link this explanation with what is happening in people's minds. We must interpret the situation as they do.

The need to understand an actor's point of view is captured in another important concept, the *definition of the situation*. We must understand an actor's **definition of the situation**, because actors will act meaningfully only in relation to their definition, not ours. Take a simple example: self-destructive behaviour. At one time or another, we have all seen a very intelligent, attractive person act in an obnoxious way. We may know he or she wants to have friends, but other people stay away in droves. We begin to wonder whether that person is irrational for acting in such a self-defeating way.

Our view may change once we get inside that person's mind. He or she may feel ugly and undesirable as a friend. The person may aim at avoiding interactions that might end in rejection. Since obnoxious behaviour poses a difficult test for anyone who wants to be a friend, someone surviving this "ordeal by obnoxiousness" would surely be worth having as a friend. So, once we understand this person's reasons, the obnoxious behaviour makes perfect sense and does not seem irrational at all.

We note one other fact about this scenario: behaviour often produces the very result that is expected or feared. A person who believes rejection is likely, often gets rejected—indeed, often causes rejection. A person believing friendship is likely, on the other hand, often gets friendship. This leads sociologists (for example, Thomas and Thomas, 1928) to conclude that "a situation that is believed to be real is [often] real in its consequences." This simple generalization applies in a wide variety of social interactions.

Social interactions produce relationships that reflect the beliefs and expectations people bring to them. How can social order emerge from two (or sometimes many more) possibly quite different beliefs, expectations, and definitions of the same situation? The answer is, through *negotiation*. According to symbolic interactionists, social arrangements require continuous negotiation, dialogue, bargaining, and compromise among all the people present. Negotiation takes place in the House of Commons when a law is being changed or a new law is being voted into effect. It also takes place when ordinary people are deciding what movie to see on a Friday night.

As you might imagine, negotiation requires a great many social skills, and we all learn these skills in interaction, throughout our entire lives. We learn them the same way we learn language, through trial and error. With practice, we all become good at *verstehen*, at understanding someone else's definition of the situation, because we have to. To reach agreement with someone, we have to see the world the way they do, however imperfectly. Reaching agreement is often easiest if we can lead someone to redefine the situation: for example, to see the interaction as a chance for cooperation, not conflict.

How the three approaches are different

EXHIBIT 1.4

THREE PARADIGMS, THREE VISIONS

How would the three paradigms we have discussed analyze the same question or topic? Consider prostitution: why it exists in virtually every known society.

The Structural Functionalist Approach

Prostitution contributes to the stability of family life by giving sexually dissatisfied men an outlet that requires no significant commitment of time, money, or affection. By releasing tension, it reduces conflict both within the family and in society at large.

The Conflict Approach

Prostitution is another means by which men subordinate and degrade women. Poor and uneducated women with few other means of earning a livelihood are the most likely to sell their bodies. In this way, prostitution is also a means by which middle-class and wealthy people subordinate and degrade the poor, while holding them responsible for their own victimization.

The Symbolic Interactionist Approach

Prostitution is wrongly supposed to characterize a profession, with a particular relationship between the prostitute and "client." Rather, prostitution includes a wide range of activities ranging from occasional sex for gifts and favours, through kept women, street walkers, and call girls. In each case, the relationship, the motives, and the meanings are quite distinct.

Note that each paradigm provides only a partial account of prostitution; all three accounts are quite compatible with one another.

There is no denying that there are many differences among these three paradigms. Students planning to continue their studies of sociology should take note of these differences. However, this book is going to blur the differences between paradigms and stress the similarities. We are going to walk down the main street of current sociology, and not the side streets. We do this for two main reasons: the fact that many differences are more apparent than real, and the fact that similarities are more numerous and important than the differences.

There is no simple relationship between the three main paradigms (functionalist, conflict, and symbolic interactionist) and the two levels of analysis (macrosociological and microsociological). True, symbolic interactionism tends to specialize in microsociological analysis and the others in macrosociological analysis. Yet each paradigm has valuable insights to contribute at both levels of analysis. This is not surprising since, as we have argued, the two levels of analysis are merely different ways of looking at the same thing.

All three paradigms have explanations for both order and change, consensus and conflict. In one situation, the structural functionalist explanation may be best. In another situation the conflict paradigm or symbolic interactionist paradigm may be best. No conclusive evidence proves that one paradigm is always or never appropriate, or that combining paradigms is misleading and fruitless. On the contrary, many sociological researchers—especially sociologists working on applied questions with a practical significance—use all three paradigms interchangeably. They would gain nothing by ignoring another paradigm. Fortunately, the connections among paradigms are strong enough that such transitions among them are easy.

Basic sociological concepts

We have already noted that the paradigms have a great deal in common. Their similarity on important points is even more evident when we look at sociology from outside: from the standpoint of a new student or a researcher in, say, physics or history. Then, the features of the discipline that unify sociologists are a lot more striking than the features that separate them. Perhaps the most obvious sign of unity would be the prevalence of key concepts which are used by almost all sociologists, regardless of paradigm.

People who have spent a lot of time being students or teaching students know that concepts are the key to understanding any field. Concepts are the tools of thought and argument: they make the work of study and research easier. You could make a pretty good guess at the nature of roadbuilding by studying a jackhammer, dump truck, grader, tar truck, and steamroller. In the same way, you can get to understand sociology more rapidly by learning the conceptual tools that sociologists actually use.

The terms *social structure* and *social relationships* refer to two basic sociological concepts used by almost every sociologist. We have used them repeatedly in this chapter. Social structure, as we noted earlier, refers to any enduring, predictable pattern of social relationships among people. "Society" in this sense is the broadest form of social structure, it is the basic large-scale human group. Members of a society interact with one another and share a common geographic territory. To some degree, they also share a common culture and sense of collective existence; they participate together in social institutions.

Social institutions are enduring, complex, integrated sets of organized social relationships, which typically achieve some intended goals for certain people—for example, for students, consumers, citizens. The family is a social institution, as are schools, churches, banks, and prisons. People within a social institution are thus part of a **social relationship**, a stable pattern of meaningful orientations to one another, such as the connections between parent and child, doctor and patient, or one friend with another.

Being a parent or a student or a doctor is one's status in the institution. **Statuses** are socially defined positions in a social institution. They determine how the individual should relate to other people (that is, the rights and responsibilities of office) and with whom the individual will interact. **Roles** are one's actual pattern of interaction with others. Being a doctor is a status, acting like a doctor is a role performance. **Role expectations** are shared ideas about how people should carry out the duties attached to a particular social position—regardless of the personal characteristics of those people. Another way to say this is that *status* refers to what a person is, while *role* refers to the behaviours we expect (and usually get) from people in that status. "Status" could be likened to a job title and "role" to a job description.

The concept of *social relationship* is the meeting point of the macro and the micro. Each of us participates in social life in terms of the statuses and roles we have been assigned or have adopted. Being a "student," for example, carries with it a lot of social baggage in terms of learned behaviour patterns, expectations, and motives. We all learned to be students—a somewhat painful process for many of us—in elementary school. Once that role is learned, we carry around with us expectations of what it means to be a student and how to do whatever it is that students do. We also carry around with us expectations about teachers and how and why teachers do whatever it is that they do.

As an individual, however, being a student does not mean carrying out some impersonal set of duties, obligations, or expectations. We each have our own reasons for doing things, our own sense of capacity, self-worth, and achievement. We may have a learning disability that makes studying for an exam a form of torture. Or we may have financial difficulties, which might mean that we have to drop out of school and get a job if we do not get a scholarship. Or we might be taking a particular course because we hope to get a chance to date one of the other students. Each of us is an individual, and we experience and act out our roles and statuses in our own particular way. And yet, despite this, classroom behaviour is still to some degree predictable.

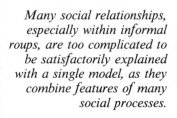

Many social relationships, especially within informal roups, are too complicated to be satisfactorily explained with a single model, as they combine features of many social processes.

However meaningful our lives are to us as individuals, most of what we do will still fit into the pattern common to all. We are still "students."

Why and how this is true is, of course, a large part of what this book is about.

SOCIOLOGY IN EVERYDAY LIFE

Pure sociology

What do sociologists do? Put simply, most sociologists teach and do research. There is very little we can tell about the teaching of sociology. You are much less likely to know much about research, however, and so we would like to give you some idea of what is involved in this aspect of sociological work.

Most of the research you read about in this book and other sociological texts is pure or basic research. Such research is aimed at testing theories about some aspect of social reality. The researcher's objective is a deeper understanding of the way social life works. Often there is little concern with the uses to which this knowledge may be put.

Sociologists usually do basic research because they enjoy the detective work, the excitement of answering hard questions they consider important. As well, their colleagues expect them to do as much basic research as time allows. This helps them stay on top of changes in the field of sociology and, in this way, to be better teachers. Finally, they do it because basic research is important to society as the foundation of all applied research.

EXHIBIT 1.5

POSSIBLE FUTURES: THE NYLON WAR

At the height of the Cold War, the Harvard sociologist David Riesman wrote a sociological fantasy called "The Nylon War." The well-known sociological notion of relative deprivation, which holds that people are stirred into protest and feel alienated not so much by their level of absolute deprivation but in relation to the standards of others with whom they compare themselves, lies at the heart of this paper. If this is indeed the case, Riesman argued, then efforts to subvert the Russian system of government might be powerfully enhanced were we to show to the Russian population at large how superior the living standards of Americans are compared to their own. What better way to do this, he argued, tongue in cheek, than to send bombers over Russia which would drop not atom bombs, but Sears Roebuck catalogs, nylon stockings, and other consumer goods unknown to the Russians. This would result in massive defections among large sectors of the Russian population. Who knows, perhaps, it would topple the Russian government, or at least force it to make major concessions to the oppressed population.

History has proved Riesman's analysis correct. It is precisely a sense of relative deprivation that has broken support for Communist party rule in the Soviet Union and Eastern Europe. Increasingly, sociologists have shown an ability to forecast future trends and outcomes, using sociological analysis.

We shall examine other examples of futures research throughout this book. Note, however, that it may take time for these theories to prove valid — in the instance above, nearly forty years.

Source: Coser, Louis A. *The Pleasures of Sociology*. Toronto: New American Library of Canada, 1980, p. 486.

Applied Research

Applied research is intended to identify and provide practical advice for solving social or organizational problems. In the last three decades, more and more sociological research has been applied research. Business and government have applied the findings of pure sociological research more often. As well, more sociologists than ever are working as paid consultants and researchers outside the teaching profession. We shall briefly explore some common types of applied research.

Market research

Market research is carried out on behalf of the producer of a good or service. Such research aims at achieving a better understanding of who purchases the good or service and why; what people do and do not like about it; what would make them more satisfied with the product; and how the producer could persuade more consumers to buy or use the good or service.

Suppose a producer of soft drinks, like Coca Cola, is losing the sales war to a competitor—in this case, Pepsi Cola. The executives at Coca Cola will want to know why more people are choosing Pepsi over Coke. Are the Pepsi-choosers young or old, rich or poor, men or women, urban or rural people?

Journalist Thomas Oliver's book, *The Real Coke, The Real Story* (1987) tells the fascinating story of a fierce contest between the corporate cola giants. It is only one of thousands of battles businesses fight with the aid of market research every year, and sociologists play an important part.

Political polling

When you think about it, political polling is a lot like market research. In one case you are discovering how to get people to drink Cola A instead of Cola B. In the other case you are discovering how to persuade people to vote for Candidate A instead of Candidate B.

Just as in product marketing, in politics there is always a natural market for a candidate. However, a majority of voters *may* vote for your candidate if you approach them correctly. Doing so requires knowing who—what kinds of

Pollsters are among the most devoted people-watchers. Public opinion polls provide up-to-date information on who is for and against each candidate, and where people stand on public issues.

people—they are and what they care about. You need to know how they view your candidate and the other candidates, and what voters consider the main issues in the election.

As political campaigns have become ever more costly and therefore risky, political polling has become an important part of political life. All major parties have their favourite pollsters. Some political figures even employ pollsters of their very own. Many of these pollsters and political advisors are trained sociologists.

Political polling, then, is a form of applied sociology that can have a powerful influence on society; and it is for this reason that ethical issues become important. Should a sociologist help a candidate or government persuade people to support his or her position? Does the answer to that question depend on whether the sociologist agrees with the politician's position? Should ethical considerations be more important in sociological research than they are in physics, chemistry, or mathematics? These ethical issues are far from settled.

Program planning and evaluation

Sociologists are also increasingly active in research that plans and evaluates social programs. Usually the client for such research is a public organization or part of government; sometimes, it is a profit-making organization.

A typical project of this kind might plan a system of half-way houses for released convicts. After a period of operation, sociologists would evaluate the program and suggest changes. The goal of such half-way houses would be to integrate ex-convicts back into normal society and keep them out of further trouble with the law. The sociologist would advise government on how such a system should work: for example, what kinds of convicts would be good candidates for early release from prison into a half-way house; what facilities and support services the system should provide; how the system might deal with the ex-convicts' needs for family, work, and self-esteem.

A second aspect of such a project is the outcome evaluation, to find out whether the program produced the results planners had intended. Were ex-convicts who passed through these half-way houses more easily integrated into society—finding jobs, friends, and independent housing, for example—than ex-convicts released directly into normal society? Finally, did these chosen convicts stay out of trouble, compared to other ex-convicts without the half-way program to help them?

CLOSING REMARKS

As you can see, sociologists are involved in a wide spectrum of research activity, much of it of great practical significance to people's lives. If you think about it you will probably realize that there are many good reasons why you should study sociology. In general, sociology will help you gain a broad perspective on the social world. There are careers in sociology for people who become interested in continuing in the field. As well, sociology—as a science—will help you see that things are not always what they seem to be. By helping you understand the social world better, sociology will help you function in that world. In short, it will provide you with some useful life skills. After studying sociology, you will be able to put your own problems in a broader context. That will help you understand and deal with your problems better. You will be better able to understand the groups you are part of—your family, friends, school classes, work groups, and so on. Sociology will give you tools that allow you to collect and analyze data about the social world. Finally, sociology will help you think about the world and its problems more objectively.

Discussion Questions

1. Have people write anonymous messages on slips of paper which, in a sentence or two, explain a personal problem they are having right now. Select one or more out of a hat, and discuss. Is this personal trouble the flip-side of a public issue? If so, what kind of issue?

2. Does sociology study different things than other disciplines, or does it simply study the same things in different ways? Support each side of this argument with examples.

3. Is it really possible for sociology to be value free, and should it be value free? Why, when people in the physical sciences (e.g., physicists, biologists) are becoming increasingly concerned about the ethics of their research and its consequences, should sociology be striving for value freedom?

4. Conflict theorists believe that most of us suffer from "false consciousness." What do they mean? Why do structural functionalists and symbolic interactionists not agree with this belief? What is your position on this?

5. If people really have "free will," as sociology seems to assume, does this mean they choose the lives they lead? Are they personally responsible for being poor, for example?

6. What are some of the main differences between pure research and applied research in sociology? Which kind of research do you consider more important to society; why? Should sociologists be prevented from doing certain kinds of pure or applied research?

Data Collection Exercises

1. Collect some data on rates of teenage suicide in Canada and other countries. Which countries rate high; which rate low? In which countries are the rates rising or falling? How might you begin to explain these differences? What additional data would you need to test your explanation?

2. How do people manage to "navigate" through crowds? Go to a crowded place (e.g., a shopping mall or busy street). Watch and record how people use their eyes, faces, and bodies to signal where they intend to walk, so as to clear a right-of-way. How do you suppose people learn to do this kind of signalling? Why does automobile traffic require other kinds of regulation?

3. Watch and record an interaction between two of your friends (or family members) as they try to resolve a disagreement. Did they reach an agreement? If so, what was the turning point in the negotiation—the point at which they began to close in on a resolution? Now that you have a hypothesis about conflict resolution, record a second interaction (observe different people, please!) and see if the same thing happens again.

4. Collect information about the way a public figure changed his or her "image" over the course of time. Can you show that the image changed in response to public opinion polls? Can you show that the changes made the public figure more popular?

Writing Exercises

1. Write a 500-word essay on one social process (a family quarrel, a union-management negotiation, a classroom lecture, a soccer game) as it might be described by an *astronomer*, who is accustomed to studying inanimate objects at a great distance. (In your explanation, ignore such psychological factors as attitudes and emotions, and focus on the ways some behaviours lead up to and result from other behaviours.)

2. Write a 500-word essay on one major event or issue (for example, the dropping of an A-bomb on Hiroshima in 1945, the social effects of acid rain, or why many people hate their job) from the symbolic interactionist perspective.

3. Write (but do not send) a 500-word letter to your province's medical association replying to their structural functionalist views on extra-billing (see page 18 above). Try the conflict perspective.

4. Write 200 words of advertising copy for a product — a good or service — you consider perfectly useless and idiotic. In doing so, keep in mind who your potential buyer (or market) is, and his or her attitudes, beliefs, motivations, and limitations. (Note: The advertisement must *seem* earnest and sincere.)

Glossary

conflict theory — a theoretical perspective that emphasizes conflict and change as the regular and permanent features of society, because society is made up of various groups who wield varying amounts of power

dyad — a two person group

groups — the primary subject matter of sociologists. On a micro level, a group is a collection of people who interact regularly face-to-face. On a macro level, a group is a category of people who share some important trait in common.

humanities — branches of knowledge concerned with studying human thought; they include philosophy, languages, literature and the fine arts.

macrosociology — the study of large social groups, social processes that characterize whole societies, and the system of social arrangements that exists in a given society

microsociology — the study of small groups, and of the processes and patterns of face-to-face social interactions that take place within these groups in everyday life

paradigm — a general way of seeing the world that embodies broad assumptions about the nature of society and social behaviour. It suggests which questions should be asked by sociologists and how answers should be interpreted.

scientific method — a systematic series of steps in research that ensures maximum objectivity. It includes a process of collecting evidence, making theories, and testing predictions against careful observations.

social structure — any enduring, predictable pattern of social relations. The participants in relations may be people, roles, groups, or institutions.

sociological imagination — an awareness of how individual experiences, values, beliefs, attitudes, and aspirations influence and are influenced by the social context

structural functionalism — a theoretical perspective that emphasizes the way each part of a society functions to fulfil the needs of society as a whole

symbolic interactionism — a theoretical perpective that studies the process by which individuals interpret and respond to the actions of others, and that conceives of society as the product of this continuous face-to-face interaction

Suggested Readings

Berger, Peter L. *Invitation to Sociology*. Garden City, N.Y.: Anchor (Doubleday), 1963. An elegantly written short introduction to the field, which generations of students have read with pleasure. However, the book ignores social conflict and gives the impression that social life is a state of mind, without historical context.

Collins, Randall and Michael Mayakowsky *The Discovery of Society*. New York: Random House, 1989. A brilliant short history of the development of sociology, set against the backdrop of 19th- and 20th-century social and political change.

Giddens, Anthony *Sociology: A Brief but Critical Introduction*. San Diego: Harcourt Brace Jovanovich, 1987. A short, interesting book on one central debate in sociology: whether contemporary social problems are due to capitalism (as Marx would say), industrialism (as Durkheim would say), or bureaucracy (as Weber would say).

Mills, C. Wright *The Sociological Imagination*. New York: Oxford University Press, 1967. This classic work in sociology is written from the conflict perspective. It emphasizes the close connection between personal troubles (private experience) and public issues (the wider social context).

Nisbet, Robert A. *The Sociological Tradition*. New York: Basic Books, 1966. Wonderfully written, this long book organizes much of the history of sociology around the "unit-ideas of sociology," or its founders' key concerns: community, authority, status, the sacred, and alienation.

Westhues, Kenneth *First Sociology*. New York: McGraw-Hill Ryerson, 1982. Written by a Canadian, this introduction to the field stresses the importance of moral as well as intellectual commitment in the study of society.

References

Durkheim, E. (1951) *Suicide*. New York: Free Press

_____ . (1938) *The Rules of Sociological Method*. Chicago: University of Chicago Press

Friedson, E. (1975) *Doctoring Together: A Study of Professional Social Control*. New York: Elsevier

Johnson, T. (1972) *Professions and Power*. London: Macmillan

Marx, K. (1955) *The Communist Manifesto*. Samuel H. Beer (ed.). New York: Appleton Century Crofts

_____ . (1969) *The German Ideology*. New York: International Publishers

_____ . (1936 [1867]) *Capital*. New York: Modern Library

Merton, R.K. (1957) "Manifest and latent functions" chapter 1 in *Social Theory and Social Structure: Toward the Codification of Theory and Research*, 2nd edition. New York: Free Press

Mills, C.W. (1959) *The Sociological Imagination*. New York: Oxford University Press

Oliver, T. (1987) *The Real Coke, The Real Story*. New York: Penguin

Parker, T. (1983) *Rules of Thumb*. Boston: Houghton Mifflin

Parsons, T. (1951) "Social structure and dynamic process: the case of modern medical practice" chapter 10 in *The Social System*. New York: Free Press

Schlozman, K.L. and S. Verba (1979) *Injury to Insult: Unemployment, Class and Political Response.* Cambridge: Harvard University Press

Sieber, S. (1981) *Fatal Remedies: The Ironies of Social Intervention.* New York: Plenum

Thomas, W.I. and D.S. Thomas (1928) *The Child in America.* New York: Alfred A. Knopf

Veenhoven, R. (1984) *Conditions of Happiness.* Dordrecht, Holland: Reidel Publishing

Weber, M. (1974) *The Protestant Ethic and the Spirit of Capitalism.* London: George Allen and Unwin

_____ . (1961) *General Economic History.* New York: Collier Books

_____ . (1958a) "Class, status, party" chapter 7 in H. Gerth and C.W. Mills (eds.) *From Max Weber: Essays in Sociology*, New York: Oxford University Press

_____ . (1958b) "Science as a vocation" Chapter 5 in H. Gerth and C.W.Mills (eds.) *From Max Weber: Essays in Sociology.* New York: Oxford University Press

CHAPTER 2

One person's meat is another person's poison. This "food" is on some culture's menu of delicacies. Just as there is almost nothing alive that some people won't eat, there are few forms of behaviour or human relationship you won't find somewhere.

CULTURE

CULTURE IS UNIQUELY HUMAN

What is Culture?

As human beings, we live in a world that is dramatically different from the world inhabited by other species on this planet. Whereas animals live within a *natural* environment to which, for the most part, they must adapt; human beings live in a *social* environment which, for the most part, we have created. This humanly created environment in which we live is culture.

Of course, human beings also live within a natural environment which, to some extent, constrains us. Like the other creatures with whom we share this planet, we breathe the air, enjoy the sights of grass and trees, swim in lakes, and run for shelter from the rain. Deprived of air, of food or water, we too will die. Our bodies catch diseases, put on weight, grow feeble and weakened with age. Nevertheless, if you look around you, you will notice that almost everything you see is the product of human activity: buildings, roads, cars—even the grass and trees in our parks and lawns are laid out as they are because people planted them that way. Culture is our uniquely human environment.

This is **culture** in its broadest sense: all of the objects, artifacts, institutions, organizations, ideas and beliefs that make up the symbolic and learned aspects of human society.

Looking at culture in this way, as a shared symbolic environment, helps to explain how and why the people of any particular society are alike. Culture structures a person's perception of the world and shapes his or her behaviour. That means that people who share a common culture share a similar way of experiencing the world. In this respect, a common culture helps to hold a society together.

We can also look to culture to account for many of the differences among us. People brought up in different cultures will experience the world in different ways. They will have different traditions, values, attitudes, and beliefs. They may eat different foods, wear different clothes, speak different languages. Even two nations as similar as Canada and the United States have significant cultural differences (see Exhibit 2.4). In addition, within one society there may be many subcultures which develop because of generational, class, or occupational differences. A **subculture** is a group that shares some of the cultural elements of the larger society, but also has its own distinctive values, beliefs, norms, style of dress, and behaviour patterns. A subculture may even, as in the case of ethnic groups, have its own language.

Because understanding its culture is so essential to understanding a society and the people who live within it, anthropologists who study relatively small-scale societies often focus on culture in order to get a picture of the whole society. Sociologists, who deal with large and complex societies, look at culture differently. We are more likely to be interested in the kinds of social differences that exist within a society—class, gender, ethnic, or other differences among people—and look at the role of culture in creating or preserving such differences.

Because we know most about other cultures that are similar to our own, everyday experience suggests that all people are pretty much the same. Despite some variations in speech and dress, the people you meet on the streets of Canada are a lot like one another. Even in the cities of Europe, you meet people like yourself. The food, the clothes, and the television programs are similar. You will see cowboy westerns on television in Paris, world-class fashion in Milan, skyscrapers in Barcelona, Athens, Vienna, and London.

The differences are more striking once we set foot outside the developed nations (especially the cities) of Europe and North America. In rural regions of Asia, Africa, or Latin America, you will see poorer versions of our own society mixed with some remnants of older, probably unfamiliar cultures. In fact you will see a puzzling mix and clash of many lifestyles, few of which can be found in North America. However, even this degree of difference from our own culture does not capture the wide range of human possibility.

Only the study of history and anthropology makes us aware of how widely cultures have varied over the ages. This variation tells us that human beings are capable of creating an extraordinary variety of social relationships and forms of social organization.

Culture and human nature

Before we begin to examine the different components of culture in some detail, let us look more closely at the distinction between culture and nature. Common sense takes culture for granted because most of us assume that our behaviour is a consequence of "human nature." We usually assume that our own ways of seeing the world and behaving in it are natural. We assume as well that our goals, motives, attitudes, and beliefs are the only sensible ones, and that everyone else would share them with us if their culture did not get in the way. However, nothing could be further from the truth. We are not born with any predispositions to any forms of cultural or social organization. Our perceptions and ways of acting are neither "natural" nor genetic, as they are with animals.

Animals, like humans, have patterned ways of thinking and behaving. They, too, have stable relationships with one another, such as parental or dominance patterns, and some even have a division of labour. A division of labour, or specialization, occurs when the different individuals gather food, reproduce, and defend the colony or group. Labours may divide along age and gender lines; for example, among bees we find a queen bee, worker bees, and drones. Like humans, very few animals live in isolation. One need only consider sea creatures—schools of fish, banks of coral, and communities of Portuguese men-of-war—to see that individualism is largely unknown among many creatures on the planet. The most complex and highly evolved species are also able to communicate information about the location of food supplies and enemies amongst their members.

However, such animal behaviour is largely genetic or inborn. That is why such behaviour does not vary much within the species; it does not change within a generation, or even scores of generations; and it is not learned, as it is in humans.

We know little about the genetic bases, if any, of human social behaviour. Likewise, researchers have so far found little ability among complex animals to learn what humans are able to learn. Despite the apparent similarities, we humans are far ahead of other animals in our abilities to change our environment, to learn from our experiences, and to pass on what we have learned to others. Unlike animals, we humans also vary among ourselves and adjust our behaviour to meet new challenges.

Our abilities to think, plan, remember and communicate ideas give humans a decided edge in creating complex social structures. Animals—like humans—do have a microsociology of their own; for example, members of most species can cooperate and communicate in some way. Animals often also have a macrosociology; for example, a division of labour and a ranking system. However, among animals, both the small "interpersonal" processes and larger social arrangements are genetically programmed. Neither is open to choice and voluntary change.

Among humans, *both* the micro- and macro-structures are negotiable and open to change. Indeed, it is human ability to change micro-structures—to imagine, plan and set about creating new futures—that permits us to change our larger social structures.

Is there anything that does limit how widely human cultures can vary; and if so, what is it? The search for an answer to this question has led generations of sociologists and anthropologists to look for and document cultural universals. **Cultural universals** are, in the simplest terms, practices or traits that are found in every known human culture. Anthropologist George Murdock (1945: 124) listed many cultural universals, including the following general attributes:

- athletic sports
- bodily adornment
- cooking
- dancing
- funeral ceremonies
- gift giving
- language

- laws
- music
- numerals and counting
- personal names
- religion
- sexual restrictions
- toolmaking

Because these activities are universal, we must allow for the possibility that they meet universal human needs, whether physical, emotional, intellectual, or spiritual. Nevertheless, however "natural" these needs might be, all humans appear to devise cultural means of meeting them, and to do so in a great variety of ways.

Take, as an example, religion. Religion consists of the collection of thoughts and practices that puts people in touch with the supernatural. The followers of some religions believe the supernatural dwells in all of nature, in natural objects like the ocean and natural forces like the wind. Other people conceive of distinct supernatural creatures – gods, goddesses, nymphs, devils, and so on. Some religions have many gods, some have only one. Some believe in an afterlife or in reincarnation while others do not. There are also differences in spiritual values – ideas of good and evil, for example – and ritual practices that distinguish the religions of the world.

To say that all human cultures contain religion is to point to something that unites human beings and (so far as we know) separates us from other animals. Yet religions vary enormously. The same is true for all the other cultural universals which have been found: the processes by which a common need is met differ between cultures.

Because culture is connected both to social structure and to personality, the concept of culture is an important link between the macro and micro perspectives on society and personality we discussed in the first chapter. Cultures reflect and order the social relationships that have grown up within a society while at the same time providing the means to allow new relationships to form. At the macro level, social institutions express the dominant **values** of a culture. Through socialization, which we will discuss in the next chapter, culture works at the micro level to shape personalities – the relatively stable combinations of traits that make up the way particular individuals view the world and interact with others.

One set of social relationships with which most of you are familiar is the family. Because the family is such an important social institution, the dominant values in our society that relate to the family provide us with an idealized version of family life, one which often does not fit the real circumstances in which we find ourselves. The failure to distinguish between "ideal culture" and "real culture" leads us to misinterpret public issues – the dramatic social and economic changes which are transforming family structures – as personal troubles – our personal inability to live up to the cultural ideal of what a family should be.

Real culture and ideal culture

Ideal culture is that aspect of culture that lives in the minds of the people who adhere to it. It is the set of values people claim to believe in, not the culture they express in their actual behaviour. People express their ideal culture in many forms: in holy books, laws, social institutions, novels, and television programs, for example. They adhere to an ideal culture and try to build social arrangements around it, even when their lives belie that ideal.

People express their **real culture** in their actual behaviour – how they dress, talk, act, and think. What they do may differ markedly from the values and norms people claim to believe in. Christians, for example, claim to adhere to values and norms spelled out in the New Testament, yet how many Christians actually turn the other cheek or love their neighbour as they love themselves? Not very many. In reality, Christians are no less selfish and no more compassionate or loving than Jews, Muslims, or Hindus.

Where real and ideal culture differ, it does not necessarily mean that the real culture is inferior. In some cases *ideal* signifies "pure" or "abstract" rather than desirable. If we return to our example of the family, it is clear that we pay lip service to an ideal of the family that scarcely exists any more. That ideal family includes a man and woman, married for the first time, and two or more children born to that couple, who are living at home. The man is the family bread-winner and the woman a housewife who earns no income. Television programs, popular novels, and social movements like REAL Women and Pro-Life promote this ideal family. Social welfare policies that view single mothers with distrust and treat them with contempt act as though the ideal version of family were a reality.

Yet, in fact, a large proportion of Canadian adults are single, separated, or divorced. Many adults live together without marrying, others are married for a second time. A great many married couples have no children or only one child, are raising children of another marriage, or have borne children who have since left home. In a majority of Canadian families of all kinds, adult women earn a weekly income: they too are bread-winners.

The split between ideal culture and actual behaviour leaves many people feeling abnormal, guilty, or disadvantaged. This feeling, that life is not what it should be, results from a lack of cultural integration. **Cultural integration** is the tendency of the various parts of a culture to fit together and complement one another. The more integrated the various elements of a culture are, the more likely a change in one element will have repercussions for other elements.

The lack of cultural integration with respect to family life keeps social policies—laws, regulations, and welfare practices, for example—from catching up to social and cultural changes that have already occurred. Similar problems can be found throughout our society: our ideal culture is always far behind real culture.

In the past, cultures were much more integrated than our own. Pre-modern, small-scale, traditional societies were more integrated, if for no other reason than that most people's lives had so little variety and held out so few possibilities that there was almost no distinction between what people expected and what they attained. The rapid pace of change in modern societies prevents that level of integration.

In North America, technology and the marketplace shape our culture. New goods and services always find their way into people's lives, even if they do not square with the ideal culture. This leads to vast variations in people's real lives, for example by region, ethnic group, and social class, and to vast differences between what people say they want—their expressed values—and what they actually do (and buy).

Material culture and non-material culture

We learn a great deal about what people actually want and do by studying their material culture—the physical and technological aspects of their lives. Material culture includes all the artifacts and physical objects that members of a culture create and use. Non-material culture is that part of a culture that goes on in people's minds. Non-material culture includes values, beliefs, philosophies, and patterns of government: in short, all the aspects of a culture that do not have a physical existence. So, for example, the material culture of Christianity includes Christian churches, hymnbooks, crucifixes, statues and art objects depicting Jesus and his family and followers. The non-material culture of Christianity consists of a body of ideas about Christ's mission on earth: especially salvation possible through acceptance of Jesus Christ, rewards for good behaviour and punishments for bad behaviour, and ways of thinking about the relationship between humanity and God.

The gap between real and ideal culture often expresses itself in a gap between material and non-material culture. In a culture as committed to a high standard of living and to consumer goods as ours is, we can learn a great deal about culture from the physical objects that surround us. They are as much our cultural masters as our servants. Material goods also shape social interactions. The cellular telephone, the fax machine, and the computer bulletin board have each had a major impact in a very short period of time on how we communicate with each other, while the "Walkman" has had an equally significant effect on preventing or inhibiting interaction.

Imagine Grok, a future sociologist who is trying to understand our culture by examining its physical artifacts. Grok would be able to learn a lot about our central values by studying a teenager's room. First, Grok would note the presence of information-saving and information-transmitting devices: books, magazines, televisions, records, tapes, radios, telephones, VCRs, videotapes, computers. From these, Grok might conclude that teenagers in our society depend on information flow for their education, recreation, social life, and livelihood.

Second, Grok would notice a wide variety of time-keeping devices: clocks, wristwatches, calendars, schedules, and datebooks, among others. From these, Grok might conclude that teenagers in our society use time efficiently and precisely.

Third, Grok would observe many objects of adornment: clothing for different occasions, jewellery, cosmetics, and false body parts (wigs, braces, false eyelashes and nails, contact lenses). From this, Grok might conlude that teenagers in our society have to look good if they value their friendships and romances.

Grok might find a great many other clues to Canadian culture by examining the material objects in an average Canadian home or workplace. Grok might even guess from the objects of adornment that Canadian teenagers value friendship, being loved, and success. From the timekeeping devices, Grok would guess they value hard work and reliability. (These are good guesses, as we shall see later in this chapter.)

Grok would be unlikely to find material clues that Canadian teenagers value freedom, honesty, or cleanliness. There is no one-to-one fit between material and non-material culture. At the same time, objects of material culture tell us a great deal about what people *really* value. That is because people have to spend valued time and money to acquire these objects.

EXHIBIT 2.1

THE CULTURAL BASIS OF CRICKET

The English game of cricket is played so slowly that it makes baseball—let alone hockey—seem almost reckless. What's more, players do something we would find amazing if it happened in a North American team sport: they applaud opponents for an excellent performance.

The cricket player's view that winning is not everything points to an interesting cultural difference between the English people and North Americans: a love of sport for its own sake. In cricket, everything depends on playing by the rules—on playing gracefully and, if possible, winning gracefully. Cheating is unacceptable because without manners, cricket is nothing. The essence of cricket, then, is the cultural outlook that underlies the game.

Even in the stands, good manners are considered important. While Australian cricketers recently beat an English team, easily and by a wide margin, English fans continued to applaud the Australians' virtuosity.

Yet all of this has started to change. There has been a decline in willingness to play by the rules and a greater tendency, by players, to question the decisions of umpires—previously considered an unsporting act. Behaviour has been changing in the stands, too. At a recent game in Leeds, many in the crowd were drunk, noisy, threatening, and disruptive; they even seemed indifferent to the play. In short, they behaved like a typical North American sports audience.

How would you account for this loss of the traditional cricketer's outlook in England? And how would you account for the historical fluctuation in, say, hockey violence—the fact that during some decades, the sport is much more violent than in other decades?

Adapted from John Gray, *The Globe and Mail*

CULTURE SHAPES BEHAVIOUR

Shared symbols and meanings

In addition to examining its material objects, a good way to start understanding a culture is by studying its shared signs and symbols. **Signs** are anything—gestures, artifacts, or words—that stand for, signify, express, or meaningfully represent something else. A "stop sign" stands for the legal command "Stop!" just as the word "woman" stands for a human female. A symbol is a sign whose relationship with something else expresses some value or generates some emotion. For example, a picture of a dove not only stands for a particular species of bird but also for the idea of peace; a flag not only identifies a country but embodies the sense of pride and identification with the country felt by its citizens.

Cultures differ widely in their symbols for the same thing and in the meanings they assign to the same object. Something you and I might consider a simple design or pattern might mean a great deal to someone else. For example, Muslims in Tongi, Bangladesh, ransacked a Canadian-owned Bata shoe store to protest against the sale of sandals bearing a logo they considered blasphemous. The logo resembled the Arabic word for *Allah*, or God. Police fired tear gas and rifles to disperse the group. One person was killed and 50 were injured in this upset over something Bata Shoes had never intended to have symbolic meaning.

Closer to home, a recent Quebec law requires that all public signs in the province must be in French. If the same information is provided in English, the French signs must be dominant. Legislators wrote this law to signify the dominance of French- over English-Canadian culture in that province. The passing of this law followed a great deal of emotional expression and political argument on both sides of the issue.

Such examples show that artifacts, words, and actions can—intentionally or unintentionally—signify important cultural meanings. These meanings can stir people to action, even to risking their lives. Their willingness to pay such a price is also a measure of the symbol's meaning. In people's eyes, protecting and honouring these symbols is the same as protecting and honouring their own group. Sharing and protecting these symbols and signs is considered central to a culture and the society. Actively opposing hated signs (for example, a swastika, or hammer and sickle) also honours a person's own group and strengthens group solidarity.

Because simple objects can be endowed with such powerful meanings and emotions, learning to participate in another culture is a slow, often difficult process. People can only learn the meanings of signs and symbols by immersing themselves in a culture—through observation, trial and error.

The importance of values

As we have seen, signs and symbols are used to express, or to challenge, the values of a society. Values are socially shared conceptions of what a group or society considers good, right, and desirable. Because they are internalized—learned and endowed with emotion and meaning—values influence peoples' behaviour and serve as standards for evaluating the actions of others.

In a classic study of the rise of capitalism, the German sociologist Max Weber (1974) argued that the *economic behaviour* we associate with modern life in the West would not have been possible without a major shift in the *religious values* which were dominant in medieval Europe. Today it is hard to believe that people once thought life on earth less important than life after death, or that hard work, thrift, and saving were considered unimportant or wicked. Yet people in the medieval, Catholic societies of Europe thought a concern with worldly activities, wealth, and profit-making through the investment of money at interest was immoral. Weber linked the rise of capitalism in the West with the rise of Protestantism, and particularly with a type of Protestantism—Calvinism—that developed in northwestern Europe in the 16th century.

Weber explained as follows: Calvinists believed that all people are predestined to go to either Heaven or Hell. Since they believed that salvation was already determined, their religion strongly emphasized the autonomy and independence of the individual, and reduced people's dependence on organized

IT'S MILLY TIME

What do these advertisements tell us about our cultural conceptions of happiness and how happiness can be attained?

religion (that is, the Church, priesthood, and ritual). Autonomy, independence, and the acceptance of new business activities all played a key role in the historic rise of capitalism.

Just as important to the emergence of capitalism was the development of new attitudes toward economic success among Calvinists, and their compulsion to make as much money as possible, which would then be re-invested in an enterprise. Weber suggested that because they believed salvation was predestined, Calvinists searched for a sign from God that they were among the "elect." Since they already believed that they were working for God, it made sense to see success at work as a sign of their good standing with God. By working hard and re-investing their profits, Calvinists sought financial success as a sign of God's favour.

What was critical about Protestant Calvinism, Weber said, was that it justified and encouraged activities that the Catholic Church had frowned on. By doing so, it allowed people to consider themselves moral and be rationally acquisitive at the same time. It offered a new, moral basis for the economic behaviour we call capitalism. This, says Weber, is why capitalism developed in Protestant Europe, not India, China, ancient Israel, or Catholic Europe.

The link between the rise of Protestantism and capitalism shows how changes in one cultural element (in this case, religion) may unintentionally bring about changes in another (in this case, the economy). What Weber called the **Protestant Ethic** is a doctrine formulated by Protestant reformer Martin Luther, who believed that everyone should work very hard for the glory of God. Calvinist Protestants took this doctrine of Luther's, combined it with the belief in predestination, and unwittingly created a new economic system: capitalism.

Do these Protestant values still guide people's lives? Bibby and Posterski (1985) surveyed Canadian teenagers and asked them what they were looking for in life. Over 80% cited friendship, being loved, and freedom as goals in their lives. Other values that two-thirds or more of the teenagers cited were success, a comfortable life, and privacy. By contrast, only a minority valued being popular, recognition (that is, fame), or acceptance by God.

When asked how they thought people ought to live, over two-thirds cited honesty, cleanliness, hard work, reliability, and forgiveness as appropriate means to their goals. They put imagination in last place; politeness and intelligence were also relatively low on their list of values.

Yet the Protestant ethic appears to live on in Canadian teenagers' *values* to some extent. Sixteenth century Calvinists would have agreed with the teenagers' assessment of honesty, cleanliness, hard work, and reliability. Like today's teenagers, they probably would have considered imagination, politeness, and intelligence much less important. On the other hand, Calvinism does not seem to live on in teenagers' *life goals*. Teenagers consider God much less important than people did four centuries ago, and they consider love, privacy, and freedom much more important.

However, bear in mind that our sample is made up of teenagers. Young people in Canada are more likely than older Canadians to dwell on the importance of privacy and freedom, since they do not have much of either. In time, these young Canadians may become more like their parents and give greater value to family life and economic security.

What is striking is the strong commitment of teenagers to values developed over 400 years ago in another part of the world. In any society, cultural continuity is at least as striking as cultural change. What's more, people start learning their culture's values at a very young age and never stop. We shall discuss this process of learning a culture in the next chapter.

Norms, folkways and mores

Few of our everyday-life activities are directed toward fundamental goals and values. For this reason sociologists use the concept of **norms** to indicate the less abstract sets of goals and expectations which guide behaviour in everyday life. **Norms** are expectations which serve as common guidelines. They tell us what is appropriate or inappropriate, normal or abnormal. There are many different types of norms. **Folkways**, a term Graham Sumner (1906) invented at the turn of the century, refers to the popular habits, traditions, and ordinary usages and conventions of everyday life. People expect others to conform to the folkways, but do not punish their violation formally. Because they do not regard a violator of folkways as being immoral, they punish the violator with stares of contempt and exclusion—nothing worse.

For example, consider teenagers' reaction to "nerds," portrayed in many movies of the last decade. The nerds do not violate teenage values. After all, nerds are just as committed to privacy, freedom, and friendship, to honesty, cleanliness, and hard work as anyone else. (In fact, they may be too serious about these goals!) Where they differ from other teenagers is in the way they dress, talk, and look. Nerds devote too little concern to their appearance, to taking part in popular activities or being popular. In these ways, the nerds stand guilty of violating the folkways of teenage behaviour. The others punish them with exclusion, ridicule, and contempt.

Mores, another term attributed to Sumner, are norms that do carry moral significance. People believe that mores contribute to the general welfare and continuity of their group. Because mores have a moral undertone, their violation is considered a serious matter and people punish it severely. Indeed, mores are often formalized into law.

In every society most people follow the appropriate norms of behaviour most of the time. This is not as easy as it sounds because norms are often situation-specific. They set standards for how people ought to act in a given situation. For example, the government hands out medals to people who kill enemies in wartime but prison terms to people who kill their enemies in peacetime. The act—killing another person—is the same in both cases, but the situations vary, as do the norms governing this behaviour.

To see more clearly how situation-specific norms work, think about how many behaviours which are considered appropriate in one situation would be considered inappropriate in another. You would be violating norms if you wore a bathing suit while eating in a classroom, wore pyjamas to Church, or sank to your knees in prayer in a hotel lobby with your shoes and socks off. Just think of how people would react to you—what they would say and do.

For the most part, we conform to the norms of our culture unquestioningly. We have internalized these norms and made them part of our personality and outlook on life. Also, because we are social beings, we need the approval of others for a feeling of self-worth. In this sense, most of our conformity to the rules of our culture is self-imposed and unconscious.

Nevertheless, norms do not determine behaviour; they are merely expectations. Deviation from norms is possible and all of us deviate from some norms, some of the time. Usually this deviation is relatively minor or is temporary, and leads to nothing too serious in how other people respond to us. Someone who violates serious norms, however, or who continuously violates norms may find the consequences very serious indeed. Such people may be labelled mentally ill.

People reward conformity to norms and punish deviation by social **sanctions**. There are two kinds of sanctions: positive and negative. A positive sanction is a social reward for the conformity to a norm, or for approved behaviour. A negative sanction is a punishment for behaviour that violates a norm. Sanctions reinforce the norms by controlling people's social behaviour.

Some behaviour is strongly prohibited and the prohibitions are strongly enforced. These prohibitions, **taboos**, are powerful social beliefs that a particular activity, food, place (and so on) is totally repulsive. The taboo, then, strictly prohibits certain activities. Infringement of the taboo is supposed to result in immediate punishment, either by the social group or by a supernatural force. An example of such a powerful taboo in our society would be cannibalism, the eating of human flesh.

Researchers once considered the "incest taboo," a supposed universal revulsion against sexual relations between two close relatives (for example, father and daughter, brother and sister, or first cousins), a cultural universal. Virtually every society does forbid certain kin from marrying each other, in the belief that such unions are immoral. However, societies differ markedly in which kin they forbid marrying in this way. Moreover, incestuous behaviour appears to be just as universal as the taboo itself. Certainly, the data (for example, Canada, 1984) suggest incest does occur in our own society, though it is illegal behaviour and considered child abuse when one of the participants is a minor.

As is true of other sociological concepts, culture is understood differently by sociologists using different perspectives. Because culture orders behaviour, those sociologists who emphasize order, such as structural functionalists, will typically look to culture and socialization to explain consensus and stability. But cultural values, norms, and taboos do not tell us what is actually going on in a society. In some instances, formal disapproval may mean that an action, such as incest, is occurring more frequently than many people would like. Conflict theorists would suggest that it may also indicate a conflict between two groups within the society: one that approves of the action and another that does not. The ongoing public debate and disagreement over abortion is a good example of this.

Finally, because human being are not robots, we should not think of values or norms as commands which people are programmed to follow. Symbolic interactionists emphasize how people make creative use of values and norms in the course of everyday-life interaction. For example, two of you may share the same cultural values and norms about love and loving relationships, but you have to work out the actual details of your relationship between you. This can be a thrilling process or it can be a painful one — often it is both — but is never exactly the same twice.

EXHIBIT 2.2

WHAT'S "IN" AND WHAT'S "OUT" IN OUR SOCIETY

In November, 1988, interviewers from Contemporary Research Centre (Toronto) asked a random sample of 2029 Canadians to tell them what, in their opinion, is currently "in" (modern or contemporary) and what is "out." What do their replies tell you about Canadian culture and the direction it is changing?

Reprinted by permission of Contemporary Research Centre.

	Percent who say "IN"		Percent who say "IN"
Buying lottery tickets	92	Summer cottages	70
Mothers who work outside the home	92	Winter vacations in the Caribbean	69
Personal computers	88	Car phones	67
Reading books	87	Designer clothes for "kids"	66
Cycling	87	Sunbathing	59
Fuel-efficient cars	87	Automobile racing	56
Condoms	84	Sending Christmas cards	50
Saving money	80	CFL football	49
Skiing	80	Summer vacations in Europe	47
Belonging to a health club	78	Attending religious services	46
Dancing	78	Fur coats	41
Bilingualism (French & English)	77	Drinking scotch	36
Eating in fast-food restaurants	76	Gin and tonic	31
Aerobics	75	TV dinners	30
Jogging	75	Earrings for men	29
Taking vitamins	74	Playing bridge	27
Drinking wine and spirit-based coolers	74	Smoking cigarettes	22
Breast feeding	73	Drinking and driving	18
Women's rights movement	72	Having a large family	10

Source: CRC Omnibus, November 1988. Face to face interviews with a random probability sample of 2029 Canadians, 15 years of age and over interviewed in their homes by CRC interviewers. A split sample technique was used so that approximately 1000 respondents categorized each of the 38 activities shown above.

LANGUAGE

One component of culture to which Canadians are particularly sensitive is language. As a multicultural nation made up of people from many different ethnic, religious, and linguistic backgrounds, the issues surrounding culture and language hold a central place in Canadian society. We will consider these issues in detail later in this chapter and in Chapter Six.

Language is an abstract system of sounds (speech), signs (written characters), and gestures (non-verbal communication) by which members of a society express their thoughts, feelings, ideas, and desires. This means that language, whether spoken or written, verbal or non-verbal, is the means by which the achievements of one generation are passed on to the next.

Like other signs and symbols, words carry intended and sometimes unintended meanings. We learn both kinds of meanings as active members of a culture, as much through observation and through trial and error as by formal instruction.

According to anthropologists Sapir and Whorf (Sapir, 1929), language helps us express our thoughts but also structures them. Because language is the most important means we use to communicate, the way in which a language is structured has immense significance for how we experience the world. Different languages provide different conceptual tools with which their speakers organize and interpret reality. A language does this by providing us with ready-made categories through which speakers "see" the world. Colour, for example, is one such set of categories. We see one object as "red," another as "green," still another as "blue" because our culture assigns objects to these categories. Other cultures assign colours differently. In many cultures, for example, what we see as two distinct colours, "blue" and "green," are seen as two shades of a single colour; similarly, we see two shades of red as being "pink" and "red." As children learn to speak the language of their culture, they also adopt the assumptions that pervade their language.

Cultures make words to describe, and thereby teach members of a society to see, what the society cares about. The Slave, a native group of the Northwest Territories and Alberta, have a culture that traditionally involved travelling and fishing on ice. They developed a complex vocabulary related to describing ice conditions, one that included separate terms for ice that is thin, thick, brittle, muddy, wet, hollow, slippery, blue, black, white, seamed, cracked, or floating. On the other hand, the English language has dozens and possibly hundreds of words that describe machines of various kinds. Eskimo and other pre-industrial languages have very few such words, and often adopt words from English for referring to these items.

Most of the assumptions embodied in language are tacit; that is, they are known but remain implicit, sometimes not even recognized. These tacit assumptions lurk everywhere in our language. A good example is the use of sexist language in English. We are all accustomed to using the words "*man*kind," "police*man*," "chair*man*," and other words that include the word "man." Historically, many of these words have aptly described the role in question; for example, police*men* and chair*men* really were men, not women.

The view that people should switch to gender-neutral terms such as "police officer" and "chair person" is more than a quibble. If the Sapir-Whorf hypothesis is valid, our continued use of the masculine words implies that women are still absent from these roles, and perhaps should be. If we continue to see women in these roles as being deviant, we may end up discouraging women from seeking the roles. Wittingly or unwittingly, the use of these terms today serves only to affirm the traditional subordination of women to men.

The inability of certain languages to name and talk about certain kinds of things makes communication across cultures very difficult. It also makes rapid cultural change very difficult. A person from a pre-industrial culture who wishes to assimilate into an industrial society will have to learn new speaking and thinking patterns which may differ considerably from those of his or her own culture.

All languages have their strengths and weaknesses, when it comes to perceiving and communicating about the world. None is absolutely better than any other, although some may be better than others for thinking and talking about certain kinds of things. The English language is a flexible tool for communicating information about modern life. However, there may be shades of meaning, states of mind, and types of feelings that the English language steers us away from understanding. People who must give up another language to live their lives in English will be more aware of this loss than anyone else.

CULTURAL INTEGRATION

The mass media

An important source of cultural integration in the modern world are the mass media. As our imaginary sociologist, Grok, would have noticed, we all consume mass media to a degree that no one would have imagined a century ago. **Mass media** are forms of communication which impart information to, or influence the opinions of, large audiences, without any personal contact between the senders and receivers of the messages. Examples of mass media are television, movies, newspapers, and radio.

The invention of the printing press by Gutenberg in the 1430s made possible the mass distribution of printed books, and initiated a revolution in the nature and effects of communication. One effect was the spread of literacy, the growth in numbers of people who could read and interpret information for themselves. People no longer needed to rely on the village priest to teach them what the Bible said; they could do it for themselves. This change supported the breakaway of Protestants from the Catholic church in 16th-century Europe.

The spread of printed information through newspapers, handbills, and manifestos also helped people to mobilize for political action. Information, and the sense of power it conveyed, helped to support the French and American revolutions of the 18th century and other rebellions of the 19th century.

The rise of technology in the 20th century that conveys information through sound and image—the camera, radio, telegraph, telephone, and television—has brought whole populations into awareness. Even people who are are illiterate and who live in distant parts of a country can know what is going on by listening to a transistor radio. This development of information technology has made cultural integration and political rebellion equally possible. We have yet to see what impact the next generation of information technology – computers – will have, although some have claimed that the dramatic changes which swept through Eastern Europe in 1989 were in part a consequence of information technology freely crossing national borders.

This century has seen both cultural integration and political rebellion realized through the use of mass media. The media's potential both for maintaining and for overthrowing order has made its control a central concern in the 20th century. In the Third World, many countries are going through the same steps of national unification that Europe and North America have centuries earlier. This has made the mass media central to their economic and cultural development too.

Canadian thinker Marshall McLuhan (1965) has written that "the medium is the message." By this he means that the type of medium – whether written word or visual image – will determine the cultural impact and interpretation of a message. Television and movies have a different impact from the written word. As a result, new technologies have started a second revolution in mass communications.

Economist and historian Harold Innis (1972) goes even further, stating that the medium of communication – whether verbal or written – will determine the form a society takes. An oral tradition supports a rich and flexible civilization, based on custom and training. A written tradition supports standardization, discipline, and political unification, says Innis. Writing on paper, not stone, is the means of communication leaders need to use if they want to build empires.

Ethnocentrism

Though one language may fit a given situation better than another, most people would agree that no language is necessarily better than any other. Yet it would be hard to persuade people that no particular values were better than any others. People are so emotionally involved with their culture that often they cannot see that their own values, like other cultural traits, are merely one approach to human life. Their **ethnocentrism** leads them to view everything from the point of view of their own culture.

Ethnocentrism refers to a tendency to use one's own culture as a measuring stick for evaluating all other cultures. One's own culture is taken to be the norm, and is therefore considered superior to all other cultures, which deviate from that norm. Ethnocentrism leads people to assume that what is true of one's own culture should be true of another.

Ethnocentrism is particularly dangerous in a world in which nations with different cultures and institutions must cooperate to achieve common goals. Cooperating means crossing cultural boundaries and, increasingly, governments have been willing to look for ways of doing this. However, accepting cultural variation as a fact of human life and avoiding ethnocentrism are not easy matters. Ethnocentrism is not only cultural short-sightedness; it is sometimes rooted in people's upbringing and values.

CULTURAL VARIATION

Subcultures and countercultures

We noted earlier the doubt that a unified Canadian culture really exists. Instead, a variety of ethnic, linguistic, and regional groups seem to co-exist in Canadian society. However, people who belong to these distinctive cultural groups may still share a great deal with other Canadians. So, it makes more sense to speak of many subcultures co-existing within Canadian society, than it does to speak of many cultures.

A subculture emerges when a particular segment of society faces problems or pressures, or enjoys privileges unique to its social and economic position. Members of a subculture may share a common age, religion, ethnic heritage, belief system, occupation, interest, or hobby. Or, they may share exclusion from the larger society (as, for example, is true of prison inmates).

A **counterculture** is a subculture that rejects conventional norms and values and adopts alternative ones. It is fundamentally at odds with the culture of the larger society. Such a subculture is often found among younger and less advantaged members of a society. A counterculture develops among people with little reason to conform to the main culture. Such people are not likely to get rewarded with praise, good jobs, or high incomes even if they value what people are supposed to value and do what people are supposed to do. They may be victims of prejudice and discrimination, like many visible minorities. Or they may not be taken seriously because they are considered too young or very old.

A counterculture helps people solve their problems by rejecting the majority values. In effect, a counterculture rejects conventional morality and makes deviance—the more outlandish, the better—the new standard of behaviour for this group. Keep in mind, though, that members of a counterculture do not reject conformity to everything, only conformity to some of the primary goals that most Canadians believe in pursuing.

Like every subculture, a counterculture has its own beliefs, material culture, and problems of cultural integration. Even members of the Hell's Angels have their loyalties; even anarchists own personal possessions. Delinquents, punk rockers, and skinheads too have their ideals. Just like any group, every counterculture is full of contradictions between what members say and what they do.

A good example of a subculture that is *not* a counterculture is the gay subculture. The gay subculture provides homosexual people with social supports for living the lifestyle they prefer. This subculture is not, in principle, opposed to the "straight" lifestyle of heterosexuals; in their own subculture, gays simply show no interest in living the "straight" life.

However, it is often difficult to distinguish a subculture from a counterculture. For example, is the often-studied delinquent or gang subculture merely designed to support the delinquent lifestyle of its members? Or is it a purposeful rejection of the values that underpin law-abiding, middle-class society? Sociologists disagree about this. There is less disagreement that certain politically militant groups—for example, the Palestine Liberation Organization, or Solidarity—are based on countercultures and not merely subcultures.

High culture and popular culture

Not all subcultures consist of the disadvantaged or the victimized. At the upper end of the social scale, we find people with quite different subcultures. These are not countercultures but neither are they part of the cultural mainstream. High status people—who benefit most from the way society is organized—do not necessarily conform to the majority culture.

It is people in the middle class, rather than the upper class, who stand to gain most by conforming to the rules and values of popular culture. If they conform, they may be able to move up the social ladder; if they do not, they may slide down. People at the bottom of the social scale stand to gain least from conformity. They also have the least to lose from noncomformity: that is why they can risk forming countercultures.

As for people at the top of the social scale, they run little risk of losing their power, wealth, and position, and they stand to gain nothing by conforming to ordinary standards. So many people of the upper class create a culture that is just as outlandish as a delinquent or bohemian counterculture.

Another segment of the upper class participates in what is sometimes called "high culture." **High culture** refers to the set of preferences, habits, tastes, values, and norms that are characteristic of, or supported by, high status groups in society; they include the fine arts, classical music, ballet, and other "highbrow" concerns. Of course, wealthy people are not the only ones who attend symphony concerts, read poetry, or visit art galleries. If they were, audiences would be too small to keep the shows open. These activities are called high culture, first, because people with more than average formal education—that is, a high education—are most likely to patronize them. Second, supporters believe these activities require a higher intellectual level than, say, bowling or reading *TV Guide*. Third, the financial support of upper-class donors keeps these arts alive in Canada. Upper-class philanthropy provides much of the operating budget for many of these activities.

Historically, the high culture that painters, poets, and composers created for wealthy patrons dignified the aristocracy's image of itself. According to art historian John Berger (1972), classic works of art

> supplied the higher strata of the ruling class with a system of references for the forms of their own idealized behaviour. . . . They offered examples of how the heightened moments of life—to be found in heroic action, the dignified exercise of power, passion, courageous death, the noble pursuit of pleasure—should be lived, or, at least, should be seen to be lived. (Berger, 1972: 101)

High culture excludes many more people than it includes. By the images it conveys and the views it ennobles, high culture has traditionally cut ordinary people off from their own history.

Instead, middle- and working-class people develop and make use of a popular culture of their own. **Popular culture** is the culture of the masses, and includes those objects, preferences, and tastes that are widespread in the population. Popular culture is a blanket term for any element of culture that is distinct from the culture of high-status groups.

Like all forms of culture, popular culture is fragmented along age, sex, and social-class lines. We can see this fragmentation in market surveys that identify the viewers of different kinds of television programs: educational television *versus* soap operas *versus* sports, for example. Similar fragmentation is found in people's preferences and tastes in leisure, dress, eating, and even living-room decoration.

At the same time, popular culture reflects the influence of high culture. We see this influence in mass advertising. John Berger has identified some of the images that advertising has borrowed from classical oil painting such as the poses used to denote stereotypes of women: serene mother (madonna), free-wheeling secretary (actress, king's mistress), perfect hostess (spectator-owner's wife), and sex-object (Venus, nymph surprised). There are also physical stances which convey the wealth and power of men.

The mass media and popular culture have developed hand in hand. They reflect the rise of new technologies for reaching large numbers of people. They also reflect the rise of enormous new audiences with a great deal of money to spend. Trends in high culture reflect the growth of new audiences too. The fine arts began to change as early as the 19th century with the rise of middle classes who were anxious to establish their social worth by buying pictures (White and White, 1965).

Dominant ideologies

People make their own cultures, it is true. However, in every society, some people have more influence over their culture than others, because they can more easily control communication and the flow of information. The cultural ideas they promote may come to dominate people's thinking, and for this reason some sociologists refer to these ideas as the dominant ideology of a society, as we discussed in Chapter One. An **ideology** is a coherent set of related beliefs about the nature of the world and the people in it. People use ideologies to guide their interpretation of, and reactions to, daily events. An ideology influences the use and exercise of power, and may explicitly guide political action. Revolutionary ideologies like communism and fascism are examples. Also, an ideology may be moulded by, or react against, the ruling class in society.

A **dominant ideology** is an ideology that supports the dominant group. Most of us accept its validity because we have learned and believe this dominant ideology. Our schools, churches, and mass media teach the dominant ideology of our society, which serves to justify the position, power, and rewards of the members of the ruling class.

Consider the ways we learn to think about the rich and powerful members of our society: political figures like the Prime Minister, and important business people like bank directors and wealthy investors. We are taught to think that they are smarter, harder working, more knowledgeable, more public-spirited and therefore more deserving of rewards than the rest of us. People like them, not people like us, make history. The well-being of our culture, government, and economy depends on the wisdom and kindness of these people. We owe them everything.

The dominant ideology glorifies the rich. It also pacifies the poor by making them feel responsible for their own dismal condition. The schools, churches, and mass media all promote the idea that our society doles out rewards to people who deserve them most. In effect, they suggest that life is like school: the smartest and hardest-working people get the best grades, while the "dumbest" and laziest fail. So the ideology says; but most of life is not like school at all: you can inherit a fortune and social connections from your parents. In school, no one ever inherited an A-plus or flunked out on the first day of classes.

The imagery of free and fair competition, which justly rewards the rich and justly punishes the poor, is all around us. It is even part of the language we use to discuss current events.

For example, newspaper and television commentators use the same words to describe business activities, political campaigns, and military offensives as they do football games. The descriptions are all morally neutral and imply that no actions are good or bad in themselves. All events—whether a bombing, a hostile takeover, or the discovery of political corruption—are described as though they took place outside a social context, without any historic meaning or ethical significance. They are no different from scoring touchdowns or fumbling the ball: mere competitions fought according to their own rules, using their own particular weapons and strategies. Winning generals, tycoons, and quarterbacks always deserve a pat on the back.

This style of thinking leads people to blame themselves for personal troubles like poverty or unemployment. They feel that they deserve to lose because they are losers.

Cultural capital, cultural literacy

Dominant ideologies are not the only ways in which powerful people use culture to their own advantage. There are many ways cultural advantage is spread unequally throughout the population. Two sorts of advantages which are unequally distributed are cultural capital and cultural literacy.

French sociologist Pierre Bourdieu (1977) coined the term **cultural capital**. It refers to a body of knowledge and interpersonal skills that helps people to get ahead socially. Familiarity with high culture is one form of cultural capital. This familiarity can help in establishing good social relations with wealthy and powerful people. A study of American high-school and college students by DiMaggio and Mohr (1985) shows that young people with more cultural capital—more familiarity with good books, opera, and art, and also a tendency to identify themselves as "cultured"—do better in life than similar young people with less cultural capital. Cultural capital affects their educational attainment, college attendance, college completion, graduate-school attendance, and even choice of marriage partners.

Cultural capital includes a wide variety of skills that enhance social relationships. They include knowing how to speak well and interestingly, what topics to discuss, how to order and eat graciously, what beverages to drink, how to dress stylishly but tastefully, how to play a variety of games and sports that others may want to play (e.g., tennis, sailing, bridge, chess, polo), knowing how to compare scotches or wines or race-horses or hotels in different European cities, and so on.

Few people learn these things in school. To learn them requires a wide variety of personal experiences, indulgent parents, devoted teachers, and a great deal of time and money to spare. Cultural capital helps people get ahead because it marks them out from the rest of the field. They end up with more advantages because they start out with more.

Middle-class parents often try to provide their children with experiences that will provide them with cultural capital. These may include ballet lessons, private schooling, foreign trips abroad, instructional summer camps, and so on. Working-class parents are rarely able to give their children these experiences. As a result, working-class children are less likely to get ahead socially than middle-class children. Indeed, among the poorer members of society, cultural literacy, not cultural capital, is often the issue.

Unlike cultural capital, which is a luxury, cultural literacy is an absolute necessity in our society. **Cultural literacy** is a solid knowledge of our own traditional culture—the building blocks of all communication and learning. To be culturally literate is to have enough general knowledge about the world to be able to communicate effectively with any adult member of the society.

Historian E.D. Hirsch (1988) argues that schools ought to provide their students with such a store of cultural knowledge, rather than abstract thinking skills. He cites research to show that effective learning does not depend on general intelligence, creativity, or an ability to solve problems. It depends on an ability to understand words and concepts and to quickly recognize common patterns of meaning.

This means that experience is more important than ability. A chess grandmaster, Hirsch claims, is much better than anyone else at identifying traditional game strategies and responding to them. Outside a chess game—say, in fixing a car, filling out an income-tax form, or preparing a meal—the grandmaster is no more capable or creative than you or I. On the other hand,

All humans communicate meanings and intentions with their bodies, although "body language" differs somewhat from one culture to another. See if you can tell what each of the bodies is "saying". How did you learn this "language"?

the experienced chef is extraordinarily creative in the kitchen, but no more creative than anyone else outside it. So creativity and problem-solving abilities depend on concrete knowledge.

This suggests that, before people can learn anything else, they need to master a body of information. What's more, this body of information they need for everyday life is easy to identify. In North American culture it is the storehouse of common knowledge—a few thousand names, dates, concepts, and expressions to which most people refer in their thinking and communication. The vast majority of items in this storehouse date back 50 years or more. So the storehouse of common knowledge is not only useful and widely known; it is also slow to change. All of us know (or ought to know) what is meant by an "Achilles heel," for example, an expression which refers to a hero in a Greek myth which dates back well over 3000 years. Cultural items in this storehouse are known and used nationally by literate people from every ethnic and racial group, region, and social class.

The culture of poverty

People without access to cultural capital or deprived of cultural literacy nevertheless have their own distinctive, enduring pattern of values, ideas, and behaviours. Anthropologist Oscar Lewis (1961), who carried out extensive field research on poor people living in slum communities of Mexico and other less developed nations, found what he called a *culture of poverty*. This **culture of poverty** is the "structure, rationale, and defense mechanisms" of people "who are at the very bottom of the socio-economic scale, the poorest workers, the poorest peasants, plantation labourers, and that large heterogeneous mass of small artisans usually referred to as the lumpen proletariat" (Lewis, 1961: xxiv, xxv).

The culture of poverty lacks cultural integration. Perhaps more than any other form of culture we have discussed, it patches together traditional and modern, rural and urban traits. Old beliefs and new practices, ancient superstitions and streetwise dodges make up the culture. The people who live in this culture of poverty lack the resources they would need to make their culture richer and more consistent. Like an often-repaired household tool, the culture of poverty stays on because it still works, even if badly.

It works because the culture of poverty reflects the experience of these people as victims of inequality and social change. Important cultural elements include a belief in luck, magic, and destiny. Males learn to show off and take careless risks with their lives. People rarely plan and prepare for the future. They seek excitement and bravado in a life that is otherwise filled with drudgery and deprivation.

The culture of poverty is full of defeats and self-defeating actions. It steers people away from cultural literacy and a middle-class, industrial lifestyle. In this way the culture perpetuates victimization and lets the rest of us off the hook. We can feel blameless and virtuous in our enjoyment of prosperity. In our own society, the culture of poverty is found among poor urban immigrants, some native peoples on reserves, and impoverished groups who have migrated to cities from northern Canada and the Maritimes.

HOW CULTURES CHANGE

A great many factors go into changing the culture of a society. New technologies for sharing information and ideas play an important part. Also, changes in the balance of ethnic and regional groups, of rich and poor, rural and urban, young and old, make a difference. This is because people's cultures not only shape but also reflect their life experiences. Different groups have different typical experiences and, as some groups become larger or smaller, their experiences become more or less common in society. In that way, different cultural traits become more or less common.

Changes in the natural environment affect our culture as well. As the dangers to human survival through pollution and environmental damage become more and more obvious, our values and behaviours are bound to change.

For the most part, cultures change through innovation and diffusion. With **cultural innovation**, people invent and introduce new ideas, objects, or methods of doing things into a culture. There are two forms of cultural innovation: discovery and invention. Discovery involves finding out about and making known the existence of something that was always there, but whose existence was not known. Examples of this include the discovery of radium by Marie Curie and her husband, and of the medicinal properties of penicillin. On the other hand, invention is the creation or design of something that did not exist before—for example, a car, television, or form of jewellery.

Cultural diffusion is the process by which cultural elements spread from their point of origin to other points or areas—from group to group within a society, or from one society to another. The adoption of ideas, technology, and customs from other cultures is very common, and it increases with the spread of mass communications. Cultural diffusion also occurs through trade, exploration, military conquest, missionary work, and tourism.

It is often no simple matter to determine whether a cultural change has come about through innovation or diffusion. Sometimes researchers can trace the historic spread of a new tool or idea (or even word) from one part of the world to another. They do this by studying traces of the flow of people—including warriors, traders, and colonists—who might have carried the tool or idea from one place to another. Often, they look for material artifacts along the path of this flow. As well, researchers look for formal similarities between the tool or idea as it exists in places A and B. The greater the number of similarities, the less likely the thing in question could have been invented anew in both places.

Elements of both the material and non-material culture undergo cultural diffusion. However, receiving cultures are more likely to resist the spread of foreign ideas and values than they are to resist new technology and consumer items. New ideas, belief systems, philosophies, and ideologies are much more threatening than new ways of cultivating the land, making cars, or healing the sick. Adopting a foreign belief may force people to question their fundamental assumptions about the way the world works. Such cultural change makes people much more uncomfortable than changing the way they use tools, wear clothes, or cook food.

When a culture changes very rapidly, whether through innovation or diffusion, culture shock may result. **Culture shock** is a term that normally describes the disorienting effect of a totally foreign culture on a newcomer.

Futurist Alvin Toffler (1971) has used the term "future shock" to describe the disorientation people experience as a result of the speed-up of social and cultural change in modern societies. With modern information technologies, each generation must deal with and absorb information which increases in quantity and undergoes changes (including changes to theories, ideas, and facts) faster than any generation before it. When things are changing quickly, it is hard to know what to believe—what values, norms, and behaviours are appropriate and workable. The confusion people feel is future shock, a type of culture shock.

CANADIAN CULTURE

Multiculturalism and cultural pluralism

Issues of cultural change and conflict are particularly pressing in a country like Canada, which contains a wide variety of cultural groups. In addition to all of the various ethnic groups there are regional subcultures, religious groups, occupational groups, and a host of others. Because of Canada's historical origin as a political union of the British and the French, however, ethnic subcultures are particularly significant. In Canada, cultural pluralism is not only a reality, it is an official policy. **Cultural pluralism** is a social arrangement under which several distinctive cultures, or ethnic subcultures, co-exist within a society. The members of these subcultures share some cultural elements with the larger society of which they are a part. At the same time, they maintain their own identities and some unique cultural traits.

Multiculturalism is the name of a federal government policy that supports cultural pluralism in Canada. As an official policy, muticulturalism is only about 20 years old. It grew out of attempts to deal with Canada's historic problem of bilingualism and biculturalism.

Canada became a nation through the signing of the British North America Act of 1867. The BNA Act assured that French Canadians living in Quebec would retain a great deal of control over cultural and educational matters, although French Canadians living outside Quebec would have less certainty

These children do not have much cultural capital or cultural literacy. So what will they have to work with as adults?

EXHIBIT 2.3

WHY CITY LIFE IS OVERWHELMING

People who leave farms or small towns for large cities often remark on the difference in lifestyles they experience: the coldness or aggressiveness of big-city people, the hectic pace of life there, and the difficulty they have establishing close relationships. Writing nearly a century ago, sociologist George Simmel was one of the first scholars to discuss this problem in his classic work, "The metropolis and mental life."

Simmel (1950:422) notes that, because of a city's size, economic function, and complex division of labour,

> the individual has become a mere cog in an enormous organization of things and powers which tear from his hands all progress, spirituality, and value in order to transform them from their subjective form into the form of a purely objective life. . . . On the one hand, life is made infinitely easy for the personality in that stimulations, interests, uses of time and consciousness are offered to it from all sides. They carry the person as if in a stream, and one needs hardly to swim for oneself. On the other hand, however, life is composed more and more of these impersonal contents and offerings which tend to displace the genuine personal colorations and comparabilities. . . . [The individual] has to exaggerate this personal element in order to remain audible even to himself.

Paradoxically, preachers have repeatedly condemned the modern city's excess of wealth and "objective culture" and lack of "subjective culture"—that is, of personal values and spirituality. Yet this very lack of subjective culture in the city is

> also a reason why these preachers are so passionately loved in the metropolis and why they appear to the metropolitan man as the prophets and saviors of his most unsatisfied yearnings.

Source: *The Sociology of George Simmel*, K.H. Wolff, trans., ed., and introduction. New York: Free Press, 1950

their culture would survive. By leaving culture, language, and education out of federal political control it was assumed that each provincial community had the means and the will to preserve its own culture. What this really meant, however, was that Canada's federal government could not resolve ethnic or linguistic disputes and that these were often left to fester. Inevitably, a number of problems arose both inside and outside Quebec which showed that French-Canadian culture would have trouble surviving.

These problems were amply clear by the early 1960s, when the process of modernization in Quebec set in motion wide-ranging political, social, and economic changes usually called the "Quiet Revolution." This process strengthened the Quebec government within Confederation and better equipped French Canadians within Quebec for economic and political competition with English speakers. Nevertheless, despite their gains, significant numbers of Quebeckers began to question whether Quebec really had a place in Canada. Many Canadians, both English- and French-speaking, realized that it was time to reassess the nature of Canadian Confederation and to rethink the role both of Canada's ethnic groups and of the federal government. When Lester Pearson became Prime Minister, he pledged to investigate and solve the problem of cultural inequality.

Pearson established a Royal Commission on Bilingualism and Biculturalism to study the disabilities associated with being a French Canadian in a predominantly English-Canadian country. After several years of research, the Commission's Report (Canada, 1969) recommended many changes, and some were adopted. For example, the federal civil service now pursues an active policy of bilingualism and more equal hiring of francophones and anglophones. In the area of education, the federal government has expanded its funds for what is a provincial responsibility, to make francophones more competitive.

However, other ethnic communities resented the federal support for francophones, even though the BNA Act had never guaranteed these groups cultural protection. Communities of Ukrainian, German, and Italian Canadians, among others, wanted federal recognition that they, too, contributed to Canadian life. They also wanted financial help to make sure their cultures survived. For several reasons, the federal government came around to their way of thinking. First, it wanted to defuse opposition to all the changes that would help francophones. Second, it recognized that Canada had always been a mix of ethnic groups that kept their cultures. Formal policies supporting cultural pluralism would simply strengthen what already existed. Finally, ethnic minorities had traditionally supported the Liberal Party, the party in power when the policy was formulated. When he became Prime Minister, Pierre Elliott Trudeau was reluctant to lose the support of the ethnic minorities by denying their request. That is why the federal government today regularly funds multicultural events, and ethnic cultural and social organizations: what we call "multiculturalism."

Is there any standard we can apply to judge whether cultural pluralism or multiculturalism benefits the whole society? For example, is there any evidence that cultural pluralism increases the cohesion of Canadian society, the degree of cooperation among different groups, the effectiveness of the federal government, or the economy's ability to change and compete in world markets?

It is doubtful cultural pluralism has any of these functions or outcomes. On the contrary, cultural pluralism is likely to reduce cohesion and cooperation between groups (Porter, 1979). Indeed, Canada has been faced by a series of political crises since the late 1960s brought about by the lack of cultural consensus and cooperation: the October Crisis in 1970, the election of the Parti Québécois in 1976, the Quebec Referendum on Sovereignty Association in 1980, the Constitutional Crisis of 1983, the invocation of the "notwithstanding" clause by Quebec in 1989, and the Meech Lake constitutional debates of 1989 and 1990. Much of Canada's political discord is thus partly cultural in origin.

On the other hand, some believe that this unassimilated mix and clash of varied cultures is basic to Canada. To have a country like Canada—as distinct from an American "melting pot"—means putting up with a hurly-burly of competing cultures. To value Canadian society is to value cultural pluralism and to support multiculturalism. In their eyes, cultural pluralism *is* Canadian culture.

EXHIBIT 2.4

ARE CANADA AND THE UNITED STATES DIFFERENT?

Canadian and American cultures are very similar, as anyone who has travelled in the two countries will have noticed. Yet the two cultures are also very different.

The differences show up in different kinds of laws, ways of solving political conflicts, and even interpersonal behaviour. Canadians particularly have made a common practice of comparing themselves with Americans, to make sure they are no worse. Yet it was an American sociologist, Seymour Martin Lipset, who had the greatest influence on the way Canadian sociologists view differences between the two cultures.

During brief stays to research a book on the CCF in Saskatchewan and teach at the University of Toronto, Lipset formed some very definite views about Canada. His analyses started with what he saw and experienced. Lipset was intrigued, for example, that faculty and students at the University of Toronto used different washrooms. This difference from American practice suggested to Lipset that Canadians are more elitist—more anxious to maintain a social distance between people in authority and others—than Americans.

People who are elitist readily submit to authority. They are likely to place a greater value on the group (or society) than on the individual. In general, such people are more traditional and conservative in their habits and views than Americans.

Using a variety of data, ranging from novels and literary criticism, through historical analyses to modern survey data, Lipset tested his theory. Can you prove it wrong? Others have.

Source: S.M. Lipset *Continental Divide: The Values and Institutions of the United States and Canada.* New York: Routledge, 1990

Images of Canadian culture

Cultural pluralism is one way people view Canadian culture and what sets Canada apart from the United States, England, or other Western nations. However, it is not the only one. Exhibit 2.4 gives another vision of Canadian culture, developed by the American sociologist Seymour Martin Lipset (1990). It is the image of Canadian culture as elitist, traditional, and focused on the group rather than the individual.

Lipset's vision of Canadian culture is one that a great many observers of Canada would accept. However, support for this view comes largely from outside Canadian sociology: from novelists (like Margaret Atwood), journalists (like Richard Gwyn, Pierre Berton, and Andrew Malcolm), literary critics (like Northrop Frye and George Woodcock) and historians (like Ramsey Cook). There is some evidence, however, that the validity of Lipset's thinking has declined in the last two decades. While Canada's institutions have tended to preserve its cultural history, and Canada was, historically, more traditional and group-oriented than the United States, recent survey data find little support for Lipset's cultural analysis. Where researchers do find cultural differences between Canadians and Americans, they run in the wrong direction. For example, in both our social policies, such as medicare, and our attitudes

Cultural artifacts express people's values. Paintings done in the late 19th century force us to wonder why fine artists then often portrayed women as sickly, sleeping, or dead. Why did they, and their audience, equate sickliness with femininity and virtue?

Tissot, James, *The Convalescent*, 1872

towards the disadvantaged, Canadians are much more egalitarian than Americans (Baer, Grabb, and Johnston, 1990).

People, then, hold at least two images of Canadian culture. One is that Canadian culture is a mosaic of competing ethnic cultures. Another is that Canadian culture is a traditional, largely British culture with American influences thrown in.

Yet other observers will say that neither of these images aptly describes Canadian culture. They would argue that Canadian culture may not exist at all, and if it does, it is no more than a collection of regional cultures: a Newfoundland culture, Maritime culture, Quebec culture, central Canadian anglophone culture, Prairie culture, and British Columbian culture.

Books by George Woodcock (1970), a western literary critic, and Joel Garreau (1981), an American journalist, have argued this idea persuasively. These authors claim that the real vitality in North American culture is found within, not across, its regions. Each region has its own history, natural environment, economic base, and traditional concerns. The people of each region have their own values and way of life. Trying to prove these distinct regions make up a unified Canadian culture is an impossibe and fanciful task, according to these writers. Survey data support this view with evidence of strong variations in attitudes across Canada's regions (Blishen and Atkinson, 1982).

Whether a unified Canadian culture exists and, indeed, whether there should be one, are actually important questions. Nationalists argue that without a unified Canadian culture it will be impossible to escape economic, cultural, and political assimilation by the United States. Others, like Richard Gwyn, say that Canadian culture is already strong enough to resist that possibility. Others still, like George Woodcock or some Quebec nationalists, would argue that unification could only come at the expense of lively ethnic and regional cultures that people really care about.

These disagreements over Canadian culture point to the fact that culture in a modern industrial society is far too complex to allow for easy generalizations or facile simplifications. Canada really is made up of all of these and many more subcultural elements. As a nation created through the political union of two different groups and then further settled by large numbers of immigrants from many different countries, Canada's culture is difficult to study, but all the more interesting. Moreover, what we learn about Canada helps us to understand the nature of ethnic and cultural relations throughout the world.

CLOSING REMARKS

At the beginning of this chapter we suggested that culture could best be understood as a symbolic environment within which we live. As we looked more closely at this environment, however, we discovered that it differs radically for different people. The culture of poverty is literally a different world from that of high culture. The world of the successful professional is different from that of the adherent of Hare Krishna. The world of the Italian Canadian is in many important ways different from the world of the Inuit. All of us, living together in the same country, are living at the same time in different worlds. Understanding these different worlds and understanding how and why they *are* different is an important task for sociology. Understanding how it is that people are socialized to live in their worlds is the topic we turn to in the next chapter.

What conclusions would extraterrestrials draw about our culture from these common everyday objects? Would they be wrong?

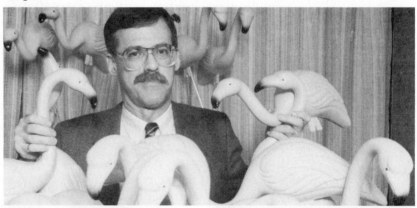

Discussion Questions

1. Self-destruction in various forms—for example, setting oneself on fire, self-imposed starvation—is an increasingly common way of dramatizing political frustration. Are all self-destructive acts, like suicide and anorexia, symbolic? That is, are they all likely to have different meanings in different cultures?

2. Are people using less sexist language in the media today? What about in private conversation? Have changes in use of language changed people's behaviour toward women?

3. Is multiculturalism a good thing for Canada, a waste of money (that is, with no effects either way), or positively harmful to the country?

4. What conditions are likely to produce a subculture? For example, are you likely to find subcultures formed by drug addicts? antique collectors? people who love pizza?

5. How does the widespread belief that "winning is everything" support the ruling class? Is it possible for Canadians to compete economically and politically with other nations if we reject that belief?

6. Given the ways our technology and population are changing today, what changes in cultural values do you think will occur before the year 2010? What do you think it would take to get a really major cultural change?

Data Collection Exercises

1. What are the folkways and mores of your own friendship group? Try breaking one of the rules—for example, make a date and don't show up; borrow some money and refuse to pay it back; or continue talking about something long after everyone is bored stiff by it. How do you *think* they will react? How *do* they react? What have you learned from the discrepancy between these two?

2. Give five of your friends (who are not members of this sociology class) the "I AM ..." Test. Ask each one to print the numbers 1 through 10 down the left hand side of a page. Then, beside each number, have them write a word or phrase that (they feel) describes who they are. When you have all the data, analyze these responses to determine which of your friends are ethnocentric.

3. Look through three kinds of magazines: *True Romance* (or *Soap Opera Digest*), *Life* (or *Macleans*), and *The New Yorker* (or *Harpers*). Describe the elements of high and popular culture you find in each one. What differences do you see in the physical appearance of each—the print size, layout, number and type of pictures, and so on. How about the content: how do they differ in *what* they talk about?

4. Pretend you are a participant observer. View a video on street gangs (e.g. *Colors*) and record the evidence that a "culture of poverty" exists among these young people.

Writing Exercises

1. Write a 500-word address to a high-school graduating class, reminding them why they ought to work hard after they graduate. Make sure your speech touches on values that are important to these young people.

2. Write a 500-word essay describing one particular kind of difficulty a newcomer might have learning Canadian culture: for example, learning how to get a date, talk to a teacher, or work out a disagreement with a neighbour.

3. Write a 500-word essay on what the word "family" conveys to people in our culture.

4. Prepare a 500-word message from the Prime Minister, to be delivered on television on Canada Day. This message should convey the impression that everything is wonderful in Canada, and people should do their best to keep things just as they are.

Glossary

counterculture—a subculture that rejects conventionally accepted norms and values in favour of alternative ones

cultural capital—a set of beliefs and social skills that help people get ahead in an unequal society

cultural literacy—a solid knowledge of our traditional culture; the ability to learn and communicate in our society

culture—the objects, artifacts, institutions, organizations, ideas and beliefs that make up the symbolic and learned aspects of human society

ethnocentrism—a tendency to view social life from the point of view of one's own culture, which enters into both common thought and also social research

material culture—the artifacts and physical objects created or used by members of culture, to be distinguished from what goes on in the minds of the people (**non-material culture**)

norm—a social expectation about "correct" or "proper" behaviour in a particular situation, which serves as a guideline for individuals' action. **Folkways** are norms that, when violated, are not punished formally. **Mores** are norms that carry moral significance, and are therefore cause for severe punishment when violated.

subculture—a group in society that shares some of the cultural traits of the larger society but also has its own distinctive values, beliefs, norms, style of dress and behaviour

symbol—a sign—for example, a gesture, artifact, sign or word—that can meaningfully represent something else and generates some emotion

values—social shared conceptions of what is considered good, right, and desirable, which influence people's behaviour and serve as standards for evaluating the actions of others

Suggested Readings

Arendt, Hannah *Eichman in Jersusalem*. New York: Viking, 1964. This brilliant account of the trial of a prominent ex-Nazi official raises the question, *Who was responsible for the extermination of the Jews, and who is to be punished?* If notions of "right" and "wrong" vary from one culture to another, no easy answer is possible.

Bell, David V. J. and Lorne Tepperman *The Roots of Disunity: A Look at Canada's Political Culture*. Toronto: McClelland and Stewart, 1979. A short book on Canada's political culture, the values and beliefs that underlie our political life, how history and geography have helped to disunify Canadian society.

Bibby, Reginald and Donald Posterski *The Emerging Generation: An Inside Look at Canada's Teenagers*. Toronto: Irwin Publishing, 1985. This survey of Canadian teenagers relates adolescent values to adult Canadian culture and also to the particular stresses teenagers have to face in a modern society.

Fussell, Paul *Class*. New York: Ballantine Books, 1983. A witty book on culture in general, and upper-class culture in particular, this book shows—among other things—how you can judge a person's class from living-room decoration.

Hirsch, E. D. *Cultural Literacy: What Every American Needs to Know*. New York: Vintage Books, 1988. Hirsch has collected data to demonstrate that there really is a storehouse of common information. People who do not master this information have serious difficulty in a competitive, information-oriented world.

Lewis, Oscar *The Children of Sanchez: Autobiography of a Mexican Family*. New York: Vintage, 1961. A poignant story of a poor Mexican family, told in the family members' own words. This book illustrates, in real-life terms, the experience of a culture of poverty.

References

Baer, D., E. Grabb, and W. Johnston (1990) "Reassessing differences in Canadian and American values" in J. Curtis and L. Tepperman (eds.), *Images of Canada: The Sociological Tradition*. Toronto: Prentice-Hall, pp. 86-97.

Berger, J. (1972) *Ways of Seeing*. New York: Viking

Bibby, R.W. and D. C. Posterski (1985) *The Emerging Generation: An Inside Look at Canada's Teenagers*. Toronto: Irwin

Blishen, B. R. and T. H. Atkinson (1982) *Regional and Status Differences in Canadian Values*. Toronto: York University, Institute for Behavioural Research

Bourdieu, P. (1977) *Reproduction in Education, Society and Culture*. Beverly Hills: Sage

Canada, Government of (1969) *Report of the Royal Commission on Bilingualism and Biculturalism*. Ottawa: Supply and Services

_____. (1984) *Sexual Offenses Against Children*, Report of the Committee on Sexual Offenses Against Children and Youth. Ottawa: Supply and Services

DiMaggio, P. and J. Mohr (1985) "Cultural capital, educational attainment and mate selection" *American Journal of Sociology*, 90 (6), pp. 1231-1261

Garreau, J. (1981) *The Nine Nations of North America*. New York: Avon

Hirsch, E.D., Jr. (1988) *Cultural Literacy*. New York: Vintage Books

Innis, H. (1972) *Empire and Communication*. Toronto: University of Toronto Press

Lewis, O. (1961) *The Children of Sanchez: Autobiography of a Mexican Family*. New York: Vintage Books

Lipset, S.M. (1990) *Continental Divide: The Values and Institutions of the United States and Canada*. New York: Routledge

McLuhan, M. (1965) *Understanding Media: The Extensions of Man*. New York: McGraw-Hill

Murdock, G.P. (1945) "The common denominator of cultures" in R. Linton (ed.) *The Science of Man in the World Crisis*. New York: Columbia University Press, pp. 123-142

Porter, J. (1979) "Ethnic pluralism in Canadian perspective" in *The Measure of Canadian Society: Education: Equality and Opportunity*. Toronto: Gage, pp. 103-137

Sapir, E. (1929) "The status of linguistics as a science" *Language*, 5(4), pp. 207-214

Sumner, W.G. (1906) *Folkways*. New York: Ginn

Toffler, A. (1971) *Future Shock*. New York: Bantam Books

Weber, M. (1974) *The Protestant Ethic and the Spirit of Capitalism*. London: George Allen and Unwin

White, H. C. and C. A. White (1965) *Canvases and Careers: Institutional Change in the French Painting World*. New York: Wiley

Woodcock, G. (1970) *Canada and the Canadians*. Toronto: Macmillan of Canada

CHAPTER 3

We are all being socialized [all] the time, whether we know [it] or not.

SOCIALIZATION

SOCIALIZATION IS A LIFELONG PROCESS

In the last chapter we described culture as the socially constructed environment within which we live. We showed that most of the objects around us—whether real or ideal, material or non-material—are cultural objects. People, too, are cultural objects, not only in terms of appearance, in how we display ourselves to others, but as socialized members of our society. This means that all of us are to a large extent a product of our society: in the way we think, the way we act, the things we say, and the values and norms we hold dear. But it also means that in important ways we are free to create ourselves, that much of who we are and what we do is a product of our own activity. Both of these tendencies—freedom and determinism—are features of socialization.

Socialization is often defined as the social learning process through which an individual becomes a capable member of society. The process is a social one because it is through social interaction that the individual acquires the culture—the language, perspective, and skills, the likes and dislikes, the cluster of norms, values, and beliefs—that characterize the groups to which he or she belongs, both the immediate groups and the larger society.

Primary socialization is the learning that takes place in the early years of an individual's life. Many believe primary socialization to be extremely important in forming an individual's personality and charting the course of future development. Although primary socialization almost always takes place within the context of the family, even a relatively young child will learn many of the social skills necessary to participate in a wide variety of social institutions.

Because primary socialization is a fundamental social process both for individuals and for society as a whole, it is of interest to both macrosociologists and microsociologists.

Among macrosociologists, the structural functionalists see primary socialization as the means whereby individuals are integrated into society, coming to take their allotted role and learning to fulfil socially necessary functions. In their eyes, human babies are a "blank slate" waiting to be imprinted with socially meaningful information. It is only through effective social imprinting—for example, the teaching and learning of language—that society can manage to survive. (We shall discuss such learning further in this chapter.)

Conflict theorists, in contrast, emphasize the ways in which socialization teaches and perpetuates forms of domination. They see socialization as teaching people their "place" in society and convincing them that this "place" is inevitable. Poor people learn to blame themselves for failure and praise the rich for their success. In this way, socialization contributes to the survival of the dominant class. We will have much more to say about this "legitimation" of power in the chapter on social inequality.

Microsociologists, such as symbolic interactionists, study the actual interactional processes whereby individuals are socialized, particularly, as we will discuss later in this chapter, those that lead to the development of a social "self." Through these processes people come to see themselves as others do. In this way, they come to think of themselves as good or bad, competent or incompetent, normal or deviant, and so on. We will have more to say about these processes in the next chapter on deviance and control.

Socialization does not end during childhood; it is a lifelong process because we continually undergo new experiences. There are new social roles we take on, new social institutions in which we participate, new stages of life to adjust to and identify with. The socialization that occurs after childhood is called **secondary socialization**. Unlike primary socialization, secondary socialization is much more limited, involving the learning of specific roles, norms, attitudes, or beliefs.

In addition to the socialization we undergo, our individual ability to adjust will vary for a number of reasons: our character and temperament, past experiences, behaviour patterns, and whether our social setting encourages change, for example. What is remarkable about humans is our huge variety and almost endless ability to adjust and change.

BECOMING SOCIAL: NATURE *VERSUS* NURTURE

Where does this human adaptability come from? How much of it is because of our genetic makeup, unique among animals? How much is because of the training we receive that helps us learn and re-learn as we pass through life? What, ultimately, makes each of us the kind of person we are? These questions are at the heart of a centuries-old debate that is often called the "nature *versus* nurture" debate. Are personality and social behaviour the products of our genetic makeup—our inborn nature—or of our environment—our social nurture? Are we destined at birth to become who we are, doing the kinds of things we do? Or is our character a consequence of our upbringing, the culture into which we have been born?

People holding to the "nature" position believe that human behaviour is genetically determined. Such **biological determinists** argue that the diversity found in individuals and cultures exists because nature has selected for them—in the same way nature has selected for our enlarged brains and upright walk.

A notorious recent example of this approach has been advanced by psychologist Philippe Rushton. Rushton claims to show that racial differences in mental ability and sexual behaviour are genetic in origin. In particular, Rushton asserts that Asians are more intelligent, more law-abiding, and less sexually active than Caucasians, who in turn are more intelligent, more law-abiding, and less sexually active than Blacks. The implications of this are clear: if Blacks are less intelligent, less law-abiding, this difference is "natural"; it cannot be altered because it is genetic. Rushton is saying that Blacks are doomed by their genes to be intellectually and morally inferior. Rushton's argument goes on to claim that Blacks are intellectually and morally inferior because they are more primitive, having evolved earlier in the course of human evolution, whereas Caucasians and Asians, who evolved later, are morally and socially advanced.

Both scientists and non-scientists have reacted strongly against Rushton's so-called theory, but only partly because it is fundamentally, completely, and transparently wrong. They have reacted strongly because this kind of thinking has historically masked racist thinking and provided support for horrifying "social experiments," most notably by the German Nazis during the 1930s and 1940s.

We will note in Chapter Eleven that scientific research must meet objective standards acceptable to the scientific community if it is to be considered good science. Scientific reviewers have, almost unanimously, declared that Rushton's work is filled with logical errors and faulty data. Despite Rushton's claims, no research has ever been able to demonstrate acceptable scientific evidence of a genetic origin for social differences among races. For example, how could there be a genetic predisposition for being "law-abiding" when the law is a fairly recent social and cultural product in human history, not a genetically determined process? In any case, the term "law-abiding" is a moral judgment, not a scientific description. The example of courage and determination provided by Chinese students during the illegal demonstrations and subsequent massacre in Beijing's Tienanmen Square in 1989 shows us the irrelevance of discussing "Asian law-abidingness" removed from the social, political, and moral context of any particular law. Rushton's work ignores history, ignores social, economic, and political forces, and ignores the motivation, character, and reasoning of the individual.

An advocate of the "nurture" position would take the opposite tack to Rushton's, attributing all character traits and the diversity among different cultures to learning. According to this point of view—social or **cultural determinism**—infants are born largely as blank slates, with no significant genetic predispositions, drives, or instincts and no innate personality. As children, they learn the "*do*s and *don't*s" of their culture. Culture, rather than genes, determines behaviour.

Most social scientists have put this debate aside. They recognize that both factors—nature and nurture—tie together in real life. Members of a group share genetic characteristics because, over a long time, they live and reproduce together. This makes it likely that genes do influence personality somewhat, but this influence is usually limited to forming a behavioural potential. The extent to which people realize this potential will depend on the social setting within which they live and learn.

Consider language as a case in point. The capacity to use language is genetic in origin. Human beings have the vocal cords necessary to produce the sounds out of which words are formed, and the human brain has the capacity to differentiate those sounds and identify their appropriate meanings. But while the capacity to use language is genetic in origin, language itself is not. Language is a product of culture which is learned: if language *were* genetic in origin—that is, if the sounds used and their appropriate meanings were innate — there would be only one language used by everyone in the same way. Not only are there hundreds of different languages, but everyone uses language in their own way. Few of us talk about things in the same way. Moreover, a language constantly changes as new words get added, meanings get altered, and old words are dropped.

The example of language is particularly important because, as we saw in the last chapter, language is the means whereby we communicate our experience of the world. We not only learn our language; language itself is the means by which we learn from others and with which we teach others. Language is the key to socialization.

Perhaps no example illustrates the importance of primary socialization as well as the case of feral children. These are children who have been raised with little or no contact with other people. They have not undergone the typical patterns of socialization, and in some crucial ways most of them never quite become full-fledged members of society.

Feral children

History has recorded many tales and anecdotes about "feral" children, that is, children supposedly raised outside society, unaffected by human relationships and values. An early example is the Roman legend about a pair of children, Romulus and Remus, whom the Romans considered the founders of their civilization. In the legend, a female wolf raised these children. Recent fictional examples include Tarzan — raised by apes.

However, there are also recorded cases of real children being found who were considered feral. One of the best documented examples is the "Wild Boy of Aveyron" — well documented because a doctor, Itard, studied him closely and recorded what he found. The boy, briefly called Joseph and later Victor, emerged from the woods in southern France on a winter morning in the year 1800. He had been caught digging for vegetables in a terraced garden.

The boy, who seemed to be about 11 or 12 years old, was almost naked, showed no modesty, and was totally unhousebroken — he would relieve himself wherever he wanted, squatting to defecate and standing to urinate. He could not speak and made strange, meaningless cries.

Three or four months after Doctor Itard took over his training, the boy became responsive. Victor could pay attention, understand and follow verbal instructions, play games, care for himself, and even invent things with familiar objects. He wore clothes and used a chamber pot to relieve himself, but still felt no shame or modesty. He kept up many of his earlier habits, continuing to avoid other people and escaping company when he could. His old, "wild" reactions to nature — to wind, the moon, and snow — never disappeared. In Doctor Itard's hands, the boy's training was, at best, a superficial success. Still, Victor showed affection to people who protected him and he did what they expected.

After five years with Itard, Victor lived another 22 years with a devoted woman named Madame Guerin in a little house near an institute for deaf-mutes. In this period, no one — Itard included — tried to train Victor further and no one followed his progress. By 1816, his civilization had largely eroded. The young man was once again fearful and half-wild, and still could not speak. He had few links to the rest of the community. A state pension kept Victor alive and finally he died, unnoticed.

What does the story of the Wild Boy teach? One obvious lesson is the importance of primary socialization. Despite the attempts made to teach him, there was much that Victor never learned, and he never seemed to adjust to civilized life. There is no way of knowing now, of course, what Victor's capabilities were, but we suspect that by missing the crucial years of childhood socialization he was never able to achieve his capabilities. We may think that socialization imposes society on the individual and that is true. But by providing us with knowledge and skills it also provides us with the tools and resources to think independently, to act creatively, and to take advantage of our opportunities. Was Victor better off after his capture than before? Perhaps not, but as a wild, naked, asocial creature digging for vegetables Victor was much less than a full human being. That is the most important lesson Victor's case teaches us. We are social beings who only fulfil our potential and achieve our goals as members of society.

ACQUIRING SOCIAL KNOWLEDGE

Learning and behaviour

Since socialization is a form of learning, understanding how socialization works requires that we know something about how people learn.

For one thing, learning is a natural human process. It is natural in the sense that the ability and the will to learn are part of our nature. Researchers have found that a newborn reacts differently to its mother's voice than to that of a nurse or doctor. The infant learned to recognize that voice even before birth, while still in the womb. This shows that, as in the case of language, *what* we learn is not determined, but the desire to learn is present at least from birth. This means that all of us learn and do so without anyone forcing it upon us. In fact, as you know from school, things we are forced to study are not really learned. They may be memorized, but will only be remembered until the next test, then quickly forgotten. In contrast, what we learn will be something that is meaningful for *us* or that is of use to us. When we learn, we are gaining knowledge or skills we can use.

Learning can occur in many different ways. We learn by observation, by experiment, or by imitation. We learn from friends, from parents, relatives, and passers-by. We learn from television, radio, books, and billboards. Throughout most of human history, when few people had any formal education, almost all learning occurred in informal ways, from others.

Perhaps the most simple type of learning is **conditioning**, which involves learning to associate particular stimuli or conditions with particular consequences. This type of learning was studied by the Russian psychologist Ivan Pavlov, who found that he could get dogs to salivate after hearing a bell. Pavlov would ring the bell, then feed the dog. After a time, the ringing of the bell was enough to begin the dog salivating.

Although conditioning is an important form of learning among animals, few human experiences involve learning through conditioning. Sometimes we come to associate some sound, smell, or other stimulus with some memory, but this is of little significance in our daily lives, and little of our behaviour is a

Social scientists have learned some of what they know about socialization from the study of higher animals.

consequence of such associations. Because human behaviour almost always involves the interpretation and use of symbols, our learning is much more complex.

Cognitive development

Since humans think and communicate symbolically, we need an approach to socialization that takes this difference into account. This is where theories of cognitive development are valuable. The term *cognitive* refers to intellectual capacities such as thought, belief, memory, perception, and the ability to reason. **Cognitive development**, then, refers to the development of these various capacities.

A **developmental approach** to learning focuses on both the inner workings of the individual's mind and on observable behaviour. As individuals go through the socialization process, they are active, not passive, participants in learning. They do not merely respond to rewards and punishments as dogs or trained seals might. They respond on the basis of their interpretations of situations. Learning is more than a matter of knowing what to do, how to do it, and when; learning also involves understanding *why* we do, or fail to do, certain things in certain situations.

Remember the discussion in the previous chapter that concerned inappropriate behaviour in a given situation—praying in a hotel lobby or eating pizza during church services, for example. Most of us avoid violating norms in these ways because we have figured out the rules and what happens when we violate them. We know *why* the rules exist and to what other situations they may apply. Somehow, we are able to generalize from past experience, and to apply these generalizations to future experience. This learned ability is a key part of socialization.

Being able to think—to solve an arithmetic problem, write an essay about Shakespeare, or figure out what to wear to a party—requires an ability to reason, to wonder about and ponder over things. These skills do not develop through external conditioning or imitation, but through a continual development of the mind.

Language learning falls into this category. It is unlikely a child ever heard another speaker say "he runned" or "it's the goodest" or "my foots hurt." Children make such mistakes because they do *not* copy what they hear others saying. Instead, they imperfectly detect and apply rules in our language, and make up words according to those rules. Mistakes arise because speakers are not consistent: they break the rules in idiomatic ways.

Idioms are the hardest part of a language (and culture) to learn. The following phrases would puzzle a non-English speaking person trying to understand what the word "gets" really means:

> John gets his ideas across
> John gets along very well with Sarah
> John gets around at night
> John gets at Sarah when he is drunk
> John gets away with murder
> John gets back at Roy when they are together
> John gets by quite nicely
> John gets me down with his moods
> John gets down to work when he wants to
> John gets in with the important people
> John gets off lightly
> John gets on with everyone
> John gets out of everything
> John gets round his parents
> John gets over a broken heart quickly

You could never learn the proper use of English idioms (like those above) by following rules: there are just too many exceptions. The learning of social and cultural behaviour is the same. Some of it is based on past reinforcement, some on imitation, and some on following rules. Yet even so, some is the result of trial and error and cognitive processing.

There are many examples of cultural idioms. On some occasion, you have probably visited the home of someone you want to impress: for example, a teacher, a boss, or the parents of a girlfriend or boyfriend. Then you may have become painfully aware of your ignorance of relevant rules. You may have wondered how to dress for the visit. Should you bring a gift, and if so, what? Should you arrive on time, or early, and if early, how early? If offered alcoholic beverages, how many should you accept? Most troublesome of all, since you do not want to offend the hosts by leaving too soon or bore them by staying too long, how will you know when it is the right time to leave?

The Swiss psychologist Jean Piaget (1951) devoted most of his life to the study of cognitive development in children. He emphasized that young children are **egocentric**. This means that they put themselves, literally, at the centre of the world. They assume that everything happens because of them, that everyone is interested only in them, and that whatever they experience is all that there is. Above all, an egocentric child is unable to think about itself objectively.

A good example of egocentric thought can be found in children's ideas about the "movement" of the sun or moon. Children of about age three will tell you that the sun or moon follows them around. When they move in one direction, the moon does too. When they stop, it stops. When they move in another direction, so does the moon. We adults know that this illusion is caused by our great distance from the sun or the moon, relative to our distance from objects such as trees or buildings near us, and we do not even notice it. An egocentric child, when asked why the sun or moon follows them, however, is likely to say something like "it wants to know what I am doing."

By about the age of seven, egocentric thought is replaced by socialized thinking. Then, a person begins to see him- or herself in relation to others, as object as well as subject of actions. A properly socialized person will take into account the thoughts, desires, experiences, expectations, and reactions of other people.

When you are deciding what to wear to Saturday's party, for example, you will review information such as the following:

(1) What have I worn to other parties that people have liked (or ridiculed)?

(2) What will people I consider good dressers be likely to wear?

(3) What "kind" of party is this—who is going to be there, what is the occasion, how do people usually dress for such an occasion?

If you can think through questions such as these and come up with answers—and you do, every day, in one version or another—then you have reached a fairly high level of cognitive development.

Moral development

If we have difficulty describing the acquisition of social manners and language, think how much more difficult it is to find the roots of moral behaviour.

An early researcher in this area was Sigmund Freud. Freud was a Viennese physician who studied people suffering from mental disorders and founded a school of thought and treatment called psychoanalysis.

Psychoanalysis is a theory of personality that stresses the role of unconscious or subconscious desires, fears, and memories—especially childhood memories—in guiding our behaviour. It is also a method of therapy that seeks to uncover these unconscious forces, so that the individual can gain control over his or her life.

Freud (1962) postulated that the human psyche is made up of the **id, ego**, and **superego**. The **id** consists of an individual's most primitive urges, including sexual and aggressive drives. Some urges, like the sex drive, demand continual and instant gratification. The id is essentially an irrational force in the human mind that searches for pleasure.

The **superego** is that part of the self which has **internalized** society's demands and rules of conduct. The superego acts as a watchdog, regulating the individual's behaviour so that it measures up to the dictates of society. It controls by punishing the individual with guilt, shame, and fear. For Freud, the superego is formed in early childhood through a struggle between the child and a dominant parent (in 19th-century Vienna, usually the father) which typically leads the child to adopt the father's values as his own. The father's values form the content of a child's superego. Where this struggle has failed to occur, or has taken a particularly inconclusive or violent form, superego development may be abnormal.

In Freud's theory, the **ego** is the conscious self. It composes a person's conscious thoughts and emotions, and carries out his or her rational actions. Often the ego has to come between the id and the superego. It reconciles the id's unconscious wishes and urges, and the superego's equally unconscious internalized inhibitions against pursuing them. At any given moment, an individual's behaviour and thoughts may reflect an underlying conflict between the id and superego. "Cutting loose" and "getting serious" respectively show the id and the superego gaining an upper hand in this ongoing battle.

Freud considered the neuroses associated with repression of the id a normal part of civilization. However, when a person's ego has failed to establish and maintain a balance between the id's and superego's demands, these neuroses get out of hand and require treatment.

A great deal of research and therapeutic practice have grown out of Freud's original conception. Debate over whether Freud was right is far from over. A particular difficulty is the need to believe that one and only one conflict—the conflict between infant and more powerful parent—generates an adult's morality. In effect, this is a one-stage theory of moral development. What's more, Freud generalized to all society what he found in 19th-century Viennese society women and in himself.

Since Freud's death, more researchers have adopted a multi-stage theory of moral development. For example, Erik Erikson (1950), a disciple of Freud, saw personality development as a lifelong process marked by many critical turning points. How an individual resolved each challenge as it came up would determine his or her ability to deal with the next.

As well as concerning himself with cognitive development in children, Jean Piaget (1932), too, studied the development of morality. Piaget researched the way children think about social norms by asking them to discuss a game of marbles. He studied their moral thinking by telling them stories and asking them for comments. From these simple methods, Piaget drew powerful conclusions.

Among children from four- to about eight-years-old, Piaget found what he called *heteronomous* morality—a respect for adult authority. Young children conceive of right and wrong in very specific and objective terms. Behaviour is "wrong" if they have seen adults punish or threaten to punish such behaviour. Young children consider adult rules and moral values absolute and unchangeable. They favour punishing deviation severely, rather than repairing harm done to the injured party. They also show little interest in the motivations of wrong-doers: why they did what they did.

Among older children Piaget found that *autonomous* morality prevailed. These children had already begun to think about and follow their own rules of morality and conduct. Older children viewed rules as products of group agreement that advance cooperation within the group. Justice is a matter of mutual rights and obligations which, they believe, is sometimes served best by repairing harm done, rather than punishing the wrong-doer. In their eyes, moral ideas are relative rather than absolute, and may change as the group sees fit.

Interestingly, the differences Piaget found between younger and older children are similar to the difference the sociologist Emile Durkheim (1964) found when he compared laws in pre-industrial (or primitive) and industrial societies. Societies appear to develop morally in the same way that individuals do, and for similar reasons. Although no general theory has been accepted that applies to all social structures, we observe that micro and macro development seem to mirror each other. In both cases, cognitive or information-processing complexity—Durkheim called this *moral density*—increases. In a specialized society people need to cooperate more and rigid, simple rules prove unworkable. We shall return to Durkheim's findings in the next chapter, and reconsider social evolution at the end of this book.

Canadian sociologist Bernd Baldus used a method similar to Piaget's to study the moral development of Canadian children. Using drawings, he and Verna Tribe (Baldus and Tribe, 1978) found that by Grade Six, a high proportion of children have learned to consistently match social class indicators such as clothing, type of housing, and quality of car with one another. Fancy clothes, a nice house, and a new car go together in children's minds.

Moreover, children learn to believe that people with good clothes, houses, and cars care more about their appearance and try harder to succeed than other people. Richer people are also nicer and better people: more honest and better behaved, in children's minds. Even children from poor families hold these views that rich people are morally superior.

Baldus' research shows that moral assessments of others do not develop in a social vacuum. Rather, they reflect the society's dominant ideology, which attaches a positive moral value to successful people. In this scheme, what is right is what succeeds.

Development of self

While all sociologists consider socialization to be a social process, some, such as symbolic interactionists, are more concerned with understanding the process than the result: how does socialization actually work? How do people come to take on the norms, values, attitudes, beliefs, and behaviour patterns of the people around them? How do they, in technical terms, internalize their culture? And how do they do so while maintaining their own personal identity and sense of worth? Many sociologists believe that the key to answering these questions can be found in the concept of the *self*.

Everyone has a sense of self. By the **self**, we mean the individual's experience and awareness of oneself, of having a distinct personal identity that is separate from and different from that of other people. Sociologists believe that the process by which a person develops this sense of self is also the process by which they internalize their culture.

A child is not born with a sense of self. As Piaget showed in his research on egocentrism, young children have no sense of self distinct from other people. They come to be aware of themselves as they become aware that other people (such as their parents or siblings) are distinct from them, that these other people have expectations about them, and that they are expected to adapt to other people's ideas and instructions.

This means that the self is a social product. It emerges in the course of an individual's interaction with other people, even with those he or she admires from afar (such as movie stars or heroic ancestors). The individual's experiences in life, the groups to which he or she belongs, and the socio-historical setting of the group all shape one's sense of self.

Because the self is a social product, it is subject to change throughout the life cycle. People's experiences and self-conceptions change throughout their lives. We can usually trace these changes back to the influence of particular social institutions or people on the individual. Social theorists may differ in their accounts of the emergence of the self, but on one thing they agree: social interaction is central to the growth of the self.

The looking-glass self

American sociologist Charles Cooley (1902) was the first to emphasize the importance of the self in the process of socialization. Cooley developed the notion of the **looking-glass self**, which emphasizes the role of the social environment in the development of a self-concept. According to Cooley, individuals form concepts of themselves as they observe other people's reactions to them. Research suggests that people live up (or down) to the expectations others (such as parents or friends) have of them. They come to see themselves as these **significant others** do. A little girl will traditionally be told to "act like a lady," and will come to see certain activities such as playing baseball, climbing trees, or taking up boxing as inappropriate or beyond her capacities.

EXHIBIT 3.1

THE LOOKING-GLASS SELF

About the looking-glass self, Cooley has written:

> A social self of this sort might be called the reflected or looking-glass self. . . . In imagination we perceive in another's mind some thought of our appearance, manners, aims, deeds, character, friends, and so on, and are variously affected by it.
>
> A self-idea of this sort seems to have three principal elements: the imagination of our appearance to the other person; the imagination of his judgement of that appearance; and some sort of self-feeling, such as pride or mortification. . . . The thing that moves us to pride or shame is not the mere mechanical reflection of ourselves, but an imputed sentiment, the imagined effect of this reflection upon another's mind. . . .
>
> [For example] we are ashamed to seem evasive in the presence of a straightforward man, cowardly in the presence of a brave one, gross in the eyes of a refined one, and so on. We always imagine, and in imagining share, the judgements of the other mind. A man will boast to one person of an action — say some transaction in trade — which he would be ashamed to own to another.

Source: C.H. Cooley, *Human Nature and the Social Order*. New York: Scribner, 1902, p. 184

The **looking-glass self**, then, is the name Cooley gives to a phenomenon we all know intuitively: the process of seeing ourselves through the eyes of others, seeing ourselves as others see us. The way we think and feel about ourselves reflects the way we believe others think and feel about us. We shape our behaviour to elicit a favourable response from the people who matter most to us. We do this because we rely on others to provide us with a positive self-image.

Thus, the looking-glass self, or reflection we see in our social mirror, both tells us who we are—gives us an identity—and tells us how good we are—provides an evaluation.

The notion of the looking-glass self is very limited, however. We are not merely puppets who act out the expectations of others, no matter how significant they may be. Every parent knows how few of their expectations for their children come true, just as children rebel and reject many of their parents' expectations. This rebellion is not limited to adolescence; child-care experts refer to a two-year-old child as being in the midst of "the terrible twos," a stage also called *negativism*. Cooley's views are an example of what is called an *oversocialized* view of the individual (Wrong, 1961). It fails to account for individual spontaneity, creativity, or independence. Moreover, if a looking-glass does exist, then it is one we can see right through, for parents who socialize are as affected by their children as their children are by them. Socialization is a two-way process.

Mead and internalization

A more complete approach to socialization can be found in the work of the American social philosopher George Herbert Mead (1934). Mead's particular interest was in the process of internalization. How, he wondered, are the rules, norms, and values which are imposed on the child by others internalized so that the child becomes committed to them and feels guilt or shame if they are violated?

Mead suggested that there are a number of phases a child goes through as it learns to internalize social expectations. The first phase is called the **preliminary phase** because the child does not yet have the capacity to engage in true social behaviour or to understand people's expectations. During this phase, which takes up the first year or so of life, the child's social behaviour is largely limited to imitation. Infants imitate their parents, their siblings, even themselves, repeating gestures or sounds they may have made at first by chance. A game such as peek-a-boo illustrates the repetitive and imitative nature of an infant's social interaction.

A higher level of social behaviour can be observed in the **play phase**, during which the child engages in solitary play. This stage is roughly equivalent to the egocentric stage described by Piaget. Both Mead and Piaget emphasize that play is solitary, even if children are playing in each others' presence, because it involves no real interaction. Two little girls of three playing with their dolls are each taken up with her own doll; each talks to her doll, feeds it, and scolds it. They are incapable of playing together by, for example, having one little girl be the "mother" and the other the "child." For this reason Piaget referred to conversation among children at this level of development as *collective monologue*.

Social behaviour during the play phase is still largely imitation, but what are now being imitated are social roles: patterns of behaviour appropriate to being a "mother," "father," "Ghostbuster," "nurse," or whatever. In this way roles and expectations are being learned as children play, imagine, and create.

The next phase, the **game phase**, involves a still higher level of social behaviour: coordinating social roles. Games differ from play because, whereas play is largely spontaneous, games have rules which must be followed. Moreover, games always involve others, so each participant has some role to act out. A good example of an early game is hide and seek. Here children learn to take on one of two roles, those who hide or the one who is "it." There are rules to follow: the person who is "it" must count to ten, must say "ready or not, here I come," must find someone before they return to "base," and so on. All of this involves coordinating one's own actions and expectations with those of others.

You may not realize it, but learning to hide is quite an achievement. An egocentric child cannot hide because he or she fails to take other people into account. Young children playing hide and seek will not know how to hide. They will hide behind some object, but have their feet or other part of their body showing; since they cannot see whoever is "it," they assume that they cannot be seen either. Or they may always hide in the same place, or giggle so that they will be heard. Hiding requires that we take the other person into account: If I hide here, what will the other see or do?

This process of taking the other into account was called by Mead *taking the role of the other*. It is the prerequisite for competent social interaction. We take the role of the other during interaction in two senses. First, we orient our actions toward others so that we can be understood. When a teacher stands in front of a class, for example, he or she has to ask themselves how to get the lesson across so that the students will understand it. The teacher will then monitor the responses of the students to see if they do understand what is being said.

The second sense of taking the role of the other is essential to the development of the self. It is a process of coming to see yourself as others see you, of being able to view yourself objectively and think about yourself in terms of your relationship to other people.

Obviously, this process begins first in childhood as we learn to take the role of the significant others around us. We learn not to bite our sister if we are angry because she will hit back; not to spill our soup when eating because Mommy will get angry; not to run down Grandpa's hallway because he will get upset. But taking the role of the other in this manner means that the rules are still external to us, they are still being imposed on us by others. They are not yet internalized. That requires an ability to take the role of the **generalized other.**

George Herbert Mead coined the term **generalized other** to refer to an individual's general idea of society's attitudes and perspectives, and of how the larger social group expects him or her to behave. Having such a concept of a generalized other is possible because the majority of the members of a society or subculture to which we belong agree on most role expectations, values, and norms. It is in relation to this sense of generalized other that we develop our conceptions of ourselves: how we are similar and how different from other people. When we take the role of the generalized other it is no longer Mommy who gets upset when we spill soup; now we are the ones who get upset. We will look around quickly in embarrassment hoping no one has noticed how clumsy we have been. Since it is we who have these feelings and expectations, taking the role of the generalized other means that the norms and values have now been internalized.

Mead's theory of internalization has been used by structural functionalists to emphasize how individuals learn to accept the values, goals, and norms of the society around them. Mead's theory is not an example of social determinism, however. If the self develops in the course of interaction, then we can distinguish between the individual's personality and temperament which *precede* the socialized self, and the different roles we act out in the course of our lives. We go from being a child and daughter to being a student, physician, mother, adult; but there is something more in us than the socialized player of these internalized roles. Mead tried to incorporate this "something more" into his view of the individual by distinguishing between **the I** and **the Me**. All of us have an aspect of the self that Mead calls the **I**, an aspect that is spontaneous, impulsive, and self-interested—in many respects, like Freud's id. All of us also have a **Me**, an aspect of the self that is the result of socialization and is therefore conscious of social norms, values, and expectations. The Me is the socialized player of social roles. When we interact with other people, for example, we learn through socialization to hide or repress our true feelings about others, showing them a "Me" which may be very far removed from the "I." We may also be unaware of our real feelings; like Freud's id, we tend to be unaware (unconscious) of the "I."

GENDER SOCIALIZATION

Mead's ideas on the social self, on the importance of the symbolic in interaction (such as the notion of the generalized other) and his insistence that there is always a spontaneous I engaged in interaction, were key ideas in the development of symbolic interactionism; most symbolic interactionists look to the work of Mead as the foundation of their perspective.

Sociologists pay a great deal of attention to primary socialization. It is during this phase of your life that you learned all the really fundamental roles of our society and learned to think and act like a competent member of society. Just think for a moment what one learns in the first few years of life. We not only learn such fundamental skills as speaking our language, thinking and reasoning, or interacting competently; we learn such basic facts about ourselves as whether we are male or female and what that means about *who* or *what* we are. Indeed, gender socialization can well stand as an example of how primary socialization proceeds.

Masculine and feminine ideals

Gender roles are the set of socially defined expectations we have of appropriate behaviour for individuals of each sex. What we mean by **gender socialization** is simply socialization into gender roles. It is the process of learning the attitudes, thoughts, and behaviour patterns that are appropriate for members of each sex.

When people are asked what makes males and females different, they usually refer to physiological characteristics such as genitals, and to personality differences such as aggressiveness. But physiology only partly explains differences between males and females. In everyday life we almost never make use of physiology to decide who is male or female because there are very few people whose genitals are visible to us. We decide who is male or female on the basis of appearance, which is really a matter of social convention. As for personality differences, the differences we witness between males and females in our society are primarily social and cultural constructions. We know this because gender roles change over time and vary considerably from one culture to another.

People learn gender roles very early in life. Infants are identified as male or female at birth. Little boys and girls are playing separately, at different kinds of games, by the age of three. Already, they have learned to want certain toys, enjoy certain games, and avoid fraternizing openly with the opposite sex: those who violate this last rule are ridiculed. From this motivation to perform gender roles correctly, it is but a small step to actually learning them.

In our own society, the masculine ideal has traditionally included toughness, reason, and action. Conversely, the feminine ideal has traditionally included softness, emotion (or intuition), and passivity. The masculine image is epitomized by popular culture characters like Rambo and Dirty Harry. Perhaps male images are also being epitomized—exaggerated for mass consumption—because this ideal is on its way out. Many men, as well as women, oppose this ideal of masculinity. Few see a value in it and few want to live up to it. Instead, masculine and feminine ideals, and male and female gender roles, are starting to blur.

The blurring of gender roles

The blurring of gender roles takes a variety of forms. First, few women today—with the possible exception of members of fringe groups like REAL Women—are trying to live up (or down) to the traditional image of femininity. Likewise, few men today are trying to live up (or down) to the traditional image of masculinity. The male ideal mainly persists among boys in the five- to fifteen-year-old range. They are the ones who watch violent cartoons and movies, read violent comic books, and purchase fighting equipment (martial arts gear, video war games, military clothing, and miniature soldier figures).

Second, in practice men and women are sharing more duties and activities than in the past. More women work for pay in jobs that, in the past, only men were allowed to hold. In their work settings, women prove as able as men to be tough, rational, and active. Men, at the same time, are assuming a somewhat greater responsibility for child care and housework than they did in the past. In the domestic setting, men are learning to master softness, emotionality, and, if not passivity, then at least some greater tranquillity.

An increasing number of roles are gender-blind, in the sense that we do not automatically associate a particular gender with the role. Still, progress in gender equality is slow. Society may change, but these changes have no direct effect on the socialization of the next generation. This is because social changes are filtered through the particular agents of socialization which are actually engaged in the socialization process.

AGENTS OF SOCIALIZATION

Agents of Socialization are the institutions and other structured relationships within which socialization takes place. Some of the most important of these are the family, school, peer group, and mass media. In modern industrialized societies, these institutions socialize almost everyone. However, religious groups, work settings, and voluntary associations also play a significant role as agents of socialization. The effects of various agents of socialization on the individual are often complementary, or reinforcing. Yet conflicts among them (for example, between the family and the peer group) are common too.

Families

Most of us are born into families and have some idea of what family life means. As we shall see later in this book, there is a great deal of variation in the Canadian family and it is changing rapidly. Whatever the family's form, however, a child's first emotional ties are usually to family members. Families provide the basic necessities of life, and often provide love, security, comfort, and emotional support as well. Sometimes, unfortunately, they provide the opposite: abuse and neglect. In these cases, the effects on child development are often very harmful. Family members also teach the child the language, norms, values, and expectations of the culture or subculture to which the family belongs.

Very little of what a family transmits through socialization is transmitted consciously. The child learns a great deal simply by observing the manner in which family members interact with one another, the roles they act out, and the attitudes and values they exemplify. We first learn the meaning of "woman," "wife," and "mother" by watching our own mother, for example. Later, after an opportunity to observe other versions of "woman," "wife," and "mother" in friends' homes or on television we can begin to generalize. Once generalization begins, conscious choice becomes possible and the self begins to develop more rapidly and uniquely.

So the family is important in laying down a bed of concrete experiences on which we can build or against which we must fight. It is the starting point for our social knowledge, the place we experiment with our vision of the generalized other. It is in the family setting that we also form our first close attachments and learn to communicate openly.

Schools

Schools are important in our society for many reasons. They provide us with information and teach us skills designed to help us to better understand ourselves and the world and to function effectively as citizens and workers. Schools also provide their students with at least a minimum level of cultural literacy and cultural capital (although elite private schools provide much more of both). In this way, the school system prepares people for careers, helps some people overcome the disadvantages of their birth, and reinforces the advantages of others.

However, from the standpoint of basic socialization, schools perform another important function. They open the door to a strange new social world. Unlike the family, a school is populated by strangers. Some of these strangers—the teachers—hold positions of authority. Obedience is expected and deviation is punished. Teachers exert control without delivering affection. They expect compliance without exception. They will not make special deals of the kind that children and their parents usually make. In these respects, teachers are the first truly impartial rule-enforcers children are likely to have met. The school is a child's first exposure to the "rule of law."

The school also offers a child his or her first exposure to political life. The classroom is a structure of unequal power, over which the teacher presides. This power is not shared and, at least in theory, not up for negotiation. In practice, of course, social order within the classroom is constantly negotiated between the teachers and class. This is good training for the way power actually operates in adult political systems.

The school is also a child's first experience of economic life. Like every economy, the school distributes scarce resources. Some children will get more of the teacher's time and attention, others less. Some children will get high marks and special honours; other children will consistently do poorly and end up in a slow learning track. Students are fully aware of this unequal allocation of rewards and punishments. They know who the "teacher's pet" is and who is the "class victim," as Wilfred Martin (1984) found in a study of Newfoundland schoolchildren. What's more, they have strong views about the way the teacher hands out rewards and may rebel if they feel an injustice has been done.

At least in the first years of schooling, the academic curriculum—reading, writing, arithmetic—is far less important than this "hidden" curriculum. The school is a world that more or less predictably rewards conformity, good behaviour, and effort. Children learn this new, non-familial behaviour. By exposing children to the first large organization in their lives, the school experience challenges earlier ideas. Despite the many injustices found in every school, there are few other institutions that strive so self-consciously to be fair and consistent.

Not all of the learning at school takes place within the classroom. In the schoolyard, many children have their first exposure to bullies, team games, much older and younger children, and same-age children of the opposite sex. The school population provides experiences that are unlikely within the family. The variety of students present forces children to re-assess the rules and roles they learned in infancy.

Schoolyard games are a time for learning skills, values, rules, cooperation, and subordination.

Peers

Peers are important agents of socialization and are particulary influential from late childhood through adolescence and early adulthood. The **peer group** is a group of interacting companions who usually share similar social characteristics (for example, age, gender, social class, or religion), interests, tastes, and values.

Members of a peer group relate to one another as individuals. As individuals, they are able to get to know one another in terms of similar interests, activities, and tastes. This is the foundation for close friendships (as well as strong enmities). The friendships of youth are particularly intense because children and adolescents spend so much of the day together, usually in school, engaged in identical or similar activities.

Like parents and teachers, peers are also part of our **reference group**, people to whom we will mentally refer when evaluating our own thoughts and behaviour. A reference group provides the standards against which people and behaviour are evaluated. All reference groups act as agents of socialization by giving us clear examples of how to behave and, sometimes, by rewarding us for behaving that way.

A familiar example can be seen in the attempts young children make to dress like their older siblings, their peers, their parents, and often the people they see on television. Their sense of "beautiful," "cool," or "radical" appearance comes from these sources, and often their excessive efforts are laughable. Yet, by their effort to dress like "the big guys," these children are declaring a desire to *be* like the big guys: indeed, to be accepted by them, and also to be accepted as one of them by others.

One's peers start to be a very important reference group as soon as a child starts school, and become more important through high school and college. In the work setting, one's workmates or professional colleagues continue to provide an important peer influence throughout adulthood.

EXHIBIT 3.2

SOCIALIZATION INTO THE STUDENT ROLE

Have you ever wondered what kindergarten was *really* about? You probably did not learn very much in kindergarten that you did not already know: just more singing, fingerpainting, hearing stories read, and other similar activities. Why do schools keep kindergarten going—why not simply start students in Grade One?

Sociologist Harry Gracey (1977:217) studied kindergarten classes to find the answer. He found the classes very much like a marine "boot camp":

> The unique job of the kindergarten in the educational division of labor seems rather to be teaching children the student role[:] . . . the repertoire of behavior and attitudes regarded by educators as appropriate to children in school. . . . The teachers expended most of their efforts, for the first half of the year at least, in training the children to follow the routines which teachers created. The children were, in a very real sense, *drilled* in tasks and activities created by the teachers for their own purposes and beginning and ending quite arbitrarily (from the child's point of view). . . . Classroom routines were introduced gradually from the beginning of the year in all the kindergartens, and the children drilled in them as long as was necessary to achieve regular compliance. By the end of the school year, the successful kindergarten teacher has a well-organized group of children. They follow classroom routines automatically, having learned all the command signals and the expected responses to them. They have, in our terms, learned the student role.

Do students have to un-learn this role when they go into higher grades? Or does all schooling—including post-secondary education—demand automatic obedience, even if more subtly demanded than in kindergarten? And is this kind of training a good or bad preparation for the world of work?

Source: H.L. Gracey "Learning the student role: Kindergarten as academic boot camp" in D.H. Wrong and H.L. Gracey (eds.) *Readings in Introductory Sociology*, 3rd edition. New York: Macmillan, 1977, pp. 215-226

There may be many issues on which members of a reference group may not agree. In fact, parents and peers often do not. Though both parents and peers belong to the same reference group, a child may take their respective opinions into account on different occasions or in relation to different issues.

Mass media

The last chapter noted the importance of mass media in shaping and transmitting culture. So it stands to reason the media should play an important role in socialization. Socialization by mass media is a major type of secondary socialization, which influences people's behaviour through modelling and imitation.

In their survey, Bibby and Posterski (1985) found that 90% of Canadian teenagers reported they listen to music "very often," and 57% reported they watch television "very often." By contrast, fewer than 40% play team sports, work out, read a book, spend time on a hobby, or take part in a youth group "very often." Because so many consume media messages, the lyrics of songs, the stories on television, and plot lines of music videos likely have a significant influence on teenagers' behaviour.

The ways mass media influence behaviour, and whether this influence is good or bad, are popular issues. A lot has been written about the way news reporting seriously distorts reality, creating fears that are unwarranted and support for certain policies or candidates that reduce these fears. The effect of violent and pornographic programs on interpersonal relationships has also been studied.

Other writing on the effects of mass media has to do with the way advertising secretly manipulates our desires. Products are advertised in ways that appeal to people's longing for social acceptance or status. Sex is also a powerful attention-grabber; advertisers even imply that their product will increase a user's quality or quantity of sexual experiences.

One television advertisement for a soft drink became notorious for its use of sexual display. It showed a parade of young people marching, singing and dancing down the street with the product in hand. At one point, an attractive young cheerleader did a cartwheel toward the camera. This was the dramatic high point of the advertisement, though it was hard to say why. It became easier when network censors slowed the ad down to reveal that the young cheerleader had no underpants on.

However enjoyable in its own right, such advertising discourages us from thinking rationally about the merits of the product advertised. Rationally, we should buy Beer X because it tastes better or is cheaper than Beer Y, not because the ad turns us on. By encouraging us to behave irrationally, the mass media undo much of what our other agents of socialization – especially parents and schools – try to accomplish.

Other agents

There are many other agents of socialization in our society. Because modern societies have so many different social institutions, secondary socialization, particularly within professional schools and work groups, is very important. Here the socialization process centres more on specific goals and activities than is the case in a peer group, family, or public school.

These agencies prepare people for a coming change of roles. As such they provide anticipatory socialization. **Anticipatory socialization** prepares people for roles they may eventually perform. Most adult socialization is of this character. For example, occupational training programs prepare people for the work they will have to do after graduating.

Equally important, these programs teach the attitudes, values, and beliefs asociated with a future activity. A law school education, for example, teaches students the values of the legal profession and trains them to a style of thinking about legal problems. It also teaches students how to speak, dress, and deal with clients in an appropriate professional manner.

Medicine, too, requires professional socialization. Medical school teaches students the parts of the body, types of diseases, diagnoses, and possible cures.

As well, medical students learn the ethics of medical practice and ways to give a reassuring show of competence to the patient in every situation (Haas and Shaffir, 1977).

During anticipatory socialization, students motivate themselves to learn new values and skills. They have selected themselves into the form of training that will help them go in directions they want to go. Accordingly, anticipatory socialization is often self-training.

Workplace socialization is the process of learning what is and what is not acceptable behaviour, and how things ought to be done, within the context of a workplace. It includes the process of adopting the values, goals, and perspectives of those with whom a person interacts at work. Workplace socialization may also include picking up the specialized terminology (or argot) of the people at work. This helps give the new worker a sense of belonging and of loyalty to the group.

In work settings, ambitious junior executives often pay close attention to the way senior executives dress, speak, and act, and model their actions after them. The person who prepares for career advancement in this way is more likely to advance than the one who does not. On the other hand, such anticipatory socialization may isolate the ambitious person, psychologically and socially, from people he grew up with. **Social marginality** may develop. Marginal people are no longer a part of the group they come from, nor yet members of the group they aspire toward.

Social marginality can be painful and perplexing. Researchers have found that it afflicts a great many children of immigrant parents. These children find themselves cut off from their ethnic roots yet still not fully accepted by the society they want to join. Anticipatory socialization, then, is a two-edged sword that is dangerous to wave around.

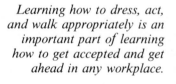

Learning how to dress, act, and walk appropriately is an important part of learning how to get accepted and get ahead in any workplace.

SOCIALIZATION OVER THE LIFE CYCLE

What is the life cycle?

We have already noted that the development of the self and the learning of social behaviour is lifelong. Personal change is the only constant in life. And we have noted that current theories of socialization see development occurring in many phases or stages. The notion of developmental stages implies that people's lives follow a pattern as they age and pass through typical social roles. Sociologists call this pattern the life cycle.

The **life cycle** is a socially recognized, predictable sequence of stages through which individuals pass during the course of their lives. Each stage is characterized by a set of socially defined rights, responsibilities, and expected behaviour patterns.

The recognized sequence in North American society includes infancy, childhood, adolescence, maturity, and old age. Remember, though, that stages of the life cycle are socially and not biologically defined. For example, adolescence is not a biological fact, it is a social invention. Adolescence as we know it today did not exist before the 19th century. Two hundred years ago, fifteen-year-olds spent their time in the same ways as people who were 25 or 35: in adult work. If unmarried, they were all equally subject to domination by the head of the household.

Likewise, old age is not a biological reality so much as a social and psychological one (Dychtwald and Flower, 1990). Today, few people of 50, 60 and even 70 years of age think of themselves as old, or do the things old people used to do. People of these ages are much more physically active, travel more, and enter new roles more readily than people of the same age did 50 years ago; they even divorce and remarry with some frequency. It is the behaviour of eighty- and ninety-year-olds today that is similar to the behaviour of sixty-year-olds a century ago.

Because the life cycle is socially defined, life cycles vary across cultures as well as over history. Different cultures and periods identify different stages, and expect them to last different lengths of time. Our own society has recently recognized a distinct stage between adolescence and mature adulthood. People are calling it the "youth stage," or "young, single, and independent stage." This new stage has emerged because fewer young people are moving out of their parents' homes to marry and form new families. Instead, many are moving out and living on their own, or with a roommate. They are delaying marriage while they find themselves, learn to be independent, or simply have fun.

Even this modified picture of the life cycle is too simple. It gives the impression that people pass through life in only one way and doing otherwise is wrong or abnormal. In fact, the life cycle is just a statistical summary of what people are doing, and not a social law. People vary around the average enormously and they are varying more all the time. Sociologist Denis Hogan (1981) analyzed data on American men over the past half century and found a growing tendency to deviate from the average life cycle.

For example, the typical male 50 years ago finished his formal education, got a job, then married. The proportion of men who took another path—for example, married, finished school, then got a job—was extremely small. Since then, the proportion of men following these alternative patterns has increased dramatically. As a result these once deviant patterns are much less deviant today. It is much easier today than it once was to marry while still in school. In fact, two incomes make finishing school easier, not harder, for people who do not live with their parents. And people are increasingly moving between work and education over the life course. People no longer feel that when you have started working for pay, your education is over for all time. Women are particularly likely to keep moving between school and work in this way, and they are doing it more and more (Jones, Marsden, and Tepperman, 1990).

So the notion of life cycle is no more than a simplifying device that helps us think about behaviours that relate to aging in a general way. Looking at the development and changes in the concepts of childhood and adolescence may help to illustrate how the course of our personal lives matches up with the experiences of many others.

Childhood

Childhood as we know it today is a social category dating from modern times. According to Philippe Aries, author of *Centuries of Childhood* (1962), until the end of the Middle Ages parents treated children like small adults almost as soon as they were weaned and able to get around on their own. Children worked and played, mingled and competed, with mature adults.

Only gradually did parents come to see a value in separating children from adults. The new distinction between childhood and adulthood was part of a new family relationship and new attitudes to childhood and education. The change included special games and skills for children, and the rise of schooling with curricula specially tailored to the abilities of children. The change is revealed in people's diaries and in the painted portraits of families and children as they changed over the centuries.

Four main changes accompanied this rise of childhood as a social category. One is the change from communal, extended family life to a single-household, nuclear family containing only a father, mother, and children. Another is a change in thinking about children. No longer do people view them as little adults. Rather, they are "natural beings" with an innocence and purity that needs careful nurturing through formal education.

The third and fourth changes have to do with the rise of urban, middle-class life. After the 17th century, the economy had ever less need for children's labour and considerably more need for educated adults. This change in the character of work placed a greater importance on literacy and interpersonal skills than in the past. Finally, the new urban middle-class was able to pay for their children's education and forego the income their children might have otherwise earned.

This invention of childhood as an ever-lengthening period of economic inactivity and dependence also led to a long decline in child-bearing that has not yet ended. Children have become ornaments of the family—objects of conspicuous consumption. As such their value increases with their absence from activities that would benefit the family economically. As the lengths and costs of childhood increase, parents are ever less willing to bear children. It is for this reason that more and more Canadian couples are having fewer children than their parents did, or no children at all.

The social responsibilities of childhood suit the uses to which people put childhood. While enforcing their children's dependence and economic uselessness, parents expect their children to remain emotionally infantile. They pamper and spoil their children, but also control them closely. They expect their children to do well at school, as proof of their future worth and to justify parental investment.

Adolescence

The invention of the adolescent stage is part of a general extension of childhood ever deeper into the age span. At one time, childhood ended and adulthood began in the early or mid-teens. Today the transition occurs more and more often in the late teens or early twenties. The extension of childhood results from the same forces as those which led to the invention of childhood in the Middle Ages: namely, the stretching out of formal education, the need for literacy and special skills in an urban, industrial labour market, and parental ability and willingness to pay for longer economic dependency.

According to the American historian Joseph Kett (1977:5,6), it was psychologists, urban reformers, educators, youth workers, and parent counsellors who defined the concept of adolescence. What is significant here is that the invention of adolescence was largely a matter of professional interest. Today we are accustomed to the regular discovery of new behavioural problems that only highly specialized professionals can treat: stress, type-A behaviour, anorexia, and so on. Our society respects professionalism and a specialized treatment of problems that may have been around since the beginning of time. The invention of adolescence and the scientific study of that life stage coincides with the start of professional social science.

The professions most involved in creating adolscence were interested in staking out a socially important turf within which they might appear useful. Specifically, the rise of adolescence and the professional problem-solving that

In our society, traditional gender ideals are hanging on, but they have to share centre stage with some new, radically different ideals.

EXHIBIT 3.3

POSSIBLE FUTURES: FAMILY LIFE

Have you ever wondered why you and your parents (or, if you are a parent, why you and your children) get into so many arguments? The answer is not personal, but societal, sociologist Kingsley Davis told us 50 years ago. Part of the problem is rapid social change, and it raises questions about the future of the family:

> Our rapid social change . . . has crowded historical meaning into the family life-span . . . thereby [giving] the offspring a different social content from that which the parent acquired, and consequently [adding] to the already existent intrinsic difference between parent and youth, [thus doubling] the chance of alienation. Moreover, our great societal complexity, our evident cultural conflict, and our emphasis upon open competition for socio-economic status have all added to this initial effect. . . (Davis, 1940: 532)

Davis continues that if our society were stable and "simple," like earlier rural societies based on the family; if young people won their freedom from parental authority in gradual and definite stages; if adolescence was unhindered by sex taboos and the postponement of marriage; and if competition for status was absent; *then* parents and youth would not be in conflict.

> Hence, the presence of parent-youth conflict in our civilization is one more manifestation of the incompatibility between an urban-industrial-mobile social system and the familial type of reproductive institutions. (ibid)

Davis implies that parent-child conflict is inevitable in our kind of society. In turn, this helps us understand recent dramatic changes in the family: for example, the reasons why, over the past century, Canadian women have (each) been bearing fewer and fewer children and why, in the last 20 years, people have become less likely than ever to marry and (if married) more likely than ever to divorce. As industrialization and urbanization have increased, conflict within the family has increased; as conflict has increased, people have found new ways of avoiding or escaping family life.

What do you think family life will be like in the year 2040, if Davis is right?

Source: K. Davis "The sociology of parent-youth conflict" *American Sociological Review*, 5(4), August 1940, pp.523-535

accompanied it suited the needs of psychologists, educators, and social workers for status-enhancing work.

This is not to say that many teenagers do not require help and advice or deserve extended education and economic support. Rather, adolescent interests coincided with the professional ambitions of applied social science. In a similar way, Freud's promotion of psychoanalysis (around the same time) coincided with the "discovery" of new forms of neurosis. In both cases, people with a solution to offer looked for a problem to solve.

IS THERE ANYONE YOU CANNOT BE?

Resocialization and social structure

Throughout life we change our goals and values. We even change very fundamental facets of our personalities. Strictly speaking, such **resocialization** is a learning process that involves a reshaping of the individual's personality, not merely a change in some attitudes or skills. So fundamental a change comes about through the teaching of radically different values, norms, and role expectations from those previously learned. Resocialization causes the individual to hold a different outlook on the world and a different sense of self.

Resocialization can be voluntary or involuntary. People who undertake psychological counselling are often seeking resocialization—a remaking of their personality. In this case, resocialization is voluntary. However, resocialization may also be involuntary, as it is for people who live in total institutions.

A **total institution**, as described by sociologist Erving Goffman (1961), is an organization which is set apart, either physically or socially, from the rest of society. Examples are prisons, mental hospitals, boarding schools, concentration camps, military barracks, and convents. Inmates in these institutions have little, if any, contact with the outside world. Within them, they learn new modes of thought and behaviour that the people in charge deem appropriate.

People do change fundamentally when they are in fundamentally different settings, especially if they have entered them freely. Does this mean there are

EXHIBIT 3.4

SOCIALIZATION IN CRIME

Even deviance and crime require socialization, as Peter Letkemann shows in his book *Crime as Work*. He writes

There are, essentially, two classes of criminal skills. There are, first of all, those that appear to be extensions of the legitimate order, that is, skills available to all members of society. Such skills include the ability to detect when home owners are not home, or to pose as a customer when not really interested in buying. These skills are systematized, sharpened, and refined by the criminal who consciously uses them.

Secondly, some criminals possess skills that are not easily available to the average citizen. Indeed, access to such skills is also differentially distributed among those criminals who seriously desire them. Such skills include the mechanical procedures for safeopening, or the organizational know-how necessary for successful bank robbery. . . .

The learning of technical skills takes place, basically, by experiment and experience. Formal teacher-student relationships are rare; partners in crime, whether experienced or inexperienced, tend to be equals. . . . Prisons are schools of crime, particularly in providing associations with other criminals who may later choose to work as partners, or who serve as advisors both during and following the prison experience.

Source: P. Letkemann *Crime as Work*. Toronto: Prentice-Hall (Canada), 1973, pp. 117, 156

conditions under which a gentle person might willingly become a killer? Or a loyal person, a traitor?

The answer to this question is often "yes." Warfare, for example, commonly teaches people to kill. As a total institution, the military service programs people to kill efficiently and enthusiastically. And during wartime, the mass media and political leaders whip up even ordinary citizens into blood-lust, under the guise of patriotism and self-defense. Under such circumstances, most people find ways to justify their change of attitude and behaviour.

So we have evidence that sometimes people do respond to new opportunities and dangers by radically changing their thoughts, actions, and relationships. Yet we also have evidence that sometimes people do not: in particular, they resist changes they consider immoral. There were the people who could not learn to hate the enemy soldier, and even people who went to prison for refusing to fight. There were the people who could not inform on their friends, and paid a price for that.

CLOSING REMARKS

Throughout this chapter we have tried to avoid presenting an oversocialized model of the individual (Wrong, 1961). Because sociologists study the social bases of individual behaviour, it is easy for us to fall into the trap of assigning too much weight to conformity and socialization. Yet most of the evidence points away from the individual as the passive subject of socialization. The work of Jean Piaget, for example, has shown the important role experience plays in the course of cognitive development. We do not simply absorb what we are taught; we must creatively assimilate the new material in a way which makes sense to us and which allows it to work for us.

George Herbert Mead, too, presented an active model of socialization. By interacting with others we not only come to understand them, we also come to have a sense of ourselves. The individual in Mead's model cannot be oversocialized, because socialization is a process of interaction, and not some quantity of knowledge to be absorbed or a finite set of norms to be followed. As long as we continue to interact with others and meet new people we continue to be socialized: to discover new things about others and about us. Good sociology – the kind of sociology which never loses sight of either the broad social processes which affect all of us, or of the many intricate sets of circumstances which are unique to each of us – avoids social determinism.

In any case, social determinism raises more problems than it solves. How, for example, could we explain deviance if we assume that everyone is socialized to conform to society's norms and values? Some have tried to deal with this by claiming that deviance results from incomplete or imperfect socialization, others by arguing that deviance itself is conformity to the expectations of particular subcultures. However, by this time, it should be clear that what we call "deviance" is a normal part of social life: something that people learn and unlearn, as conditions permit. It is also something that people define and redefine, as conditions change. We shall explore these issues further in the next chapter.

Discussion Questions

1. Everyone pays the cost of having people in society who have been inadequately or harmfully socialized, since they may end up criminals or mentally ill as adults. Should this give society the right to direct the ways parents socialize their children?

2. What is the strongest evidence that people really do have an *id* that is struggling to overcome reason and order? What would you offer as an alternative explanation for the same evidence?

3. "If the school exposes a child to rules that apply equally to everyone and rewards for merit, is this doing the child a disservice? After all, it is preparing the child for a world that does not exist outside the school." Discuss this statement.

4. Currently, childhood is a time of play and freedom from responsibility, while adulthood is a time of little play and a lot of responsibility. How might lives be organized in future to mix play and responsibility throughout the life cycle? How would childhood gain from this? How would adulthood gain?

5. Old people seem more satisfied with life than younger people, though they may have less money and poorer health. How do they learn this approach to life, and could younger people learn it too?

6. Is there any change people cannot make through resocialization? Give examples of where this change is limited or impossible.

Data Collection Exercises

1. Try a small experiment on one of your friends and report the results to class. Think of something he or she really does not want to do, then see if—through casual conversation and bargaining—you can get that person to do it for a certain reward. What does the outcome of this experiment teach you about the interactionist approach to socialization?

2. Try another small experiment on one of your friends and report the results to class. If the theory of the looking-glass self is valid, you should be able to change your friend's behaviour by changing the way you reflect his or her behaviour. Try persuading your friend that he/she is acting really strangely today and ask if anything is the matter. What does the outcome teach you about the looking-glass self theory?

3. Interview six mature adults you know, to find out what are their main goals in life. Did they always want these things, or did they change their goals from earlier ones? If so, when and why? What evidence can you collect that they are likely to change again?

4. Study advertisements in magazines and newspapers to see what proportion contain a blurring of gender roles. In which types of advertisements (i.e., for what kinds of products) is gender blurring more or less likely? How would you explain this relationship?

Writing Exercises

1. Write a 500-word essay that demonstrates there are no essential differences between teaching a dog to roll over, a baby to eat with a spoon, and a friend to drive your car.

2. Write a 500-word essay on the way your family taught you the difference between right and wrong. Focus on a particular incident that was especially important in your childhood socialization.

3. The year is 2000 A.D. Write a 200-word advertisement for a new psychological counselling service that promises to break people of a bad habit that went untreated by professionals in 1990.

4. You have just been admitted to a total institution where they are trying to change the way you think about something. Choose your institution (e.g., prison, mental hospital, boarding school, military barracks, convent) and write a 500-word diary showing what they are doing to you, when, and with what effects.

Glossary

agents of socialization – institutions and other structured relationships within which socialization takes place

anticipatory socialization – socialization that prepares a person for roles they may eventually have to perform

cognitive development – the development of abilities to think, believe, remember, perceive, and reason

generalized other – a person's general idea of how the society, or surrounding social group, expects him or her to behave

I and me – "I" is the part of the self that is not socialized; "me" is the part that is.

id – in Freud's theory, a part of the personality that includes the individual's most primitive drives, such as sex and aggression. According to Freud, the **ego** is the part of the personality that keeps a person aware of the facts of reality. The **superego** is the conscience, or part of the personality that keeps a person aware of ideals, values, and norms, and causes feelings of guilt and shame for wrong-doing.

internalization – the process by which a person learns and accepts as binding the norms and values of a group or society

life cycle – a socially recognized, predictable sequence of stages through which individuals pass in the course of their lives

looking-glass self – a sense of oneself formed through interaction with others, by assessing how they view us

peer group – a group of companions with whom one interacts, particularly from late childhood through adolescence into early adulthood, and who relate to one another as equals

resocialization – a learning process that reshapes the individual's personality by teaching radically different values, norms, and role expectations, often within a total institution

significant others – people who play key roles in our early socialization and whose approval is important to us (e.g., parents)

social determinism – a theoretical approach that denies human free will and assumes that social structure causes people to act the way they do

socialization – the social learning process through which an individual becomes a capable member of society

Suggested Readings

Brim, Orville G., Jr. and Staton Wheeler, eds. *Socialization after Childhood: Two Essays*. New York: John Wiley, 1966. One of the early statements on the way people learn and change as they pass through the life cycle.

Freud, Sigmund *Civilization and Its Discontents*. London: The Hogarth Press, 1963 [1930]. Here Freud applies his sometimes confusing theory to social life and shows that abnormality is normal in a repressive society.

Goffman, Erving *Asylums*. Garden City, N.Y.: Anchor Books, 1961. A classic statement of the ways total institutions destroy and construct identities for inmates. Contains a rich collection of evidence from many types of institution.

Haas, Jack and William Shaffir, eds. *Shaping Identity in Canadian Society*. Toronto: Prentice-Hall, 1978. Essays that focus on identity formation in ethnic groups and large organizations. Also includes analyses of wrestling and premarital sex.

Sennett, Richard and Jonathan Cobb *The Hidden Injuries of Social Class*. New York: Vintage, 1973. A beautifully written statement of how it feels to grow up in the lower class, feeling inadequate. Discusses how the mind deals with these "hidden injuries" in adult life.

Shattuck, Roger *The Forbidden Experiment: The Story of the Wild Boy of Aveyron*. New York: Pocket Books, Washington Square Press, 1980. Critic and poet Shattuck makes this case history into a general enquiry on the meaning of civilized life: what it gains us, and what it loses.

References

Aries, P. (1962) *Centuries of Childhood: A Social History of Family Life*. New York: Vintage

Baldus, B. and V. Tribe (1978) "Perceptions of social inequality among public school children" *Canadian Review of Sociology and Anthropology*, 15 (1), pp. 50-60

Bibby, R.W. and D.C. Posterski (1985) *The Emerging Generation: An Inside Look at Canada's Teenagers*. Toronto: Irwin

Cooley, C.H. (1902) *Human Nature and Social Order*. New York: Charles Scribners

Durkheim, E. (1964) *The Division of Labor in·Society*. New York: Free Press

Dychtwald, K. and J. Flower (1990) *Age Wave*. New York: Bantam Books

Erikson, E.H. (1950) *Childhood and Society*. New York: W.W. Norton

Freud, S. (1962 [1930]) *Civilization and Its Discontents*. London: The Hogarth Press

Goffman, E. (1961) *Asylums: Essays on the Social Situation of Mental Patients and Other Inmates*. Garden City, New York: Anchor

Haas, J. and W. Shaffir (1977) "The professionalization of medical students" *Symbolic Interaction*, 1 (Fall), pp. 77-88

Hogan, D. (1981) *Transitions and Social Change: The Early Lives of American Men*. New York: Academic Press

Jones, C.J., L. Marsden, and L. Tepperman (1990) *Lives of Their Own: The Individualization of Women's Lives*. Toronto: Oxford University Press

Kett, J.F. (1977) *Rites of Passage: Adolescence in America 1790 to the Present*. New York: Basic Books

Martin, W.B. (1984) "Student perceptions of teachers' pets and class victims" *Canadian Journal of Education*, 9 (1) Winter, pp. 89-99

Mead, G.H. (1934) *Mind, Self and Society*. Chicago: University of Chicago Press

Piaget, J. (1932) *The Moral Judgement of the Child.* New York: Free Press

_____ . (1951) *Play, Dreams and Imitation in Childhood.* New York: W.W. Norton

Wrong, D. (1961) "The oversocialized conception of man in modern sociology" *American Sociological Review*, 26 (April), pp. 183-193

CHAPTER 4

Sociologists have always bee[n] fascinated by the reciprocal relationship between crime and punishment, deviance a[nd] control. The question is, wh[ich] causes which?

DEVIANCE AND CONTROL

DEVIANCE AND SOCIAL CONTROL

When most people think of "deviance," they visualize behaviour committed by some person they would characterize as a "degenerate," "low-life," or sexual "pervert" – abduction, torture, rape, murder, use of illegal drugs. However, deviance is found everywhere and takes many forms. On April 25, 1990, an electric transformer station in Toronto blew up shortly after 8:00 p.m., plunging 750 000 people into darkness. Soon, police were reporting chaotic traffic conditions everywhere and looting along Yonge Street (Toronto's main street) and in the downtown Eaton Centre. Yet despite the cover of darkness, such deviance was rare. In middle-class North Toronto, people lit candles and sat on their porches joking with neighbours. Others on lawn chairs listened to hockey or baseball games over their portable radios. People got re-acquainted with their spouses and children, since television viewing was impossible. Most Torontonians continued to behave in ordinary, orderly ways. By the time electricity was restored several hours later, most people could look back on a pleasant and different, but not deviant, evening.

Why did some Torontonians loot stores while others a mere five kilometres north of them sat and joked with neighbours? Why are violent crimes and property crimes more common in some neighbourhoods, countries, or periods of history than other times and places? What factors lead some people to break the law and others to obey it, whether law enforcement is strong or weak? These are the questions sociologists ask and answer when they study the topic of deviance.

To sociologists, **deviance** is a general term referring to behaviour of any sort that leads to a negative reaction or response on the part of a community or group. This would include crimes such as robbery or vandalism; forms of behaviour such as mental illness or juvenile delinquency; and the violation of institutional rules, such as cheating on an exam or smoking in a non-smoking area. It also includes behaviour that simply does not conform to social norms, such as dressing in a peculiar manner (for example, wearing your clothes inside out) or only taking a shower once every two weeks. Obviously, deviance is a very broad category of social actions.

The study of deviance has long been one of the more contentious areas of sociological research. Because it covers such a very broad range of behaviours, deviance is a difficult term to define and sociologists have been unable to come up with a specific definition agreeable to all. Sociologists have also found it difficult to specify exactly what behaviour is considered deviant because deviance is always relative to a particular group or community. Different people have different conceptions of what behaviour they consider deviant. For example, being a homosexual is not deviant to the community found in a gay bar, but being "straight" might well be. In a pluralistic society such as Canada, there are few behaviours that almost everyone would agree are deviant other than murder, child molesting, mutilation, and rape, and there is a great deal of disagreement on behaviour such as abortion, homosexuality, and recreational drug use.

What all behaviours termed or *labelled* deviant do have in common is that they are perceived by the members of some group to pose a threat to their cherished values, or to individual or group security. This is more serious than merely considering behaviour to be uncommon or eccentric. In those cases where people do not feel threatened by uncommon behaviour, they are likely to see it as simply an expression of a person's individuality. In fact, there is a lot of room in North American popular culture for the acceptance, even the admiration, of people who are eccentric or who "rebel" in fashionable ways.

This means that reactions to behaviour considered uncommon depend, in part, on how the behaviour is perceived. But perception by itself is not enough; it must then be transformed into action. Whether perception carries weight and how much will depend on how much power the observers have to *enforce* their own definitions of normal or acceptable behaviour.

Enforcement at the microsociological level translates into a pattern of social control at the macrosociological level. **Social control** refers to the institutions and procedures used to make sure that members of society or of some group conform to expected and approved behaviour. The effects of social control are obvious when that control is *formal*, especially the enforcement of laws through the courts and the police. **Formal social control** is institutionalized control by which specific persons (such as police officers) have been assigned the task of enforcing specific rules or laws using specific procedures.

Most people have relatively little contact with the courts or other agencies which exercise formal social control, and our familiarity with this form of control usually comes through the media rather than personal experience. But that does not mean that we do not experience social control. Social control is also present in everyday life when ordinary people exercise **informal social control** through gossip, praise, blame, example, and other interpersonal means. Since we are social beings who seek the approval of others for a feeling of self-worth, informal social control usually works well to keep people conforming to the rules. These informal controls are the kinds of social sanctions we discussed in the chapter dealing with socialization. They teach us to obey the rules and gently prod us in the direction of conformity when we show signs of backsliding.

Still, deviance does occur frequently in society and all of us at some time or other deviate from some rule. The fundamental issue for sociologists is understanding the social processes that produce deviance and that determine the relation between deviance and social control. Because there are so many different forms of deviance, chances are that there are many different reasons that people engage in deviant behaviour. Nevertheless, sociologists have been able to develop some simple generalizations to explain the relation between deviance and social control. Not surprisingly, each of the major theoretical perspectives—functionalism, conflict theory, and symbolic interactionism—has developed its own explanation of deviance.

The functionalist approach to deviance

From a common-sense point of view we might expect the relation between deviance and social control to be relatively clear cut: some form of deviance occurs which leads to attempts at social control. This social control either reduces or eliminates the deviance. There is some truth to this common-sense

EXHIBIT 4.1

SOCIAL CONTROL IN A RURAL SETTING

The following vignette from Valloire, a tiny 400-person village in the French Alps, illustrates how gossip can control behaviour in a small community.

> Housewives in Valloire avoid being seen talking to one another. . . . If they need something from the shops, they try to find a child who will run the errand for them. There is no reason why the husbands should not do the shopping, and if they happen to be around, they do so . . . [But] if women are seen talking together . . . very likely they are indulging in *mauvaise langue*—gossip, malice, 'character assassination'.
>
> Even when the spring and summer come and the snow has cleared away, [women] still observe some caution and restraint. . . . There are three reasons for not wanting to meet people: One is that you might bump into someone with whom you are not, at the moment, on speaking terms, and this would be very embarrassing for both of you. Secondly, if you do meet someone with whom you *are* speaking, then good manners require you to stop in the [damp and chilly] street and exchange some remarks about the weather . . . and about births, marriages and deaths and other bits of family news . . . Anyone who sees you talking in this fashion is likely to make assumptions about *mauvaise langue* and so your reputation suffers. [As well], everyone knows almost everyone else, and many of them are relatives, and at least some of them are on speaking terms with one another, so that a trip to the shops could turn out to be very time-consuming. If you try to cut the meetings short by being brief, or, worse still, by ignoring the other person, then you deliver a deadly insult. . . . You earn yourself a reputation for being *fière*, that is, 'stuck up'.
>
> There is, however, one device which allows a woman to hasten past her acquaintances, calling out a greeting but not stopping to chat: that is to wear an apron. The apron indicates that there are pressing tasks at home to which she must get back and that the people whom she meets must not think she is cutting them because she does not stop and talk. In other words, the apron signals that the woman is politically 'off-stage'. (Bailey, 1971: 1, 2)

How do people in large cities avoid being the topic of gossip? Or avoid seeming stuck up?

Source: F.G. Bailey, "Gifts and poison" pp. 1-25 in F.G. Bailey (ed.) *Gifts and Poison: The Politics of Reputation*. Toronto: Copp Clark, 1971, pp. 1, 2

view, but the relation between deviance and social control is far more complex. Structural functionalists, for example, argue that social control does not arise in response to deviance, nor can deviance be eliminated; both deviance and social control have significant social functions of their own.

In one of the earliest functionalist theories of deviance, Emile Durkheim (1938) noted that deviance can be found in every society and in every social group. This means that deviance is a "normal" aspect of social life. Why, Durkheim asked, is society incapable of eliminating deviance? One explanation, which Durkheim rejected, is that some people are naturally wicked or have an innate tendency to break the rules. Another explanation, which Durkheim promoted, is that deviance is in several important ways functional to human groups and societies. Deviance, in other words, benefits society.

There are a number of ways, Durkheim suggested, in which deviance benefits society. For example, people who are identified as deviants may serve as scapegoats for social ills—as targets for repressed aggression and tension. Having a common enemy helps to unite the rest of the group. Durkheim also suggested that deviants provide us with vivid examples of how not to act. A society needs deviance to define the boundaries between good and evil, right and wrong, and what is or is not acceptable. Also, since the exercise of social control increases social cohesion and group solidarity, the enforcement of rules upon deviants ties the group more tightly together. To the degree that deviance both calls forth and justifies social control, then, deviance is "good" for society.

There are other positive functions deviance performs in society. Deviant behaviour calls attention to flaws in the social system that need mending. Deviance may also represent new and improved ways of getting things done, or better ways of adapting to changes in the social environment. Minor forms of deviance may serve as safety valves, allowing individuals to let loose in a socially controlled and acceptable manner (for example, getting drunk at a weekend party). In all these ways, Durkheim believed, both deviance and social control help society to survive and change.

Durkheim's discussion of the functions of deviance and social control provided sociologists with a new way of thinking about deviance, one that remains important today. It contradicts the common-sense bias that deviant behaviour is intrinsically "wrong," "bad," or "evil," and directs our attention to the social processes that produce and maintain deviance. In particular, it helps us understand why certain forms of behaviour, such as prostitution (discussed in Chapter One), continue despite being considered both immoral and illegal.

There are, however, a number of flaws in the functionalist approach, the most glaring having to do with the issue of "benefits." Who exactly benefits from some particular form of deviance? Who is harmed? Why, for example, did Nazi Germany decide on Jews as scapegoats for the country's problems rather than the many Polish agricultural workers living in Germany? It is simplistic to say that "society" benefits from any particular form of deviance because it is always specific people who benefit while other specific people are harmed. In any case, how can we argue that society "benefits" from rape, child molesting, or murder? The functionalist perspective has failed to deal effectively with these kinds of issues.

Conflict theories of deviance

Another perspective, adopted by many sociologists, is that both deviance and social control are the outcome of conflicting interests. This conflict perspective takes as its starting point the recognition that the creation of rules and their enforcement leads to people being defined as deviant. If there were no rules, or if rules were not enforced, there would be no deviance. Deviance only springs into existence through the application of rules to human activity. Understanding how, why, and by whom rules are created, then, is the key to understanding deviance.

This view holds several interesting implications. The first is that societies plagued by deviance really suffer from the application of too many rules. If we lived with fewer rules and less rule-enforcement—that is, if we adopted a live-and-let-live approach to other people—we would not have to worry about deviance. Our controllers, the government and law-makers, cause our problems by trying to enforce laws that create more problems than they solve. The current debate over the legalization of narcotics and other illegal drugs makes this very point: keeping these drugs illegal creates an enormous criminal drug industry which does more harm than would the drugs themselves if legally available.

Conflict theorists usually take this analysis a couple of steps further. They argue that social control extends social inequality into the realm of law. In every society, some people have more power than others. These people will seek to use this power to protect their own interests and possessions, which means seeing that the government makes, and the police enforce, laws that protect the interests of the powerful.

From this standpoint the study of deviance and control is the study of law-making: why governments make certain laws at certain times, and whom these laws favour. By this reasoning, neither deviance nor control is functional to society. Rather, social control serves one particular group in society at the expense of everyone else. Deviants are the main victims of this control.

Again, as was the case with the functionalist approach, there is much about deviance that this perspective helps us to understand. Yet, when we look at the controversies and conflicts of interest surrounding deviance, it is hard to interpret many of them as involving the "powerful." Instead we find conflicts based on religious beliefs, as is the case with abortion legislation; or on personal security, as in the demand by police that the death penalty be re-introduced for the killing of a police officer. Instead of seeing the deviants as the "real" victims, many would suggest that the real victims of crime are the poor and powerless who are the most likely to be robbed, murdered, exploited, or raped.

The labelling perspective

The interactionist approach to deviance examines how the social processes which generate deviance and social control have impact on the experience and self-identity of the individual. One particularly significant attempt to understand deviance which emerged out of this interactionist approach is referred to as *labelling theory*. **Labelling theory** starts from the assumption that deviance is determined not by the behaviour itself but by the reactions of others to the behaviour. When someone is labelled as deviant, the rest of society will treat that person as a deviant, often locking them into a deviant lifestyle and leading them to identify themselves as deviant.

Labelling theorists do not try to explain primary deviation—why an individual engages in deviant behaviour in the first place—but study secondary deviation—what happens to people after they have been identified or labelled deviant. This shift in focus has significant consequences both for what labelling theorists study and for how they go about doing their research.

Labelling theorists are uninterested in why people first engage in deviance because they see everyone as being deviant to some degree. From their point of view, the population is not split into two camps, conformists and deviants. Rather, most people conform to most norms most of the time and everyone violates some norms at some times in their life. The question is not why some violate norms but why some get locked into a pattern of repeated norm violation or criminal behaviour.

This means that labelling theorists do not study the factors that might lead people to commit deviant acts or the social characteristics of the typical deviant. Labelling theorists begin by looking at the act of labelling itself. They show that the application of a label is stigmatizing. A **stigma** is a social attribute that acts as a mark of shame or social disgrace, and that discredits an individual or group. The stigma that accompanies being labelled deviant serves to remind others of what happens to people who violate social norms.

Applying Cooley's concept of the looking-glass self, labelling theorists point to the importance of the audience in forming an individual's self-image. A person seen as deviant by others may come to see himself or herself that way. Ironically, the individual will then be more likely to engage in deviant behaviour, because that fits in with his or her new self-image. This new deviant behaviour and self-image is what labelling theorists call **secondary deviation**.

Labelling theorists are not saying that deviant behaviour is wrong only if you get caught. They are emphasizing that deviance does not exist without control. People who have not committed any crimes or engaged in any deviant behaviour, and are falsely accused of doing so, will be treated as deviants by the community and social control agencies. At the same time, many "nice, respectable" people whom others have trusted and treated as trustworthy have turned out to be embezzlers, mass murderers, or leaders of satanic cults.

Labelling theorists focus on the processes of interaction, negotiation, and enforcement which lead some people to be defined as deviant. They ignore the issue of why people may engage in deviance, such as "predisposing" motives or causes, because being labelled deviant does not necessarily prove that the person being labelled did participate in deviant acts; they may be falsely accused. By observing people, talking to them, and participating with them in some of their activities, the labelling theorist discovers how people defined as deviant organize their lives, develop a self-identity, and come to terms with the public's definition of them.

EXHIBIT 4.2

HOW'S YOUR MENTAL HEALTH?

	Often	Sometimes	Never
A. Have you ever been bothered by your heart beating hard?	☐	☐	☐
B. How often are you bothered by an upset stomach?	☐	☐	☐
C. Do your hands ever tremble enough to bother you?	☐	☐	☐
D. Are you ever troubled by your hands or feet sweating so that they feel damp and clammy?	☐	☐	☐
E. Have you ever been bothered by shortness of breath when not exerting yourself?	☐	☐	☐
F. Do you ever have spells of dizziness?	☐	☐	☐
G. Do you feel weak all over much of the time?	☐	☐	☐
H. Do you feel healthy enough to carry out the things you would like to do?	☐	☐	☐
I. Do you feel you are bothered by all sorts (different kinds) of ailments in different parts of your body?	☐	☐	☐
J. Do you ever have loss of appetite?	☐	☐	☐
K. Do you have any trouble in getting asleep and staying asleep?	☐	☐	☐
L. Has ill health affected the amount of work you do?	☐	☐	☐
M. Have you ever felt you were going to have a nervous breakdown?	☐	☐	☐
N. Are you ever bothered by nightmares?	☐	☐	☐
O. Do you tend to lose weight when important things are bothering you?	☐	☐	☐
P. Do you tend to feel tired in the mornings?	☐	☐	☐

Answer these questions to assess your own mental health. They measure how often you experience symptoms of anxiety and depression and, hence, distress. A total score is obtained by "weighting" the items and adding up the weighted scores. For example, give yourself 2 points if you are often "bothered by your heart beating hard," 1 point if it only happens sometimes, and 0 points if it never happens. After scoring all 16

Continued

of your answers this way, get your total score.

This method of data collection is too crude to diagnose mental illness, but good enough to identify signs of trouble. If you are scoring above 16 on this test, you are experiencing a lot of symptoms and may want to consult a doctor.

However, sociologists look for revealing social patterns in these data. For example, Statistics Canada (1981: 130-131) reports that people with high scores on this set of measures are likelier to be

- old—not young
- female—not male
- widowed, separated, or divorced—not married
- poor—not rich
- poorly educated—not well educated

What conclusions will a sociologist draw from these findings—for example, what conclusions about the causes of poor mental health? And what conclusions about how "deviant" poor mental health really is?

Source: Statistics Canada, *The Health of Canadians: Report of the Canada Health Survey.* (Catalog 82-538 E.) Ottawa: 1981, pp. 130, 131, 209. Reproduced with the permission of the Minister of Supply and Services Canada, 1990.

The labelling perspective does not directly contradict either the functionalist or the conflict approach to deviance. By ignoring "why," the labelling perspective leaves open the question of whether deviance has broad social functions or reflects conflicting sets of interests. The implication is clear, however, that labelling theory assumes the consequence of social control to be more significant than its cause. What this means, however, is that labelling theory is not really a "theory" at all because it fails to explain deviance. At best, the labelling approach is a corrective or addition to other theories.

CAUSES OF CRIME AND DEVIANCE

In addition to the explanations of crime provided by the major sociological perspectives, there are several theories developed specifically as explanations of crime and delinquency. Two of the main theories in this area are anomie theory and differential association theory.

Anomie theory is a sociological theory of deviance developed by Robert Merton (1957). According to anomie theory, the cause of deviance does not lie in the individual but in the unequal opportunity structure found in society. It explains crime and deviance as a product of the discrepancy between culturally defined *goals* and socially approved *means* for attaining those goals. Merton suggested that one of the primary goals of American society is success, particularly in obtaining money, material goods, and "the good life." Almost everyone has been socialized to value success. Yet the reality of inequality is that most people do not have access to the legitimate means and resources that allow one to obtain success. People therefore are impelled to seek alternate means of achieving their goals. Merton referred to this discrepancy between goals and means as **anomie**.

There are a number of alternatives, which Merton called *adaptations* to anomie. Some people simply ignore the reality of inequality and continue to conform to society's rules even though these never do pay off in personal success. Merton called this adaptation *ritualism*. Other people recognize that they will never achieve their goals and just give up. They become *retreatists* (for example, alcoholics, drug addicts, or suicides). Still others *rebel* against the inequality and try to change the political order.

However, one common non-conforming adaptation to anomie is *innovation*. Innovation is developing one's own, non-legitimate means for achieving goals, such as crime. Merton suggested that this adaptation is most likely among lower-class individuals who have been well socialized to desire success but have been poorly socialized to respect the legitimate means available.

Merton's explanation of deviance is macrosociological. It explains deviance as a consequence of structural factors. Yet there is a serious gap in this type of explanation, an inability to specify who will engage in deviance. After all, a great many people face the conditions of anomie Merton described, yet only a minority become criminals. Why is that?

Differential association theory was first advanced by Edwin Sutherland (Sutherland and Cressey, 1978) 50 years ago to explain why some individuals, but not others, become criminals. Sutherland theorizes that criminal activities are as much the product of learning and socialization as is conformity. The individual learns the attitude, thought, and behaviour patterns—including the techniques, motives, and rationalizations—of the group to which he or she belongs. If the members of the group are prone to crime, the person socialized into that group will be as well. This theory emphasizes the importance of the group to which the individual belongs in producing a deviant or criminally inclined person.

Unlike Merton, who sees deviance as an individual adaptation to anomie, Sutherland sees deviance as a group or subcultural activity. To understand why one person is a plumber, another is a social worker, and a third is a bank robber, we must know how each learned the skills and gained the necessary credentials. We start by studying the social milieu in which each person grew up and the reasons why it was easier for the bank robber to learn bank robbing than plumbing or social work.

Sutherland's theory assumes that becoming a deviant means conforming to the norms and values of a particular group. Deviance, even crime, is not proof in itself of a personal pathology or disorganization. We shall have more to say about that assumption shortly.

None of the major sociological perspectives and none of the special theories of crime do full justice to the phenomenon of deviance. It is not that these perspectives and theories are wrong; each provides us with valuable insights on some aspects of deviance. But as we stated at the beginning, there are many different forms of deviance and many different social processes at work. Different factors result in different forms of deviance, and generate different kinds of social control. We see that there are some forms of deviance, particularly certain crimes, over which there is basic consensus in our society, which most people consider wrong and believe should be punished. Then there are forms of norm violations, such as mental illness, that most people would see as neither criminal nor requiring punishment. Finally, there are social diversions such as pornography, which some see as a social problem and others consider a fundamental right. An examination of these different forms of deviance and their different characteristics is therefore necessary before we can go on with our analysis.

KINDS OF DEVIANT BEHAVIOUR

Crime

Crime is usually considered the most serious form of deviance. A **crime** is any act formally prohibited by law, specifically by the Criminal Code of Canada. Defining certain acts as crimes gives the state the authority to punish offenders, and the Criminal Code specifies an appropriate range of punishments for each crime.

Although all crimes are defined by the Criminal Code, there are many different kinds of crime. There are some crimes considered extremely harmful by most people, such as murder, armed robbery, extortion, arson, sexual assault, selling drugs, and kidnapping. In general we can say there is widespread consensus in Canadian society, and in most other societies, that these forms of behaviour are unacceptable and should be severely punished.

In contrast, there are some crimes over which there is so much disagreement that the law has, in effect, lost jurisdiction. The best example, at the time of this writing, is abortion. A series of court decisions have struck down Canada's abortion law and the issue is so contentious that the federal government seems unable to draft legislation on abortion to either clearly criminalize or clearly legalize it.

Then there are the more standard crimes that most people consider wrong, but for which most people are not particularly concerned with the severity of punishment. These include offenses against property like breaking and entering, automobile theft, and shoplifting; minor assaults and drunken driving; also "white-collar" offenses like embezzlement and fraud. All of these offenses have a victim or (as in the case of drunken driving) run a serious risk of victimizing someone. In each case, a victim may have pressed charges against the offender or the police may have done so, especially where public order was being violated.

Another category of crimes are **victimless crimes**, from which no one suffers directly, except perhaps the people engaging in the behaviour. Examples of victimless crime are gambling, prostitution, and illicit drug use. These are all crimes because the Criminal Code defines them as crimes, and their perpetrators are subject to legal action. However, in practice the police do not enforce these laws consistently or energetically, and the courts are unlikely to hand out stiff penalties. Instead, the penalties for these crimes may range from a light prison sentence down to probation, a fine, or a community-service order.

We know a great deal about the prevalence of certain crimes because a high proportion of murders, robberies, and kidnappings are reported to the police and are recorded as official data. Of these, a relatively high percentage result in arrests and convictions. By comparison, people are much less willing to report other crimes, especially sexual assaults. Many women—the majority of victims—are reluctant to undergo the psychological, legal, and public humiliations that often accompany such reporting. In addition, of the sexual assaults reported, only a small percentage result in convictions because judges and juries are often reluctant to believe the victim, and convictions often result in less than the maximum sentence.

Another category of crimes that are likely to go unreported are those committed by professional criminals for gain, such as robbery, arson, selling drugs, and assault with a deadly weapon. For example, victims are often afraid to report attempts of extortion—demands for money with threat of physical violence—because they fear revenge by the criminal or his colleagues.

Still, criminologists know enough about crime to permit several generalizations. First, the incidence of crime seems to be increasing, with crimes most common in big cities. Second, crimes that are not committed for gain usually result from disputes between spouses or friends. Third, crimes that are committed for gain are often connected directly or indirectly to organized crime.

Because they are so common, easily investigated, and inexpensively

EXHIBIT 4.3

WHY YOU ARE NOT A CRIMINAL

In an effort to understand why some people had become criminals, sociologist Joseph Rogers got the imaginative idea of asking other people why they had *not* become criminals.

His results suggest that ordinary, law-abiding people may have far more in common with convicted offenders than we normally suppose. Consider the following statement by a female student in sociology:

> Crime never seemed to be a very good way of life, so I didn't want to make my living at it. I figure that it is better to have a legitimate job and do it well than an illegal job, no matter how good.
>
> Most criminals are always on the move. One can never settle down and be happy because the police are always right behind you. Too, if people find out how you make a living they won't want to live near you or have anything to do with you—sounds like a lonely life to me.
>
> A person might say, "But the money is great." Well, I'd compare it to being an actress. The chances of making it to the big time are very slim and most of the dollars you will make will be few and far between. Personally, it is much nicer to know that there will be a cheque every week and that I won't have to worry about getting caught spending it. . . . You ask why I, myself, am not a criminal. Well, I weighed the pros and cons of criminal life and it came up sadly lacking in the pro department. (Rogers, 1977: 80)

What are *your* reasons for not becoming a criminal?

Source: J.W. Rogers *Why Are You Not a Criminal?* Englewood Cliffs, NJ: Prentice-Hall, 1977, p. 80

prosecuted, a small number of crimes represent the bulk of our criminal statistics at any given time. This suggests that recorded rates of crime most closely reflect the reporting and prosecution of specific crimes. Changes in the crime rate may therefore reflect changes in the victims' willingness to report crimes and the willingness of the police to investigate them.

Norm violations

Norm violations are not defined as crimes in the Criminal Code; nonetheless, people may see them as significant and serious forms of deviance. In the past, many of these forms of deviance were considered crimes; we would consider the perpetrators mentally ill or alcoholic and they would be locked up in prisons. Today, we tend to view such social deviations as illnesses in need of treatment. Still, the courts have felt little need to limit the state's powers over the socially deviant, the way they do when dealing with regular criminals, because they see the state's role as parental and benevolent. This means that the court can put a person defined as mentally ill in a hospital indefinitely against his or her will. It is only recently that patients have been sure of legal representation and due process in court proceedings that affect their lives. One consequence of this recent development is that professionals in deviance such as psychiatrists, psychologists, and social workers have won a dominant role in dealing with social deviants.

Thus, changes over time in the kinds of deviation reported and in their frequency largely reflect changes in the procedures for defining, detecting, and processing deviants. If we discovered that reported rates of mental illness were twice as high this year as ten years ago, we could not fairly conclude that mental illness is twice as common. Possibly, all that had changed was the official definition of mental illness and the procedures used for its detection.

Much of the deviant behaviour in Canada is simply one or another form of social "diversion." Many people commit these deviant acts for pleasure, not gain, and many in the community see nothing wrong with these acts, if done in moderation.

Social diversions

A third class of deviant acts consists of social diversions. **A social diversion** is an act that only some people would regard as violating norms and that fewer still would consider a serious violation. The Criminal Code does not forbid any of these social diversions, nor do formal institutions—the courts, hospitals, or health professionals—try to control them. They are largely recreational activities whose main purpose is personal stimulation and subcultural integration (Hagan, 1984: 19).

One major category of social diversion is that of sexual behaviour. There are many forms of sexual behaviour that may be viewed by most people as "odd," "weird," or "sick" but in which a significant number of people engage. The most obvious example is homosexuality, simply because it is today the most visible and most accepted form of alternative sexuality, but other examples would be sado-masochism, fetishism, or cross-dressing. When Prime Minister Trudeau came to office in the late 1960s, he declared that the Canadian government had no business in the bedrooms of the nation. He meant that official efforts to control homosexuality, non-marital or marital sex were going to disappear; and they have. Today, condom use is publicly promoted to combat AIDS, birth control is readily available, and gay rights are protected in the Human Rights Code of Ontario and, possibly, by the Canadian Charter of Rights.

To a large degree, informal controls on these behaviours have also diminished since the 1960s. Yet sexual variations remain deviation, and some of the less common forms still raise eyebrows among many Canadians.

Another class of social diversions includes styles of dress, speech, and behaviour that are uncommon among middle-aged, middle-class people. Such deviations are more common among young people than among the old. Eccentric clothes and speech often signify membership in a group holding values and norms that are uncommon and may offend other people. We call some of these groups **deviant subcultures**.

We have little accurate information about changes in the rates of social deviation, including sexual behaviour, gang behaviour, or other subcultural deviation. This is partly because no one gathers systematic statistics on a regular basis. Also, people's willingness to discuss their deviations varies over time and place, and by their nature many social deviations are faddish—they come and go very quickly.

As we see, deviant behaviour takes many forms, and often it exists mainly in the eye of the beholder; therefore, we sometimes learn more by studying the beholder than we do by studying the supposed deviant. However, most sociological interest and research has focused on those who are defined as deviant. Understanding how people come to be engaged in deviant acts, who these people typically are, and what happens to them after they begin to participate in deviant activities, is an important area of sociological concern.

PARTICIPATION IN DEVIANT ACTIVITIES

A **deviant subculture** is made of people who conform to certain norms and hold certain beliefs that the larger society considers deviant. Members of the subculture may dress, behave, and speak in a way that emphasizes the boundaries between that group and competing groups (e.g., rival gangs) or "straight" society.

Deviant subcultures

The discovery of deviant subcultures was an important achievement in sociology. Up through the 1930s, social scientists assumed that a properly socialized individual would not engage in deviant behaviour. They thought deviant behaviour was therefore the result of social and personal disorganization, which prevented proper socialization. They viewed gangs, for example, as evidence that the slums within which most gang members lived were lacking agreed-on norms and values. From this standpoint, they viewed the behaviour of gang members as individual pathology: a sick adaptation to personal deprivation, broken homes, and lack of moral guidance.

Research on gangs showed sociologists that this was not a valid interpretation. First, research by Thrasher (1937) and others on gang behaviour showed that gang members were far from being unsocialized non-conformists. In fact, they did conform to rules – gang rules, which were often the exact opposite of society's rules. This is the opposite of disorganization.

Second, research reported by William Foote Whyte (1961) in his classic *Street Corner Society* went even further. Whyte showed that gangs were an integral part of the slum community's organization. Gang activities linked young people into both organized crime and the corrupt political party structure of the neighbourhood. Gang members carried out important criminal and political work for well-established organizations. Whyte demonstrated that people had not only misunderstood gangs, they had misunderstood the slum-dweller's way of life.

Such findings remind us that gang behaviour, like all subcultural behaviour, is open to interpretation. Middle-class observers were ready to see gang activity as pathological because they knew few of the facts. They also had an ethnocentric view of how communities *should* operate. For our part, we are not arguing that gangs and slums are wonderful. All we can say is what Whyte was saying: people in poor communities are no better or worse, no more or less organized, than people in other communities. Our social programs should not be directed toward changing the people, but toward changing the conditions of their lives.

Deviant subcultures, with their distinctive forms of behaviour, dress, and speech, emerge whenever people with something in common feel a need to insulate themselves from the larger society. An example is the jazz musicians' subculture, with its own language, in-jokes, idols, and sense of alienation from non-musicians (Becker, 1963). Deviant subcultures also emerge when the rest of society discriminates against or endangers people who behave in unusual ways. An example of this is the gay community. In most cities the local gay community has established its own networks and hang-outs to compensate for discrimination. As Durkheim said, a need for group cohesion strengthens the demands for conformity within the group. The less contact there is between members of a deviant subculture and the rest of society, the more stable, complex and "strange" the deviant subculture is likely to be.

So crime and deviance are "normal" after all, but not everyone becomes a criminal or a member of a deviant subculture. What kinds of people *do* become criminals or career deviants, and why? We begin with the first question first.

Who commits crimes?

In the case of serious crimes, the most common criminals by far are young, single males.

The statistics for murder show that more than two-fifths of murder suspects are between the ages of 20 and 29 years and another quarter are between 30 and 39. Almost nine out of ten suspects are male and almost half are single. As for robberies and non-sexual assaults, or offenses causing bodily harm, they too are carried out primarily by males. In incidents where they could estimate age, at least half the victims said their assailants were under age 25. Young males also dominate larceny, or theft such as shoplifting. About one in seven offenders is under age 15 and five in eight are under 25 years of age.

Why are criminals so often young, unmarried males? In the case of homicide, many believe the reason to be that young males lead an unstructured lifestyle and are accustomed to expressing physical aggression. Additionally, in poor communities a high proportion of young men are unemployed and may feel a high degree of frustration. This also makes them more likely to feel and express aggression.

EXHIBIT 4.4

MALE VIOLENCE IN THE HOME

By their own admission,

> Almost one in five (18%) married or cohabiting men had committed at least one of eight listed violent acts [against their spouses in the preceding year]. The figure rose to about 30% among divorced or separated respondents. Considering only the five most serious acts—[kicking, biting, or hitting with a fist; slapping; hitting or attempting to hit with an object; beating; using or threatening to use a knife or gun]—each of which carries a high risk of serious injury, about 10% of married and cohabiting men reported at least one such incident. (Lupri, 1989: 20)

Abuse of a female partner was more common than average among men with low incomes.

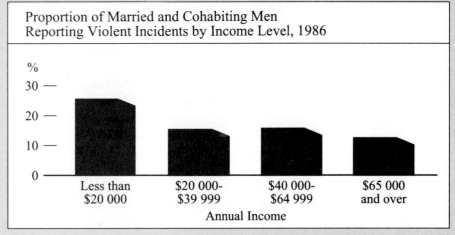

Proportion of Married and Cohabiting Men Reporting Violent Incidents by Income Level, 1986

Source: Canadian Social Trends – Autumn 1989.

Continued

It was also more common than average among younger men, though not absent from any age group.

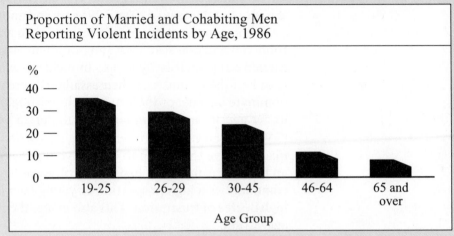

Proportion of Married and Cohabiting Men
Reporting Violent Incidents by Age, 1986

Source: Canadian Social Trends – Autumn 1989.

Younger men with the least education reported the most incidents. As well, self-confessed violence was commoner than average among men who had experienced many stressful events—such as unemployment, bankruptcy, a wage drop, the need to work additional hours, a move to less expensive accommodations, demotions or career setbacks—during the year. About one man in three experiencing six or seven such stresses admitted to domestic violence, compared with only one man in thirteen who experienced none of these stresses.

Source: Eugen Lupri "Male violence in the home" *Canadian Social Trends*, Autumn 1989, p. 20. Reproduced with the permission of the Minister of Supply and Services Canada, 1990.

The victims, too, are disproportionately young unmarried males, students, and the unemployed. They are most likely to be out in public places and engaged in evening activities outside the home, the circumstances often associated with assault and robbery.

Juvenile delinquents seem to have a different motivation. Delinquency often reflects a desire for adventure, thrills, and the respect of peers. Many delinquents also make use of drugs and alcohol, which are seen to loosen inhibitions against socially disapproved activities. Delinquent activities by teenage boys and young men focus on activities which display a tough, active, unemotional masculine image. They also display characteristics associated with the culture of poverty discussed in an earlier chapter: a focus on fate, danger, luck, and taking risks. The delinquent activities range in seriousness from vandalism, petty theft (such as shoplifting), breaking and entering, illegal alcohol and drug use, auto theft and dangerous driving, up through drug dealing, robbery, and gang fighting. Some of these acts are aimed at making money but most are intended to gain or defend status, protect gang turf, or demonstrate manliness. Their symbolic value lies precisely in their lack of practical payoff and in their danger to life and liberty.

Relatively few juvenile delinquents become career criminals although, once police have recorded a contact with a juvenile, the probability of another recorded contact is high. It may be that police only make records for juveniles they think are bound to get into more trouble, or it may be that a recorded contact predisposes the police to keep a closer watch on a particular juvenile. With closer observation, chances are the police will detect more deviance. Yet, for all this, most delinquents stop breaking the law when they become mature adults.

A small group we might call *violent predators* do not stop. These are criminals who commit a variety of serious crimes: typically robberies, assaults, and drug deals. These offenders are also quite young, on average less than age 25 when first imprisoned. By their mid-twenties they have been committing violent crimes for six years or more. Evidence suggests they are less socially stable than other offenders — for example, less likely to hold a steady job or be married. Drug use is very common among these violent predators.

But, despite the social harm caused by violent predators, the legal system focuses its main attention on *street crimes*, such as theft, auto offenses, and victimless crimes. It is also less pro-active in dealing with domestic crimes and with *suite crimes*, or white-collar crimes, like fraud, forgery, tax evasion, price-fixing, work safety violations, and embezzlement of funds.

White collar crimes are committed by high-status members of the community, often in the course of their work. While poverty may breed crime, it seems that greed does the job equally well. The difference in types of crimes committed by members of different social classes is related to a variation in their opportunity to commit them. It is easier for an executive in a large company to embezzle money than it is for the average person on the street.

Corporate crimes, like domestic crimes, are hard to detect and almost impossible to prevent. They are also hard to punish, because the business community closes ranks to prevent the criminalization of acts that Goff and Reasons (1978) say should be considered serious crimes. Corporate deviance, such as waste dumping, bribery of officials, and work safety violations, has many victims. In that respect, such business acts deserve prosecution and punishment more than many acts we consider crimes.

Unlike white-collar and domestic crimes, crimes by violent predators are rare, constituting less than 10% of all Canadian criminal acts. The media and government have led us to fear and punish the rarest crimes and to focus on crimes whose perpetrators are most easily detected and convicted: street crimes and, secondarily, domestic crimes. They also ignore deviant acts of equal (or possibly more) significance — white-collar crimes — that, for political reasons, would be harder to punish.

Female criminals

Women are less likely than men to engage in much crime, although evidence shows a recent increase in female criminality. This may reflect a blurring of gender roles: for example, more social and economic activity outside the home than in past generations or, as criminologist Freda Adler (1975: 30) notes, a decline in women's acceptance of "dated notions of femininity." As women's circumstances have changed, Adler suggests, their abilities and opportunities for crime have increased. Adler (1975: 95) writes that "Girls are involved in more drinking, stealing, gang activity and fighting – behaviour in keeping with their adoption of male roles." Not only are deviance rates increasing among females but the kinds of deviant acts they commit are changing too. True, women remain less likely than men to commit violent crimes such as murder, robbery, assault. Yet they seem to differ very little from men in their willingness to commit white-collar crimes (for example, embezzlement, theft, or fraud) when the opportunity arises.

The rise in female crime may also reflect a greater willingness among police to apprehend and lay criminal charges against female offenders, who in the past benefitted from a popular belief that they were "the gentler sex." Earlier in this century, female criminals were more likely to be thought mentally ill – hence, blameless – than criminal. Accordingly, boys might be delinquent but girls were "wayward."

Leaving crime

Efforts to rid people of their tendencies towards crime have had notoriously little success. The violent predators resist all attempts at change through treatment. Indeed, every day the prison subculture undoes any efforts at reform. Professional criminals, too, have no desire to change and good reason not to do so. Others, however – the amateur criminals who make up the vast majority – do gradually draw away from criminal activity.

Unless they are professional criminals, people have less time and opportunity for crime as they get older. They have less time to spend with friends in public places, for example. On the other hand, they spend more time at home with their families.

As they age, they also have a greater *stake in conformity*, a stronger motivation to stay out of trouble. They may have a family they care for and want to support, a mortgage to pay, a job they like, or income they need. They may feel less at odds with society at age 35 than they did at 15. Certainly, the costs of losing what they have will be higher. So they will obey the rules more consistently, whether they believe in the rules or not.

EXHIBIT 4.5

Possible Futures: Preventing Mass Murders

Sociologist Elliot Leyton has analyzed the characteristics of sexual mass murderers and tabulated some of his findings in the chart below.

	First Scan (Social Characteristics)	Second Scan (Behavioural Traits)
John Bianchi (Hillside Strangler)	Adopted	Mr. Perfect, Policeman
Cliff Olson (B.C. Murders)	Institutionalized (Juvenile home)	Boxer

Continued

David Berkowitz (Son of Sam)	Illegitimate and Adopted	Mr. Crazy, Security Guard
Earle Nelson (Manitoba Murders)	Adopted	Insuff. Data
Ted Bundy (Seattle)	Illegitimate	Mr. Perfect
Albert Fish (Prewar children)	Institutionalized (Orphanage reared)	Mr. Perfect
Albert DeSalvo (Boston Strangler)	Institutionalized (Juvenile home) and Violent Kin (Both father & brother charged with assault)	Boxer
Peter Sutcliffe (Yorkshire Ripper)	Violent Kin (Brother twice charged with grievously wounding police)	Mr. Perfect
Dean Coril (Houston Murders)	Ruptured Maternal Bond (Mother thrice married)	Insuff. Data
"Norman Collins" (Michigan Murders)	Ruptured Maternal Bond (Mother thrice married)	Motorcycles
William Bonin (Freeway Murders)	Institutionalized (In juvenile home from age of eight)	Mr. Crazy
Ian Brady (Moors Murders)	Illegitimate and Institutionalized (Both foster and juvenile homes)	Nazi Buff
Richard Speck (Chicago Nurses)	Institutionalized (Juvenile home)	Insuff. Data
Robert Irwin	Institutionalized (Juvenile home)	Insuff. Data
William Heirens (Chicago Murders)	Institutionalized (Juvenile home)	Nazi Buff, Gun Nut
Edmund Kemper III (Santa Cruz Murders)	Institutionalized (Mental hospital from age of 15) and Ruptured Maternal Bond (Mother thrice married)	Gun & Knife Nut
Fritz Haarmann (Prewar German)	Institutionalized (Juvenile home)	Insuff. Data
Robert Carr III	Institutionalized (Juvenile home)	Insuff. Data
Antone Costa (Cape Cod Murders)	Not Fit	Not Fit
John Christie (London Prostitutes)	Not Fit	Policeman

Mr. Perfect—a social manner (or way of presenting oneself to others) that suggests good grooming, a willingness to conform to rules, and extremely high personal standards of behaviour. Psychiatrists might call this "psychopathic behaviour".

Mr. Crazy—a social manner (or way of presenting oneself to others) that suggests unpredictability, an inability to conform to rules, violent mood shifts, and communication with invisible beings. Psychiatrists might call this "psychotic behaviour".

Continued

Gun Nut, Knife Nut, Motorcycles, Boxer, Martial Arts, Nazi Buff—evidence of a fascination with "power sports" and, more generally, with power gained through physical aggression against others.

Note how well elements of these profiles fit Marc Lepine, the murderer of 14 Montreal women. Like the others Leyton studied, Lepine was described as "Mr. Perfect," was fascinated with guns and the military, and was the witness to frequent domestic violence by his father against his mother.

If Leyton's analysis is correct, we may already know enough about mass murderers to start preventing mass murders. But what social, legal, and cultural changes will be needed to prevent them? And what ethical problems are likely to arise if we undertake this course of action? Sociological expertise has no particular value in answering that question.

Source: E. Leyton, "A social profile of sexual mass murderers" in T. Fleming and L.A. Visano (eds.) *Deviant Designations: Crime, Law and Deviance in Canada.* Toronto: Butterworths, 1983, pp. 98-107

For dealing with most criminal activity, prevention may prove much more effective than punishment. Sociological findings have strengthened the view that attempts to reduce crime must focus on social development. There is no doubt that criminals who get caught are more likely to be *poor* than rich. Providing people with more opportunities may help keep them from being motivated towards crime in the first place, and may give them a stake in conformity.

CLASS AND JUVENILE DELINQUENCY

Is crime primarily a lower-class adaptation to inequality, as Merton thought? Are lower-class youths the most likely to be socialized into criminal subcultures, as Sutherland assumed? Or are sociologists and others biased in how they think about crime and how they think about class?

As in many other areas of deviance, research in juvenile delinquency was hampered for a long time by the assumption that delinquency is almost exclusively a lower-class problem. Much of the effort given to policing and preventing delinquency has, therefore, focused on lower-class life and lower-class youth. A prime example was the costly program the United States government mounted during the 1960s to prevent delinquency, by offering lower-class youth opportunities for advancement through legitimate means: in a word, a job-creation program.

The program did not work. Perhaps lower-class youth did not really want to conform to the socially accepted norms, even if doing so brought them a weekly paycheque. Perhaps the inducement offered them—a dead-end job at low pay—was too slight to lure youth into law-abiding middle-class life. Perhaps Sutherland was right and the youth had learned delinquent skills and values, which they were unable or unwilling to renounce. Or perhaps the program ended too soon for us to know whether it might have worked.

Whatever the reason, juvenile delinquency remains a problem in large North American cities. However, our understanding of delinquency is greater than it

Sociologists have been studying delinquent gangs for well over 60 years and find their organization far more revealing than their (supposed) disorganization.

once was. We now have better measures of how much unreported delinquency occurs. We also have theories that help us see how very similar delinquent culture is to the dominant culture.

More and more criminologists have been using self-report surveys to measure delinquent behaviour among middle-class youth. Obviously, respondents may misreport their behaviour in this kind of survey, as in any other. Some forget past misdeeds; others may under-report their misdeeds, to seem more virtuous than they really are; others still may exaggerate their misdeeds to seem more rebellious.

John Hagan has reviewed the many studies of the relationship between social class and delinquent behaviour. He finds that the self-report studies show a weaker relationship between social class and delinquency than do studies based on official records. Indeed, unofficial studies of many types of deviance generally do. Still, Hagan (1984: 79) concludes that while official records may over-represent the connection between social class and rates of deviant behaviour,

> evidence reviewed indicates that forms of deviance considered serious and treated as such are unequally distributed through the class structure, with the lower class experiencing more than its fair share of serious crime and delinquency, hard drug use, problems of alcohol abuse, and mental illness.

However, which forms of deviance are considered "serious" is subject to social influence. As certain types of deviance—for example, recreational drug use—become more common in the middle and upper classes, people redefine them as less serious and treat them as such. Once behaviour comes to be more acceptable as part of the dominant culture, it is less likely to be defined as a feature of the delinquent subculture.

One explanation of how delinquent subculture connects to the dominant culture is *neutralization theory* (Sykes and Matza, 1957). This theory focuses on the way the delinquent thinks about his or her own behaviour in the context of dominant cultural norms, how the delinquent redefines delinquent actions to make them seem normal and blameless. Neutralization theory assumes the deviant rationalizes his or her behaviour in order to violate the norms while displaying a belief in the system. This process of rationalization, or **neutralization**, makes delinquency morally possible. If the neutralization succeeds, a person is psychologically free to commit the delinquent acts.

Techniques of neutralization include the following:

(1) denial of responsibility—"I can't seem to stay out of trouble, no matter how hard I try";

(2) denial of injury—"He could spare the money, he's rich" or "She does it with other guys all the time";

(3) denial of the victim—"He made me do it," "She was asking for it," or "He left his keys in the car, so he's to blame too";

(4) condemnation of the condemners—"The police don't give people an even break," and "The courts favour rich people over poor ones"; and

(5) appeal to higher loyalties—"They're my buddies, so right or wrong, I do what they do."

These techniques of neutralization are not limited to delinquents. Similar techniques are part of our dominant culture. Though most of us pay lip service to telling the truth, we all lie at some time or another. People find ways to justify lies of all kinds—white lies, lies to the sick and dying, lies parents tell to children, lies people tell to their enemies, and lies intended to protect clients and peers.

Whether intended or unintended, lies and other forms of deception are part of our dominant culture. We practise them because they often pay dividends. As Merton said, people want to obtain what our culture values—wealth, power, esteem. They will find ways to get these things, illegitimately if necessary, without giving up the idea that they are good, even upstanding people. Like crime and delinquency, techniques of neutralization and deception work.

Our culture teaches everyone that it is important to succeed at any price. It also teaches people how to lie effectively. So it is hard to understand why delinquent behaviour, indeed any criminality, should be more common in the lower classes than in the higher ones. To a large degree, variations in the societal response are wider than class differences in deviant behaviour.

Biases in selection process

Hagan (1984) points out that the perceived seriousness of a deviant act and the number of prior convictions in an offender's past record often allow us to predict the type and severity of societal response. Nonetheless, an important part is played by what we call *social resources*.

Middle- and upper-class people have more **social resources**—more knowledge of the law, more self-confidence, more money for lawyers, better social connections, a more respectable appearance and successful demeanour—than people in the lower classes. Social resources include cultural capital that can be used in the legal context. As we already know, our society distributes cultural capital unequally among the social classes.

Social resources help people avoid labelling and punishment by the police and courts. Often, as in assault or property-damage cases, the police and courts try to interpret behaviour and assess blame before taking any action. They are more likely to label people with few social resources as criminal or delinquent; they are more likely to label people with more resources as alcoholic or mentally ill for a criminal act. Middle- and upper-class people are also more aware of how and why to press for the latter labels, and more likely to succeed. Though being labelled "sick" is embarrassing, in the long run it is far less harmful than being labelled "criminal."

Erving Goffman (1964) calls the use of such social resources **impression management**, a set of techniques to avoid stigmatization or to impress others with our own positive virtues. Everyone practises impression management, and people with more social resources and cultural capital are more successful at it.

In giving preferential treatment to people who are better at impression management, police and judges are doing nothing but what the school children were doing in the study by Baldus and Tribe (1978) reported in Chapter Three. They are inferring moral worth from visible class position—from manner of dress, speech, and demeanour – and from managed impressions. As members of our culture, police and judges are no more or less likely to do this than anyone else. Though anecdotes are plentiful, there is no hard evidence that officials prefer people with more social resources because of any bribery, threats, or discrimination other than the kind we have described.

The process we are describing is a circular one: some have called it a self-fulfilling prophesy, others a revolving door. Official rule-enforcers (including police and judges, but also social workers, psychiatrists, and the whole correctional and treatment establishment) define as serious the deviance in which poor people engage. They define the serious deviant acts that rich people commit as evidence of illness, not crime, and find those actions morally blameless.

No wonder, then, that criminals and delinquents are people who start out and end up without social resources. The act of labelling them criminal completes the circle and creates a secondary problem, recidivism.

RESPONSES TO CRIME AND DEVIANCE

Repressive and restitutive laws

In his classic book, *The Division of Labour*, Emile Durkheim (1964) examined the relationship between forms of solidarity and forms of legal sanctions. For Durkheim, legal sanctions serve to indicate the gravity people attach to moral precepts, and the place these morals hold in the public conscience. He classifies sanctions into two types, repressive and restitutive. **Repressive** laws or sanctions inflict loss of life, liberty, property, honour – in short, suffering – on the deviant. **Restitutive** laws or sanctions attempt to return social relations to their original state following the deviant act, and do not necessarily inflict suffering.

Solidarity, which Durkheim also refers to as "cohesion" and "integration," is the cooperation and drawing together of people. Durkheim theorized that in societies whose institutions are not complex and which have little division of labour, solidarity is based on people sharing allegiance to common values. This kind of society is based on "likeness," and everyone thinks and acts alike. Such a system, Durkheim suggested, will be characterized by repressive sanctions. On the other hand, a society made up of people who are different but interdependent will be more pluralistic, and sanctions against deviance will be restitutive, not repressive.

The evolution from a society based on likeness to one based on difference should be evidenced by a changing ratio of restitutive to repressive laws. Existing laws could become less repressive, or restitutive laws could be added to existing repressive ones.

In fact, both processes have occurred. First, repressive law has diminished. Today, modern democratic societies do not use torture to punish crime, and people are not branded or mutilated for an offense against property. Additionally, ever fewer countries apply the death penalty for offenses against persons, like murder. Second, most new law is restitutive. Fewer offenses against property result in imprisonment, and time spent in prison tends to decrease. More offenses result in a fine or a requirement that the offender make restitution to the injured party. Some offenders are made to serve "community service orders," which require a specified number of hours of beneficial work for the community.

How, then, are we to make sense of the continuing popularity of capital punishment among the general public? If Durkheim's theory is valid, societies and communities supporting capital punishment—a repressive sanction—will differ from societies and communities rejecting it. Individuals who express support for capital punishment will belong to subcultures that are more homogeneous, in which people are more alike.

Public opinion polls on support for the death penalty show support for these assumptions. In a modern society, support for repressive law is a subcultural value characterizing people who live a traditional life in a homogeneous community. When these people explain their support for repressive law, they make clear that law, for them, serves a different purpose than it does for others. As Durkheim suggested, in a modern society law aims at resolving conflicts and making good the damage someone has done. Restitutive law is instrumental: an instrument for social improvement. Laws are valued if they are effective and are scrapped if they are not.

However, in a homogeneous community, law has a different purpose. Law expresses moral sentiment and rallies public outrage against the deviant. In this way it strengthens social solidarity among the conformists, whether it improves cooperation and makes good damage or not. Laws are not valued because they achieve desired goals; they are valued if they express popular sentiment (Chandler, 1976).

This difference in views about law helps to explain some of the on-going conflict in modern societies over what should or should not be considered deviant and punished. Yet there is often more to this conflict than a mere difference of views, as findings on moral enterprise indicate.

Moral enterprise

Moral enterprise is the process by which individuals or groups strive to influence the passing of rules or laws, in order to impose their own definitions of deviance on others. Such individuals or groups often see themselves as fighting a "moral crusade" against behaviours they view as evil.

By this definition, the pro-capital-punishment lobby is made up of moral entrepreneurs. So is the Pro-Life (anti-abortion) lobby, and the groups who press for prayer in the schools or the banning of certain books from school libraries. So are groups that demand censorship of books and movies.

Of course, many groups lobby in Parliament and elsewhere for their particular point of view. They include representatives of business, labour unions and manufacturing associations, exporters and importers, and various ethnic, racial, and regional interests. Moral entrepreneurs are distinguished from these other lobby groups in several ways. First, moral entrepreneurs are not motivated by personal gain. They gain nothing but satisfaction if their morality becomes law. Second, moral entrepreneurs hold an expressive, not an instrumental, view of the lobbying process; that is, their approach to law-making is aimed at expressing moral principles rather than at achieving results and changing behaviour. The lobbying technique of moral entrepreneurs is no more designed to achieve the desired results than is the law they are proposing. On the contrary, their entire approach to social engineering is emotional. That is why they often fail.

In these respects, moral entrepreneurs on the "right" are no different from those on the "left." Historically, such groups have been less successful in imposing their views here than in other societies. In pluralistic systems like ours, political leaders tend to avoid repressive laws because they alienate large blocs of voters. Political parties adopt very similar viewpoints in order to win the votes of large, differentiated electorates. So it is rare that a strongly moralistic law gets legislated.

The most famous example to the contrary was Prohibition in the United States. Prohibition consisted of a ban on the sale and public consumption of alcohol in the United States lasting from 1920 to 1933. Sociologist Joseph Gusfield (1963) argues that the successful lobbying effort organized by the American Temperance Movement leading to Prohibition was an example of what he called "status politics." **Status politics** are a particular kind of moral enterprise, and not simply an expression of moral outrage at drinking. They demonstrate "a struggle between groups for prestige and social position." Defending one's position in the status order is as much an interest as protecting or expanding economic power; indeed, the two are often related.

Specifically, the clash between drinker and abstainer dramatized a profound conflict in American society. Between the 1880s and about 1920 the United States underwent profound social changes. As the United States was transformed from a largely rural, small-town society to an urban, industrial power, enormous numbers of immigrants poured into American cities. This shifted economic and political control of American society away from the native-born, white Protestant, small-town middle class, which had run America up through the 19th century. The new American immigrants were foreign-born city dwellers, mostly Catholic, whose numbers, ambition, and cultural difference were considered by many Americans to be menacing. Whereas American Protestants made a virtue of "temperance," the new immigrants saw nothing immoral in the use of alcohol. Indeed, to the small-town, middle-class American, the new immigrants came to be associated with the consumption, manufacture, and distribution of alcohol: Italians with wine, Germans with beer, Irish with whisky, and Poles with vodka. The attempt to impose temperance through Prohibition was an attempt to turn back the clock to a homogeneous society dominated by middle-class Americans. It was designed to show the immigrants who ran the country.

The success of the American Temperance Movement serves as a valuable lesson of how moral enterprise works. Prohibitionists had strong personal interests to protect, even if they were unaware of how closely linked those interests were with prohibition. Also, they used strategies that were calculated to succeed, and succeed they did, for a time. The Eighteenth Amendment to the American Constitution, also called the Prohibition Amendment, was ratified in 1920 and prohibited the manufacture and sale of alcoholic beverages. By the time the Amendment was repealed in 1933, however, it had proved unenforceable and almost universally unpopular.

The North American fascination with organized crime is really a love-hate relationship. Our culture views crime bosses as business innovators, to be admired if they are successful. Pictured here are "Scarface" Al Capone (left) and U.S. Marshall Henry C.W. Laubenheimer.

Prosecution

From an instrumental view, a law is useless if it does not command public respect and if even law enforcers oppose it. Widespread practices and difficulties in enforcing the law have played a large part in the repeal or neglect of laws against drinking, drug use, abortion, and certain sexual behaviours.

At the same time, law enforcement—policing and the prosecution of charges in court—is hampered by the unwillingness of victims to report crimes and of witnesses to testify. Rules protecting the rights of the accused often make gaining the required evidence very difficult and run the risk that evidence collected improperly will lose the case for the prosecution. As well, crown prosecutors with heavy case-loads must often argue against well-paid, well-staffed private lawyers, or against legal-aid lawyers whose case-loads are even heavier. These are reasons why only a small proportion of all reported crimes result in arrest and the laying of charges. However, a large proportion of arrests and charges laid result in convictions, since prosecutors only lay charges if they believe a conviction is likely. Indeed, the prosecutor's belief in the strength of his or her case is likely to lead judges and juries to assume that the accused is guilty unless proved otherwise, though, by law, the opposite assumption should be made.

Still, the charges on which a criminal is tried may not be the charges originally laid. Instead, the final charges are often the result of **plea bargaining**, a process in which prosecuting and defense attorneys reach agreement on the charge to which the accused is willing to plead guilty. The accused, through his lawyer, agrees to plead guilty to a lesser charge than the one originally laid.

The plea bargained for in this way is often to everyone's advantage. Because it is a guilty plea, the court can deal with it more quickly and cheaply than if a trial was needed to prove guilt or innocence. The easier procedure saves the overburdened judicial system time and money. It also saves time for the defense attorney, and gets around the need for the prosecution to gather evidence if it wishes to press the original charge. And it wins the accused a lighter penalty than he or she would receive if the prosecution won its case.

Plea bargaining will not benefit the accused if he or she is innocent, or if the prosecution cannot gather enough persuasive evidence to convict on any charge. The prevalence of plea bargaining means that the law is likely to punish the poor more frequently and heavily than it does the rich, who can afford to pay for a longer, more effective defense in court. Again, a differential in social resources translates into class inequalities before the law.

Judgment

As criminologist John Hogarth (1971) has pointed out, sentencing is a human process. The same forces that influence our own ways of evaluating evidence and people influence judges and magistrates.

It should come as no surprise, then, that judgments for the same crime vary widely among Canadian judges and magistrates. They vary across provinces and they vary with the social characteristics of the judge. For example, it is not accidental that the judge who granted an injunction to stay a woman's abortion on the request of a boyfriend in 1989 is a pious Catholic. A Protestant or Jew might never have granted the injunction, which was overturned on appeal.

Hogarth's survey of magistrates shows that a variety of social and cultural perceptions go into a magistrate's decision whether an accused person is guilty of the offense charged. They also influence how punitive the magistrate's judgment is. Magistrates differ in the rehabilitative value they attribute to punishment and whether they believe punishment should express the moral outrage of the community. In this respect, punitive magistrates turn out to be similar to ordinary citizens who favour capital punishment.

The attitudes, beliefs, and values of magistrates and judges play a part in judgments they render because the law allows a judge discretion – sometimes, considerable discretion – in the sentencing process. This discretion is not intended to allow the judge to express his or her personal biases, though it has that effect. Rather, it is intended to allow the judge or magistrate to take a wide variety of circumstances into account and weigh them up in a professional way. In this respect, the law is aiming to have the punishment suit the criminal and not merely the crime.

Despite our media-induced fears of murder by a stranger, murder by a loved one is far more common. Courts are faced with judging motive and blame in these recurrent domestic dramas.

EXHIBIT 4.6

THE SELECTIVE APPLICATION OF RULES

Consider the Dubin inquiry into steroid use in amateur sports, which centred on Ben Johnson's loss of his Olympic gold medal in 1988. The inquiry heard a bewildering array of evidence. Some witnesses claimed that almost everyone in world-class sports uses steroids; others, that Coach Charlie Francis and physician Jamie Estaphan were particularly vigorous in forcing steroids on their athletes. Some have contended that Ben Johnson is a childishly naive victim who never knew what he was injecting; others, that Johnson was seeking success at any cost because he liked to win and enjoyed good living.

All of this is confusing enough. But ask yourself, why is the government spending so much money to get to the bottom of this matter. Is Canada's international image at stake? Probably not. Is the future of amateur sport in Canada in danger? Perhaps, but many other things affecting many more people are also in danger. Why is there no commission of inquiry into unemployment, housing, or poverty, for example?

Deviant acts get the maximum official response and media attention when they reveal *least* about most people's personal troubles. Many believe the aim is to shift attention away from important social issues, not toward them. In Roman times, it was called giving the people "bread and circuses." What do you think?

However, the result may be unfair. Two similar criminals committing an identical crime may receive quite different punishments depending on the sentencing norms in the court, city, or province in which they are appearing. Whereas individualized justice has a lot of merit in principle, at the extreme it demands and allows judges to show the absolute wisdom of Solomon—a challenge they are no better at meeting than is anyone else.

CLOSING REMARKS

Deviance is one of those topics that tend to be very popular with students. Like a course on cultural differences, there is something exotic about the study of deviance. Because most of us do not view ourselves as deviant, we tend to find the underside of social order fascinating. Yet to the sociologist deviance is not exotic, rare, or peculiar, but is a common, recurrent, and normal feature of everyday life. All of us engage in some form of social deviance at some time or other. As we noted earlier, the issue for sociologists is to understand the social processes that produce deviance and that determine the relation between deviance and social control.

In many ways, deviance is just the flip-side of social order. Society creates deviance by expecting, insisting upon, or enforcing social order. If you keep all your books on a shelf in no particular order, then no book is out of order when you place it back on the shelf. But if you keep your books in alphabetical order, then a book must be put back correctly or it is out of place. Creating order creates the possibility of deviance. Deviance, then, is not some special topic of study but an aspect of how society itself is organized. Understanding crime requires not only understanding the legal system but also the political and religious interests which created that system. It requires understanding as well how inequality is organized in our society and how inequality leads to crime. Sociologists disagree on what deviance is and how it works because they disagree on how society is organized.

The issue of the social organization of inequality in our society is one whose significance goes far beyond the issues of crime and deviance. In fact, understanding the social organization of inequality is a major step towards understanding Canadian society. It also helps us to understand our own, personal place in this broader society.

Discussion Questions	1. *Grokking* is a particular form of deviant behaviour that was unknown 20 years ago, was barely mentioned 10 years ago, yet today is apparently as common as halitosis. We have limited funds to study this change. To understand most about the rise of this new behaviour to prominence, should we spend our money studying Grokkers or the Grok-police?

2. Some believe sociology took a great stride forward when it rejected the social- and personal-pathology explanations of deviance in favour of subcultural theories. Others believe it was a step backward. What do you think?

3. How might Merton and Sutherland go about explaining the observed differences in consensus-crime rates between Canada and the United States? What evidence would we need to test which one was right?

4. Many kinds of crime and deviance are apparently more common in the lower classes than in the higher ones. Given what we know about the reasons for this, for which kinds of crime and deviance would class differences be *least*?

5. The debate over how to reduce crime and delinquency keeps polarizing people. One group says punish the criminal, the other group says treat the criminal. Where do you stand on this issue? Now, organize the most persuasive argument you can for the *opposite* position.

6. Why don't we put organized crime out of business by decriminalizing all the goods and services they offer?

Data Collection Exercises

1. Pairs of students should go to a busy public place (for example, a park, shopping centre, subway station) and station themselves six to fifteen metres from each other. They should observe and record all deviant activities there for a period of one hour. Then they should report on their findings and the reasons why their findings are not identical.

2. Design a small questionnaire or interview schedule to measure the attitudes of fellow students to various types of sexual behaviour. Then analyze the data, looking for patterns: specifically, (a) what kinds of people have the greatest tolerance for sexual deviation, and (b) what kinds of attitudes group with which other attitudes.

3. Sutherland says people are not criminal because they lack association with criminal skills, attitudes, and values—in short, with criminals. Conduct unstructured interviews with your family and friends to determine whether they know any criminals and, if so, which kinds. Would they know how to fence stolen property? Get illegal drugs? Rob a bank?

4. Try a simple, harmless experiment on a friend to see if you can change his or her behaviour by labelling him or her differently. For example, can you get your friend to behave more politely by praising his politeness? Can you get him to behave more rudely by commenting repeatedly on his rudeness? (Be sure you brief your friend on the reasons for your experiment, and your findings, when you are finished.)

Writing Exercises

1. Write a 500-word essay demonstrating that it is social control that produces deviance in a family. Be sure to mention who benefits from this control.

2. You are the attorney defending (or prosecuting) a poor, young man accused of committing a serious crime. Is there anything you want to tell the jury about poor, young men that may help bring about an acquittal (or conviction)? Write a fiery 500-word statement to the jury.

3. Try to recall if you ever suffered an attack of anxiety and depression, as indicated by the measures in Exhibit 4.3. Write 500 words describing this episode: what led up to it, how long it lasted, and how it ended.

4. Write a brief (300 word or less) restitutive law that will govern shoplifting offenses. Now, write a brief restitutive law that will govern bodily assaults.

Glossary

crime—any act formally prohibited by law

deviance—behaviour that leads to a negative reaction or response from a community or group

deviant subculture—a subculture whose members conform to norms, values, and beliefs that the larger society considers deviant

moral entrepreneur—a person who strives to influence the legal process in order to impose his or her own definition of deviance on others

neutralization—the deviant's rationalization of deviant acts which makes deviance morally possible while belief in the system is maintained

organized crime—a centralized and formal structure within which individuals devote themselves to the pursuit of goals by illegal means

recidivism—a repeated lapse into crime and delinquency

secondary deviation—deviance by a person who perceives him- or herself as deviant, because of reactions to **primary deviation,** the initial deviant behaviour

social deviation—an act not defined by the law as criminal, but nonetheless viewed as a deviation from social norms and subject to official control

victimless crime—a category of crime from which no one suffers directly except perhaps the persons engaging in the behaviour

Suggested Readings

Becker, Howard S. *Outsiders*. New York: Free Press, 1963. In this widely read classic, Becker spells out the labelling theory of deviance, then applies the theory to a variety of outsiders including jazz musicians and marijuana smokers.

Erikson, Kai T. *Wayward Puritans*. New York: Wiley, 1966. The early Puritans in Massachusetts "created" deviants where none really existed. As Erikson shows, this strengthened their solidarity and sense of normality.

Goffman, Erving *Asylums*. Garden City, New York: Doubleday, 1961. Through the eyes of participant-observers and inmates, we learn about life in "total institutions" which dramatize the boundary between insiders and outsiders.

Gusfield, Joseph *Symbolic Crusade*. Urbana: University of Illinois Press, 1969. This book analyzes the American temperance movement as a clash between rival cultures and status groups. Law-making and enforcement are mere tactics in this battle for social dominance.

Hagan, John *Disreputable Pleasures*, 2nd edition. Toronto: McGraw-Hill Ryerson, 1984. A lucid and comprehensive look at the main theories in the field of crime and deviance, illustrated with recent Canadian data.

Prus, Robert and Styllianos Irini *Hookers, Rounders and Desk Clerks*. Toronto: Gage, 1980. This book describes the social organization of a hotel community in a major Canadian city and looks at the deviant careers that flourish there.

References

Adler, F. (1975) *Sisters in Crime: The Rise of the New Female Criminal*. New York: McGraw-Hill

Baldus, B. and V. Tribe (1978) "Perceptions of social inequality among public school children" *Canadian Review of Sociology and Anthropology*, 15 (1), pp. 50-60

Becker, H.S. (1963) *Outsiders: Studies in the Sociology of Deviance*. New York: Free Press

Chandler, D.B. (1976) *Capital Punishment in Canada: A Sociological Study of Repressive Law*. Toronto: McClelland and Stewart

Clairmont, D.H. and D.W. Magill (1974) *Africville: The Life and Death of a Canadian Black Community*. Toronto: McClelland and Stewart

Durkheim, E. (1938) "Rules for distinguishing between the normal and the pathological" chapter 3 in *The Rules of Sociological Method*. New York: Free Press

———— . (1964) *The Division of Labor in Society*. New York: Free Press

Goff, C.H. and C.H. Reasons (1978) *Corporate Crime in Canada*. Toronto: Prentice-Hall (Canada)

Goffman, E. (1964) *Stigma: Notes on the Management of Spoiled Identity*. Englewood Cliffs, NJ: Prentice Hall

———— . (1961) *Asylums: Essays on the Social Situation of Mental Patients and Other Inmates*. Garden City, NY: Anchor

Gusfield, J. (1963) *Symbolic Crusade*. Urbana: University of Illinois Press

Hagan, J. (1984) *Disreputable Pleasures: Crime and Deviance in Canada*, 2nd edition. Toronto: McGraw-Hill Ryerson

Hogarth, J. (1971) *Sentencing as a Human Process*. Toronto: University of Toronto Press

Merton, R.K. (1957) "Social structure and anomie" chapter 4 in *Social Theory and Social Structure*, revised edition. New York: Free Press

Sutherland, E.H. and D.R. Cressey (1978) *Criminology*, 10th edition. Philadelphia: Lippincott

Sykes, G. and D. Matza (1957) "Techniques of neutralization: A theory of delinquency" *American Sociological Review*, 22 (December), pp. 664-670

Thrasher, F.M. (1937) *The Gang*. Chicago: University of Chicago Press

Whyte, W.F. (1961) *Street Corner Society*. Chicago: University of Chicago Press

CHAPTER 5

Sociologists study the ways which people create, symbolize, and transmit inequality from one generation to the next.

SOCIAL INEQUALITY AND STRATIFICATION

THE REALITY OF INEQUALITY

Inequality is a fact of life for all of us. Sociologists are fond of using the term *life chances* to describe the effects of inequality, and few terms capture the link between macrosociological social processes and personal life circumstances as well. When you pass some homeless "street person" huddled among old newspapers while taking shelter from the weather, you probably realize that this person's life chances are few in number and quite bleak. Where will they be in ten years? If they are not still on the street they are very likely to be dead. Think, too, of all the poor in Canada. What chances do they have to improve the quality of their lives in the coming years? You can be sure that they are not spending much time deciding which restaurant to eat in, what movie to see, or where to go on vacation. As for the rich, life is not so much a matter of chances as of options. Being rich means you have the choice to live your life pretty much the way you want, doing the things you want to do, with few of the limitations that other people must take into account.

Now think of yourself. Even though few of you are rich—most students are typically middle class—"chances" are, your life still holds many options. But because you are not rich, whether you take advantage of these options and have the sort of life you want will depend, in large measure, on the choices you make and the actions you undertake now. Yet even the best choices you make today will not give you everything you want later.

Canadians are not in the habit of thinking much about inequality. We live in one of the wealthiest, and freest, countries in the world. But that does not mean that inequality is absent, only that it has a somewhat gentler and more reserved face. One consequence is that Canadians are more likely than people in other nations to assign either praise or blame to the individual rather than "the system" for success or failure in life. Nevertheless, inequality, in Canada or anywhere else, is largely a consequence of a "system"—the stratification system—and learning to recognize inequality as a feature of social structure rather than as a consequence of personal character is an important part of learning sociology.

TYPES OF SOCIAL INEQUALITY

Social inequality includes all the differences between individuals, groups, or regions that arise out of social characteristics or relationships. It includes differential access to social rewards like wealth, prestige, and influence. The characteristics affecting inequality are social because they have meanings attached to them that members of a group share and transmit to future generations. These meanings are also the basis on which people act and react towards others.

For example, inequality of wealth is a social phenomenon because it arises out of unequal access to wealth or out of unequal opportunities to acquire wealth. By contrast, differences in athletic ability are probably genetically based and not an example of social inequality. However, the prestige our society accords to superior athletes can be used to obtain a great deal of wealth, so that athletic ability, too, becomes part of a system of social inequality. There is a meaning attached to athletic ability, which people share and transmit culturally.

In recent years, sociologists have come to think of inequality as the unequal distribution of resources. These resources are of three types: material resources, such as wealth or those things which bring wealth; symbolic resources, such as cultural capital; and authoritative resources, such as the police officer's right to tell people what to do. This means that there are three interrelated but somewhat different systems of inequality: class, based on the distribution of material resources; status, based on the distribution of symbolic resources; and domination, based on the distribution of authoritative resources. Other forms of social differentiation, such as gender, race, and ethnicity, combine with class, status, and domination to form an integrated system of inequality called a **stratification system**. In this chapter we will examine all three forms of inequality, beginning with domination, the ability to control the actions of other people.

PATTERNS OF DOMINATION AND SUBMISSION

Whether you are aware of it or not, almost all of the social relationships in which you have taken part are unequal. In childhood, your parents were able to control your behaviour much of the time and, within limits, to get you to do what they wanted you to do. The same, of course, was true in school when teachers told you where to sit, when to speak, what to say, and what to do. These personal experiences simply reflect the fact that in most social relationships one person or set of persons dominates the others. In that respect, domination is a universal feature of social life, one found in every society. What is more, patterns of domination persist over decades, generations, and even centuries.

By **domination**, we mean the exercise of control over an individual or group of people. Put in simple terms, domination is the ability to get other people to do what you want them to do. The flip side is **submission**, the act of yielding to the control of another, or doing what others tell you to do. Because there are different ways of getting people to do what we want them to do, there are different forms of domination. Power, authority, and charisma are different types of domination. As for submission, this often takes the form of acts that symbolize a subordinate status and acceptance of the other's domination. The military salute is a good example of such an act.

Charisma is a term which is often used by the media to express "popularity," "style," or other intangible personal qualities. As originally developed by Max Weber (1964), however, the term *charisma* refers to domination based on extraordinary (usually magical) personal qualities or abilities. In the past, charisma was more important as a form of domination than it is today. Few of us today are willing to follow leaders because of their supposed magical or supernatural abilities, although occasionally leaders such as Reverend Jim Jones appear who still display charismatic domination over their followers. Reverend Jones was the leader of the People's Temple, a religious group based largely in California which moved to Guyana to establish Jonestown. Like many charismatic leaders, Jones insisted that his followers display loyalty to him and be willing to die at his command. On several occasions he informed his followers that, because of some crisis affecting the Church, they were all to commit suicide together. These all proved to be false alarms until 1978 when Jones and about 900 of his followers finally did commit suicide after Jones had a visiting U.S. congressman killed. That so many of his followers were willing to commit suicide at his order gives us an indication of how strong charismatic domination can be.

Power and **authority** are the two forms of domination that characterize modern industrial societies, and we will focus our discussion in this chapter on these. **Power** is the capacity to exercise one's will despite resistance—to alter the behaviour of an individual or group, with force if necessary. In the case of power, one submits to the force or the threat of force, not to those who exercise that power. This means that power is impersonal. When a bank robber demands money from a teller, it is the gun that compels the teller to submit, not the personal charm or other qualities of the robber.

As for authority, this refers to the willing submission to domination. By **authority**, we mean the ability of an individual or group to issue commands and have them obeyed because people perceive this exercise of control as *legitimate*; that is, as justified and fair. **Legitimate authority** is a general and unquestioned belief that the exercise of control by government and other officials (for example, police and judges) is valid and justified. It is also a belief that people in positions of authority have a right to be there—a right to rule—and citizens have a duty to obey the rules that are set out.

A familiar example would be the authority of an instructor in a classroom. The relationship between teacher and students is no more equal now between adults than it was in childhood. Students still quiet down and sit when a professor enters; the opposite is rarely true. Instructors feel free to call students by their first names; the opposite is rarely true. When a student meets an instructor, each knows roughly how to behave and who is dominant. The instructor tells you what to do, but chances are you go along both because you have been taught that the teacher has that right and because you believe that the teacher's commands are ultimately in your best interest. Like power, authority is an impersonal form of domination. The authority of the professor is a consequence of his or her position, not personality, character, or individual abilities. We obey a teacher, a police officer, a judge, or a boss because of their position.

We noted earlier that Canada is one of the freest countries in the world, and this is certainly the case in terms of political rights and freedoms. There are some political and constitutional problems concerning rights—such as the recent decision by the Quebec government to invoke the "notwithstanding" clause in order to prevent the use of English on outdoor commercial signs—but generally few Canadians feel politically oppressed. This does not mean that domination is any less pervasive in Canadian society. It merely means that domination in our society most often takes the form of authority rather than power. Most of us feel that those who dominate us, such as our teacher, our boss, or our Prime Minister, have the right to do so. Make no mistake, however; authority is as much a form of domination as is coercion. Indeed, Max Weber, the German sociologist, argued that the "rational" bureaucracy is the most highly developed form of authority and the most effective and efficient form of domination found in any society. The good bureaucrat never questions orders and gives little thought to the results of his or her actions (Weber, 1964).

One sign that domination plays a much greater role in our society than most people would credit is the prevalence of many symbols of domination in our society. Examining the symbolic display of power and authority makes the hidden reality of domination more apparent.

The symbols of domination and submission

Domination and submission are symbolized in a variety of ways in our culture, ranging from the tangible and material to the intangible and behaviourial.

Many social roles require particular clothing (often uniforms) and a particular manner. The military is the obvious example, in which the uniform indicates each individual's rank. Another example is the hospital, in which the outfits worn by doctors, nurses, orderlies, and patients are all clearly different and readily recognizable. Even where there is no uniform, symbols of status are readily visible. The executive office, the embossed business card, an expensive German car, an in-ground swimming pool: these are accepted symbols of high status and success in our society. Workers with little authority typically wear jeans or work clothes to work every day. Those with more authority wear business suits. Our reliance on such symbols for information explains why it is often confusing for students who see some of their teachers dressing in business suits while others dress in jeans; when we receive such mixed messages, we become aware of how closely authority and the symbols of authority are tied in our society.

Our culture places a high value on intelligence and planning, and we more readily justify rewards to people we think have more intelligence and plan more. Our culture portrays higher-class males as being smarter and more highly motivated than working-class people. The varieties of symbol here are many: brain *versus* brawn, head work *versus* hand work, diligence *versus* sloth.

Racial and sexist prejudice combines with these assumptions about intelligence to justify and explain why white males have higher status than non-whites or women. One research study (Rainville and McCormick, 1977) compared the ways American sportscasters report the achievements of white and black football players. White television announcers tend to criticize black NFL players more and praise them less than they do white players with similar abilities, playing the same positions. More importantly, the commentators describe black players more often as targets of aggression and white players as

EXHIBIT 5.1

SHOOTING AN ELEPHANT: WHO DOMINATES?

For a brief time in the 1920s, George Orwell was subdivisional police officer of a town in Lower Burma, then a colony of the British Empire. Anti-European feeling was very bitter and "I was hated by large numbers of people," he reports. One day a "tiny incident" gave Orwell a "better glimpse than I had had before of the real nature of imperialism—the real motives for which despotic governments act."

An elephant had entered the town and was rampaging the bazaar; Orwell was asked to do something about it. Seeing the elephant peacefully eating grass, he knew "with perfect certainty that I ought not to shoot him." But an "immense crowd, two thousand at least and growing every minute" had followed him. They expected him to shoot the elephant.

> I perceived in this moment that when the white man turns tyrant it is his own freedom that he destroys. He becomes a sort of hollow, posing dummy, the conventionalized figure of a sahib. For it is the condition of his rule that he shall spend his life in trying to impress the 'natives,' and so in every crisis he has got to do what the 'natives' expect of him. He wears a mask, and his face grows to fit it. I had got to shoot the elephant. I had committed myself to doing it when I sent for the rifle. A sahib has got to act like a sahib; he has got to appear resolute, to know his own mind and do definite things. To come all that way, rifle in hand, with two thousand people marching at my heels, and then to trail feebly away, having done nothing—no, that was impossible. The crowd would laugh at me. And my whole life, every white man's life in the East, was one long struggle not to be laughed at.

In the end, Orwell shot the elephant, to avoid looking like a fool. But he never forgot that domination makes the jailor and the jailed both prisoners of their unequal relationship.

Source: George Orwell "Shooting an elephant" in *Shooting an Elephant and Other Essays*. New York: Harcourt Brace, 1950

initiators; and white players as more intelligent—having better cognitive as well as physical skills. By inference, the choices and tactics of black players are determined by instinct or luck, for which they deserve no credit.

We ascribe "higher" qualities to higher-class whites, and in this way justify their receiving more rewards. Inequality is no more due to unequal intelligence and planning than it is to fair competition. However, people who believe they lack intelligence or the right values are easy to dominate. From the standpoint of those who dominate, these beliefs are helpful and justified.

As for gender, again domination and submission are symbolized in ways that make existing inequalities seem appropriate, even desirable. For example, most people expect women in our culture to be submissive. Even religious teachings put forward this idea. For a woman to behave otherwise is to risk being labelled unfeminine or a "bitch." Conversely, people expect men to be dominant. For them to act in a submissive manner is to risk being called a "sissy" or a "wimp."

Some of the most common ways of expressing gender inequality are also the least tangible. One way of expressing domination is to assume decision-making powers in a relationship. In a marriage, one spouse may control the way money is spent. In a dating couple, one person may decide how to spend an evening or whether there will be sexual intercourse. In conversation, one person – typically a male – will cut off or break in on the speech of another. So it should come as no surprise that, generation after generation, men hold dominant roles in the economy and family, and women, subordinate roles. Cultural values and symbols do not create inequality between the sexes, but they make it appear natural and right.

Gender, of course, does not determine inequality. Upper-class men and women are both advantaged over lower-class men and women. Indeed, many argue that it is class that is the major determinant of life chances in a modern industrial society such as Canada.

CLASS

The modern theory of economic and social class was first developed by Karl Marx as part of his theory of society and social change. This theory of class is often described as a form of *economic determinism*, because Marx saw the stratification system as determined by the means of production to be found in a society. The means of production are the tools, objects, techniques, or skills that are used in the production process. In a simple hunting society such as the ones almost all humans once lived in, the means of production would include objects such as bows, arrows, and spears. For an industrialized society such as Canada, the primary means of production are machinery, technology, labour, and capital. People's position in the stratification system, or **class**, depends on their relationship to the means of production.

Marx (Marx, 1936; Marx and Engels, 1955) described our society as a capitalist society because of the important role capital plays in the production process. Capital consists of money or other material goods which are invested in an enterprise in order to generate production. In Marx's description of capitalism some people – the **bourgeoisie** – own the means of production and thereby control the labour of everyone else. As owners, they have the means to create and destroy jobs, hire and fire people, and to extract "surplus value," or profits, from other people's work. This profit becomes capital when it is re-invested in the enterprise. A second group, the petty (or petite) bourgeoisie, includes small-business owners who have so few employees that they do most of the work themselves. Like the bourgeoisie, they own the means of production. Unlike the bourgeoisie they do not extract profits from other people's labour. The vast majority – the **proletariat** – work for the bourgeoisie. They own none of the means of production but their own labour power, which they sell to their bourgeois employers.

People in the same social class share the same relationship to the means of production. So they have similar, even if not exactly the same, wealth, authority, and prestige. For Marx, variations in income, education, and job prestige within a class confuse the class issue. All members of the proletariat, or working class, are vulnerable to the power of the bourgeoisie. They all – construction workers, sales staff, secretaries, and professors alike – sell their labour for wages. All could be thrown out of work, find themselves without an income, and have to rely on savings, welfare, or charity to survive.

Objectively Marx has to be right: it *has* to make a difference whether a person controls the work of others or is controlled by others. The person who controls—the person with large amounts of capital to invest and the power to decide other people's fate—must have more in common with other people in the same position than with the people he or she controls. Likewise, people subject to control must share more experiences with one another than they do with the controllers.

Still, several problems arise when we apply class analysis as Marx formulated it. First, people's subjective reality may not square with their objective reality. A great many people in the proletariat do not consider themselves proletarians, or workers, and identify instead with the bourgeois or capitalist class. They model their attitudes, goals, and lifestyles on capitalist, not working-class, ideals. Marx was aware of this subjective identification, calling it "false consciousness" because it leads people to identify falsely with another class. He assumed that class consciousness would eventually overcome false consciousness. There is, however, little sign of this happening among Canadian or most other workers in modern industrial societies. Accordingly, they tend not to vote for working-class political parties and instead seek social acceptance by the bourgeoisie.

Second, in modern industrial capitalism, ownership and control have largely separated. Millions of small stockholders own a great many large business organizations. Effectively, senior management and elected directors, not stockholders, control these organizations. Often, the controllers may own some of the corporate stock. In any event, they operate the company in their own interest, not that of the small stockholders. However, they may not constitute an inherited upper class in the sense of Marx's concept of the bourgeoisie.

Third, many wage-earning people may be right in assuming they differ from others who seem to share the same relationship to the means of production. Not all wage-earning people really share the same market position: they differ dramatically in material rewards and life chances, such as pay, security, and opportunity for promotion. Not all share the same work situation, i.e., similar work tasks and production technology, including supervision on the job. Some have both better market rewards and better working conditions than other wage-earners.

In analyzing classes in modern society, Max Weber (1958) added to Marx's list. He included the propertied class (Marx's bourgeoisie); the traditional petty bourgeois class of small business people, shopkeepers, and farmers; and the working class (Marx's proletariat). As well, he identified a wage-earning intellectual, administrative, and managerial class. Within each of these four classes we find more of the similarity (and awareness of similar interests) that Marx expected to find.

Neither Marx nor Weber believed that any particular way of measuring stratification would apply to all societies. On the contrary, they both argued that changing historical conditions would produce different structures of domination and submission. For Marx, the crucial changes were those in the means of production. The development of new means of production creates new classes which are in conflict with the old. History, to Marx, was the record of class conflict and revolutions in which new classes overthrow old ruling classes. For Weber, many more factors could lead to changes in stratification, including changes in cultural and religious values. More importantly, Weber was the first to emphasize the independent significance of status and domination for stratification. Although Weber agreed that class has the greatest impact on life chances, he nevertheless argued that in a modern state both the spread of politics and the development of government bureaucracies give domination a role independent of class. As for status, Weber claimed that most of the important forms of stratification in the past, such as caste systems and slavery, were examples of stratification based on cultural and religious values rather than class.

Other explanations of inequality

Both Marx's and Weber's analyses of class can be considered examples of the conflict perspective on stratification. Another explanation of stratification is the one put forward by functionalist sociologists Kingsley Davis and Wilbert Moore (1945), known as the *functional theory of social stratification*. This explanation sees social stratification as inevitable and even desirable. Their argument goes as follows: There are certain positions in all societies that are functionally more important than others. Performing adequately in these positions requires special skills, but few individuals have the talent and motivation to invest the time and money necessary to acquiring the skills. As a result, a society needs a system of rewards and privileges, which motivates individuals to get the necessary skills to fill the important positions. These rewards include wealth, prestige, and (to some degree) power.

The functional theory has led to a great deal of debate over whether it is possible to rank occupations objectively, according to their importance to society. Even if we could agree that doctors are more important to society than truck drivers, and therefore should be better paid, we would have trouble applying the same logic to explaining the salaries earned in organized crime, professional sports, and popular entertainment. And even if we could get past *that* hurdle, we would have difficulties using the functional theory to account for other *non*-occupational inequalities: why men dominate women, whites dominate non-whites, rich nations dominate poor nations, and so on. Inequality is too complex for the functional theory to handle.

To date, symbolic interactionists have not done much work on class or other forms of inequality. Some interesting work was done by Gregory Stone (1970) on how appearance, especially clothing, can be used to establish and display one's social status, but this line of research has not been consistently followed up. There has also been some interest in what is sometimes called *micropolitics*, such as Erving Goffman's (1961) study of the mental hospital as a total institution and the "underlife" which develops in such an institution as a way of "working the system." While a microsociological perspective may not be suitable for developing a full-fledged theory of inequality, interactionists and other microsociologists can make significant contributions to our understanding of the symbolic and interactional manifestations of domination, status, and

EXHIBIT 5.2

A CASTE SYSTEM IN OUR OWN BACKYARD

Only 50 years ago, the American South was no less a caste society than India or South Africa. Unlike the Indian one, this caste system was based on colour:

> All privileges and opportunities, as well as duties and obligations, are unequally distributed between the two groups. The whites receive by far the larger portion of all economic and social rewards, while the Negroes have an undue share of the more onerous duties. Both Negroes and whites recognize the fact that the white group is superordinate in power and prestige, and they exemplify this awareness in both their behaviour and thought. Furthermore, each of the groups is endogamous; that is, marriage between them is absolutely forbidden, and any children of extralegal sex relations are automatically relegated to the subordinate Negro group. Each individual is born into the Negro or white group and must remain in it for life. He may neither earn nor wed his way out. (Davis, Gardner, and Gardner, 1965: 15)

Whites saw the unequal arrangement as due to Negroes' inherent inferiority and believed their system was the will of God. They considered the blacks unsocialized beings whose childlike behaviour imposed a burden on whites, to which they must adjust with parental firmness. They judged black physical characteristics to be badges of subordinate status and believed the light-coloured blacks were less primitive and animal-like than blacker ones.

Nothing showed the inequality and social distance more clearly than the taboo on sex between races. White men often broke that taboo by having sex with black women (though never marrying them). Yet white women were never to have sex with black men. The white women risked ostracism and the black men lynching, if they broke this rule.

Just think how easily Philippe Rushton's theory of innate racial differences (discussed in our earlier chapter on culture) could be used to justify this racist social order.

Source: Davis, A., B.B. Gardner, and M.R. Gardner *Deep South: A Social Anthropological Study of Caste and Class*, abridged edition. Chicago: University of Chicago Press, 1965 [1941]

class differences in everyday life. A good example is Gusfield's study of the symbolic crusade that led to Prohibition in the United States (discussed in Chapter Four).

The class system in Canada

As we noted earlier, the class system is based on differences that develop in people's relationship to the means of production. And, as Weber pointed out, class is also influenced by market position and workplace conditions.

Erik Olin Wright (1985) has modified the Marxian scheme of class analysis to incorporate Weber's modifications, especially the emphasis Weber places on domination. In Wright's scheme, as in Marx's and Weber's, there are capitalists and petty bourgeoisie. However, the wage-earning majority includes four subtypes. Some wage-earners exercise workplace control over other wage-earners and some do not. Some wage-earners are controlled at the workplace and others are not.

The wage-earners who are controlled but control no one else – call them *workers* – are most similar to Marx's proletariat. Like them in many respects are *supervisors*, who are closely controlled at work but who also control (or supervise) other workers. Two other wage-earning groups differ from the supervisors and proletariat in their social origins, educational attainment, pay level, and workplace autonomy. One is the group of *managers and technocrats* that controls other workers but enjoys a great deal of freedom from control on the job. Another is the group of workers – academics, salaried professionals, and technical personnel – who enjoy a great deal of freedom on the job and have no control over other workers. Call them *semi-autonomous employees*.

In research using a 1981 survey of the Canadian population, Michael Ornstein (1988: 194) found that only 2.8% of all employed people fell into the capitalist class. The petite bourgeoisie made up 11.8% of all employed people. Managers and technocrats comprised 7.0%, supervisors 10.9%, semi-autonomous employees 8.1%, and workers the vast majority at 55.9% of the employed population.

The capitalists averaged the highest rate of pay, twice that of all wage-earners and nearly three times that of workers. To some degree this difference reflected the fact that capitalists had attained a higher level of education, were older, and were more often men than the wage-earning population. However, even controlling for, or equalizing, education, age, and gender, an average capitalist earned more than twice as much as the average worker and nearly twice as much as the average wage-earner.

Ornstein also found large differences in background, pay, and working conditions between manual and nonmanual workers. Manual workers are more likely to be men than women: in fact, less than a quarter are women. Manual workers have less education (on average) than nonmanual workers: fewer than half had graduated high school and only 2% had completed a university degree. Manual workers also report a much less settled work history than nonmanual workers: nearly a third had been unemployed and one-quarter had been laid off in the preceding two years.

Finally, manual workers are more closely supervised than nonmanual workers. Roughly one in three has to meet a quota at work and only one in three Ornstein sampled said they could leave their work at any time to run an errand. Nearly half of the manual workers sampled reported frequent supervision.

By contrast, about three-quarters of *nonmanual* workers are women. Nearly three in every four have graduated high school, with one in seven even graduating from university. Rates of recent unemployment are about the same as they are for manual workers; but less than half as many nonmanual (than manual) workers had been laid off in the previous two years. The nonmanual workers were also half as likely to report frequent supervision or having to meet a quota at work. In keeping with this greater flexibility, nonmanual workers have more freedom to leave work at any time to run an errand.

In short, nonmanual workers have more freedom and somewhat more job stability than manual workers. However these typically "pink collar" (female, nonmanual) workers earned about 20% less than their "blue collar" (male, manual worker) counterparts.

The effects of gender point to the fact that a person's place in the stratification system is not simply a consequence of the relations of production. Women doing the same jobs as men are typically paid less than men, often by a substantial amount. Also, women doing the same work as men usually have less chance for promotion than do men. In this case, gender serves as a form of status, the social ranking of individuals and groups in determining a person's place in the stratification system. Another way to put this is that gender is a symbolic resource that males can use to acquire material resources, but constitutes a social stigma that women must overcome to obtain those same material resources. Status, then, is a separate component of stratification in our society.

STATUS AND SYMBOLIC RESOURCES

The term "status" has two related meanings in sociological literature. One is *status* as a position in a social system—for example, daughter, parent, or professor—that embodies a cluster of rights, responsibilities, and role expectations. In this way, a status shapes role relationships and social interactions among people. The second meaning, derived from the work of Max Weber, is of status as a measure of social worth or honour.

There are two important implications of Weber's view of status for the study of inequality. One is that status is a relative term; one person's worth or honour is always determined by positive or negative comparison to someone else. This makes status much harder to measure than material wealth. Put differently, our desire for status has no limitation. Just as people who have high status often try to cash it in for material resources, so people who have wealth are willing to spend vast sums of money on philanthropic projects to obtain status.

Second, status is a symbolic relationship. This means that status can be seen as the unequal distribution of symbolic resources. Some of these resources, such as cultural capital, allow a person to acquire status; others, such as the symbols of wealth and conspicuous consumption, allow a person to display status.

Ascribed and achieved statuses

Sociologists typically refer to status as ascribed or achieved. An **achieved status** is based on characteristics over which the individual exerts some control—for example, educational attainment, type of job held, or marital status. Becoming Pope would be an example of achieved status. An **ascribed status** is based on the position into which an individual is born, or on characteristics over which the individual has no control—for example, age, sex, ethnicity, or caste. By this definition, the social stratum into which a person is born is an ascribed status. Prince Charles' position as Prince of Wales is an example of ascribed status.

Is the social stratum to which an adult belongs also an ascribed status? Can we guess what a newborn child's life chances are going to be, given his or her class of birth? The answer is, sometimes yes and sometimes no.

Among children born into very rich or very poor families (say, the top 10% and bottom 10%), most will still remain in precisely the same social stratum when they are an adult. In this case, people's social position – whether we are considering their wealth, status, or ability to dominate others – is ascribed. Among children born into the middle 80% of the population, few will remain in precisely the same social stratum as their parents. In that sense, their social position is achieved, not ascribed. Nonetheless, all children are more likely to end up in a stratum close to their parent's than one that is very distant.

Of course, because ours is a multi-dimensional stratification system, an individual can occupy two distinct positions which confer different amounts of social status. This means that some people experience **status inconsistency**. For example, an individual who is highly educated yet works in a low-paying job, belongs to a racial minority, or has a criminal record, will experience status inconsistency.

However, major inconsistency is relatively rare. In a multi-dimensional stratification system like ours, people are ranked along more than one dimension – for example, on income, job prestige, authority at work, educational attainment. Individuals ranked similarly on a number of dimensions belong to the same stratum or level. Within each stratum, individuals share similar life chances and perhaps even outlooks.

What further integrates an individual's position in the stratification system is that not all dimensions are equally important. Sociologists use the term socio-economic status to refer to a social ranking which combines various dimensions of stratification: particularly prestige and wealth. It takes into account a number of factors that determine a person's social status: income, type of occupation, level of education attained, and place of residence, among others. Sociologists have measured and combined these variables in a variety of ways. One way has emerged as the most commonly used: occupational prestige.

Criteria for determining who is and who is not worthy of prestige varies across cultures. Within cultures, it varies among subcultures and over time. In our society, wealth, power, intelligence, athletic competence, and physical attractiveness are all highly valued and all sources of prestige. **Prestige** is social honour. As such, it is a way of measuring social status and how much respect people will show someone. In our society, a person's job is his or her main source of income, authority, and prestige.

Being the president of a large corporation is a very prestigious position, and provides a person with great authority. Winning an Olympic gold medal is also prestigious. As a result, both the president of a corporation and an Olympic athlete enjoy relatively high social status, but different amounts of authority.

Sociologists have found that people who hold different jobs receive different amounts of prestige, because the jobs themselves are more or less prestigious. The most prestigious jobs are typically best paying and filled by the most highly educated people. We can predict how much prestige a person will receive from a job by knowing what the job pays and how much education the average jobholder has attained.

Despite some variations and exceptions, occupational-prestige rankings are very similar from one industrial country to another and change slowly over time. The gaps in prestige between medical doctor, door-to-door salesman, machinist, and unskilled construction worker are similar in Canada, Britain, Germany, and Japan. They are similar in 1990 to what they were in 1970 and 1950.

Unequal conditions and opportunities

We have stressed that there are many different types of social inequality but also many connections among them. Indeed social inequalities often overlap and reinforce each other. As a result, advantaged people enjoy a great many advantages and disadvantaged people suffer a great many disadvantages.

How would we go about eliminating these advantages and disadvantages so as to ensure more equality? Our answer depends on what we mean by equality.

Many people favour **equality of condition** – equality in the distribution of wealth, prestige, power, and other rewards among all members of society. Other people favour equality of opportunity – equality of access to those things valued by society. Equal opportunity means that all positions in society are equally open to everyone, regardless of age, race, gender, religion, or political affiliation. Recruitment, then, is done according to merit, or on the basis of personal talent.

However, in our society as in every other, what everyone wants is unequally distributed. Such inequalities of condition include differences of wealth, authority, and prestige that translate directly into differences of physical and material well-being: food, shelter, physical security, good health, and so on. Indirectly, they also translate into differences of mental health and happiness. Inequalities of opportunity are differences in the chance that people (or their children) will get to enjoy an improved social condition: more wealth, authority, and prestige; better health; more happiness.

Inequalities of condition and opportunity are not scattered randomly among members of a society. Rather, they vary from one social stratum to another. People in the same social stratum have similar conditions and similar chances for changing those conditions. People in higher strata have both better conditions and better chances for further improving those conditions. What is more, their children also have better chances than the children born into lower strata.

Better conditions and better opportunities for improving those conditions go together. People cannot have an equal opportunity to get what they want if they start out with vastly unequal wealth, power, and respect.

Thus, a society cannot equalize opportunity without greatly reducing the range of unequal starting points. If everyone were born with the same wealth, social position, and social connections, a great many people would have much more chance of getting what they want out of life than they do today.

The Assets and Locus of Control of Canada's 17 Largest*
Nonfinancial Enterprises

Enterprise Name	Nonfinancial Assets ($ Billions, 1987)	Who Controls?
Bell Canada	35.5	Management
Edper/Brascan	29.1	Bronfmans (Toronto)
Olympia-York, etc.	24.7	Reichmann family
Canadian Pacific	20.6	Management
Campeau	16.1	Robert Campeau
CEMP/Seagram, etc.	14.4	Bronfmans (Montreal)
Nova	10.2	Management
Thomson Group	9.5	Thomson family
Irving	9.0	K.C. Irving
McCain	8.0	McCain family
Unicorp Canada	6.2	George Mann
Power Corp.	6.1	Paul Desmarais
Falconbridge-Placer	4.8	Management
Eaton's	3.9	Eaton family
Trans Alta Utilities	3.7	Management
Weston Group	3.5	Weston family
Atco Ltd.	3.2	Southern family

Total Assets:
Top family-controlled firms $133.7 (billion)
Top management-controlled firms $74.8 (billion)

* Largest as measured by assets

Source: These data were provided by R. Jack Richardson, Department of Sociology, McMaster University.

SOCIAL MOBILITY: MOVEMENT WITHIN STRATIFICATION

Although there is no "Canadian Dream" equivalent to the "American Dream" of upward social mobility, most people tend to consider upward social mobility to be a realistic goal and devote much of their time and energies to getting ahead, improving their position in the social hierarchy. It is this ideal that has kept enrollments at colleges and universities increasing while the actual number of traditionally school-aged persons has declined. Education is seen as a means of social mobility. But how realistic is this goal given the context of unequal conditions we have discussed so far? The answer is that it depends on where you are starting from and how far you expect to rise.

Social mobility is the movement of individuals among different levels of the social hierarchy. Usually these levels are defined occupationally. There are many types of social mobility: horizontal and vertical, upward and downward, intergenerational and intragenerational. Sociologists have identified these different types of social mobility because each type often has very different causes from the others and will also often have different consequences for individuals.

Horizontal social mobility is the change from one occupational status to another that is roughly equal in rank: for example, change from school teaching to middle management, or from driving a bulldozer on a construction site to driving a truck on a highway. **Vertical social mobility** is the change from one occupational status to another that is higher or lower in rank: from lawyer to bartender, nurse to doctor, or short-order cook to architect.

Vertical mobility may be upward, to a higher level or stratum than the individual (or the individual's parents) held before, or downward. Typically sociologists who want to discover the pattern of social mobility in a society will measure the relative amounts of upward and downward mobility: whether more people move up than down, for example.

Some upward mobility is *structural mobility*, due simply to a growth in the number of good jobs available in the economy. Other upward mobility is *exchange mobility* and requires that one person move down for every person that moves up. Again, sociologists look for a pattern by learning what proportion of upward mobility is structural and what proportion is exchange mobility.

Finally, social mobility may be intergenerational or intragenerational. **Intergenerational social mobility** refers to the difference between the rank an individual currently occupies, and the rank his or her parents occupied. **Intragenerational social mobility**, also called "career mobility," refers to an individual's movement among various positions over the course of a lifetime.

The most commonly studied patterns of social mobility are those of vertical, intergenerational mobility among males.

Social mobility in Canada

How common is upward social mobility in Canada? Let us start by considering only mobility among males, since the patterns of mobility for females are quite different. How many men get ahead in Canadian society, in the sense that they hold a higher social position than the one into which they were born?

This question is hard to answer precisely, because both measurement procedures and rates of mobility change somewhat over time. Fortunately, however, research in most Western countries has turned up similar results. Heath (1981: 47) summarizes sociologists' conclusions in the following way:

(1) Most social mobility is short-range. Long-range movement from rags to riches, or riches to rags, is very rare.

(2) There is a barrier to movement across the manual/nonmanual line.

(3) There is a high degree of self-recruitment, "inheritance with a vengeance," at the top end of the social scale.

Each of these statements, however, is subject to modification. First, most upward mobility is structural mobility resulting from the creation of new jobs. This means that mobility is more likely to be short-range, rather than long-range. Long-range movement is more common in periods of great economic expansion than in periods of economic stagnation or decline. In addition, long-range movement is most likely in sectors of the economy and regions of the country that are expanding most rapidly.

Getting ahead is a major concern in our culture. We tend to blame people who fail to do better than their parents did, or even do significantly worse. Yet downward mobility is also widespread in our society.

Second, as more children of manual (blue-collar) workers get post-secondary education, there is more upward mobility across the manual/nonmanual line. Conversely, certain skilled blue-collar jobs are becoming more attractive in comparison with unskilled white-collar jobs. As a result, there is some movement of "nonmanual" children into blue-collar jobs. However, the chances that a "manual" child will take a blue-collar job and a "nonmanual" child will take a white-collar or professional job are higher than the reverse.

Third, managerial and professional jobs have increased rapidly in the past few decades and a great many working-class people have entered these jobs. This was entirely structural mobility, however; it displaced no upper-class people.

Further, the top end of the social scale contains a variety of desirable positions. This level recruits very different kinds of people in very different ways. The owners of large businesses and self-employed professionals are much more likely to come from the families of large business owners and self-employed professionals than from any other social origin. On the other hand, senior business managers and government bureaucrats are much more likely to come from working-class backgrounds. The *top* positions in the *leading* banks, industrials, and law firms are likely to go to people whose parents occupied similar positions.

So this is the answer to the question as put (How common is upward mobility in Canada?): quite common, especially in periods of economic expansion; but don't expect to become a millionaire. Being realistic, the chance your job will be slightly more prestigious than your father's, if you are a male, is about 40% (Creese, Guppy, and Meissner, forthcoming).

Women's mobility *versus* men's

Until very recently women's mobility was very different from that of men. A generation ago most women spent little of their lives in the paid work force. Those who did worked for pay before having children or after all their children were in school full-time. Even so, they fitted their work lives around their family responsibilities and avoided careers requiring too much time away from home. As a result, the majority had jobs, not careers. As well, women suffered discrimination in the labour force. This made it harder for women to get good jobs or promotions when they competed with men, or even equal pay for equal work.

Under these circumstances, most married women held the social rank their husband, the "breadwinner," had been able to attain. As a result, women would gain their greatest social mobility by marrying and supporting their husbands' efforts. Some women married up while others married down. British data analyzed by Heath (1981: 114) show that "a woman's class fate is more loosely linked to her social origins than is a man's."

Up until very recently, women's fates in the job market have also been more "loosely linked to social origins" than men's fates. In enormous numbers, women have filled a small variety of low-to-medium-prestige jobs. These jobs are chiefly in sales, clerical work, service, light manufacturing, and semi-professional work (like nursing and school-teaching). To women from working-class backgrounds, these jobs have often meant upward mobility. To women from middle- or upper-middle-class backgrounds, these jobs have meant downward mobility. Again, women have been less likely to inherit their parent's class position than men.

These patterns have begun to change as women attain higher levels of education, have fewer children, spend more years in the labour force, and experience less discrimination. Increasingly, women's patterns of social mobility grow more similar to those of men. Yet there is no doubt equal mobility exacts a higher toll from women than it does from men.

Canadian research by Katherine Marshall (1987) shows important differences between women who hold jobs, enter traditionally female careers, or enter traditionally male careers (like law, medicine, architecture, and engineering). Of the three groups, women who enter traditionally male careers—which offer the greatest opportunity for upward mobility—are least likely to marry. If they do marry they are least likely to bear children and most likely to divorce. This pattern suggests that even today family obligations limit the social mobility of women in ways they do not limit men.

Who is most and least mobile in Canadian society?

Within the broad band of people—the middle 80%—that is neither desperately poor nor fabulously rich, the most mobile are well-educated people.

Repeated studies of social mobility in Canada have confirmed results obtained elsewhere. They show that education is the single most important factor in overcoming the inheritance of class position. The more and better education a person obtains, the more likely that person is to move upward socially. This is because the best paying, most prestigious and secure jobs increasingly require educational training and credentials.

Status attainment studies show that people with the same amount of education are likely to get jobs of equal prestige, whatever their class of origin. Higher education provides skills and credentials for getting a good job, and also cultural capital which is useful in advancing a career. Post-secondary education is better than a secondary education in this respect. A university degree—especially a professional degree—is better than a community college diploma.

However, this simple conclusion is subject to a number of qualifications. First, people born into lower-class positions are less likely than average to get a higher education. For these people, the psychic and financial costs of remaining in school are much greater than for a middle- or upper-class student.

Second, a higher education does not guarantee a high prestige occupation. In periods of economic stagnation or decline, the risk of underemployment, if not unemployment, is high even for university graduates. Underemployment was particularly common in the late 1970s and early 1980s when large numbers of young people belonging to the "baby boom" generation flooded the job market. It should be less common in the generation born since 1965, especially if the Canadian economy continues to grow.

Third, there is no doubt that job discrimination limits the opportunities of even highly educated women and ethnic minorities. With human rights legislation, affirmative action, and the growth of ethnic subeconomies, these disabilities have started to diminish. Still, visible minorities do much worse, despite higher education, than equally educated white males. We shall discuss this issue further in the next chapter.

In short, the most upwardly mobile Canadian is likely to be a professionally educated white male born into a middle-class family in central Canada. The least upwardly mobile person is likely to be a member of a visible minority with high-school education or less. He or she will live outside central Canada, in a small town or city where opportunities are more limited.

ELITE DOMINATION

We noted earlier that mobility into the top ranks of Canada's stratification system is unlikely. These top ranks are often referred to as the elite. An **elite** is a small group that has power or influence over others and that people regard as being, in some way, superior. The top few percent in a larger social group—in a society, political party, or other collection of individuals—is that group's elite.

In his study of elite domination in American society, C. Wright Mills (1956) argued that what he called the *power elite* dominates American society. Typically the elite make decisions that affect the larger group and set the trends the larger group follows. Mills suggested that the elite does not form a "ruling class" because they are not a class—they come from different sectors of society, especially the military and political in addition to the economic elite—and they do not "rule." The exercise of power in a modern society, Mills argued, is no longer based on the use of force but by the elite reserving for itself the ability to make or influence the crucial political, economic, and military decisions that affect society. They are able to do this not only because of their own positions, but because by and large the public is unaware that these decisions are even being made. Moreover, those who do know are convinced that those at the top are best suited to be making these decisions. In effect, the elite dominates as a consequence of the ignorance and indifference of the public.

The situation in Canada is similar, although it is complicated by the influence exerted on Canada by our powerful American neighbour and the comprador

elites. Where federal legislation is concerned, the economically powerful influence politicians by calling in old favours, offering new ones, contributing to campaign costs, and lobbying in Ottawa. They also embarrass politicians by publicly questioning their competence or honesty. Sometimes they do the same thing indirectly by privately funding research by any of a number of friendly scholars, pollsters, or think tanks.

Many politicians are indebted to corporate sponsors. Like Brian Mulroney, they may have served corporate interests as lawyers or businessmen before assuming political office; and they may intend to return to the corporate world after leaving office. So it is easy to understand how the economic elite can exert great influence over political leaders who define what policy the government will follow.

It is more difficult to understand why average Canadians are unaware of the way elites influence government policies. The answer is that a great many Canadians are uninformed, misinformed, and confused about what to believe, even in their personal lives. A large proportion are ambivalent or confused about their opportunities for achieving what they want. Survey data show that nearly half feel people should set goals that are hard to achieve. Over two-thirds say that what you get out of life is your own doing, not the result of luck or chance. Accordingly, eight in every ten respondents feel that people should try to improve their position, rather than accept it. Just as many think that people's problems are never too big to keep them from running their lives the way they want to.

On the other hand, nearly two Canadians in three say that people should reduce their desires to prevent disappointment in life. Almost as many feel that people should be content with what they have, since you never know the future. Despite their rhetoric about choices and challenges, most people quickly resign themselves to limits on their opportunity.

Canadians show what Mann (1970) called "pragmatic acceptance" of the facts of social inequality. Mann concludes there is little evidence people generally agree with the beliefs and values of liberal democracy: the belief that people are rewarded for hard work and merit, or that the competition for society's rewards works fairly. There is neither consensus nor consistency in their views. To a large degree, it is this ambivalence that makes the system work.

> Cohesion in liberal democracy depends on the lack of consistent commitment
> to general values of any sort and on the 'pragmatic acceptance' by subordinate
> classes of their limited roles in society. (Mann, 1970: 423)

If people are so confused, ambivalent, and resigned about their own lives, think how much truer this is when it comes to the big issues over which media wars and political campaigns are fought. Most Canadians are still confused about the implications of Canada's free trade agreement with the United States, and the debates on the Meech Lake Accord in 1990 were filled with lots of threats and dire predictions, but almost no facts.

In conclusion, elites are able to dominate because they are more unified and less confused about their interests than are other groups in Canadian society.

Is there mobility into the elite?

Societies vary in the extent to which their various elites (political, intellectual, economic, and so on) form a cohesive whole or ruling group. Where such a group exists, the ruling elite makes decisions affecting everyone else. In most societies, the children of people who are elite members have the best opportunity of entering the elite themselves. Ruling elites differ in the extent to which they are open to entry from outside—that is, by children of non-elite parents.

In Canada, the dominant elite is the **corporate elite**, the group of top executives of the major or largest Canadian corporations. By virtue of their positions, these people hold the most economic control in the country. Their decisions affect economic trends and, through them, touch many lives. The group includes both owners or controlling stockholders in major compa-

EXHIBIT 5.3

THE MAKING OF A CANADIAN FORTUNE

Today, the Toronto Bronfmans control assets worth nearly $30 billion, and the Montreal Bronfmans assets worth nearly $15 billion. As journalist James Gray tells us in his book *Booze*,

> Of all the 3 500 000 immigrants who came to Canada between 1885 and 1914 a few may have come with less, but none went further than the family of Yechiel and Minnie Bronfman who in 1889 fled from the pogroms of Bessarabia to a homestead north of Wapella in what would become Saskatchewan. . . . When it became apparent to Ekiel that there had to be a better way of making a living than homesteading at Wapella, he loaded his family and his possessions on his farm wagons and moved to Brandon, a town of 3 500 located 120 miles to the southeast. (Gray, 1972: 101)

From there, two sons, Abe and Harry, went to Winnipeg to learn skilled trades—cigar-making and harness-making, respectively—but they scarcely practised the trades. By age 21, Abe had taken over the Balmoral Hotel in Yorkton, Saskatchewan. Two years later, Harry joined him in running it.

> The choice of the town and the hotel was a felicitous one on every count. As one of the earliest settled villages in eastern Saskatchewan, its population doubled and redoubled during the next decade, and so did the population of the surrounding countryside. The railway construction boom would give Yorkton, which was on both the Canadian Pacific and the Canadian Northern railways, direct connection with all the important centres of Manitoba and Alberta. The hotel itself was on Livingston Avenue, directly across the street from the C.P.R. express sheds through which Bronfman whisky would flow by the carload. (Gray: 104)

Eventually brother Sam joined Ekiel, Abe, and Harry in the family businesses—first hotels, then booze, then property and assorted investments. Doesn't it sound easy? Nothing helped the family fortunes more than Prohibition—find out how.

Source: Gray, J.H. *Booze: The Impact of Whisky on the Prairie West*. Scarborough: New American Library (Canada), 1972

nies—Canada's leading capitalists—and senior executives who may own smaller blocks of stock but may exercise more control. The corporate elite exercises its economic power largely by voting on boards of directors of the major corporations.

We have already noted Heath's finding that, in Britain, elites recruit new members mainly from within their own ranks. Yet the recent rapid growth in positions at the top has made structural mobility into the elite possible for more people born into lower classes.

In general, these findings hold for Canada as well as for Britain (which Heath studied) and other Western countries. However, certain peculiarities of Canada make it necessary for us to study the Canadian elite more closely. In fact, some of Canadian sociology's finest research has devoted itself to this very topic. Canada is different from Britain (and indeed many other Western countries) in the following ways:

(1) there has never been a landed aristocracy in Canada;
(2) much of the Canadian economy is controlled by foreign-owned (especially American-owned) multi-national corporations;
(3) the state has always played a particularly vigorous part in Canada's social and economic development;
(4) Canada has always had a very high rate of immigration; and
(5) the Canadian population and economy has grown very rapidly and unevenly since the Second World War.

The fact there has never been a landed aristocracy in Canada has probably made it much easier for people to move up into elite positions. In Canada, as in the United States, great wealth and power are enough to gain a person entry into social circles of privilege and distinction. Converting money into social acceptance has always been harder and slower in Europe, where family lineage has counted for more.

Wallace Clement (1975) has found important differences in the patterns of movement into elite positions. He distinguishes between indigenous elites—the people who control Canadian-owned organizations (like the Bank of Montreal)—and **comprador elites**—the people who run foreign-owned or controlled corporations that are located in Canada (like IBM or General Motors). Clement found much more upward mobility into comprador elite positions than into indigenous elite positions.

This finding permits a number of different interpretations. We should note first that large foreign-owned companies are more likely to be industrial organizations while large Canadian-owned companies are more likely to be financial organizations. Clement's finding may prove that financial institutions recruit more conservatively than industrial organizations. It may prove that industrial organizations pay more attention to recruits' ability than to their social origins and connections. Or it may prove that the Canadian class structure has less influence over foreign-owned companies when they are recruiting and promoting people.

The important role of the state in Canada's economy has meant that government (especially civil service) elites would be as important as corporate elites. So mobility into corporate elite positions may have to resemble mobility into government elite positions. In the first important study of Canadian elites,

John Porter (1965) found many similarities in the backgrounds of the corporate and civil-service elite groups. They included an over-representation of upper-class people in both cases.

In recent years, governments on all levels—federal, provincial, and municipal—have attempted to hire and promote people on meritocratic principles. A **meritocracy** is a social system in which people are chosen to fill positions on their merit, especially talent and educational attainment. The problem with meritocracy is knowing how to measure talent objectively. Still, meritocracy means emphasizing achievement over ascription, and avoiding job discrimination.

Recent years have seen a great deal of affirmative action in hiring and promotion. It has aimed at increasing the proportion of francophones, women, visible minorities, and other disadvantaged people in positions of power. The corporate elite has had to follow the government's lead in order to keep up good relations with the federal bureaucracy and a good public image. Today, the proportion of francophones and females in the corporate elite is still small, but it has grown significantly since Porter first described the elite 30 years ago.

The high rate of immigration to Canada has also worked to increase mobility into the corporate elite. Facing a high proportion of the population whose ancestry is neither English nor French, corporate elites may feel pressured to admit more members of ethnic minority groups into their numbers. Immigrants and the children of immigrants have become more numerous among the corporate elite. However, this change has been primarily due to the sheer numbers of immigrants and their activity within new economic sectors. In fact, Jorge Niosi has suggested (1981: 35) that, after the conflict between foreign- and Canadian-owned organizations, "the ethnic split is the most important division in the Canadian capitalist class."

Centred on the banking industry, the traditional corporate elite has continued to draw its membership disproportionately from among white, Anglo-Saxon Protestant males. In new, rapidly growing sectors of the economy—especially real estate, manufacturing, construction, and the trust industry—ethnic minorities have been more successful. They have entered the corporate elite by building their own dominant corporations, not working up through already existing ones. Examples include the Bronfmans, the Reichmans, Bata and many others described at length in Diane Francis's *Controlling Interests* (1986) and Peter Newman's *The New Acquisitors* (1981).

What is more, with the ethnic domination of new sectors by new organizations, organizational control has often returned to family (owners') hands. These new elites stand at the head of enormously large family businesses. Indeed, as Jack Richardson (1990) points out, the Canadian economy has undergone a significant transformation in the past decade or so. Three closely related elements of this transformation are the resurgence of family controlled enterprises, the growth of huge conglomerates, and the integration within these conglomerates of financial and non-financial firms.

What the above suggests is that the Canadian elite has been changing, and so has the opportunity for upward mobility into the elite. Although Wallace Clement argues that this opportunity has shrunk since Porter's research 20 years earlier and that the elite is restricting recruitment from outside, little evidence supports that view. On the contrary, current evidence suggests many new players have entered the elite in the last 20 years and this number is likely to grow.

Still, rags-to-riches mobility remains a rare outcome, one which is not to be expected. It is unrealistic to set your heart on entering the corporate elite. Unless you are the child of a member of the elite, your chances of succeeding are tiny. The fact that some people can enter the elite from below does not prove that Canada is a meritocracy. No one has yet demonstrated that elites — people at the top — are more talented than people near the top, at the middle, or even at the bottom. The key to gaining elite status is still financial capital, cultural capital, accidents of birth, and a lot of luck.

EXHIBIT 5.4

DOWN THE UP STAIRCASE

Our society is so concerned with how people get ahead that it pays little attention to how people fall behind, and how many people do so. Yet, during the 1980s, millions of North Americans became downwardly mobile, according to recent research presented by Katherine Newman in her book *Falling From Grace: The Experience of Downward Mobility in the American Middle Class* (1989). Writes Newman,

> They are men and women who once had secure jobs, comfortable homes and reason to believe that the future would be one of continued prosperity for themselves and their children. Longtime members of the middle class, they suddenly find everything they have worked to achieve — careers, lifestyles, and peace of mind — slipping through their fingers. And despite sustained efforts to reverse the slide, many discover there is little they can do to block their descent.

One major group of downwardly mobile people included female lone parents and their children. Another included the rejected middle-managers who suddenly lost their jobs during the recession of the early 1980s when many large business organizations were "downsizing."

Downward income mobility was hard for the female lone parents to accept because it often accompanied personal rejection, a break in intimate relations and social life, and increased parental responsibility. This package of horrors shattered any illusions these lone parents may have harboured about the security of marriage.

Downward income mobility was hard for the young-to-middle-aged executives because it violated all the rules of the "culture of meritocracy" they had believed in. Their experience showed that education, effort, and cooperation did *not* guarantee success, or even security in a job. Merit was *not* rewarded. If they could no longer believe in meritocracy, they would have to completely reorganize their thinking about life; and many resisted doing so.

How would you "rethink" your life if you were one of these millions of downwardly mobile people?

Source: Newman, Katherine S. *Falling From Grace: The Experience of Downward Mobility in the American Middle Class.* Copyright © 1988 by Katherine S. Newman. Reprinted by permission of The Free Press, a Division of Macmillan, Inc.

Like people, groups and nations also compete for upward mobility. Much debate has centred on whether free trade with the United States will improve the well-being of Canadians in the long run. Some believe other competitive strategies are better.

POVERTY IN CANADA

Defining and measuring poverty

We turn now from the powerful and wealthy to the powerless and poor. Sociologists distinguish between relative and absolute poverty. **Absolute poverty** occurs when people do not have enough of the basic necessities—food, shelter, and medicine, for example—for physical survival. Researchers define **relative poverty** by general living standards of the society or social group. Because not all societies or groups within a society are equally wealthy, what people consider poor varies among different societies and subgroups within a society. In a stratified society like ours, we consider people with much less than the average income "poor."

By some reports, poverty is decreasing in Canada. Health and Welfare Canada (1989: 35) reports that "the incidence of low-income among Canadians has fallen from 26 to 15 percent." Health and Welfare Canada attributes this decline to improvements in coverage and benefits in the social security system. Whether this trend in poverty is believable depends on whether we agree with the way in which government statisticians are measuring low-income. The Low Income Cut-off Point is the income level below which a person (or family) is judged to be living in poverty. While judgments of what constitutes "poverty" may vary over time and from one region (or social group) to another, the officially designated Cut-off Points are set so low that no one disagrees the people below the line are truly impoverished. Debate focuses, instead, on whether the line ought to be set much higher, revealing that a great many more people are "in poverty" than the government would like to admit.

The Low Income Cut-off Points vary with family size and size of community in which the family lives. Larger families who live in larger communities require more income to live at the same level as smaller families in smaller communities. The guiding principle is that a low-income person or family spends 58.5% or more of its income on food, shelter, and clothing. Each year statisticians update the specific dollar cut-off lines using the Consumer Price Index, to account for yearly changes in the cost of living.

Of this mode of analysis, Methot (1987: 7) says that statisticians fail to take into account other factors such as accumulated wealth, non-monetary income, and future earnings potential. These, Methot notes, are also important in determining the economic well-being of families and individuals.

However, we have no better measure than this of poverty in Canada. At least this method allows us to compare groups within Canadian society and see which are at the greatest risk of poverty.

Who are the poor in Canada?

Health and Welfare Canada reports that among families, the incidence of low income is lowest in families without children, with multiple income-earners, or headed by an elderly person. It is highest in families with three or more children and in those headed by mothers (mostly single parents). Methot (1987: 2) agrees that nearly half of all lone-parent families headed by women have low incomes. This percentage has increased since 1981. Indeed, families headed by lone female parents make up about one-third of all low-income families.

This growing problem is what some have called the "feminization of poverty." The incidence of low incomes among families headed by lone male parents is also growing. Yet it remains about half as high as for families headed by female lone parents. What's more, families headed by a lone parent are far more likely to have a female than a male family head. After divorce or separation, women are far more likely to take responsibility for the children. So, overall this kind of low-income family is likely to remain common unless the state takes strong measures to change things.

Among unattached individuals, the incidence of low income is highest among the young (under age 25), the old (65 and over), and women. This is largely because these groups are least likely to be in the labour force or hold a good quality job. Methot reports that low incomes are more common than average among families whose head

- had completed little formal education;
- was not in the labour force at all;
- did not work full time all year long; or
- experienced some unemployment during the year.

Finally, low-income families were most common in Quebec and the Atlantic provinces (especially Newfoundland). The numbers swelled in Alberta and British Columbia in the early 1980s, with the collapse of the oil and construction boom. In general, low incomes are common in regions where unemployment and low education are common: namely, in the Canadian hinterlands.

> In Canada's many rural and remote communities . . . economies are largely based on primary industries such as fishing, forestry, mining and farming. Residents must often contend with weather extremes, physical isolation and limited access to affordable housing, food, clothing, and health and social services. They also tend to be unemployed more frequently and for longer periods of time. (Health and Welfare Canada 1989: 35, 36)

Causes of Poverty

We have failed to mention the group that is likeliest of all Canadians to experience a low income. That group gives us the most insight into causes of poverty. The group we mean is children. By 1985, about one child in five under age 16 was living in a low-income family. That percentage had increased since the early 1980s, as the proportion of elderly with low incomes was decreasing.

Of all age groups, children are the most numerous and blameless victims of poverty. Their poverty demonstrates the error in thinking that poor people have only themselves to blame. The poverty of children does not result from faulty values but from forces beyond their control. These include the inability of parents to find work and the insufficiency of social supports (like free daycare) which would permit them to do the job.

Since 1981 the greatest increase in numbers of poor children has come among children with two parents (aged 25-44) at home. Their poverty problem is not due to marital breakdown. Like the female lone parents, these parents cannot find work, or, if they do work, are not paid for their work above the low-income level.

Public attitudes to poverty

Just as public attitudes to inequality are mixed and confused, so too are their attitudes to poverty. People sometimes see themselves as victims of forces beyond their control. They are then willing to believe that poverty resulting from unemployment, age, or ill health deserves assistance. Other times people see themselves as masters of their own fate. They then hold the poor responsible for their own poverty and feel that these people do not deserve public assistance.

The amount of assistance a province makes available to a poor person varies with the perceived causes of poverty. Old people and the physically disabled receive the most help, as everyone considers them the blameless "deserving poor." People are more likely to consider single mothers and chronically unemployed people the "undeserving poor." As a result, they receive less generous and less secure assistance. Social assistance payments to this latter group fail to meet actual living expenses—especially for people living in large cities where rents are high (like Toronto and Vancouver).

Many Canadians believe that, if social assistance payments exceed the minimum wage level, unemployed people will be reluctant to get off welfare and take a job. Yet many people cannot find a job. Throughout the 1980s the unemployment rate hovered around 10%. In some regions and for some groups the rate has been very much higher. Certain groups such as female lone parents of small children cannot afford to pay the daycare costs that would allow them to take a job. Others, such as the physically disabled, cannot find a job suitable to their ability (or disability).

Attitudes to welfare and social programs do not vary widely in the Canadian population (Ornstein, 1988). It is true that working-class people are very much more likely than upper-class people to say that "high income people should pay more taxes," and agree that "government should make more effort to assist the unemployed" and "provide jobs for those who cannot find a job." The upper class are twice as likely to believe that "government should cut back further on

Some believe inequality can only be reduced by taking power away from the ruling class and reorganizing society, by means of a revolution. Pictured here is a Quebec pro-resistance poster celebrating the patriots of 1837.

social programs." On the other hand, working-class people are *not* much more likely than the upper class to say that "government should make more effort to help the poor." They are even more likely than upper-class people to say that "unemployment is too high because welfare is too easy to get." Overall, a minority of employed people are in favour of more help for the poor.

CLOSING REMARKS

We began this chapter by noting that inequality is a fact of life for all of us, but that few Canadians are in the habit of thinking much about inequality. Most of us simply take for granted that it is individual circumstances or personal character that leads some to be rich and others to be poor. The idea that Canada has a distinct stratification system and that our life chances are largely the outcome of the macrosociological processes making up that system is an idea that is foreign to most Canadians. But it is essential to understanding Canadian society and where our own lives fit into this society.

In this chapter we discussed three types of inequality—class, status, and domination. All three pervade our lives and affect our relations with others. Which of the three is most important? That depends. Domination and how political authority is divided up between the federal and provincial governments has been much in the news lately. Yet politics *per se* was not at issue in the debates surrounding free trade in the late 1980s or the constitutional crisis of the early 1990s. Rather, the economic and ethnocultural makeup of the country was at the heart of those debates. Most sociologists would see our place in the economic system as the most crucial component in our life chances. Indeed, the economic order is so important in affecting our society and our lives that we shall deal with the economic order separately in Chapter Eight. As for status, we noted earlier the significance gender and ethnicity have for inequality in Canada. Much of the politics in Canada, for example, is ethnic politics, and a person's ethnicity has a major impact both on status and on economic opportunities. Indeed, understanding ethnicity and how ethnicity pervades the structure of Canadian society is the topic of the next chapter.

Discussion Questions

1. Research shows that people who are physically attractive enjoy better opportunities than people who are less physically attractive. Why is that? Is this a "social inequality," as we have defined the term?

2. Who has control over *your* access to the necessities of life—your food, shelter, and clothing? Who has control over that person's access? Are you in the same relation to the means of production as the person who controls your access to necessities?

3. How might one argue that the failure to eliminate inequality in the Soviet Union does *not* prove Marx's theory wrong? Make the strongest case you can for that view. Then consider what evidence would be needed to prove Marx's theory wrong.

4. Would you rate your chances at entering the Canadian elite as closest to one in (a) a hundred, (b) a thousand, or (c) a million? Give the reasoning behind your estimate.

5. Are the connections between Canada's ruling class and foreign ruling classes likely to become stronger or weaker in the next 50 years? What influences are likely to strengthen or weaken these connections?

6. Is there anything you can do to reduce the risk you will fall into poverty? If so, will you blame yourself if you fall into poverty nonetheless? Which poor people do you *not* blame for their poverty?

Data Collection Exercises

1. Select two or three job categories—for example, used car salesman, hockey player, secretary, dentist, garbage collector, plumber. Design a method for measuring the functional importance of each job, or contribution each one makes to society. Then, using published statistics, measure the average income earned in each category. How well does income correlate with a job's social importance?

2. Collect data on income inequalities in the Soviet Union and compare them with income inequalities in Canada. (For example, you might try to find out whether the income gap between hockey players, dentists, and secretaries is wider or narrower in the Soviet Union than it is in Canada.) Report on any data collection and measurement problems you encounter in making this comparison.

3. Using the Canadian Encyclopedia and other biographical sources, collect data on the personal histories of a dozen randomly selected elite Canadians born since 1900. With these data, determine what proportion were born into non-elite families. Of those born into non-elite families, how important was higher education in helping them enter the elite?

4. What are the major industries, or major employers, in your city of residence? Identify the two or three wealthiest companies and find out who owns them. Do the owners live elsewhere and, if so, where? Do these companies have branches in other cities or towns and, if so, where? Other than common ownership, what connects the branch in your town with branches elsewhere?

Writing Exercises

1. Write a 500-word press release explaining why Froon Technology has decided, at its annual meeting of stockholders, to lay off 800 workers and give its 14 vice-presidents an average pay raise of 20%.

2. In a 500-word essay, draw on your own experiences to describe what it's like to be controlled or supervised at work. What, if anything, do you particularly hate about that experience? (If you have never worked for pay, discuss the subjective experience of control elsewhere—for example, at home or school.)

3. Write a 500-word review of a popular movie, book, or television program, revealing how it puts across a pro-capitalism, pro-elite, or anti-working-class point of view.

4. Write a 500-word autobiography revealing what class you were born into, what class you are in now, and what class you expect to be in 20 years from now.

Glossary

affirmative action— a type of legislation (particularly related to recruitment, hiring, and promotion practices) aimed at ensuring that certain types of people (whether women, racial minorities, or otherwise) who have previously been excluded will enjoy a slight advantage over all competitors in future

ascribed status— a social status based on the position into which an individual is born, or characteristics over which he or she exerts no control. Conversely, **achieved status** is based on characteristics over which the individual exerts some control, such as educational attainment, marital status, or type of employment.

authority— the ability of an individual or group to issue commands and have them obeyed because their control is perceived as legitimate

bourgeoisie— in Marxist terminology, the group of people who own the means of production—capitalists. Sometimes also used to refer to the middle class in a capitalist society. The bourgeoisie employ the **proletariat**, who own none of the means of production but their own labour power.

caste system— a hierarchy of groups separated from each other by rules of ritual purity and prevented from intermarrying, changing castes through mobility, or carrying out inappropriate jobs

class system— a hierarchy of groups with different market conditions, work situations, and life chances. In Marxist theory, classes stand in different relations to the means of production

domination— the exercise of control over an individual or group who must submit to that person's power. It can be seen as inequality based on the distribution of authoritative resources, as **class** is inequality based on the distribution of material resources, and **status** is inequality based on the distribution of symbolic resources.

elite—a small group that has power or influence over others and that is regarded as being superior in some way. A **comprador elite** is made up of the people who run corporations located in Canada but owned or controlled by foreign concerns.

equality of opportunity—equality of access to that which society values; a situation in which all positions in society are equally open to everyone

power—the capacity to exercise one's will despite resistance. In Marxist theory, power is the capacity of one class to realize its interests in opposition to other classes.

prestige—social honour and treatment with respect, a dimension of stratification that is separate from income, authority, or class position

socio-economic status (SES)—a method of social ranking which combines measures of wealth, authority (or power), and prestige

social mobility—the movement of individuals among different levels of the social hierarchy, defined occupationally. Movement may be vertical or horizontal, intergenerational or intragenerational.

stratification system—a system of inequality that integrates class, status, and domination with other forms of social differentation, such as gender, race, ethnicity

underemployment—employment in a job which requires far less expertise, skill or ability than the job-holder typically has. Often, this is the same as "overeducation."

Suggested Readings

Clement, Wallace *The Canadian Corporate Elite*. Toronto: McClelland and Stewart, 1975. A classic study that re-evaluates John Porter's conclusions about the Canadian elite using data that are 20 years more recent, by an author who is central to new Marxist studies of Canada.

Curtis, James, Edward Grabb, Neil Guppy, and Sid Gilbert (eds.) *Social Inequality in Canada*. Toronto: Prentice-Hall Canada, 1988. A sourcebook of reprinted articles on ownership and class, socio-economic bases of inequality, ascription and inequality, the state and inequality, and consequences of social inequality.

Curtis, James and Lorne Tepperman (eds.) *Understanding Canadian Society*. Toronto: McGraw-Hill Ryerson, 1988. A sourcebook of original articles by many of Canada's foremost sociologists. It includes articles on the political economy of Canada, the labour process, social class and economic inequality, political ideology, and collective protest.

Marchak, M. Patricia *Ideological Perspectives on Canada*, 3rd edition. Toronto: McGraw-Hill Ryerson, 1989. A popular, well-written discussion of what ideology is. It shows how Canada's dominant liberal ideology helps the establishment deflect attempts at fundamental change.

Porter, John *The Vertical Mosaic*. Toronto: University of Toronto Press, 1965. Unquestionably Canadian sociology's most important and widely read work, this book has set the agenda for research for over 20 years. The first half discusses social mobility and ethnicity, the second half ruling elites.

Tepperman, Lorne *Choices and Chances*. Toronto: Holt Rinehart Winston, 1988. This book of "sociology for everyday life" explains why people want what they want out of life and get what they get. It also suggests how the reader might close the gap between what he or she wants and gets in an unequal society.

References

Clement, W. (1975) *The Canadian Corporate Elite*. Toronto: McClelland and Stewart

Creese, G., N. Guppy, and M. Meissner (forthcoming) *Ups and Downs on the Ladder of Success: Social Mobility in Canada, 1986*. Ottawa: Statistics Canada

Davis, K. and W.E. Moore (1945) "Some principles of stratification" *American Sociological Review*, 10 (April), pp. 242-249

Francis, D. (1986) *Controlling Interests: Who Owns Canada?* Toronto: McClelland and Stewart

Goffman, E. (1961) *Asylums: Essays on the Social Situation of Mental Patients and Other Inmates*. Garden City, New York: Anchor

Health and Welfare Canada (1989) *Health and Welfare in Canada*. Ottawa: Supply and Services Canada

Heath, A. (1981) *Social Mobility*. Glasgow: Fontana Books

Marshall, K. (1987) "Women in male-dominated professions" *Canadian Social Trends*, pp. 7-11

Mann, M. (1970) "The social cohesion of liberal democracy" *American Sociological Review*, 35(3), pp. 423-439

Marx, K. (1936 [1867]) *Capital*. New York: Modern Library

_____ . and F. Engels (1955) *The Communist Manifesto*, S.H. Beer (ed.) New York: Appleton Century Crofts

Methot, S. (1987) "Low income in Canada" *Canadian Social Trends*, Spring, pp. 2-7

Mills, C.W. (1956) *The Power Elite*. New York: Oxford University Press

Newman, P.C. (1981) *The New Acquisitors*, volume 2 of *The Canadian Establishment*. Toronto: McClelland and Stewart

Niosi, J. (1981) *Canadian Capitalism*. Toronto: James Lorimer

Ornstein, M. (1988) "Social class and economic inequality" chapter 7 in J. Curtis and L. Tepperman (eds.) *Understanding Canadian Society*. Toronto: McGraw-Hill Ryerson

Porter, J. (1965) *The Vertical Mosaic*. Toronto: University of Toronto Press

Rainville, R.E. and E. McCormick (1977) "Extent of covert racial prejudice in pro football announcers' speech" *Journalism Quarterly*, 54(1), pp. 20-26

Richardson, R.J. (1990) "Economic concentration and social power in contemporary Canada" pp. 341-350 in J. Curtis and L. Tepperman (eds.) *Images of Canada: The Sociological Tradition*. Toronto: Prentice-Hall (Canada)

Stone, G. (1970) "The circumstance and situation of social status" pp. 250-59 in G. Stone and H. Faberman (eds.) *Social Psychology Through Symbolic Interaction*. Waltham, Mass.: Xerox College Publishing

Weber, M. (1958) "Class, status, party," chapter 7 in H. Gerth and C.W. Mills (eds.) *From Max Weber: Essays in Sociology*. New York: Oxford

_____ . (1964) "The types of authority and imperative coordination" section 3 in T. Parsons (ed.) *The Theory of Social and Economic Organization*. New York: Free Press

Wright, E.O. (1985) *Classes*. London: Verso

CHAPTER 6

Canada's cities are a mixtu[re] of dozens of racial and ethn[ic] groups. They form what soc[io]logist John Porter called a "vertical mosaic."

ETHNIC AND RACE RELATIONS

CANADA'S ETHNIC MOSAIC

In the last chapter we noted that ethnicity and race are closely tied into Canada's stratification system. It was this close tie that led sociologist John Porter to describe Canada as a vertical mosaic, a description that seems to have become a part of our national self-consciousness. A mosaic is a pattern made of small, distinct pieces. Sociologically, a mosaic is a society in which members of various ethnic groups are encouraged to retain their distinctive identities, customs, languages, traditions—in short, their own cultures—within a larger society. Porter referred to Canada as a "vertical" mosaic because he argued that people's ethnic backgrounds to a large extent determined their place in the stratification system. Not all groups had equal access for their members into all sectors of the economy or into the economic and political elites. The situation has changed, of course, since the time that Porter wrote, and there is evidence that ethnicity has less impact on life chances than was true in the past. But the continuing reality of prejudice and discrimination against visible minorities, including the native peoples, in Canada shows that both ethnicity and race remain significant determinants of inequality for many people.

Inevitably, the persistence of ethnic inequality has made ethnicity and race political issues. Indeed, much of Canada's recent history of recurrent political and constitutional difficulties is largely a consequence of ethnic disputes and disagreements, especially over language or aboriginal rights. As well, the political importance of Canada's many ethnic groups is indicated by the substantial resources the federal government allocates to supporting and promoting its policy of multiculturalism.

What this shows us is that ethnicity has proven itself to be one of the most powerful sources of group solidarity and intergroup conflict in Canadian society. Yet this is not only true for Canada. Ethnic and racial loyalties and conflicts are frequent topics in the international news. Despite years of "Russification," ethnic consciousness and ethnic conflict erupted throughout the Soviet Union in 1989 and posed the first serious threat to the stability of Soviet society since the Second World War. Elsewhere in eastern Europe, ethnic conflicts are also reported regularly, particularly in Yugoslavia (involving Serbs and Croations) and Romania (involving the Hungarian minority). Other places where ethnic conflicts persist with deadly frequency include Sri Lanka (involving the Tamils), India (involving Sikhs or the Moslem minority), and Ethiopia. As for racial conflict, South Africa stands out both for the high degree of racial oppression institutionalized in that society by *apartheid* policies, and for the ongoing attempts by the black majority to achieve basic civil rights.

Because ethnicity continues to play such a significant role, understanding the pattern of ethnic and race relations in Canada helps us to understand much about Canadian society. It also sets us on the road to understanding intergroup relations elsewhere in the world. Finally, because so many of us continue to find ethnicity relevant in our interactions with others in everyday life, understanding the pattern of ethnic and race relations helps us to understand much about ourselves and our social relationships with other people.

Like everything else we discuss in this book, ethnic and race relations have both a macro and micro side. On the macro side, members of particular ethnic or racial groups suffering political and economic discrimination often react by organizing themselves *as groups*. They aim to gain political power, changes in the law, or economic advantage. The institutions they create—mutual aid associations, business associations, schools and churches, to name a few—are large collective responses to "public issues."

But the other side of ethnic and race relations has to do with the unique experience of "personal troubles," and it is harder to see but no less important. In a micro-approach to race and ethnicity, we ask questions like the following:

- How does it feel to be seen as black, brown, red, or yellow in a mainly white country? In particular, how does it feel to know that all the cards may well be stacked against you when you go looking for a job?

- What problems are a "mixed" pair of lovers—black and white, Catholic and Protestant, francophone and anglophone, or otherwise—likely to run into when they start to date, think of marrying, or plan to have children together?

- How should we train our children to accept ethnic differences in dress, lifestyle, and values? (And how will a young Sikh boy respond when his classmates ridicule his ceremonial turban and dagger?)

As usual, the three paradigms of sociology have differed in their approach to ethnic and race relations. Functionalists, because of their emphasis on consensus and common values, have tended to see ethnic differences as inevitably succumbing to assimilation, or have seen ethnicity as essentially "symbolic" (Parsons, 1975). They have therefore failed to emphasize the links whereby ethnicity is tied into economic, political, or status inequality. Symbolic interactionists have made valuable contributions to understanding how "boundary maintenance" works (for example, Shaffir, 1974) but have tended to emphasize the links between ethnicity and identity rather than focusing on ethnic groups as organized communities. Because Canadian sociologists have emphasized the links between ethnicity and inequality, they have primarily made use of a conflict perspective and most of the discussion in this chapter presents concepts and research using the conflict paradigm.

THE CONCEPTS OF ETHNICITY AND RACE

The term **ethnicity** refers to the set of subjective and objective characteristics that give a group a sense of collective existence and of shared biological and historical heritage. Such a sense of collective identity usually develops among people who share a distinctive culture, language, religion, national origin, or race. Thus, an **ethnic group** is a socially defined collectivity whose members share similar cultural traits and who regard themselves, and are regarded by others, as culturally and biologically united.

In Canada, ethnicity is measured in a variety of ways. Most commonly, people are asked their *ethnic origins*—from where their ancestors emigrated to Canada; their *ethnic identity*—to what ethnic group they think they belong; or their *mother tongue*—the language they learned as children, or speak regularly at home.

A race is a group whose members are socially defined as sharing the same physical characteristics. A race may be composed of members of many different social or cultural backgrounds, so the term race is used strictly as a biological, not a cultural, concept.

Many researchers have used racial categories to divide the human species into distinct physical types. Racial categories based on physical characteristics can range from three to over one hundred, depending on the researcher making the classification. However, these categories do *not* occur in nature. The researcher creates them arbitrarily and, in that way, shapes his or her findings with assumptions about the human group. Intercultural and interracial contact, including sexual contact, has been occurring for thousands of years. As a result, racial categories do not reflect genetic realities. For, in reality, virtually all of us display a mixture of racial traits. Across the human race, we find a wide range of subtly different racial features: for example, many shades of "white" skin and a wide range of darker "white" skin colours that shade into the lighter "brown," "red," and "yellow" skin colours of other "non-white" races. This continuous variation applies to all other racial features: to shape of head, size of nose, hair texture, and so on. In fact, a continuum of human types more accurately describes the human species than categories of race: there is no such thing as a "pure" human race.

Race is, therefore, arbitrary as a biological concept. However, the concept is important to sociologists because physical differences serve as group markers; they indicate membership in some group. Group markers—whether real or imagined—carry social meanings and people act on these social meanings. If people regard themselves, and are regarded by others, as members of an identifiable biological category, then for all intents and purposes they constitute a race. As W.I. Thomas (Thomas and Thomas, 1928) said in a well-known aphorism, "if [people] define situations as real, they are real in their consequences." Race is real because its consequences are real. People choose friends, marriage partners, and places of work and residence, hire employees and elect government officials on the basis of race. In many countries race strongly influences people's life chances. People have fought wars and lost lives because of ideologies they have built around race.

ETHNIC AND RACIAL GROUPS IN CANADA

Whatever the reality of ethnicity or race as categories, then, sociologists examine the patterns of social relations generated by the use, persistence, and defense of these categories. Before we begin to look at the pattern of ethnic group relations in Canada, however, we must first look at the groups themselves to see the ethnic and racial categories typical of Canadian society.

Because Canada is a nation largely built up of immigrants, there are many ethnic and racial groups in Canada. Each of these groups has its own individual features, but sociologists and other social scientists find it convenient to classify these groups into a smaller number of categories based on some common social characteristics. The British and French groups, which have special status in Canadian society, are referred to as *Charter Groups*. The many native peoples are treated as one category, despite their cultural and social differences, because they share many common problems and a common set of life chances. Canada's racial groups—the *visible minorities*—share common problems as well, especially problems of prejudice and discrimination. Lastly, there are the many other ethnic groups—usually European in origin—who have overcome the legacy of discrimination to find their own place in Canadian society.

EXHIBIT 6.1

WHY DOES ETHNICITY SURVIVE?

The last 40 years have seen a surprising resurgence of ethnic, religious, and nationalist sentiment throughout the industrialized world, contrary to what "modernization theorists" would have predicted. Ethnic identity has become more salient, ethnic self-assertion stronger, and ethnic conflict more marked everywhere in the last 20 years. Right now, such sentiments are raging through the Eastern Bloc countries, as Communist governments lose the power to control their expression. However, these sentiments have been strong and gaining strength in North America for several decades.

Sociologists Nathan Glazer and Daniel Moynihan (1975) doubt that this new ethnic conflict is simply a new form of class conflict. Nor do they believe that ethnic conflict demonstrates an uprising of "internally colonized" peoples, the ambition of self-appointed leaders, or mere fashions and fads.

Rather, the evidence suggests that ethnic conflict is closely bound up with certain major trends in modern societies. Ethnic mobilization is an effective strategy for making claims on the ever-growing welfare state. It is also a means of fighting collectively for social status and economic rewards. These aside, ethnicity has become increasingly important when—as in Communist countries—rights to private property are limited. That is because ethnicity combines personal interests with emotional ties. With international communication increasing among members of dispersed ethnic groups (Jews, Armenians, Palestinians, Chinese, or others), this mobilization is likely to increase.

For these reasons, the chances of ethnic conflict decreasing in the near future are very slight.

Adapted from Nathan Glazer and Daniel P. Moynihan, "Why ethnicity today?" in N. Glazer and D.P. Moynihan (eds.) *Ethnicity: Theory and Experience.* Cambridge, Mass.: Harvard University Press, 1975

The Charter Groups: English and French Canadians

The term Charter Groups was coined to emphasize the important status the British and French groups have in Canadian society, a status that makes them politically, economically, and socially dominant over the other ethnic groups. Canada's **Charter Groups** are the descendants of people who obtained royal charters from the English and French kings to colonize this part of the world. Royal charters granted these groups economic and political power in the New World and legitimized their power, at least in European eyes.

The Charter Groups shaped Canada's social, political, cultural, and economic institutions during the country's first century of nationhood. However, their influence over the culture has declined with their drop in numbers. Since 1871, the proportion claiming British (that is, English, Scottish, Welsh, or Irish) origins has dropped continuously, from about 60% in 1871 to about 40% today, and the proportion claiming French origins has remained almost constant for a century or so, at about 30%. This means that about one-third of Canada's current population has ethnic origins that are neither French nor British.

Although the proportion of British and French Canadians in the population is declining, they remain dominant for a number of reasons. One is that Canada's ethnic groups are not distributed equally throughout the nation. The majority of the French Canadian population is in Quebec, for example, where they make up over 80% of the whole population. Despite this numerical majority, French Canadians in recent years have felt threatened by what they see as a decline in their numbers and have felt offended by the traditional economic domination of the British Canadian minority in Quebec. The numerical majority of the French Canadians has given them control over the provincial government and has allowed them to take steps to ensure their political, economic, and cultural domination within Quebec.

This last example illustrates an important point concerning ethnic group relations in Canada. British domination in Canada was founded on conquest – military conquest over the native peoples but also over the French. This resulted in 200 years of British domination that was as much psychological as social. The British saw Canada as "their" country and, as we shall see, they allowed others to enter Canada only if those others were seen as capable of integrating into a British milieu. Unlike the United States, where ethnic groups struggled to make it to the top, Canada's other ethnic groups were expected to retain their "entrance status," and to accept British economic, political, and social domination. The result was that almost all ethnic groups in Canada still accord high status to those of British background.

For example, Berry *et al* (1977) asked respondents in a national survey to rate ethnic groups on the extent to which each is perceived as "hardworking," "important," "Canadian," "clean," "likeable," and "interesting." As Porter might have predicted, the results show Canada's Charter Groups, the English (and Scottish) and French, topping the list with the most desirable qualities. Next come the northern Europeans (Dutch, Scandinavians, Belgians), then eastern Europeans (Hungarians, Poles, Jews, Czechoslovakians, Russians, Yugoslavians, Ukrainians), then southern Europeans (Italians, Portuguese, Spanish, Greeks), then visible minorities (native peoples, blacks, East Indians). While there are some anomalies (Japanese score well up the list, just below northern Europeans), Canadians rate the ethnic groups in the same order of preference as the Canadian government has recruited them for immigration over the past century.

As for French Canadians, Quebec's motto of *Je me souviens* ("I remember") reflects both their pride in their history and their social agenda. Canadians of French descent remember that almost all of Canada was once their country. They are determined to ensure that they are accorded the political and cultural rights to which they feel entitled. Like British Canadians, they do not really feel themselves to be an ethnic group but a "national" group. To many French Canadians, Quebec is "their" country. If they are to remain a part of Canada—which a significant minority do *not* favour—then they believe that it must be as equal partners in a state uniting two "nations," one English Canadian and one French Canadian.

Because both British and French Canadians see themselves as national groups, they have managed to get along in Canada for 200 years largely by living out separate lives. This separation was dramatized in Hugh Maclennan's renowned novel *Two Solitudes*. From a sociological point of view, however, a more apt description of British-French Canadian ethnic relations is that of *institutional self-segregation* (Guindon, 1968). **Institutional self-segregation** refers to the tendency of ethnic groups to voluntarily avoid contact by developing and maintaining separate institutions such as schools, churches, hospitals, newspapers, and even trade unions. In Quebec, where this tendency was mostly developed, the contact between British and French Canadians was limited to little more than politics and work. Otherwise, contact between the groups was minimal.

When other ethnic groups began to arrive in Canada after Confederation, this pattern of institutional self-segregation spread to these new arrivals, and to a large degree it still typifies ethnic group relations in Canada.

The native peoples

Canada's native or aboriginal peoples come from a wide variety of regional locales and cultural backgrounds. There are many variations among the groups that make up this population. They have different languages and cultural practices, and have traditionally thought of themselves as different ethnic or tribal groups. These differences are partly a result of living in different physical environments: forests *versus* plains *versus* coastal regions, for example. As well, **band** and **reserve** sizes differ greatly one from another. They differ also from one part of the country to another: for example, the average reserve or settlement in Ontario is about ten times the size of a reserve in British Columbia. Geographic distance and language differences have maintained and reinforced these cultural differences. Political, military, and economic conflicts—even wars—have also increased the differences.

Today Canada's native peoples have been divided into three main groups: Indians (both status and non-status), Eskimos, and Métis. Each of these groups includes several subgroups.

Registered or *status* Indians belong to a band. They fall under the jurisdiction of the Indian Act or, if they lack band membership, are registered with the Department of Indian Affairs and Northern Development. About 70% of

Canada's roughly 500 000 status Indians live on reserves, of which nearly 2300 exist in Canada today. Most of the others have migrated to cities, where economic opportunities are much better.

A second group of native people, *non-status* Indians, have lost their Indian status primarily through marriage to non-Indians, or as the children of such marriages. There were fewer than 100 000 in the Canadian Census of 1981. Many do not live on reserves. Bill C-31, passed in 1985 by the federal government, has allowed about 70 000 of the non-status Indians to regain their status.

The Eskimo people include the Inuvialuit of the western Arctic and the Inuit of the eastern Arctic and Labrador. Most of these roughly 25 000 people still live in their native communities. Unlike the Indian peoples, they have not moved to large cities in any significant numbers.

Métis are the descendants of native-white couples who never received registered Indian status. The 1981 Census counted fewer than 100 000 Métis. Most live in small rural communities or disperse among the non-native population. Though few live in separate Métis settlements, the Métis have an identity and culture that is distinct from that of the Indians.

Canada's native peoples experience many of the problems we typically associate with conditions in the Third World. Their rate of educational attainment is low, and they are unlikely to get a post-secondary education. They are much more likely than white Canadians to live below the poverty line. Their urban unemployment rates are far higher than the average. A large proportion of houses on reserves fail to meet national health and safety standards. Overcrowding is common, so the spread of infectious disease goes unchecked. Rates of infant and adult mortality are much higher than the national average, and life expectancy at birth is much lower. Native peoples are much more likely than average to die of infectious (especially respiratory and gastro-intestinal) diseases, and from accidents, poisoning, and violence. They are less likely than other Canadians to die from "diseases of the old," especially cancer and heart attack or stroke. Native peoples also have the highest alcoholism, suicide, and crime rates in Canada.

Recently, some sociologists have compared the situation of native peoples to that of other oppressed groups, calling their condition *internal colonization* (Frideres, 1988). **Internal colonization** is a concept describing the underprivileged status and exploitation of minority groups within a larger society.

In colonialism, the relationship between colonizer and colony is exploitative. Colonialism played a large part in the development of modern industrial capitalism. Europeans took control over African, Asian, and American lands, assumed the major role in governing them, removed valuable raw materials (including gold and silver), and forced the local people to work for very low wages. They also obliged the people to buy high-priced manufactured goods from the mother country by preventing the importation of similar goods from elsewhere and by denying the natives permission to make the goods locally.

Internal colonialism is different in one important respect: it applies to a group within the colonizing society, not thousands of miles away. Otherwise, the similarities are many. The relationship between prosperous city-dwelling whites and poor rural native peoples is also exploitative. Like the colonized people of the Third World, Canadian native peoples who remain on reserves do not have true self-government but are under the control of the Department of Indian Affairs and Northern Development.

Some would argue that these problems do not arise because whites *keep* native peoples outside the political and economic arena, as they do in South Africa. Native peoples, they maintain, are no more excluded than the Newfoundlanders who choose to live in little communities on barren land near fished-out waters. If they gave up their Indian status and entered the social and economic mainstream of Canadian society, they could have full political rights and equal access to the wealth, power, and prestige with all other Canadians. However, most native peoples are unwilling to do this. Their reluctance to leave the reserves for good, renounce Indian status, and become educated urban dwellers is because of their attachment to their land and way of life. Native peoples regard themselves as a separate society and have no desire to assimilate. In this respect, they are as jealous of their culture and political sovereignty as the francophones of Quebec.

At this time, the native peoples are insisting on achieving true self-government. The blockades erected by Mohawk Warriors at Oka, Quebec, in the summer of 1990 dramatized these demands. Although the federal government provides a broad range of services to the native peoples at almost no financial cost to them, many native peoples feel that they must take charge of their own lives if they are to control their future. Despite the apparent benevolence of the federal government, the native peoples do not forget the long legacy of military conquest, trickery, and betrayal on the part of white governments.

Even today, neither the federal nor provincial governments have honoured all of their treaty obligations. In effect, they have simply stolen away the native peoples' lands. While it is not clear that native peoples are victims of capitalist exploitation, there is no question that they are the victims of paternalism and neglect. Native peoples have little responsibility or control over their own lives—in fact, only as much as the white government yields up in a condescending spirit of parental generosity.

In the beginning, Canada belonged to Native Peoples. Representatives of the French and British charter groups took most of these lands away. Controversy rages today about the fairness of these old agreements.

European ethnics

The settlement of Canada varied with the country's changing need for labour power. In certain periods, when farmers or workers were needed, the Canadian government made more vigorous efforts to attract immigrants than at other times when land or work was in short supply. Over the last two decades, Canada has more readily accepted immigrants who are racially or culturally unlike the Charter Groups. In the early days of this country, however, there was a clear preference for people very much like the English and French: first for northern (Protestant) Europeans and secondarily for eastern and southern (Catholic) Europeans.

This preference for northern, Anglo-Saxon-like people is part of Canada's identity, part of its people's historic perception of Canada as the "true North, strong and free." The imagery of such racist myths often has long historic roots and great staying power. Historian Carl Berger (1970) finds this myth emerging first among the "imperialists" in the period 1867-1914—after Confederation, and during the first major phase of non-Anglo-Saxon immigration.

The imperialists theorized that Canada's northern climate gave our national character a high degree of energy, vigour, and strenuousness. Berger suggests that "The adjective 'northern' came to symbolize energy, strength, self-reliance, health and purity, and its opposite, 'southern', was equated with decay and effeminacy, even libertinism and disease" (Berger, 1970:129). This mythology favoured the immigration of other northern peoples. The myth-holders were grateful that Canada's harsh climate would discourage the immigration of "weaker races" such as American blacks or southern Europeans. They also encouraged southern Europeans who did come to Canada to emigrate to the United States.

This ideology was useful in several ways. First, it celebrated the difference between Canada and the United States, a matter of great concern during Canada's early nationhood. Second, it glorified Canada's dominant Charter Groups. Even the French Canadians—originally from Normandy, and therefore descendants of the same Scandinavian invaders who had conquered Britain—could be included in this mythology. Third, this ideology of northerness glamourized precisely that feature of Canadian life so many found unpalatable: the country's harsh climate and difficult terrain. It celebrated adversity, turning a sow's ear into a silk purse.

Following Confederation, the national government committed itself to strengthening national sovereignty against threats of American invasion by building a railroad from coast to coast, and by settling the prairies where population was sparse. There had already been some settlement by francophones and Métis, who had come with the fur trade and stayed. More people were needed, so the government launched a vigorous campaign to attract northern, then eastern, Europeans with promises of affordable land. In the United States, this approach was drawing large numbers of farmers to the adjacent midwestern and plains states.

But Canada was much less hospitable than the United States to the world's "tired, poor, huddled masses yearning to breathe free." Canadian labour unions and **nativist groups** clearly preferred white, northern (*versus* southern), and Protestant (*versus* Catholic) immigrants. The government's willingness to accept less-preferred groups only increased with a shortage of preferred applicants and pressure from business owners.

In the end, the demands of business for immigrant workers of "lower races" — workers who were willing to work long hours for almost nothing — won out over the concerns of the imperialists. Yet, in a way, a compromise was reached after all. Canada has permitted the large-scale immigration of racial and ethnic groups the imperialists had shunned. But the ideology that favoured northern over southern people has persisted, if below the national consciousness, to this very day.

In the first decade of this century, about one-and-a-half million immigrants came to Canada. The population Canada gained through immigration in this decade more than made up for population it had lost in the preceding four decades, when more people were leaving Canada for the United States than were coming into Canada. By 1911, large numbers of immigrants from Austria-Hungary, Germany, Russia (including Poland and the Ukraine), and Scandinavia were resident in Canada. Most lived on farms or in small towns. A majority had come to Ontario and the Prairies, and they have remained disproportionately numerous there ever since. However, even by 1911, over one-third were living in cities with populations of 25 000 or more. This attraction of immigrants to cities would grow throughout this century.

A second phase of immigration began around 1914 and continued until 1945. This phase marked a slowing in Canada's immigration; there were nowhere near as many immigrants to Canada then as before or after. Several forces interrupted immigration during this period. There were the First (1914-1918) and Second (1939-1945) World Wars, when leaving Europe was difficult and Canada was unwilling to accept immigrants. A worldwide Depression in the 1930s increased joblessness in Canada. This reduced business owners' demands for immigrant workers and also increased outmigration to the United States, with a net loss of migrant population.

In the 1920s, however, immigration to Canada was fairly brisk. The economy was booming and industrial production was demanding more and more workers. Increasing numbers came from northern and eastern Europe, as well as some from Italy and other parts of southern Europe.

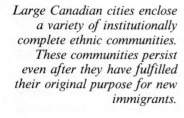

Large Canadian cities enclose a variety of institutionally complete ethnic communities. These communities persist even after they have fulfilled their original purpose for new immigrants.

Ethnic Origins of the Population, by Province, 1986

	British	French	British and French	British and/or French and some other	Other	Total
				%		
Newfoundland	89.0	2.0	4.3	2.4	2.3	100.0
Prince Edward Island	69.1	8.9	12.1	6.7	3.2	100.0
Nova Scotia	62.7	6.2	9.3	13.1	8.6	100.0
New Brunswick	46.9	33.3	10.0	6.6	3.2	100.0
Quebec	5.9	77.8	2.7	2.7	11.0	100.0
Ontario	43.8	5.9	5.7	14.3	30.2	100.0
Manitoba	29.6	5.3	3.4	17.7	44.0	100.0
Saskatchewan	29.8	3.4	2.8	22.5	41.5	100.0
Alberta	34.4	3.3	3.9	22.3	36.1	100.0
British Columbia	41.8	2.4	3.7	19.6	32.5	100.0
Canada	33.6	24.4	4.6	12.6	24.9	100.0

After the Second World War, immigration began a third phase. As before, large numbers came from Britain, northern and eastern Europe. As well, throughout the 1950s, '60s, and '70s, vastly increased numbers came from southern Europe: first Italy, then other Mediterranean countries (Greece, Portugal, and Spain). A majority of these immigrants made for the rapidly growing cities of central Canada and remained there.

Visible minorities

After 1970, the numbers of Asians coming to Canada began to increase dramatically. People of Chinese and Japanese ancestry have lived in Canada for over a century. Some immigrants came from China to work on the Canadian railways and afterwards settled in the prairies or British Columbia. As Peter Li (1982) reports, in the first half of this century just about every small town in the west had a Chinese laundry and Chinese restaurant.

However, it was in the 1970s and '80s that the numbers of Chinese immigrants to Canada swelled. A large proportion came from Hong Kong, a British colony in China since the 19th century. As well, for the first time large numbers of Asians began to come from other countries of the British commonwealth, especially India and Pakistan. By the 1980s, the numbers of immigrants from other parts of Asia (like Korea and Vietnam), Latin America, and the Caribbean were also increasing dramatically. Many of these people were fleeing poverty, desperate postwar conditions, or political oppression. Others—among them prosperous Hong Kong Chinese—were bringing large amounts of investment capital, which earned them a high priority with Canadian immigration officials. The vast majority of immigrants in the past decade have come to Canada's cities, especially Toronto, Vancouver, Calgary, and Edmonton. In this way they have increased an already rapid growth of population in those cities.

This immigration is valuable to Canada. It brings skills in manufacturing and services that the country does not supply through natural increase and training. Canada's birthrate has been dropping almost continuously for a century. (An exception was the period 1945-1965, when the Baby Boom occurred.) There is a growing shortage of people to do the work of a highly developed economy. The shortage is made even worse by limited educational opportunities for children from the working class—what John Porter (1965) called "mobility deprivation." Canadians are simply not educating enough of their children with appropriate specialized skills.

The new immigrants meet Canada's needs for a highly educated work force, but they are largely **visible minorities**, or nonwhite racial groups. They do not resemble Canada's dominant group, white Anglo-Saxon Protestants, very closely. They differ markedly in both cultural traits and physical features: because they are easily identifiable, visible minorities are easy targets for discrimination and scapegoating. Thus, the immigration of large numbers of visible minorities has forced many Canadians to confront racial prejudice seriously for the first time.

By 1980, Canada was admitting large numbers of immigrants it had turned away on racial grounds several decades earlier. The significance of this change in immigration policy testifies to two major changes in our society. One is the growth of toleration for people who are racially and culturally different from the Charter Groups. While prejudice against visible minorities persists in Canada today, such sentiments are less often voiced, less viciously expressed, and less officially approved than they once were. The change also testifies to changes in Canada's social, political, and cultural processes. Our immigration policies have always met the labour needs of big business. Today business needs the skills, hard work, and investment capital of city-dwelling visible minorities. This need has changed Canada's historic preference for white northern Europeans. In future, new needs will continue to reshape Canada's immigration policies and, in this way, change the ethnic and racial composition of Canada's population.

PATTERNS OF ETHNIC AND RACE RELATIONS
Pluralism and the vertical mosaic

As our discussion of the different ethnic groups in Canada shows, Canada has always been a **pluralist** society: one in which ethnic groups keep their distinctive cultural traits, preserve their group identity, and remain conscious of who they are and where they came from. Canadian minorities keep their heritage alive while living in harmony among members of the dominant culture and members of other ethnic groups. This pluralism is rooted in a founding fact of Canadian history: the federation of two distinct cultures, French and English.

As we noted earlier, pluralism puts the issue of ethnic group relations at the very heart of Canadian social and political life. How do the members of different ethnic groups deal with one another in a pluralist society? What rights (or obligations) are assigned to some that are denied to others? Is there a majority or dominant culture? How are different ethnic groups integrated into this culture? In a very broad sense we can say that ethnic group relations in a society take the form either of assimilation or of segregation.

Assimilation, whether social or cultural (or both), is a process whereby members of an ethnic group abandon their own social patterns and adopt those of the dominant culture. It often results in a growing similarity between the life chances of what was formerly a minority group and those of the dominant group. Thus, the economic and occupational characteristics of the two groups become similar or even the same. In time, the minority group may merge, or lose itself, within the dominant group.

There are various forms of assimilation. **Acculturation** is the process of becoming a member of a new culture – usually the dominant culture – through learning the behaviour patterns, language, customs, values, norms, and role expectations of members of that culture. This is only possible, of course, if members of the dominant culture are willing to interact with the individual. Acculturation is usually necessary if more complete assimilation is to succeed.

Amalgamation is the process whereby members of different racial or ethnic groups blend together in a new cultural mix, with all groups contributing equally. The description of the United States as a *melting pot*, in which people from a wide variety of different ethnic groups and different backgrounds come to think of themselves as equally American, is a version of this form of assimilation. In Canada, amalgamation is more likely to occur at the individual level through intermarriage among members of different groups.

The opposite of assimilation is segregation. **Segregation** is the act or process of setting apart two or more groups of people within the same territory. It may be social separation, as when one group does not associate with or interact with another. More often, it is physical separation. In this case the two groups live in separate and distinct geographic areas, whether in ghettoes or in separate but equal neighbourhoods. *Apartheid* in South Africa is a particularly extreme form of segregation.

Self-segregation is segregation chosen and practised voluntarily by the members of a given ethnic group. Neither the larger society nor the dominant group imposes it. Groups that separate themselves from the mainstream of society, such as the Hutterites, a rural religious group in western Canada, would be an example of such self-segregation. As we noted earlier, many ethnic groups in Canada are characterized by institutional self-segregation. In this case they do participate in the mainstream of Canadian life but they also seek to maintain their own institutions and their own culture.

An alternative to assimilation or segregation as a form of ethnic group relations is genocide. **Genocide** is the extermination of an entire minority population. Methods may include systematic slaughter with bombs or chemical weapons, or using gas chambers in concentration camps. In modern history, genocide has been attempted against the Jews, Armenians, and Gypsies

(Romany), to name a few. Native peoples of North and South America have also died in large numbers from infectious diseases and through conditions such as mass starvation that make survival impossible.

Elements of ethnic self-segregation

We noted earlier that certain ethnic groups are not distributed equally in all parts of the country: for example, there are many Ukrainian Canadians but few Chinese Canadians in rural Manitoba, while there are many Chinese Canadians and relatively few Ukrainian Canadians in downtown Toronto. This uneven pattern largely reflects different histories of immigration: when a particular group arrived in Canada, to what jobs members were recruited or were able to find, and where those jobs were located. They also reflect **chain migration**, the process whereby people come to areas where similar, often related, people are living.

Physical segregation also reflects choices that are fairly enduring. For example, certain groups favour rural over urban life. Typically, visible minorities (excluding native peoples), Jews, Italians, and Greeks prefer urban life in Canada. Nevertheless, within cities, they are likely to live in ethnic enclaves. Middle-class Italian Canadians are more likely to live with other middle-class Italian Canadians than with middle-class Chinese or Jewish Canadians. Working-class Italian Canadians are also more likely to live with working-class Italian Canadians than with working-class Chinese or Jewish Canadians. It is hard to say whether ethnicity or class would dominate, if people had to choose: that is, whether a middle-class Italian Canadian would rather live with middle-class Jewish Canadians or working-class Italian Canadians.

Residential segregation by ethnic and racial group (as well as class) occurs in all cities of North America: it is not uniquely Canadian. Nor is it recent; sociologists have studied the phenomenon for generations now. But the degree of residential segregation by ethnic groups in Canada is particularly high in the major cities.

This is not to deny the possibility of change or that more residential mixing may be occurring today than a generation ago. Yet ethnic segregation within each class or income level remains a fact of social life. It is largely a matter of choice, not the result of overt discrimination, although it may sometimes result from the fear of discrimination. Most likely, it is an indication of ethnic identification and communal loyalty. Therefore, residential segregation is greatest among recent immigrants, especially in groups characterized by a high degree of what sociologist Raymond Breton (1964) has called institutional completeness.

Institutional completeness

Institutional completeness (Breton, 1964) is a measure of the degree to which an ethnic group provides its members with all the services they require through their own institutions such as churches, schools, banks, and media, separate from those of the larger society. In a group characterized by a very high degree of institutional completeness, group members need not interact with or depend on members of the larger society.

Full institutional completeness is rare, however, and ethnic communities differ as much from one another as they do from the dominant Anglo-Saxon community. When many groups have a high degree of institutional completeness, many ethnic communities exist within one large society.

The extent to which an ethnic community has developed a full range of institutions, which parallel those of the larger society, may depend on such factors as the size of the ethnic population, the prosperity of its members, the strength of friendship, family, and work networks among members, the strength of a shared sense of solidarity and ethnic identification, and the range of employment opportunities that are available in the region in which the ethnic community is located.

A community's degree of institutional completeness both reflects and determines the proportion of individuals who conduct most of their personal relations within the ethnic group. Ethnic organizations such as schools, camps, churches, business associations, social clubs, mutual aid societies, and credit unions provide a context within which community members can meet and do business with other community members. These organizations make people more conscious of their ethnic origins. Like professional associations and unions, these organizations also press for group interests.

In Canada, the degree of institutional completeness developed by an ethnic community is also shaped by the number and kinds of problems immigrants face on arrival. Immigrants may be unable to speak English or French. They may be unaccustomed to urban, industrial life or lack marketable job skills and job contacts outside their own community. On the positive side, they can speak in their native tongue, and they may have social or kinship contacts brought from their homeland that they can use to develop job and business relations. So new immigrants create a community that plays to their strengths and provides assistance for their weaknesses. This is particularly true for groups that face serious discrimination on their arrival in Canada and for some time afterward. Living in a community with a high level of institutional completeness can protect immigrants in an actively hostile social and economic environment. Jews and Chinese in Canada, both victims of serious discrimination, have historically practised this self-protective strategy.

However, an ethnic community often maintains a structurally and culturally separate community even after the initial discrimination that created it has diminished or disappeared. The ethnic community not only defends its members against discrimination and pressures towards assimilation, it also sustains ethnic group cohesion by creating institutions, gaining control of resources, and providing a variety of educational, cultural, and social services. Also, institutions formed within an ethnic community generate a demand for the services they provide. Thus, the mere survival of ethnic communities does not prove ethnic discrimination is occurring. Conversely, some groups still suffering from discrimination have little opportunity to protect their own interests organizationally, despite good reasons to do so. For example, Canada's blacks by and large lack the degree of institutional completeness that would help them prosper as a community. Because blacks come from so many different cultural backgrounds and actually make up many different ethnic groups, they are unable to unite in order to develop common institutions.

At the beginning of this chapter we noted that Canada's ethnic pluralism and institutional self-segregation have led sociologists to describe Canada as a mosaic. But we also noted that it is a *vertical* mosaic, one in which ethnicity has economic as well as cultural and organizational consequences. Because of this connection between ethnicity and life chances, Canadian sociologists have made a close study of Canada's system of ethnic stratification.

Ethnic stratification

Ethnic stratification is the hierarchical ranking of groups in society on the basis of ethnicity. The hierarchy is dominated by people with the power to define which physical or cultural characteristics are most socially desirable—usually their own. Other groups are ranked on the basis of their similarity to the top group. In a society that is ethnically stratified, each ethnic group occupies a well-defined position in the social structure.

Ethnic stratification is only possible in a society whose members attach cultural meanings to various physical and cultural characteristics. There is nothing inherent in the characteristics themselves—whether skin colour or hair colour, shape of nose or cheekbones; or preferred foods and clothing—that naturally signals "good" or "bad," "smart" or "dumb," "hardworking" or "lazy." Ethnic stratification exists because people attach meaning to these characteristics and interact with others on the basis of these meanings. For example, they may assume that lighter skin indicates a higher worth than darker skin and, accordingly, treat their light-skinned slaves better than dark-skinned ones.

The study of ethnic stratification in Canada took centre-stage in Canadian sociology in 1965, when John Porter published his classic work *The Vertical Mosaic*. It provided a view of Canadian society that emphasized the connection between class inequality and ethnicity. Porter claimed that Canadian society is stratified along racial and ethnic lines, with the English and French Canadian Charter Groups at the top of the social ladder. Other ethnic groups rank roughly according to how closely they resemble Anglo-Saxons, who form the dominant group. Porter argued that you could predict a person's education, income, and job prestige by knowing his or her ethnic origin.

This correlation between ethnicity and socio-economic status arose from the patterns of immigration we have discussed. Certain groups had come to do certain kinds of work: the Ukrainians to farm the prairies, the Italians to build Canada's cities, and so on. Over time, they and their descendants had remained at the same socio-economic level—sometimes even the same industry—because of discrimination and the lack of educational opportunities.

According to Porter, Canada had always been different culturally from the United States. The United States had never been a vertical mosaic, he said. It has always been a *melting pot*, which sought and achieved near total assimilation of its members. In the United States, people considered themselves Americans first and ethnic minorities second, if at all. Canadians are less aware of their national identity than Americans. Perhaps by default, their ethnic and regional identities (which are closely tied) are much more important than in the United States.

EXHIBIT 6.2

LANGUAGE RETENTION AND GROUP SURVIVAL

People may encounter difficulties when they have to work among people of another ethnic origin, often in a second language. For francophones, having to speak English has been an inconvenience, a limit on their opportunities, and a slap at their pride. As well, it has endangered their cultural survival.

For this reason, francophone sociologists have been interested in measuring "linguistic mobility," the rates at which people are giving up one language to speak another. Francophones are afraid that the rate of mobility out of French and into English is greater than the rate of mobility out of English and into French (Lachapelle, 1980). Recent research shows that in Quebec itself, these fears are unwarranted (Health and Welfare Canada, 1989); but everywhere else, they are justified. Outside Quebec, the home use of French is very likely to disappear.

Other factors besides language mobility affect the numbers who speak French. Specifically, they are the rate of natural increase (the excess of births over deaths) of francophones and the willingness of immigrants to adopt the French language for their own use in Canada. Francophones are worried by the low and declining birth rates in Quebec, and the provincial government has already made some efforts to encourage more childbearing. The government is also making great efforts to control the selection of immigrants in favour of those who speak French or would likely do so, and to force immigrant children to study French.

Porter believed that only by increasing opportunities for post-secondary education and by encouraging ethnic minorities to get this education would ethnic inequality start to break down. He became a vigorous (and successful) advocate for the expansion of Canada's university and college systems.

Since Porter released his findings on the vertical mosaic in 1965, sociologists have researched every corner of this question. They have done so with better data and more powerful techniques of analysis than Porter had available. As a result, they have drawn different conclusions, summarized by Brym and Fox (1989: 107):

(1) Ethnicity is not a particularly good predictor of either socio-economic status or of mobility.

(2) Ethnic inequality seems to be decreasing over time.

(3) The members of many ethnic groups do experience considerable "net" upward mobility.

(4) The effect of ethnicity on "status attainment" becomes weaker as immigrants become more "acculturated."

Brym and Fox concede that "these generalizations do not hold as strongly for members of some groups—especially some racial minorities—as they do overall." Canada remains a vertical mosaic along racial, if not ethnic lines, then. Considering how much Canadian society has changed since 1965, we cannot

Racism exaggerates the extent and importance of physical differences to increase social distance between groups and to justify exploitation and scapegoating.

now know if Porter was simply wrong in his analysis of Canadian society or if his analysis was right for the period of time in which it was produced.

Porter may also have been right about some groups and wrong about others. Simply being a member of a non-Charter Group—an ethnic minority—does not guarantee low chances for mobility in Canada. Some ethnic groups do much better in Canadian society than others do. In fact, membership in an ethnic group helps some Canadians quite a great deal. In many workplaces, employers recruit people with ethnic backgrounds that are similar to their own. As a result, people of the same ethnic origins control specific organizations and even entire industries. An ethnic group can monopolize an economic activity, allowing access to that activity only or primarily on the basis of ethnic background. This benefits members of that ethnic group. Of course, in a complex industrial society such as our own, this is relatively rare, and the industry cannot be one that is *too* lucrative, or it would attract more competition from members of other ethnic groups. The near monopoly Italian gardeners have on their occupation in some cities is an example.

The fact that Porter's findings do not apply to some groups tells us that we must study how ethnic groups act on their own behalf to protect themselves and further their own interests, not merely how they react to the actions of the Charter Groups.

ETHNIC BOUNDARY MAINTENANCE AND SURVIVAL

Language and culture

In a study of the survival of ethnic communities in Canada, sociologist Jeffrey Reitz (1980) surveyed ten groups in five Canadian cities. He wanted to discover which factors cause some groups to remain cohesive communities and others to disappear through the assimilation of their membership.

Reitz measured a variety of indicators of people's attachment to their ethnic group. The most important included the following:

(1) ethnic neighbourhood residence—the degree of residential segregation of group members;

(2) ethnic identification – the degree to which members emphasized their ethnic ancestry in identifying themselves (for example, whether a man of German ancestry called himself German, German-Canadian, Canadian-German or just Canadian);

(3) endogamy – the degree to which members of the group had married other members of the same ethnic group;

(4) ethnic church affiliation – whether and how often people attended the church most closely affiliated with their own group;

(5) in-group interaction – the proportion of friends and social contacts a person had among people of the same ethnic group; and

(6) ethnic language retention – how well a person knew and spoke the ancestral language of the group to which he or she belonged.

Reitz found that all six of these aspects of group involvement were strongly correlated with one another. However, some were more powerful predictors of community cohesion than others. In-group interaction (5) and ethnic language retention (6) were tied as the best predictors of group cohesion, and they were over 25% better predictors than residential segregation (1) and ethnic affiliation (2).

Stating Reitz's finding another way, if you want to tell how well a group is maintaining its ethnic community and culture – what its chances for survival are – look at patterns of interaction and language retention. A good example of the perceived correlation of language to cultural maintenance is the importance francophones in Quebec place on the continuance of French as the dominant tongue. In turn, in-group interaction and language retention are highly correlated with each other. What's more, they are the most important ways of staying involved in one's ethnic group and keeping up a personal identification with the group. They even increase a person's chances of marrying within the group. By contrast, living in a neighbourhood dominated by your own ethnic group is a much less important way of staying involved, *especially* if you do not speak the ethnic language. Said another way, people can remain strongly involved in their ethnic group even if they move far away from the ethnic community, *if* they keep up their ethnic language use.

Language knowledge and use, then, is a key to ethnic cultural survival. Reitz found that ethnic language knowledge and use are very common among southern Europeans and Chinese people and only half as likely among northern and eastern Europeans. In part this difference is a result of the more recent arrival of southern European and Chinese immigrants. In general, ethnic language retention declines with the number of generations since a person's ancestors immigrated or the number of years since an immigrant arrived in Canada.

However, even holding constant the time since arrival in Canada, some ethnic groups are more cohesive than others. The southern European and Chinese communities continue to be more cohesive than northern and eastern European ones. For this reason, Reitz expresses uncertainty about whether widespread language retention causes ethnic communities to be more cohesive and institutionally complete, or whether community cohesion and completeness leads to language retention. Quite possibly both forces are operating.

EXHIBIT 6.3

Chinese Restaurants On The Prairies

In settling small towns and cities in western Canada, Chinese immigrants required a pool of money to get started, so many small businesses were created as partnerships based on kinship.

Peter Li, in his article, 'Chinese immigrants on the Canadian prairie, 1910-47', quotes one immigrant as saying,

> In the small towns you don't have to know too much English. Just use your eyes to see what they want. . . . You don't have to do too much because the menu is the same from year to year. . . . The business was cheap. . . . Save all the money, and then you can buy a business. . . . As long as you had a place to sleep and some work, then it didn't matter. In the winter time it was cold and there were no people [in Goven]. Some days we had only a few people, just sold a few loaves of bread and a few cups of coffee, that's all. No, it didn't matter as long as you had a place to stay.

Another talked about the way a partnership worked in this kind of business:

> The partners get a few relatives together and just chip in some money each. . . . If there is no business and you have to leave, then you sell it and split the money, that's all. . . . Everyday [we] fixed meals, cooked the meat, made a few pies, and made some soup. Whatever you needed, we made them. . . . There's no boss. Everyone did it right. . . . Just worked for ourselves. In the end, whoever had a share [in the partnership] had a share of the profit . . . if you really don't like it and can't get along, then you can buy me out, or I can buy you out.

Source: Peter S. Li "Chinese immigrants on the Canadian prairie, 1910-47" *Canadian Review of Sociology and Anthropology*, 19(4) 1982, pp. 527-540

It makes sense that language retention would play an important part in maintaining the ethnic community. First, the use of a minority language includes only community members and excludes everyone else. In that way, it forms an invisible social boundary around the group. This is bound to influence patterns of social interaction: who is friends with whom, and how commonly people interact outside their ethnic group. Second, the opportunity to speak one's native language in Canada lessens the pressure on immigrants to assimilate. Third, as we recall from the chapter on culture, language is a mechanism that encodes particular ways of viewing the world. Use of the ethnic language maintains ethnic traditions of thinking and acting, and traditional old-country values. It also symbolizes identification with, and commitment to, those cultural values and ways of thinking.

Distinctive symbols and concerns

Language use is only one part—however conspicuous—of a community's effort to maintain a distinctive identity and tradition. Ethnic churches, schools, and other cultural institutions play the same role.

We saw earlier that ethnic church attendance is a very good predictor of ethnic community attachment. A person who attends the ethnic church regularly is very likely to live in an ethnic neighbourhood, interact regularly with other members of the ethnic group, and retain his or her ethnic language. Like language, religion encodes a system of cultural assumptions about life, the world, and the supernatural. Moreover, attending one church means not attending another: again, church affiliation draws a social boundary around the group.

Thus, involvement in an ethnic religion may limit the aspirations and opportunities of group members, thereby aiding group continuity. This effect will be greatest where ethnic religion shapes ethnic education, as it does in parochial schools. For example, before the Quiet Revolution of the 1960s, Quebec's French-language, Catholic school system played an important part in maintaining a traditional humanistic (rather than scientific or business-oriented) outlook on life. One consequence of this was to keep some Quebec francophones from either scientific or business careers by limiting their opportunities to do otherwise.

Ethnic politics

Institutional completeness is another important element of ethnic differentiation and survival. The degree of **parallelism** – or average institutional completeness of ethnic groups – varies from one society to another.

In societies like the Soviet Union, efforts have been made to keep parallelism low in order to strengthen loyalty to the nation-state. Religious as well as ethnic identification has been discouraged. However, these efforts have never met with complete success. Today, both ethnic and religious groups are making much stronger demands for communal autonomy than ever in the past.

In societies like Canada, where parallelism has always been high, many ethnic communities have a high degree of institutional completeness. Some, such as the Hutterites who live in rural parts of western Canada, are almost completely self-sufficient. Often, such groups will interact with other groups mainly through their communal leaders. Non-leaders are less likely to interact with people from other ethnic backgrounds. Even groups that are far less self-sufficient will often delegate to community leaders the responsibility for *political* contact with other ethnic groups. This fact makes the leadership of ethnic communities a very important issue in Canada. Group leaders will have to reach agreement with other group leaders. In a society made up of highly parallel structures, the politics of the country are the politics of competing ethnic groups.

The degree of parallelism has a large effect on the kinds of matters that will become issues in ethnic communities, and on the character of social bargaining. These problems arise because groups often consider themselves to be in a *zero-sum* situation, where one ethnic group gains power at the expense of another. The greater the parallelism, the more likely ethnic communities are to want access to the same resources and rewards, and the greater a threat one community represents to another. As well, the greater the parallelism, the more conflicts are likely to arise over jurisdiction and the more effort each group will make to capture control of the political system.

This is why politics in Canada are more influenced by ethnicity than by class. People are far more likely to vote for a candidate of their own ethnic origin than

EXHIBIT 6.4

CHANGING ATTITUDES TOWARDS INTERMARRIAGE

Canadian survey data show that Canadians' attitudes towards intermarriage between different racial and cultural groups—Catholics and Protestants, Jews and non-Jews, and whites and blacks—have become more tolerant since 1968. In this respect, anglophones and francophones are just about equal in leading the way. Ethnic minorities whose mother tongue is neither French nor English are less tolerant and changing more slowly. This suggests they are more worried than the Charter Groups about the problem intermarriage poses for ethnic survival.

It would be interesting to learn whether the groups who are least tolerant are those whose survival is most in danger: because of small or declining group size, low institutional completeness, or high rates of intermarriage.

Language Group Differences in Attitudes Toward Mixed Marriages: Findings from Four National Surveys of Canadian Adults[1]

Year of Survey	1968			1973			1978			1983		
Lang. Group[2]	FQ	EC	OC	FQ	EC	OC	FQ	EC	OC	FQ	EC	OC
Attitudes Toward Marriage Between:												
R.C./Prot.												
Approve	60	60	67	53	73	63	78	81	65	84	86	77
Don't Know	13	11	7	28	14	16	10	11	12	5	7	13
Disapprove	27	29	26	20	13	21	11	8	23	11	8	10
Jews/Non-Jews												
Approve	47	53	60	43	62	51	77	74	56	80	78	68
Don't Know	30	17	13	39	25	25	12	18	21	9	14	14
Disapprove	24	30	27	18	13	24	11	8	24	11	8	17
Whites/Blacks												
Approve	46	29	36	50	42	46	73	61	48	86	66	54
Don't Know	16	11	8	28	20	20	12	14	17	4	10	17
Disapprove	38	60	46	22	38	44	16	25	35	11	24	28

[1] The figures are percentages; the totals may not sum to 100% due to rounding errors.
[2] The language groups are French-speaking Quebecers (FQ), English-speaking Canadians (EC), and Other Canadians (OC) whose mother tongues were other than English or French.

Sources: Statistics Canada, 1986 Census of Canada. Reproduced with the permission of the Minister of Supply and Services Canada, 1990. Ronald D. Lambert and James Curtis "Racial attitudes of Canadians" *Past and Present* February 1985, pp. 2-4. By permission of the authors.

for a candidate of their own social class. Leaders can get ethnic communities to vote as a bloc more consistently than unions can mobilize the support of their membership. Gaining power requires controlling organizations and networks of organizations. Networks are hard to build across ethnic groups, largely because of language barriers and conflicting group interests. As a result, social networks develop within linguistic and ethnic groups. In the struggle for organizational power, people use the networks they have at their disposal. To a large degree, community leaders are the main beneficiaries of ethnic parallelism, but they are not the only ones. Some people have always gained benefits from belonging to a highly organized and powerful ethnic group.

These comments on ethnic politics apply most to the French Canadians in Quebec but, increasingly, to other large and well-organized ethnic groups like Italian Canadians, Ukrainian Canadians, and Jewish Canadians as well. As their numbers, capital, and institutional completeness grow, these ethnic groups become a more and more potent force in Canadian politics. The political party most skilled at getting the support of ethnic elites has the best chance of winning elections in Canada today.

Benefits to be gained through self-segregation—social, cultural, political— are easy to see. However, the flip side of inclusion is exclusion. What seems to one person like a mere preference for "people like myself" may seem like discrimination or even racism to someone else.

PREJUDICE AND DISCRIMINATION

Although the two terms are often confused, social scientists treat prejudice and discrimination as two distinct phenomena. **Prejudice** is a negative, hostile social attitude toward members of a particular group. All members of the group are assumed to have undesirable qualities as a result of their group membership. **Discrimination** refers to actions carried out by an individual or organization against another individual because of his or her group membership. In particular, it is the denial of access to opportunities that would be granted to equally qualified and deserving members of one's own group.

An important element in prejudice is the use of **stereotypes**—fixed, unchanging mental images that embrace all that is believed to be typical of members of a given group. When we make use of stereotypes, we categorize people or things without regard to their individual characteristics or what can be called reality-testing.

The ability to form general categories is an essential feature of human thought. Without it we could not make sense of the world. Being able to classify our experiences, the people around us, and the material objects of our culture under general headings enables us to behave in new circumstances. We can then respond in appropriate ways to things and people we have never seen before. It allows us to carry over what we have learned in one situation to another, similar situation. Usually, experience and knowledge continually modify our categories. However, unlike other forms of categorization, stereotyping provides categories that are little, if at all, modified by experience and knowledge. People will often ignore or re-interpret experiences in which an individual does not

Though slavery has played little part in Canadian history, there has been no shortage of racism and racial discrimination.

conform to the stereotype of the group, rather than change the stereotype.

Stereotypes are not the same as prejudice. Indeed, we routinely stereotype things and people in our world, to simplify our living. For example, the claim that "blondes have more fun" is a stereotype. Like any stereotype, it may not be accurate; but if we act as though it is accurate, we will make it so. Moreover, it is an unprejudiced stereotype and implies no malice against either blondes or non-blondes.

However, a great many stereotypes *are* both prejudiced and prejudicial. They rationalize our prejudices against racial and ethnic minorities, giving them shape and order. In doing so they seem to justify prejudice. There are many common-sense ways of demonstrating the wrongness and stupidity of such prejudice. Leave aside the morality of the acts, or the rights and feelings of the victims of prejudice. Consider only the consequences for the prejudiced person. We have all heard that it is foolish to "judge a book by its cover," since doing so loses us the pleasure of reading what may be a very good book. The same applies to people, only more so. There is no clearer evidence of the harmfulness of prejudice than the effect of Naziism's anti-Semitic policies on Germany itself.

The German government used up vast treasures of money and labour power administering its racist policies—money, time, and effort that would have been better spent improving the lives of average Germans. Its racism destroyed the German universities, Germany's fine arts, its professional, scientific and engineering capabilities, and it even damaged Germany's business community and civil service—all in an effort to keep non-Aryans out of public life.

Germany and the Germans had to pay a heavy price for their foolish prejudice, and most people have learned the folly of racism from that experience.

Some research suggests that racial and ethnic stereotyping has declined in the last 50 years. Through social contacts and the mass media, people are learning more about others who differ from them racially and ethnically. It is hard to stereotype a group when you know many actual people who belong to the group, yet who repeatedly violate the stereotype. Still, while it may be in decline, evidence shows us that stereotypes remain.

Social distance

Prejudice is also likely to express itself in **social distance**, a reserve in interaction between people who belong to groups ranked as superior and inferior in status. The differences in status giving rise to social distance may be based on many relationships, such as class, race/ethnicity, or authority relationships (doctor-patient or teacher-student relationships, for example).

Social distance does not imply aversion, nor does it necessarily rule out certain kinds of intimacy. However all "distant" relationships are unequal. They are governed by norms and expectations about the relationship between superior and inferior, and such relationships are possible only so long as each participant keeps his or her "proper place."

In race and ethnic relations, social distance may be accompanied by fear, suspicion, and hostility. A commonly used measure of social distance, developed by E.S. Bogardus (1959), asks people to indicate to which steps on the following scale they would admit members of various ethnic and racial groups:

1. to close kinship by marriage
2. to my club as personal chums
3. to my street as neighbours
4. to employment in my occupation
5. to citizenship in my country
6. as visitors only to my country
7. would exclude from my country

Research using this procedure generally shows that people of different income, regional, educational, occupational, and even ethnic groups display a similar pattern of preferences in rating other groups. In the United States, the most acceptable groups—those granted the least distance on average, or considered equals—are those most like the dominant white, Anglo-Saxon group: namely, the (white) English and (white) Canadians. A majority of people find them acceptable as citizens, neighbours, even kinsmen. At the other extreme, white respondents have put Hindus, Turks, and blacks at the greatest distance, on average.

In a similar Canadian study (Mackie, 1974), Albertans put "Canadians," British, and Americans (meaning the dominant WASP majority of citizens) at the least social distance, followed closely by northern Europeans and French Canadians, then eastern Europeans and finally visible minorities—in

EXHIBIT 6.5

IS THERE A RACIST PERSONALITY TYPE?

Shortly after the Second World War, the American Jewish Committee decided to sponsor a major interdisciplinary study of anti-Semitism. Its goal was, ultimately, to understand how Naziism could have arisen in Europe and, secondarily, to learn whether it could arise in North America as well. The research team was headed by expatriate German sociologist, Theodor Adorno.

Through questionnaires, psychological testing and structured interviews, Adorno and his co-researchers found that anti-Semitism is strongly correlated with generalized racism and both, in turn, are part of a larger cluster of characteristics the researchers came to call the *authoritarian personality* type.

Authoritarian personalities are politically and economically conservative, as well as prejudiced against a wide variety of ideas, activities, and social groups. They are so rigid in their thinking that they are unable to change their ethnic stereotypes even when personal experience with minority people provides contradictory evidence. Faced with a contradiction, authoritarians typically divide the ethnic or racial group in two—the good ones (whom they know) and bad ones (all the rest). For example, one female student told an interviewer that

> There are Jews and Jews. I have a very good friend who is a Jew—never enters into our relationship except that she is in a Jewish sorority. (Would you want her in your sorority?) Well . . . (pause) . . . I don't think I'd have any objections. (Would you let in all Jewish girls?) No. One Jew is alright but you get a whole mob and . . . ! (What happens?) They get into anything and they'll control it—they'll group together for their own interests—the kike Jew is as dishonest as they come. . . . I knew a lot of Jews in high school. They kept pretty much to themselves. Don't think I'm echoing. I would like Jews as long as they don't reflect typical Jewish qualities. Typical Jewish nose, mouth, voice. The presence of a Jew creates feeling of tension.

Ultimately the researchers traced authoritarian thinking to childhood experiences in a very particular kind of family: a family in which children are insufficiently loved, strongly disciplined, and ridiculed for failure or weakness. Can you see the connection between these childhood experiences and adult authoritarianism?

Source: T.W. Adorno et al *The Authoritarian Personality*. New York: W.W. Norton, 1969, pp. 625-6. Copyright 1950 by the American Jewish Committee. Reprinted by Permission of Harper & Row, Publishers, Inc.

descending order, Chinese, Japanese, West Indians, Eskimos, East Indians, native Indians, and Métis. (At the very bottom of the scale were Hutterites, who themselves try to stay a distance away from other Canadians.) On average, respondents wanted twice as much social distance from the visible minorities as they did from "Canadians."

There is some slight variation in results depending on who is doing the rating. Typically, someone will rate his or her own group higher on the list (indicating less social distance) than a person outside the group would do. For example, American blacks accord other blacks less distance than whites do. The conformity of minority groups to dominant views does not mean repudiating one's own ethnic group. Otherwise, most people choose the same prevailing order of acceptability as all other groups. Obviously the pull of majority opinion has a great influence, regardless of personal experience.

To some degree, measures of social distance simply confirm other measures of prejudice and stereotyping. We prefer being close to others we consider like ourselves, people who possess the qualities we idealize (if not possess). They may also reflect actual experiences of social distance: we may prefer to be with people we have been with. People we have not been with—people we scarcely know—are not people we want to imagine being close to. However, Mackie found that "greater social distance is *not* associated with either more frequent or more extreme attribution of negative traits." (Mackie, 1974:125).

Interestingly, social distance is often a function of geographic distance. Statistics show that intermarriage across the anglophone-francophone line is more likely the more common the contact between these groups. In turn, frequency of contact varies directly with the availability of out-group people for interaction. A city with equal numbers of anglophones and francophones is likely to have a higher intermarriage rate than a city with twice as many of one group as the other. We get to like and marry people whom we know.

Conversely, we try to keep a distance between us and people we do not know. This idea supports the view to be discussed later that racist thinking follows exploitative behaviour. Our attitudes, stereotypes, and group ratings justify existing conditions of inequality and social distance. They legitimize these conditions, in the same way that labelling legitimizes the punishment of deviance; but they do not create them.

Discrimination

Because prejudice is the outcome of many different factors, it may well be that some degree and form of prejudice is inevitable in a society like ours. Such prejudice may be tolerable as long as it does not get transformed into discrimination. After all, all of us, as human beings, have people we like and people we dislike; people for whom we feel empathy and others for whom we feel antipathy; often with no real reason for these feelings. This is true not only in terms of race or ethnicity but even among our neighbours, schoolmates, teachers, and even relatives. The danger occurs when such feelings and attitudes are transformed into action; when a teacher, for example, gives students he or she does not like an unwarranted lower grade. That is discrimination.

Discrimination takes a variety of forms: job segregation, unequal pay for equal work, or denial of promotion. It is difficult to measure the direct effects of discrimination, as they are often so subtle. However, we can show that the members of some ethnic and racial groups have advantages over the members of others. To the extent that one can show that people with the same qualifications receive different rewards for doing the same work, one can claim that, logically, discrimination exists.

Some ethnic groups, usually those which have been in Canada for some time, are better able than others to organize their community so as to avoid discrimination. For example, Jewish Canadians have managed to avoid discrimination effectively. Jeffrey Reitz has found that in work organizations that other ethnic groups control, Jews are underpaid, given the average levels of education they have attained. Jews have avoided such discrimination and moved ahead by isolating themselves from work situations that would make them vulnerable to discrimination. In short, they have created their own workplaces and, as employees, gone to work for and with other Jews. This use of an ethnic *subeconomy* has benefited the Jews and may be responsible for success among other established ethnic groups as well. As their ethnic communities have prospered, so have ethnic individuals.

Certain key institutions—for example, universities—appear to have broken traditional barriers of discrimination against ethnic and racial minorities, but others—such as the largest industrial corporations and the oldest financial institutions—remain firmly in the hands of WASP (White Anglo-Saxon Protestant) males. Until all institutions are kept from practising discrimination against minorities, minority groups will continue to discriminate in their own favour, by means of institutional completeness and the formation of subeconomies. To date, racial groups, like the blacks, still have trouble doing this. They continue to lack the wealth, connections, education and institutional completeness of the Canadians of Jewish, Chinese, Italian, Greek, and Ukrainian background. As well, they suffer serious discrimination at the hands of the dominant white group.

The extent of racial discrimination in employment was demonstrated through field experiments by Henry and Ginzberg (1985). In one set of experiments, they sent two job applicants matched with respect to age, sex, education, experience, style of dress, and personality to apply for the same advertised job. They differed in only one respect: race. One was white and the other black. In all, teams of applicants sought a total of 201 jobs in this way.

Some applicants were young male or young female students applying for semi-skilled or unskilled jobs (such as waitress, gas station attendant, bus boy, store clerk) that they might normally be expected to seek. Other applicants were middle-aged professional actors (male and female). Armed with fake résumés, they applied for positions in retail management, sales positions in prestigious stores, and waiting and hosting positions in expensive restaurants.

In a second set of experiments, callers phoned 237 telephone numbers listed in the classified employment section of the newspaper, to present themselves as job applicants. The jobs they were applying for ranged widely from unskilled labour, secretarial, and service to skilled trade and managerial. All were newly advertised jobs. Henry and Ginzberg report each number was called four times, "once by someone with no discernible accent (apparently a white-majority Canadian), once by someone who had a Slavic or Italian accent, once by a Jamaican-accented caller and finally by a person with a Pakistani accent" (Henry and Ginzberg, 1990:307).

The men who did the calling (no women were included in this study) represented themselves as having the same characteristics: same age, education, years of job experience, and so on. As before, applicants were suited in age and (imaginary) experience to the jobs for which they were applying.

With the data collected in this way, the researchers created an Index of Discrimination that combined the results of the in-person and telephone testing. They found that blacks have only a 65 percent chance of getting through a telephone screening (13 interviews out of 20 calls) and their chances of getting a job offer *after* an interview are only about 1 in 20. White applicants are able to achieve an interview in 17 out of 20 calls, and to receive three offers of employment. Henry and Ginzberg conclude that "*The overall Index of Discrimination is therefore 3 to 1*. Whites have three job prospects to every one that blacks have" (Henry and Ginzberg, 1990:308).

Dramatic as this result may be, the researchers emphasize it only begins to show the size of the problem. "Once an applicant is employed, discrimination can still affect opportunities for advancement, job retention, and level of earnings, to say nothing of the quality of the work and the relationships with co-workers" (Henry and Ginzberg, 1990:308).

Henry and Ginzberg claim that this study and others demonstrate that job discrimination is not the result of a few bigoted employers. It demonstrates a society-wide bias against hiring non-whites.

No less serious than this blatant and intentional discrimination is what people have called **systemic**, *institutional*, or *constructive* **discrimination**. This is unintended discrimination that is so deeply embedded in a society's institutions and customs that it is hard to recognize. It shows itself in practices whose legitimacy and "naturalness" are taken for granted, and whose underlying assumptions are not questioned.

Consider, for example, the height requirement for police officers and fire fighters. Because northern racial and ethnic groups tend to be taller than southern ones, this rule will unintentionally discriminate against the latter. The taken-for-grantedness of the height requirement is part of the problem. Once people realize that such a rule is unnecessary—that shorter people can do as good a job—the racial discrimination disappears.

Similar problems have arisen with respect to work scheduling. Christians will want to have Sunday off, but orthodox Jews will want Saturday off, and Moslems Friday. A rigid rule that Sunday is the only acceptable sabbath will eliminate all non-Christian applicants for the job; but often there is no reason for the rule to exist. Once it goes, unintended racial discrimination goes too.

The last decade, with the spread of provincial human rights codes and the federal Charter of Rights, has seen one victory after another over discrimination. Not only ethnic and racial minorities, but women, the elderly, the physically disabled, and homosexuals have all stepped forward to seek protection against direct and systemic discrimination. Almost without exception, the courts have found in their favour.

There is no turning back on this issue: discriminatory behaviour is no longer acceptable in Canada. The difficulties lie in uncovering discrimination, prosecuting it, and enforcing remedies. This may have little or no effect on prejudice and the quality of ethnic and race relations overall, but it will reduce some of the social inequality that results from racism.

EXHIBIT 6.6

Gross And Net Effect[1] Of Racial And Ethnic Origin On Annual Income, 1981

	N	Gross effect as deviation from grand mean ($)	Net effect, controlling for sex, nativity, occupation, age, number of weeks worked and education ($)
Jewish	159 250	+ 6 261.6	+ 2 936.0
Scandinavian	176 650	+ 1 859.8	+ 1 034.6
Portuguese	104 200	− 2 001.9	+ 626.5
Croatian & Serbian	71 600	+ 458.6	+ 378.3
German	708 750	+ 652.4	+ 274.6
Ukrainian	325 350	+ 794.7	+ 212.7
Italian	443 100	− 509.4	+ 148.5
British	5 365 250	+ 355.8	+ 103.7
Dutch	251 800	+ 311.3	+ 76.6
Czech & Slovak	42 500	+ 2 136.9	+ 62.9
Hungarian	71 750	+ 1 901.6	+ 20.4
Polish	161 500	+ 720.8	− 222.7
French	3 333 800	− 501.1	− 240.3
Other[2]	1 610 400	− 1 113.3	− 277.9
Greek	83 750	− 1 893.9	− 796.3
Chinese	168 100	− 1 294.6	− 931.1
Black[3]	85 900	− 1 588.0	− 1 679.5
Canada (all groups)	13 163 650	14 044.9	14 044.9

[1]Gross and net effects are measured as deviations from the grand mean income, using Multiple Classification Analysis (Andrews et al., 1976).
[2]Includes other single responses and multiple responses of ethnic origin.
[3]Includes African, Caribbean, Haitian, and other black
Compiled from 1981 Census of Canada Public Use Sample Tape, Individual File.
Calculations were based on those 15 years of age and over, who were employed in the Canadian labour force, excluding inmates.

These results of an analysis by sociologist Peter Li show that ethnicity and race help some groups and hurt others just as much. Even controlling for a great many factors that influence income—sex, age, education, and occupation among them—visible minority groups earn far below the average national income.

Source: Peter Li "Race and ethnic relations" chapter 14 in L. Tepperman and R.J. Richardson, *The Social World*, 1st edition. Toronto: McGraw-Hill Ryerson, 1986, Table 14-6

RACISM

What is racism?

Ethnocentrism is a tendency to view the world from the point of view of one's own culture; in effect, to use one's own culture as a measuring stick for evaluating all other cultures. Racism is ethnocentrism carried to an extreme — the belief that one's own biological group or race is superior to all others.

Over the course of human history, there have been many motives leading to racism. Most often, however, racism has served as a justification for inequality, whether it be economic, political, or symbolic inequality. It would be comforting to think that people always have *some* reason for their racism, such as political or economic domination. The case of Nazi Germany showed, however, that racism can be the manifestation of irrational, sadistic, violent emotions in which claims to be furthering political and economic domination served as an *excuse* rather than as the cause of the racism. Although Nazi Germany was a particularly vicious extreme, we should never forget the "human" side of racism: the emotional, psychological side which makes racism so ugly.

Nevertheless, despite this human — or perhaps inhuman — side of racism, conflict theorists argue that unequal racial and ethnic relations are usually a consequence of economic inequality: that is, there is inequality both in how much relative wealth various groups have (inequality of condition), and in the degree to which groups have access to opportunities to acquire wealth and power (inequality of opportunity). Because wealth is a scarce resource, it can only be had by denying it to others. People with the most wealth, prestige, and power — the dominant group — maintain their position through exploitation.

Still, this exploitation has to be justified so that the exploiters can feel good about themselves. Enter racism. Racism develops out of a group's need to justify the exploitation of another group. Members of the dominant group ease their consciences by blaming the victim. They attribute the misfortunes of the subordinate group to an inferior genetic constitution (laziness, stupidity, aggressiveness, and so on), bad cultural values, or both.

People with the most intense racist feelings are not always the ones to profit most from our system of inequality. Typically, they are people who feel they have the most to lose should the targets of their racism rise to equal status. Low status members of the dominant cultural group — "poor whites" in the southern United States, for example — are threatened most by economic competition from minority groups.

Consider the experience of Japanese Canadians on the country's west coast. How did it come to pass that in 1941 a majority of Japanese Canadians were "evacuated" from coastal British Columbia to isolated interior camps and settlements? (The excuse given was that Japanese Canadians, of whom three-quarters had been born in Canada, posed a threat to national security during our war with Japan.) And what of the Order-in-Council of December, 1945, which intended to deport ("repatriate") Japanese Canadians after the war — a plan never carried through because of the opposition to it by prominent Canadians? In fact, there had been ample evidence of hostility towards Japanese Canadians even before the war, and most of it came from lower down the social scale.

Social distance and stereotyping were evident on the west coast well before the First World War; among the victims were Japanese, Chinese, and East Indian Canadians. The success of Japanese Canadians in fishing, farming, and lumbering threatened the ordinary Canadians they competed with. Anti-Japanese feelings culminated in the Vancouver Race Riots of 1907 (Ujimoto, 1983). Concerns that the Japanese would take away their jobs led the white Anglo-Saxon majority to press for an agreement with Japan that would limit further immigration to Canada (Baar, 1978). It's against this historic backdrop of competition and dislike that we must understand anti-Japanese actions during the Second World War.

Since competition for scarce resources among unequals is the ground on which most racism grows, racist attitudes are most acute during times of economic hardship and political instability. Recessions cause domestic workers to believe that immigrants are taking jobs away from them, and thus competition for the available jobs often surfaces as inter-ethnic (or racial) conflict. Marxian theorists have suggested that these ethnic and racial divisions destroy unity among employees by diverting attention from the actual problem—a misfunctioning of the economy—to ethnic differences. One of the effects of racism is to weaken the solidarity of the working class and thus strengthen the position of employers.

Racism may develop out of a need to justify the exploitation of another group, but it does not simply disappear after the conditions that gave rise to it disappear. This is because racism's underlying economic rationale is not obvious to most people. They think social inequality reflects real differences in people's moral values or moral worth. People therefore have trouble thinking differently about the group whose oppression they used to think was natural. Indeed, they may need to defend themselves against feelings of guilt by continuing to avow that group's inferiority.

Racist attitudes and beliefs pass from generation to generation, through the process of socialization. Because they are learned at a very young age, these views will forever seem "natural" to the people who hold them. People will be predisposed to look for evidence that confirms their attitudes and ignore evidence that does not—a phenomenon psychologists call the *confirmation bias*.

If members of minority groups lack the opportunity of acquiring the necessary education to fill high-status, responsible jobs, their children will start life from unequal starting points. Not only is their range and quality of choices limited, but many members of minority groups may even internalize racist attitudes and exclude themselves from competition.

As a result of these external and internal obstacles, the racism that caused the present situation is legitimized by it instead. In a queer twist of logic, the fact that members of minority groups are often poorly educated and hold low-status jobs is cited as "proof" of their innate inferiority.

CLOSING REMARKS

As we have seen in this chapter, Canada is a society built on differences. This country was founded in part as an attempt by the British and French of North America to preserve their cultures in the face of American influence. Because ethnicity, language, and religion were so central to the creation of Canada and to how Canadians think about themselves and others, it is not surprising that ethnicity in Canada came to be intimately tied into the political and stratification systems in Canada. The result was the vertical mosaic.

Is ethnicity still so important in Canadian society? There is evidence that ethnicity has less economic significance today than it had in past, although it remains economically significant for the native peoples and for the visible minorities. On the other hand, ethnicity has become more politically significant than ever before, as the priority placed by the federal government on its multicultural policy indicates.

While racism undoubtedly exists in Canada, it seems to play a less significant role in ethnic group relations here than it does in the United States. We can speculate on why this is so. It may well be that the vertical mosaic, because it emphasizes *everyone's* differences, means that specific groups are less likely to stand out as different. Since the American melting pot de-emphasizes ethnic differences, it serves to emphasize racial ones. Of course, this is only part of the story. The American legacy of slavery is the context within which racism appeared and has been maintained in that country. The closest equivalent in Canada is our treatment of the native peoples, and they, as Mackie's research reported on above shows, are at the bottom of our social distance scales. Canadians cannot afford the self-complacent assumption that our society has no, or only minimal, racism.

Discussion Questions

1. How are Canada's native peoples like, and how are they unlike, colonized Third World peoples?

2. Given Canada's history of immigration, what kinds of people – and how many – are likely to immigrate in the year 2000?

3. How might you test whether language loss within an ethnic minority leads to a decline in ethnic group cohesion?

4. Racism is only one possible response to economic difficulty. Other historical examples have been crime, political protest, escape into drugs and alcohol, and strengthened religious belief. What determines whether racism will be the response chosen at a particular time and place?

5. Extra-terrestrials have landed in Canada. Will people feel prejudiced against them? If so, will stereotyping portray them more like Jews or blacks?

6. Is the amount of intermarriage between two groups a good measure of the prejudice one group feels for another? If not, why not? Would more intermarriage cause prejudice to decline?

Data Collection Exercises

1. Collect published statistics to show how the pattern of ethnic and racial migration to your hometown has changed in the last 100 years.

2. Select any ethnic or racial community – for example, Winnipeg Greeks, Calgary Chinese, Montreal Algerians – and measure its institutional completeness. (Hint: You may want to see how Jeffrey Reitz did this in his book *The Survival of Ethnic Groups*. That is one approach to consider.)

3. Study changes in the job segregation of one particular ethnic group between 1931 and 1981, using published Census statistics.

4. Has "northern" meant the same in other cultures as it has in Canada? Study its meaning in one other northern country (for example, Sweden, USSR) and one southern country (for example, Argentina, India).

Writing Exercises

1. Research and briefly describe (in about 500 words) ethnic stratification in a selected European, African, or Asian country.

2. Write a 500-word autobiography discussing your own ethnic identity and how strongly you feel about it.

3. Describe in about 500 words how an authoritarian personality would deal with conflict (a) at home or (b) on the job. To do this, try to imagine a particular situation and how it would get played out.

4. In about 500 words, describe a work setting where there are very few visible minorities. Explain why there are not more.

Glossary

assimilation – the process by which members of a minority group abandon their own cultural traits and adopt those of the dominant culture

band – a grouping the government has created to administer status Indians, who are typically native people under the jurisdiction of the Indian Act, who live on a **reserve** ("reservation" is the American term). This is the place an Indian band has settled, under the terms of a treaty with the Federal or Provincial government.

Charter Groups – Canadians of British and French ancestry, so named because settlers from England and France first came to Canada with royal permission to trade and settle (royal charters)

discrimination – the denial of access to opportunities that would be available to equally qualified members of the dominant group

ethnicity – an ethnic group's distinctive cultural features, such as language, religion, sense of collective existence, and shared historical heritage

institutional completeness – a measure of the degree to which an ethnic group provides its members with all the services they require through their own institutions separate from those of the larger society

nativist groups – political groups favoring the interests of native-born inhabitants over those of immigrants

pluralism – a policy whereby ethnic groups keep their distinctive cultural traits, preserve their group identity, and remain conscious of their ethnic background

prejudice – a negative or hostile attitude towards members of a particular group simply because they belong to that group, based on untested assumptions about their characteristics

race – a group whose members are socially defined as sharing the same physical characteristics. The term is used as a biological concept, rather than a cultural one.

racism – the belief that one's own race is superior to all others

segregation – the act or process of setting apart two or more groups of people within the same territory

social distance – reserve in social interaction between people who belong to groups ranked as superior and inferior in status

stereotype—a fixed mental image embracing all that is believed to be typical of members of a given group

systemic discrimination—the unintended denial of opportunities to members of particular groups because of certain physical or cultural characteristics

vertical mosaic—a society in which ethnic group membership overlaps with class or socio-economic status, such that we can predict a person's position in society from his or her ethnic origins

Suggested Readings

Breton Raymond "Institutional completeness of ethnic communities and the personal relations of immigrants" *American Journal of Sociology*, 70, 1964 pp. 193-205. This classic Canadian work on ethnic relations describes why communities become institutionally complete and how their completeness reduces contact with other ethnic groups.

Levitt, Cyril H. and William Shaffir *The Riot at Christie Pits*. Toronto: Lester and Orpen Dennys, 1987. This well-written study details an unhappy moment in Toronto's history, when Jews and Nazi sympathizers clashed at one of Toronto's downtown parks.

Li, Peter *Ethnic Inequality in a Class Society*. Toronto: Wall and Thompson, 1988. The author shows that the best explanation of racism is its usefulness to capitalists. He reviews the costs and benefits of ethnicity for minority group members themselves, using Canadian census data.

Porter, John *The Vertical Mosaic*. Toronto: University of Toronto Press, 1965. In the most widely celebrated work in Canadian sociology, John Porter shows the connections between social class and ethnic status. He explains why ethnic groups have had trouble improving their standing in the society.

Reitz, Jeffrey *The Survival of Ethnic Groups*. Toronto: McGraw-Hill Ryerson, 1980. Using data from a massive survey of ten ethnic groups in five Canadian cities, the author shows the links between different aspects of ethnicity. He explores the reasons some communities grow weaker and others grow stronger.

Shaffir, William *Life in a Religious Community: The Lubavitcher Chassidim in Montreal*. Toronto: Holt Rinehart and Winston, 1974. With data collected through painstaking observation, the author describes the lives and worldviews of a minority group who have deliberately kept themselves outside society's mainstream.

References

Baar, E. (1978) "Issei, Nisei and Sansei" in D. Glenday, H. Guindon, and A. Turowetz (eds.) *Modernization and the Canadian State*. Toronto: Macmillan of Canada

Berger, C. (1970) *The Sense of Power: Studies in the Ideas of Canadian Imperialism 1867-1914*. Toronto: University of Toronto Press

Berry, J.W., R. Kalin, and D.M. Taylor (1977) *Multiculturalism and Ethnic Attitudes in Canada*. Ottawa: Supply and Services

Bogardus, E.S. (1959) *Social Distance*. Yellow Springs, Ohio: Antioch College Press

Breton, R. (1964) "Institutional completeness of ethnic communities and personal relations of immigrants" *American Journal of Sociology*, vol. 70, pp. 193-205

Brym, R. and B. Fox (1989) *From Culture to Power: The Sociology of English Canada*. Toronto: Oxford University Press

Frideres, J. (1988) *Native People in Canada: Contemporary Conflicts*. Toronto: Prentice-Hall Canada

Guindon, H. (1968) "Two cultures: an essay on nationalism, class and ethnic tension" in R.H. Leach (ed.) *Contemporary Canada*. Toronto: Macmillan

Health and Welfare Canada (1989) *Charting Canada's Future: A Report of the Demographic Review*. Ottawa: Supply and Services, pp. 6-8

Henry, F. and E. Ginzberg (1990) "Racial discrimination in employment" pp. 302-309 in J. Curtis and L. Tepperman (eds.) *Images of Canada: The Sociological Tradition*. Toronto: Prentice-Hall (Canada)

Lachapelle, R. (1980) "Evolution of ethnic and linguistic composition" part 1 in R. Breton, J. Reitz, and V. Valentine (eds.) *Cultural Boundaries and the Cohesion of Canada*. Montreal; Institute for Research on Public Policy

Li, P. (1982) "Chinese immigrants on the Canadian prairie, 1910-47" *Canadian Review of Sociology and Anthropology*, 19(4), pp. 527-540

Mackie, M. (1974) "Ethnic stereotypes and prejudice: Alberta Indians, Hutterites, and Ukrainians" *Canadian Ethnic Studies* 10, pp. 118-129

Parsons, T. (1975) "Some theoretical considerations on the nature and trends of changes of ethnicity" pp. 53-85 in N. Glazer and D. Moynihan (eds.) *Ethnicity: Theory and Experience*. Cambridge, Mass.: Harvard University Press

Porter, J. (1965) *The Vertical Mosaic*. Toronto: University of Toronto Press

Reitz, J. (1980) *The Survival of Ethnic Groups*. Toronto: McGraw-Hill Ryerson

Shaffir, W. (1974) *Life in a Religious Community: The Lubavitcher Chassidim in Montreal*. Toronto: Holt Rinehart Winston

Thomas, W.I. and D.S. Thomas (1928) *The Child in America*. New York: Alfred A. Knopf

Ujimoto, K.V. (1983) "Institutional controls and their impact on Japanese Canadian social relations, 1877-1977" in P.S. Li and B.S. Bolaria (eds.) *Racial Minorities in Multicultural Canada*. Toronto: Garamond Press

CHAPTER 7

Many people have despaired of the "end of the family." What they have witnessed is really a dramatic growth in the variety of families we can experience.

THE FAMILY

THE FAMILY AS A CONTEXT FOR SOCIAL LIFE

The family is the only social institution we will be examining in detail in this text. There is a good reason for paying such close attention to the family, for it may well be that it is the most fundamental social institution of all. It is in the family that the vast majority of people come to be socialized, come to learn who and what they are, what others expect of them, and what they can reasonably expect of others. It is in the family that we learn to get along with others, to love and sometimes to hate them, to express our innermost feelings and to lie, to resent being subject to the authority of others, and to manipulate others to get what we want.

Family life clearly illustrates the relationship between our macro and micro social worlds. Our most intimate moments are lived within the "family" or "household" setting and, not surprisingly, some people have called the family a "haven in a heartless world." Yet what happens in the family is affected by what happens outside it: remember the cartoon where the boss bawls out the dad, dad comes home and bawls out the mom, mom bawls out the big kids, big kids bawl out the little kids, and little kids bawl out the pets. We *do* take out our workplace frustrations on people who are closest to us and most vulnerable to our rages. (More will be said about this in our brief discussion of family violence which follows.)

At the same time, our public, non-domestic lives are also affected by what happens in the home. Family conflict, separation, divorce, and other domestic stresses all influence how we perform at school and on the job. Increasingly, employers are taking family responsibilities into account, by providing on-the-job child care, greater work flexibility, and more assistance in career planning, among other things. Employers are no longer able to ignore their employees' personal troubles. The growing shortage of single young workers makes the better handling of married workers (especially female ones) a public issue and an important topic in the training of managers.

For the first few years of our life, the family is a microcosm of the larger society in which we will one day participate. In learning to be a member of a family, we learn how to be members of society. Then, soon after we finally leave the shelter (or oppression) of our family, most of us marry and begin a family of our own. The new roles we take on, the roles of husband or wife and of parent, now become a crucial part of our identity. They place us in new, intense social relationships with others which may give us both new sources of satisfaction and self-esteem as well as new constraints on what we can accomplish. Either way, the family is the context within which most of us live out our private lives and it is in our family relationships that most of us experience our greatest joys or accomplishments, frustrations or sorrows.

PERSPECTIVES ON THE FAMILY

Because the family is such a fundamental institution, it is one that has been a central focus for research by sociologists working within all three of the major sociological paradigms. One consequence is that the family is yet another topic in sociology characterized by debate and controversy. Yet the family is such a diverse social institution that all three perspectives tell us something different and valuable about the family.

The functionalist paradigm

As you might expect, the functionalist perspective on the family emphasizes the various functions performed by the family as a social unit. Functionalists note that the family's role as a key social institution grows out of our long period of dependence on others for survival. The human infant's combination of physical dependence and mental competence requires that others feed, care for, and *teach* it. Human infants rely more than those of any other species on social contacts and learning in order to later function properly as adults. These biological and social factors make the family a particularly important social institution for the survival both of the individual and of society.

Marriage, too, emerges out of a combination of biological and social factors. In all societies, women have the primary responsibility for child care, at least at the beginning. That women bear, suckle, and generally take care of infants means that they are, at least temporarily, restricted in their ability to protect and economically support themselves. The dependence of infants on women and of women on men gives rise to the universal practice of marriage. However, the form marriage takes and the set of relationships and attachments that develop among the members of the family are socially, not biologically, determined.

Functionalists identify a specific set of functions carried out by the family: "socialization of children, sexual regulation, reproduction, economic cooperation, affection, intimacy, emotional support and status placement" (Mandell, 1987: 151). By carrying out these functions, the family ensures the survival of the society and of the individual, provides the setting within which the personality of the individual is moulded, and ensures the integration of the individual into the culture and value system of the society. Because of its central role, the family is in some form or other a universal social institution, that is, it is one found in every society. We remember that marriage is a cultural universal and, as such, varies across cultures.

At the same time, functionalists acknowledge that the family has undergone significant change in the modern era. Talcott Parsons (1955), the foremost functionalist sociologist of the 20th century, argued that the major functions of the family in the past were economic. The family itself—such as, for example, a peasant family—served as an economic and productive unit. The family was also the setting within which most children learned the work they would undertake as adults, such as the tasks of a farmer, housewife, warrior, merchant, and so on. In this way, the family was the unit of economic and occupational socialization. These two major functions, Parsons said, have been removed from the contemporary family. Few people today work at home and the bulk of occupational socialization has been turned over to schools and on-the-job training.

What this shift of function means, suggested Parsons, is that the family has become "functionless" at the macrosociological level. Instead, the functions of today's family are microsociological: the family integrates individuals into society through primary socialization and by "stabilizing" the adult personality through "investing" emotional resources into family roles as parent and spouse.

The conflict paradigm

Both conflict and interactionist critics of the functionalist approach have argued that the family described by the functionalists is an ideal rather than a real family. Because the family is a microcosm of society, the range of viable family patterns displayed across different cultures is huge. There is no one necessary form or set of functions for the family, just as there is no one necessary language, form of music, or set of rituals. The many changes we are witnessing in modern family life are responses to changes in the social and economic environment. As society changes, so too does the family.

Rather than focusing on the functions of the family, followers of the conflict approach have focused on the social relationships out of which the family is composed. Marxists, for example, suggest that the family remains largely an economic unit in our society, and that the pattern of male/female relationships within the family will reflect the economic conditions and forces found in society. The modern nuclear family, they suggest, is a product of capitalism and serves to perpetuate the capitalist economic system. Once the family lost its ability to function as a self-contained productive unit, the members of the family became dependent upon the wage earned by the husband and often by the wife. The nuclear family increased the dependence of the worker on the capitalist, the wife's dependence on her husband, and the children's dependence on their parents.

Many feminists emphasize the role of the family as a microcosm of the broader patterns of male domination in society. In this respect, the family becomes a political unit within which this domination is acted out on a daily basis. The family also teaches and justifies the subordination of women through the roles and values assigned on the basis of gender and passed on to the next generation.

The interactionist paradigm

Interactionists have typically focused on the family as the context within which primary socialization occurs. As such, their orientation has centred largely on the processes whereby interaction among family members leads to the emergence of identity and the "self" (See Chapter 3). Recently, however, some interactionists have begun to pay more attention to the family as a specific social institution. As one example, Nancy Mandell (1987: 153) notes that interactionists have used qualitative interviews to discover "the strains and conflicts women encounter in juggling their multiple responsibilities of domestic and wage labour."

Another symbolic interactionist, Diane Vaughan (1987), has written a book titled *Uncoupling*, which describes the process by which marriages come apart and end in separation or divorce. Vaughan is interested in the typical stages of dissolution and the reasons why reconciliation may prove impossible in certain cases. As a result of her research, Vaughan argues *against* secrecy in marriage, and *in favour of* couples airing their grievances as they arise. The longer problems go unspoken, the more likely they will lead to marriage breakdown, Vaughan implies.

All of the issues mentioned above will reappear in this chapter as we go along, because all of them are relevant to understanding the contemporary family in Canadian society. We have here a good example of how all of the different paradigms are able to make some contribution to the sociological understanding of social institutions and social life.

THE FAMILY: A PRELIMINARY VIEW

Before we begin to examine the extraordinarily diverse forms the family can take, let us develop a definition of the family that gives us at least some common starting points for analysis. We can say that a **family** consists of a group of individuals who are related to one another through marriage, descent, or legal adoption. Family members have institutionalized roles that define what they can expect from each other, and what obligations they owe to each other. In Canada, as elsewhere, the nature of these rights and responsibilities is determined by cultural values which, in turn, may be largely influenced by economic arrangements and backed-up by the laws of the state.

Adult members of a family assume a legal responsibility for taking care of their dependent children. Such caretaking includes tending to their basic survival needs, like food and shelter; providing love, comfort, and a sense of security; and teaching them the language, customs, beliefs, norms, skills, and values they will need to fit into their society.

A family also forms an economic unit. In many cultures today, and for most of human history, this economic unit both produces and consumes goods and services collectively. In Canada, the family is no longer the central economic unit of production, and few people work as members of a family. Nevertheless, the family remains an important unit for the consumption of goods and services.

You may have realized that the above is an idealized view of families—a picture of how families are supposed to be and what families are supposed to do. To some degree, all families do all of these things. Yet real families fall short of the ideal in many ways, and this can cause problems. Just like the society at large that it mirrors, the family can display selfishness and cruelty, inequality and violence.

Much of what we know about the family in Canada today comes from information gathered by Statistics Canada. Data on the family are not gathered directly, however, for a number of reasons, including the diversity of opinions on what makes up a family. Because the family is a fundamental social institution, membership in the family is not limited to some particular time or

EXHIBIT 7.1

THE OLD AND NEW FAMILY MODELS

In the chart below, sociologist Margrit Eichler (1981) provides us with a capsule version of changes in the Canadian family.

The Old Family Model	
Ideology	Sex-role differentiation
Economic responsibility	Husbands/fathers as breadwinners, wives secondary earners or nonearners
Economic dependency	Wives/children as dependents of husband/fathers
Household composition	Assumption of congruence between household and family membership
	The nuclear family seen as normative
	Wives equated with mothers, husbands equated with fathers
Household management	Wives/mothers as full-time or part-time homemakers with sole responsibility for household management
	Husbands/fathers not responsible for household management
	Unclear distinction between spousal and parental obligations
Personal care	Mothers/wives/adult daughters(-in-law) responsible for provision of care for children and adults
	Fathers/husbands/sons(-in-law) not responsible for provision of care for children and adults

The New Model Of The Family	
Ideology	Sex equality
Economic responsibility	Husbands and wives (fathers and mothers) are both earners, equally responsible for their own support and that of the children
Economic dependency	Children are dependents of their mothers and fathers
Household composition	No assumption of congruence between household and family members
	A wide variety of family types acknowledged and accepted
	Wives not unquestioningly equated with mothers, nor husbands with fathers

Continued

Household management	Shared responsibility between husband and wife
	Clear distinction between spousal and parental obligation
Personal care	Mothers/fathers, wives/husbands, daughters/sons, daughters-in-law/sons-in-law equally responsible for provision of care for family members in need of care to the degree that this can be combined with full-time paid work

Source: Margrit Eichler (1981) "Models of the family" *Canadian Journal of Sociology* 6, pp. 367-388

some particular place. If you move to Winnipeg and the rest of your family lives in Vancouver, you still consider yourself to be a member of your family. You consider your grandparents, uncles, aunts, and cousins, none of whom may live with you, to be members of your family.

Gathering statistical data on the family, however, requires that Statistics Canada have some clearly defined unit which it can measure and to which it can refer in its comparisons. And, because the family can take on so many forms and can change so dramatically over time, this unit cannot be based on either the "legal" or the "ideal" model of the family. For all these reasons, Statistics Canada makes use of the concept of a *family household* as an alternative to the family. A **family household** is defined as an adult who shares a dwelling and maintains a household with at least one other relative, whether a spouse, child, parent, or other kin (for example, cousin). The members of a family household may be related by blood ties, by marriage, or by adoption. This definition differs from the sociologist's definition given above, because for that the family is not restricted to the walls of the dwelling. That is, family members need not live together in order to be a family.

ANALYZING FAMILY PATTERNS

Unlike Statistics Canada, which looks for some uniform standard of measurement, sociologists and anthropologists are interested in examining the many different forms the family can take. By looking at the differences we hope to recognize the fundamentals that remain the same. Also, by uncovering what social, economic, and cultural factors gave rise to these differences, we have a better understanding of how the family will change in the future and why. In order to accomplish this, sociologists focus on a small number of fundamental characteristics which may vary but are likely to be found in one form or another in all families. This allows us to look for patterns of similarities and differences to explain the cross-cultural variations that can be found in the family.

Since the family is a social institution we would expect these fundamental characteristics to be composed of social relationships. Two social relationships immediately stand out when we think of what we expect to find in a family: The first is *marriage*, the relationship between a husband and wife. The second is *kinship*, the relationship between parent and child. Variations in family form, then, will consist of variations in the relationship of husbands to wives and parents to children.

Marriage

Broadly defined, marriage is a socially approved sexual and economic union between two or more people that is expected to last for some time. People often enter this union with public formalities in a socially approved ceremony, such as a wedding.

Societies vary many ways in their patterns of marriage, family, and kinship. There is variation in the range of choice given to would-be marriage partners; in the reasons for marriage (for example, economic support, to build ties with other families, to pay back a debt owed to parents, or because partners love each other); in thinking about premarital and extramarital intimacies (that is, whether they are permitted, encouraged, frowned upon or prohibited, and whether the same standard applies to both males and females); even in the desired age at marriage and the desired age difference between spouses. These variations do not appear at random. Often they reflect the basic characteristics of the society in which they are found. An examination of some of the more important variations illustrates this point.

In some societies, people may wed more than one mate at a time. Polygamy is the generic name for this arrangement. Within this general category, **polyandry** is the marriage of one woman to more than one man, and **polygyny** the marriage of one man to more than one woman, at a time. Polygamy was common in most pre-industrial societies and is still permitted in some non-industrial nations although it is banned in industrial societies. In fact polygyny is practised in parts of Asia and Africa such as Nigeria where, as recently as 1975, half of all marriages were polygynous.

Monogamy—marriage between only one woman and one man—is the marriage form that is most familiar to us. However, variations on monogamy are becoming more and more common. One is an increasing incidence of cohabitation in a marriage-like fashion between two people of the same sex. Another is what sociologists have called serial (or sequential) monogamy. **Serial monogamy** is the marriage of a person over the life course to a series or sequence of spouses, though one at a time. In a society with high rates of divorce and remarriage such as ours, serial monogamy characterizes a growing number of individuals.

In pre-industrial societies, marriage was rarely considered to be the concern of the marriage partners alone. Rather, people saw marriage as the joining of two kin groups. Each engaged person's own family considered carefully whether the proposed match was a good one for the whole kin group. This was largely because, upon marriage, family property—land, animals, or other group possessions—would pass to the other group as *bride-price* (a gift from groom to bride or her family) or *dowry* (a gift from bride to groom or his family), or (eventually) through inheritance.

One solution to the problem of property was endogamy. **Endogamy** is the requirement or preference that people marry within their own social group. In a small village of several hundred people, this group is larger than an extended family household, but people are tied together by generations of marriages. Everyone is more or less distantly related to everyone else. In a larger village or town, one might marry someone not even distantly connected by earlier marriage. However, rules of endogamy would require a person to marry within his or her own social class, caste, religious group, ethnic or racial group, or geographic region. Kin group advantage was again the goal of such a marriage. Wherever family land or other immovable properties might be lost through marriage, the pressure toward endogamy is still strong.

Other reasons for endogamy include familiarity, discrimination against the group by outsiders, and a deliberate attempt to maintain solidarity by emphasizing group boundaries in marriage. Even today, these factors influence the likelihood someone will marry a person socially very much like themselves. Endogamy today usually reflects a preference for marriage to someone of the same religious or ethnic background.

Exogamy is the practice of marrying outside one's social group. Exogamous societies are sometimes small and based on kinship, like the !Kung bushmen of the Kalahari desert. Exogamy gives small societies a greater chance of surviving in times of famine, conflict, or other hazards, because it extends the size of the group one may call on in the event of trouble. Exogamy is a good survival strategy where group resources are few and the group does not feel endangered by outside groups. Exogamy is also practised, increasingly, in our own society. To a large extent, endogamous norms concerning ethnic and religious preference have simply broken down. People feel less commitment to marrying within their own group than they once did.

Another form of variation found in marriage is that of place of residence. There are three basic residence patterns that a new family can follow: **patrilocal** (living with the husband's family), **matrilocal** (living with the wife's family), or **neolocal** (living with neither family and, often, at some distance away from the spouses' parental families). Neolocal residence is most common in modern industrial societies, in which the family is not itself a unit of production.

One final form of variation in marriage we will mention is that of authority structure. Families differ in whether they are equalitarian (or egalitarian), patriarchal, or matriarchal. The **patriarchal family** is a type of authority structure in which the husband/father is formal head of the household. He has the final say in all important matters because of his role, not because he has demonstrated more wisdom, or has more skill or more experience. In this type of family, maleness confers authority. In societies where such families are found, women have a limited or nonexistent role in public life. In all spheres of life, maleness confers authority.

Patriarchal authority relations characterized family life in many pre-industrial societies, and some patriarchal tendencies remain in our own society. Yet, compared to other societies, ours is much more equalitarian. Likewise, families in our society are much closer to equalitarian than to patriarchal families in form and function.

In an **equalitarian family**, the wife and husband make the important decisions jointly. Their opinions are equally important and mutually respected. Neither has authority over the other in the eyes of the law, and both have a roughly equal say on important (and not-so-important) family matters.

This is not to say that all families today are equalitarian. To some degree, the growth of spousal equality reflects the growth of an ideal more than a change in practice. As well, it is difficult in a great many households to know if a family is equalitarian or not. Within a family, spouses may have different rights and responsibilities which are equally important: the wife, a responsibility for child rearing and domestic decisions; the husband, a responsibility for earning an income and making major purchases, for example. However, the trend is clearly away from patriarchal family relations, or even separate but equal roles, and towards equalitarian ones. The blurring of gender roles in the workplace and elsewhere is making this outcome inevitable.

The extreme alternative to patriarchal families, a matriarchal family, is less likely to develop. A **matriarchal family** is one in which the woman/mother is formal head of the household. No doubt, we can find examples of such families in our society. They may be found where a marriage breakdown has left the wife the head of a single-parent family. Sociologists (for example, Moynihan, 1965) report this pattern has historically characterized the black family in America, in a subculture where males have been particularly transient. However, there is no record of an entire society in which the matriarchal family was a dominant or idealized family form.

Before we turn to the relationship between parent and child, one important feature of marriage in our society remains to be examined: the nature of the attachment between husbands and wives. In pre-modern societies, as we noted, marriage was a relationship between two kin groups rather than two people. Usually, the kin groups arranged the marriage and the people involved had little, if any, choice in the matter. That is not how it works in our society, where *individuals* get married and both their motivations for marriage and the attachments which tie them together are considered to be personal. Understanding the nature of these attachments as they occur in our society, especially the ideal of romantic love, helps us understand some of the pressures to which marriage as a social relationship is subjected in our society.

Romantic love

A central feature of family formation in Canada is romantic love. Love and marriage do not necessarily go together. Yet most people do get married and do so because they believe they love their partner. Nothing seems as natural to us as falling in love. In our culture, we recognize Mr. or Ms. "Right" – the person we want to marry or to be with – by falling in love. Messages such as "If you love someone, that's all that matters" and "Love will save the day" are constantly being sent to us in books, movies, television, and popular music. Yet, for all our belief in the inevitability of love, we feel we also have to give the process a hand. How else to explain the enormous amount of time and money single people spend on personal display ("advertising themselves"), searching for the right mate, and dating candidates for the position of Mr. or Ms. Right!

Romantic love plays a very small role, if any, in mate selection and marriage in many parts of the world. Instead, marriage is usually seen as a practical arrangement, one in which love is irrelevant or a matter of luck. What is relevant is whether the potential husband will be a good provider, whether the potential wife will be a good homemaker, and whether the union will be able to supply the family with sons.

The ideal of romantic love is an ingrained feature of the Canadian family that distinguishes it from the family types found in some other societies. In our culture, people are expected and expect to marry for reasons of love. Another way of stating this is that ideal Canadian families are founded on *expressive* exchange not *instrumental* exchange. **Exchange** is a process of on-going interaction between interdependent spouses. The exchange perspective sees

EXHIBIT 7.2

CHANGING NEEDS, CHANGING INSTITUTIONS

It is sometimes easy to forget how much gender relations, marriage and sexuality have changed even in the last 25 years.

Consider the following, drawn from an analysis of American sorority life as it existed up through the mid-1960s. Scott (1965) argues that a central function of sororities – hence, the reason why they survive – is to ensure that young women from good families get married to young men from other good families (or, at least, to men who are ambitious and upwardly mobile). About the importance of "timely marriage", Scott writes

> Women are constrained, if they contemplate marriage at all, to be timely about it. Whether endogamous or exogamous, arranged or romantic, marriage is an exchange in which (among other things) the sexual attractiveness of women is offered in return for status and support from men. Men can confer status and extend support for relatively many years; women are sexually attractive for relatively few. Since youth and nubile beauty are such important aspects of women's exchange, the problem of avoiding an undesirable marriage cannot be solved by postponing marriage indefinitely. Demographically, late marriage is associated with a high proportion of spinsters.

> Among all the age-graded statuses through which a woman passes, the period of nubility is the most rewarded; indeed, the rewards are so great relative to other periods that 'feminine youth' is not simply an abstract age-graded status but a veritable institution, consciously recognized, celebrated in folklore and literature, the object of anticipatory socialization of female children and a time to which later memories return. This situation favours the sororities, for they are explicitly designed to maximize the rewards of nubility, to enhance with symbol and ceremony a high valued yet ephemeral status, quite apart from the services they offer to endogamy.

What aspects of mating and marriage have changed in the last 25 years, and why? Given Scott's theory, will these changes have eliminated the need for sororities?

Source: John Finley Scott (1965) "The American college sorority: Its role in class and ethnic endogamy" *American Sociological Review*, 30 (3) June, pp. 514-527

marriage as a give-and-take situation, in which each spouse gives and gets. The stability and well-being of a relationship depends on how well a balance is struck and maintained in this exchange between spouses.

Expressive exchanges in marriage are exchanges of emotional services between spouses. They include hugs and kisses, sexual gratification, companionship, a shoulder to lean on, empathy and understanding. Such exchanges affirm the affection and love each spouse has for the other. By contrast, **instrumental exchanges** are non-emotional. They maintain a household in practical ways, such as sharing the domestic workload, earning a living, and spending the household's money.

Clearly, every marriage is a mixture of expressive and instrumental exchanges. As well, every culture values both types of exchange. However, cultures differ in the relative importance they attach to each. In our society, instrumental exchanges have always been important, particularly in marriages where children are being raised. However, our culture considers expressive exchanges to be more important in marriage than instrumental ones. People are urged to marry partners they love, not just people who would help out in practical ways. If Parsons is right and the family has lost most of its functions, as discussed above, then the modern family is primarily expressive, directed to satisfying emotional, psychological, and personality needs.

Mate selection

Naturally, the emphasis on romantic love in marriage has placed a great emphasis on careful mate selection, and the choice of a spouse who is emotionally compatible. Yet, despite our avowals of "love at first sight" and that "love is blind," social scientists have discovered that there is a method to our mating madness. As a general rule, people fall in love with and marry people who are similar to them in important ways.

Homogamy is what sociologists call this tendency for like to marry like — for people to marry others who are similar in important respects such as their racial, ethnic, national, or religious background; and their age, physical attractiveness and appearance, class and social status. The reasons for the tendency toward homogamy are easily understood. First, people have always been more likely to meet others who are (at least socially) like themselves than to meet those unlike themselves. This is simply a consequence of the social circles within which people move and interact with others. Second, we tend to like people who think the way we do, who act the way we expect them to, and in whose presence we feel comfortable. To the extent that people like themselves and the people they know, they are apt to love people who are similar to them. Third, to the extent that marriage is an exchange, the spousal exchange is easier to balance where like is marrying like.

By contrast, heterogamy is marriage between people who differ in important respects, whether socially or psychologically. There are also many reasons for modern heterogamy. First, marriageable people are meeting a wider variety of potential mates than they did in the past, especially at college or university. This wider variety gives them a wider range of choice, if they want to exercise it.

Second, many people want to escape from the groups and communities in which they grew up, and marrying an outsider is a good way of escaping their past. In particular, heterogamous marriage offers the chance for upward mobility. Third, heterogamy offers a larger range of possible exchanges in marriage. It allows a mate to trade off one quality or characteristic for another: for example, youth and beauty for wealth and status.

How do notions of romantic love fit into the picture? Well, considerations of trading off youth and beauty for wealth and status relate to romantic love in a number of ways. First, remember that romantic love is an ideal. By personalizing social relationships, it serves to motivate us to look for and find people who are "compatible." The search for compatibility, however, often results in us being attracted to a person who meets our assumptions (emotional and practical) about an ideal mate. Second, romantic love serves to justify for us the choices we make, even when these choices are based on practical considerations. By explaining our choice on the basis of love, we make it acceptable to others, and to ourselves.

However, the ideal of romantic love does place burdens upon us. Many of us expect others to meet our unrealistic expectations of love, emotional attachment, and a life of perfect happiness, just as we are expected to meet theirs. Because marriage and raising children are practical and often unpleasant matters, these romantic notions often lead to dissatisfaction and divorce. The high divorce rate in Canada is an indication of a widespread gap between our expectations and the reality of married life.

Parent and child

Historically, the relationship between parent and child was the kernel of a broader set of relationships called *kinship relationships*. We are related to many more people than our immediate family. The total network of people related by common ancestry or adoption is called a **kin group**. Relations among members of this network are called kinship relations.

In our society, relatives from both sides of our parentage are considered kin. In many other societies, however, people trace their descent through one line only—either their father's or mother's line. In a **matrilineal** society, a person traces his or her descent (or kinship) through the mother's line only. The father, his parents, brothers and sisters, and their children are not included in the person's kin group. Said another way, in a matrilineal society, you will only have cousins through your mother's sisters, not through your father's. In a **patrilineal** society, this pattern is exactly reversed. All descent is traced through the father, his brothers and his father.

Our society is neither matrilineal nor patrilineal—it is **bilateral**. This means that relatives of both of our parents are considered kin. We have maternal and paternal aunts, uncles, grandparents, cousins, and so on. The use of bilateral descent fits very well with an equalitarian authority structure in which father and mother have a roughly equal say in family matters.

In many societies, what we consider the family is embedded in a much broader web of kin relationships, and a household will encompass numerous kin. In others, such as our own, a household usually consists of parents and their unmarried children. These two main forms of family household are referred to as the extended family and the nuclear family. The common type of family household in our society is a **nuclear family**. It consists of two generations living together—typically, one or two parents and their child(ren). The nuclear family is a **conjugal family**, in which priority is given to marital ties over blood ties. The fundamental relationship is between spouses, not between one or more spouses and their parents, siblings, and more distant kin (like aunts, uncles, and cousins).

An **extended family** is one in which more than two generations of relatives live together. For example, it may include grandparents and/or grandchildren, and relatives connected by other relations than marriage and parenthood, such as uncles, aunts, and cousins. The extended family is a **consanguine family**, since priority is given to blood ties over marital ties. Consanguine families stress the importance of relationships between parents and their children, among siblings, and with other "blood-related" members of the kin group.

Each of these forms has its advantages and disadvantages. The extended family usually serves as one big productive unit, with all able-bodied members contributing to the common good of the family. The members of this unit cooperate in such productive activities as agriculture, craft work, hunting and gathering, building shelters, and other activities related to subsistence.

Moreover, members of an extended family are able to rely on one another when they need emotional support. For example, children can go to aunts and uncles, cousins and grandparents when they need to resolve a problem they feel they cannot talk about with their parents. Spouses can rely on their parents and siblings for comfort and support. This puts less strain on each other and the marital relationship. And, in an extended family, grandparents can be sure they will be taken care of in their old age.

The nuclear family also has its advantages. Such a family is not obliged to remain in any particular location: it can take advantage of job opportunities in another part of the country, or another country entirely. In industrial societies, few people own the means by which they make a living. They are wage labourers, working for that tiny fraction of the population who own the means of production, and therefore must live where they can find employment rather than where the family work is based.

In other words, the family in industrial societies is *not* a unit of production as it is in non-industrial (hunter-gatherer or agricultural) societies. There is no need for a large group of kin to live together and there are good reasons (like the need for geographic mobility) why they should not. Many of the functions the extended family once performed have been taken over by the state or profit-making organizations. They include child care (by daycare centres), education (by schools), care for the elderly (by nursing homes), and income and health supports (by state-run social service agencies).

However, the nuclear family also has its disadvantages. It offers its members too few people to rely on in times of financial trouble or emotional stress. Family members are liable to expect too much from each other, because they

Recent changes in the family reflect basic long-term changes in our society that go back at least to the last century. In a traditional, agriculturally based society, most activities, including work activities, take place in the household. In a modern urban society, most activities, especially work, are carried on outside the household. Men's activities have been moving out of the household (represented here by agricultural work) for more than a century. Women have been making the same shift (represented here by their labour force participation), although with a delay of several decades compared to men. Finally, household size has been declining in parallel with its loss of economic functions, from an average of 5.2 in the late 19th century to 2.8 today.

Similar paths have been followed by all societies, as technological advances have led to increased industrial productivity and economic development. Increasing numbers of men, then of women, began to work outside the home as work there became more productive and hence more remunerative. Changes in technology in the home have also meant that through the years fewer and fewer hours were needed to be devoted to home production. The duration and the strength of the forces reflected in this graph underline the importance of understanding the trends in the modern Canadian family, for it is very unlikely that these trends will be reversed.

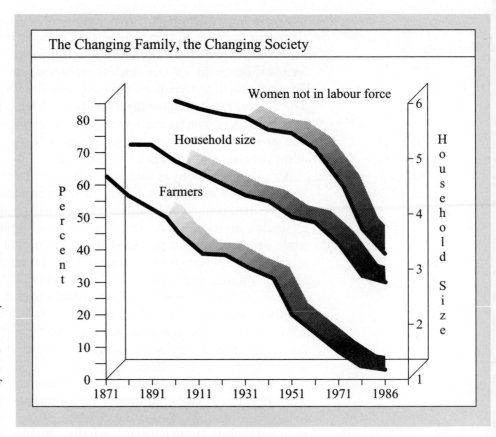

The Changing Family, the Changing Society

Source: *Charting Canada's Future: A Report of the Demographic Review.* (1989) (Catalogue No. H21-105/1-1989) Ottawa: Health and Welfare Canada, p. 16. Reproduced with the permission of the Minister of Supply and Services Canada, 1990.

have no one else to turn to. This reliance may put too much strain on relationships between spouses, or between parents and children.

Not only do kinship systems define who is a member and who is not; they also define how individual members relate to one another both within and outside the group. In fact, the two aspects of kinship are related—they are macro and micro aspects of the same thing. Our interpersonal relations—what we expect of, and get from, other people—depend largely on whether society defines those people as kin. If we have few close kin nearby, we will depend more heavily on the few kin who *are* available, often re-thinking our relationships with spouse, siblings, parents, and children. Sometimes, we develop substitutes for kinship, using friends or neighbours to provide the support and human contact we need. As family life changes, so do many other aspects of our lives, both big and small.

And, family life is capable of taking on a wide variety of forms. There is no single, universal form of family life. For this reason, family relations tell us a great deal about the unique total pattern of social patterns and values of a given society.

MARRIAGE AND FAMILY IN CANADA

Is there a distinct "Canadian" family?

Focusing on the variations outlined above, we can see that the typical Canadian family is nuclear, its residence is neolocal; marriage is monogamous, descent is bilateral; and increasingly the authority is equalitarian. The selection of marriage partners is usually endogamous, although not as restrictive as in pre-industrial societies, and homogamous.

In all of these respects, the Canadian family is very much like families we would find in other industrial countries: in the United States, West Germany, Italy, or Japan, for example. And, like the family in these other nations, the Canadian family is undergoing a great many changes both in norms and in structure. Three recent changes are particularly significant: the dramatic rise in the divorce rate, the increase in the number of single-parent families, and the growing acceptance of **cohabitation** before (or instead of) legal marriage.

Cohabitation and marriage

Cohabitation is a living arrangement in which an unmarried couple lives together to find out if they are compatible, to cut down on living expenses, or for other reasons. The major difference between marriage and cohabitation is that the former is an explicit legal commitment and the latter is not. Even so, the law regards cohabitation that continues more than three years as a legally binding relationship in certain respects (thus a common-law partnership). Long-term cohabiters owe each other support obligations (though not the sharing of community property) in the event of a breakup. So even here, the difference between marriage and cohabitation has blurred.

New housing patterns make living together easier than ever for unmarried people. By 1984, about one adult respondent in six had been in a common-law partnership at one time or another (Burch, 1985: Table 4A). Among young people aged 18-29, the proportion was much higher: about one man in five and one woman in four.

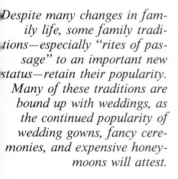

Despite many changes in family life, some family traditions—especially "rites of passage" to an important new status—retain their popularity. Many of these traditions are bound up with weddings, as the continued popularity of wedding gowns, fancy ceremonies, and expensive honeymoons will attest.

Often, common-law partnerships are a prelude to marriage. The 1984 Family History Survey revealed that just under half of the people ever in a common-law union ended up marrying their common-law partner. This suggests that, increasingly often, common-law unions serve as trial marriages (Burch, 1985: Table 5), an interpretation supported by evidence (Burch, 1985: Table 4A) that less than 2% of all respondents report having been in more than one such relationship. Indeed, 46% of males and 43% of females who ever cohabited report marrying their common-law partner.

Younger men and women are also more likely than older ones to have ever cohabited. For example, in 1984, 21% of men aged 18-39 had, at some time, cohabited with a woman, compared with less than 7% of men aged 50-64.

EXHIBIT 7.3

THE STEPS OF MARRIAGE

Although marriage can be considered a cultural universal, the customs associated with it can vary drastically, depending on the culture.

Below is a table that contains information provided by 201 pregnant or newly delivered women from Harare, the capital of Zimbabwe. The events are the elements of "marriage" to the baby's father, and are listed in chronological order.

Twelve Life Events Related to Union Formation in Harare, Zimbabwe

1. met baby's father   (201)
2. discussed with him introducing him to your family   (112)
3. discussed him with your tete (aunt) or relative   (173)
4. introduced him to your family   (148)
5. negotiation with your family of payments to them   (125)
6. first payment made to your family   (137)
7. District Court registration obtained; marriage ceremony performed   (12)
8. first slept with him   (had sex with him)   (201)
9. began to live with him   (190)
10. became pregnant with this child   (201)
11. exchanged gifts   (121)
12. tizira ("captured" by the man's family)   (90)

The numbers to the right indicate how many respondents ever experienced each event.

How many of these events are steps of the marriage process in your culture? What steps are not included by the Zimbabweans, or are not always taken? Prepare a chronology for marriage (or union leading to the birth of a child) in our society.

Source: J. Richard Udry, Nancy Dole Runkle, and Karen Gleiter "The process of reproductive union formation in urban Zimbabwe." Paper presented to the Population Association of America, Toronto: May 3, 1990.

Divorce

A second significant change in Canadian society is the increase in divorce. **Divorce** is the legal, formal dissolution of a legal marriage, freeing the spouses to remarry. Divorce is increasingly accepted as a valid and appropriate way out of an unhappy marital situation. When children are involved, many people feel that they are better off with single parents than in a family filled with conflict and, sometimes, violence.

The divorce rate is often used to measure the numbers of failed marriages, or marital breakdown in our society. It is a convenient measure and provides a basic index of changes that have taken place in Canadian family life. The Family History Survey shows that about one in ten ever-married males and one in eight ever-married females have had a marriage end in divorce.

The situation is changing, though. A larger proportion of both males and females aged 30-49 have experienced divorce than those aged 50-64. These data help to explain why most demographers project that newly married couples run a roughly 40% risk of future divorce. Their projections assume that rates of divorce will continue to rise, or at least will remain high among young and middle-aged people.

Data gathered by Statistics Canada show that rates of divorce remained fairly steady at about 200 divorces per 100 000 married women aged 15 and over each year from 1952 through 1968. With law reforms that made divorcing a spouse easier after 1968, the rates shot up five-fold to 1000 divorces per year per 100 000 married women by 1978. Rates levelled off in the 1980s, then started to fall (Statistics Canada, 1987: 22).

The recent decline in marital breakdowns may be more apparent than real, though. Some couples may have been waiting for recent amendments to the Divorce Act before starting proceedings. Other couples may be breaking up and forming new (common-law) unions without going through the formalities of divorce.

The overall divorce rate is by no means a reliable index of marital breakdown. For example, the Family History Survey has found important regional differences in the prevalence of divorce. The percentage of those ever married who had a divorce is markedly lower than average in the Atlantic provinces and in Quebec, and higher in British Columbia. The difference in Quebec, chiefly seen in the older generation, probably reflects the past influence of the Catholic Church. The higher prevalence in British Columbia may reflect the character of in-migration to the province. Divorced people are more apt than average to move, and this province attracts large numbers of migrants, including large numbers of divorced ones.

There are reasons not to use the overall divorce rate as a measure of family well-being in Canada. We all know (or know of) couples who were incompatible but stayed together—did not get divorced—"for the sake of the children" or because they feared what the neighbours or family and friends would say.

As we noted in our discussion of romantic love, our expectations concerning our marriage partners have a major bearing on the chances of divorce. One of our culture's great myths is that, if you are lucky, you will find a mate—Mr. or Ms. Right—who will be perfect for you and go on being perfect. Yet everyone changes. People break up marriages because they are no longer the same people who decided to marry in the first place. Other unhappy spouses—who feel guilty about breaking up or worry about the impact of divorce on the children, who cannot afford the costs of two separate households or fear they would miss their children if they left—stay together. They do not become a part of the country's divorce statistic, but their marriage is no less broken for all that.

There is definitely a higher incidence of marital breakdown than the divorce statistics would lead us to believe. Still, the statistics allow us to compare groups. These comparisons allow us to draw conclusions about the risks of divorce, if not the prevalence of marital dissatisfaction. They allow us to ask *Why do some people get divorced, while others don't?* Analyses of divorce data show that divorce rates are highest among couples who married when they were very young, or knew each other for only a short time before getting married. They are highest among people who live in the city, were previously married, or have friends and relatives who did not look favourably on the marriage. Finally, divorce is more likely where the wife is economically independent than where she is not.

What causes marital breakdown, whether it ends in divorce or not? Sociological research suggests that these are some of the factors:

(1) too much pressure on the nuclear family. In the event of a crisis, there are few people to rely on for comfort and support. The spouses often end up taking out their anger at the world on each other.

(2) unfulfillable expectations of a love that would last forever. People feel their marriage has failed when it loses its romantic lustre. This is easy to understand: our culture has taught us to expect that love-feelings will run high for years, if not forever, despite all the daily troubles that afflict people who live together. Rather than blaming the harsh effects of routine and daily conflict, people are liable to think they chose the wrong mate.

(3) The growing economic independence of women means that more women can leave unhappy marriages today than in the past. To the extent that a rising divorce rate is due to freer choice, it simply reflects women exercising more control over their own lives and not necessarily more marital breakdown.

Today, there is wide and growing recognition of the pitfalls of early marriage:

> The divorce rate among such young marriages is estimated at from two to four times that among persons who marry after 20 years of age. The divorce rate is related to low educational levels, low economic levels, premarital pregnancies, and possibly to personality difficulties. (Leslie and Korman, 1985: 396)

For all these reasons, both males and females marrying early have higher rates of marital instability. It seems likely that men or women who marry early are often unprepared for the reality of married life. Young women who marry and/or procreate before completing their education pay an even heavier price than men. Data from the 1984 Family History Survey (Pool and Moore, 1986: 49) suggest that female lone parents are more likely than others to have become parents too soon, before acquiring the education and job skills to make themselves economically independent. The authors continue, "In the longer run, this lack of job-related resources may have limited their power within a marriage or union and, thus, may have predisposed its termination."

Another question, which has received little sociological attention to date, is *What causes marital success?* Because of the way data are collected we know little about the conditions and circumstances of marital success. This is one area in which the sort of qualitative research engaged in by microsociologists might well prove indispensible. Qualitative interview and observation might well allow us to identify some of the negotiations and strategies developed by people to get along with one another, to defuse crises, and to maintain their relationships.

Single-parent families

As more marriages end in separation or divorce, single-parent families become increasingly common. A **single-parent family** is a family in which only one parent lives with his or her dependent children; however, child care and child support may be coming from both parents. The great majority of these families are headed by women.

Single-parent families are rapidly becoming a common form of family life. By 1984, more than one adult woman in six reported having been a lone parent at some time in her life. The proportion was one in four among women aged 40-49 and 50-65. In fact, the experience of single parenthood, though transient,

---

EXHIBIT 7.4

THE SOCIAL CONSEQUENCES OF REMARRIAGE
Statistics Canada (1987: 21) reports that

> In 1967, in 1 out of 8 marriages, one of the spouses had been married previously. Seventeen years later, in . . . roughly 1 in 3 [marriages], one of the spouses had been married before, and in 9 out of 10 of these cases, they had been divorced.

Increasingly, it has been divorce—not the death of a spouse—that has preceded remarriage. This means that recent remarriers are likely to be younger (on average, in their thirties) than past remarriers. Because they are younger, they are also more likely to start a second family than remarriers in the past. As a result, the "reconstituted" households they form are likelier to contain children from two marriages than in the past. This will make certain family relationships, like half-brother (or sister) and step-brother (or sister), more common than in the past.

Children will also have a wider variety of adult kin—step-grandparents, step-aunts and -uncles, for example—than in the past, due to remarriage. A child whose parents divorce and remarry can easily have eight living grandparents. Cultural norms governing these multiplied kin—what rights and duties are to be expected—have not yet evolved. As a result, everyone is trying to make their own sense of the new family relationships.

Source: Statistics Canada (1987) *Current Demographic Analysis: Report on the Demographic Situation in Canada, 1986.* (Catalogue No. 91-209E) Ottawa: Supply and Services. Reproduced with the permission of the Minister of Supply and Services Canada, 1990.

is an experience a great many Canadians will have experienced by the end of their lives.

Already, single-parent families constitute a high proportion of all family, and especially all childhood, experiences of poverty. They are a stark reminder of what sociologists call the **feminization of poverty**: the "poor" in Canada are predominantly women. They include single mothers living on welfare, who cannot work because they cannot afford daycare for their children; and elderly women who spent their lives as homemakers and could not, therefore, contribute to a pension plan that would support them decently in their old age.

Just as the nuclear family once represented a separation of the tasks of production from the family, Moore (1989) points out that, "the lone-parent family represents the separation of marital and childrearing processes. As the adult adapts to movement between lone, nuclear and **reconstituted families**, children provide the continuity as they grow through all the developmental stages" (348). For both mother and child, then, family living is a series of changes and adjustments. The most reliably constant relationship is that between parent and child, and even that will change significantly when the child leaves home.

PROBLEMS OF THE MODERN FAMILY

Spousal inequalities

Inequalities between spouses are bound to result from the structural characteristics of marriage, particularly in a society like ours. These inequalities do not arise from the personal characteristics of the spouses themselves: they are relatively uniform across families. They arise out of the need for sacrifice in families, and the unequal allocation of sacrifices by gender; that is, from a traditional gender-based division of labour.

Assigning certain tasks on the basis of some social characteristics, and not personality traits, is a common feature of every society—indeed, every social institution. The particular tasks and the characteristics for assigning them may vary. However, every known society has a division of labour that is based on gender and on age. This division of labour is considered natural because of certain physiological differences between young people and older ones, and between men and women.

Yet cultures differ in their interpretation of these differences. Historically in our society, women had been assigned the role of child rearing and domestic duties. Now increasingly women have demanded a more equal access to public life and well paid work, and a more equal sharing of domestic duties. In effect, they have rebelled against a division of labour in society, and in the home, based on gender. This demand is in keeping with our culture's general commitment to individualism.

The result is a gender-based difference in women's and men's experience of marriage. Sociologist Jesse Bernard (1973) calls this a difference between *his marriage* and *her marriage*. According to Bernard, marriages contain two often very different views of the relationship: the wife's and the husband's. The two perspectives are different enough, and equally distant from the objective reality, to constitute two different marriages.

These divergent perspectives, or definitions of the situation, come from the different insitutional roles women and men are required to play as wives and husbands. Males are expected to dominate women, and women are expected to subordinate themselves to men. Given this, different perspectives are inevitable: the world looks different if you are looking up or looking down.

The structural inequalities between spouses leading to different perspectives on a marriage produce other outcomes as well. For example, for men, marriage is mentally, emotionally, and physically beneficial. That may be one reason suicide rates and mental illness are less common among married than among unmarried men. For women, on the other hand, marriage is often the *cause* of mental, emotional, and physical problems.

These differences in marital experience have, if anything, been reinforced by women's large-scale entry into paid work. Now married women inhabit what sociologists Hugh and Pat Armstrong (1978) call a "double ghetto." Unlike men, married women work a double day. Their freedom to work for pay, pursue a career, and be economically independent does not mean freedom from domestic work. Women continue to do most of the household chores after they put in a full day's work outside the home: theirs is a double burden. A great deal of evidence from around Canada and elsewhere shows that when married women go out to work for pay, their husbands do *not* significantly increase the time they spend on domestic duties, even if young children are present in the household. Moreover, this inequality is apparently not lessening.

Women experience subordination—indeed segregation—in low-status "women's work" both on the job and at home. Their ghetto is double in that their work experiences of subordination reinforce their domestic experiences, and vice versa. The result is that the disadvantage resulting from domestic duties is a very serious impediment to women's economic progress.

For whatever reason, *patriarchy*—the domination of women by men—is part of our cultural heritage (Fox, 1988). It has a very long history, and some part of the male domination that persists today is simply a holdover from an earlier, agricultural period when a sexual division of labour may have been more necessary and was, in any event, more easily imposed.

It is a problem for which there are only so many solutions, if we accept the idea that only women are responsible for domestic work. Wives can try to compel their spouses and children to cooperate more, but so far such attempts have met with little success. Wives can work harder and risk their mental and physical health. They can opt for part-time rather than full-time paid work—especially while their children are very young—and there is evidence that many women are doing this. They can rely increasingly on paid domestic and child-care services (daycare, fast food, house cleaners, and so on). Or they can set their aspirations and expectations very low: that is, think of what they are doing as a job, not a career.

Evidence suggests that in traditionally male-dominated careers, where women would have the greatest difficulty lowering their aspirations and expectations, women's domestic lives are at the greatest risk. Marshall (1987) shows that, compared with women in traditionally female careers, women in traditionally male careers are less likely to marry; if married, less likely to remain married; or, if they remained married, less likely to bear children. It is virtually impossible to have a serious career *and* a serious marriage if you are a

Today, children are learning new ways of being adults by seeing their parents blur the traditional gender roles

woman, since you are expected to carry your full weight in both activities. Men, by contrast, have been culturally forgiven their lack of domestic involvement.

Part of the problem, again, is cultural and long-standing. It has to do with the way we value time. By assigning women a double day, we are saying several things about time, and about women. Mainly, we are saying that housework is worth little in comparison with other kinds of work and since women's time is worth less than men's time, women should do the housework. As Margrit Eichler (1990: 404) has written, "when we cease to define women as dependents, or when the power position of a group of people changes, the value of their time will change."

If women accept the heavy domestic responsibility currently foisted upon them, they will find it hard to compete effectively with men at work. Moreover, if employers, too, expect that women are accepting this domestic responsibility, they will see females as less valuable—since less available—employees. Continued gender inequality at home will almost ensure continued gender inequality in the workplace.

Thus, just as there is a world of work that includes a female ghetto, so there is a world of marriage that includes a female ghetto: the ghetto of wives. Wives experience marriage differently from husbands, they experience parenthood differently from husbands, and they experience paid work differently from husbands. Because their daily experience (in every important particular) is different, their perception of the world is different. They live in a different world.

Child care and child raising

Most people marry with the idea of having children. What they rarely know, or admit, is that—for all its pleasures—parenthood imposes a great many burdens. There is evidence to suppose that much family instability and dissatisfaction arises out of the trials of parenthood.

The onset of parenthood is a particularly trying time. "Both men and women express more feeling of strain at this stage than at any other period of their married lives" (Campbell, 1979: 187). Raising small children strains the marriage: disagreements become more common, both husband and wife feel they get less companionship from their mate than they once did, and both marital satisfaction and enjoyment of parenthood are declining or low. "Two out of five of these mothers of small children go so far as to admit they sometimes wish they could be free of the responsibilities of being a parent, a much larger proportion than is found among mothers of older children" (Campbell, 1979: 188).

In some ways, this period is the hardest parenthood will ever be. Once a mother is in a position to take a job, financial anxieties start to diminish. Two-income parents feel less tied down, less strained or burdened by parenthood, and more likely to enjoy it. With children in the age range 6-17,

> parents ... disagree less often about spending money and they feel they understand each other better. But they do not regain the strong sense of companionship ... they had as young couples until they reach the next stage of life when the children have grown up (Campbell, 1979: 189).

A comparison of families by Lupri and Frideres (1981: 300) shows that, at all ages (and marital durations), married women without children are more satisfied with marriage than are women with children. Whether or not a woman works outside the home also affects the pressures of parenthood: employed wives reach a lower level of marital satisfaction than nonemployed wives; conversely, the husbands of nonemployed wives reach a lower level of marital satisfaction than the husbands of employed wives do.

In all cases, the low point occurs roughly when the children are adolescents. Parenthood hits employed wives harder than it hits their spouses because of heavier dual responsibilities of work and parenthood. On the other hand, husbands of nonemployed wives will be harder hit than their spouses because of the heavier financial burden as the children enter adolescence. This greater need for money in middle age, at the very time when a husband's income has started to level off, is often called the "life cycle squeeze." Two kinds of marital conflict arise as the children reach adolescence. A wife who does not work outside the home may start to feel more satisfaction with marriage at the very time her husband, smarting under a greater financial burden, is feeling the least satisfaction ever. A wife who does work outside the home will feel declining marital satisfaction, resulting from pressures at home and on the job, at the very time her husband is starting to feel greater marital satisfaction.

How long these conflicts go on is determined by the length of time it takes all the children to pass through adolescence and leave home. The fewer the children and the more closely they are spaced, the shorter the period of minimal satisfaction for one or both spouses and the briefer the marital conflict parenthood produces.

The sociological evidence leaves no doubt that parenthood strains the relationship between husbands and wives. This in itself is a good explanation of

EXHIBIT 7.5

WHO'S DOING WHAT AROUND THE HOME?

Time budget data collected by Statistics Canada show that the division of tasks between male and female spouses is still very unequal. There is still HIS work and HER work—and more of HER work than HIS work—though somewhat more gender blurring and work sharing than in the past.

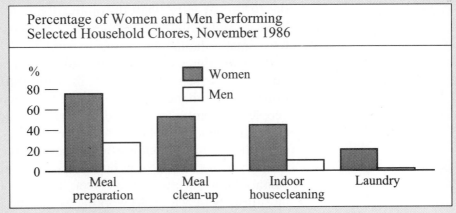

Percentage of Women and Men Performing Selected Household Chores, November 1986

Source: Statistics Canada, General Social Survey, 1986.

Continued

Daily Participation in and Time Spent on Household Chores, November 1986

	Participation rate		Average time spent by participants	
	Women	Men	Women	Men
	%		Hours/Minutes	
Age				
15-24	65	40	1:50	1:12
25-44	89	53	3:02	1:50
45-64	93	55	3:24	2:17
65 and over	90	61	3:00	2:11
Total 15 and over	85	52	2:57	1:53
Main activity				
Paid work	83	51	2:16	1:44
Looking for work	84	65	2:43	2:27
Student	57	36	1:28	1:04
Keeping house	97	91	3:52	3:35
Retired	88	62	2:51	2:21
Presence of children under age 19				
Children at home	94	53	3:22	2:01
No children at home	80	51	2:39	1:49

Source: Statistics Canada, General Social Survey, 1986.

Source: K. Marshall (1990) "Household chores" *Canadian Social Trends* (Spring), pp. 18, 19. Reproduced with the permission of the Minister of Supply and Services Canada, 1990.

why many couples are reducing or eliminating childbearing, but not the only one. The decline in parenthood has been going on for over a century for other reasons: chiefly, it has become progressively harder to live a comfortable, middle-class urban life with many children. Given the choice between more children and more disposable income, most people in Canada over the last hundred years have been choosing the latter. With the economic recession of the 1970s and early 1980s the motivation to further restrict childbearing grew stronger and, with the development of new contraceptive technology, the wish for a smaller family was easier to fulfil.

If, as we argue, childbearing tends to increase marital tension and reduce satisfaction, then the decline in childbearing should increase people's satisfaction with marriage and reduce the divorce rate. But, for the time being, people are bearing fewer children because children are increasingly expensive and of no economic value to their parents. They make marital dissolution more difficult and costly than it would otherwise be. Finally, they create enormous strains on the two-income family, especially around problems of finding a balance between family and career. These problems of finding a balance fall most heavily on wives. As working women become more committed to career advancement, children become more and more of a problem.

The generation gap

For most of you reading this book, marriage and its problems are still some time off in the future. Your family is one in which you are likely the son or daughter rather than the mother or father. Here too, as most of you are aware, the modern family is an arena of tension and conflict, inequality and dependence. Parents and children, like husbands and wives, have different perceptions of the family, perceptions that reflect structural features of our society rather than individual personality differences. These differences of perception are often referred to as the **generation gap**.

Perhaps the most significant of the structural features that promote the generation gap is the lengthening of the period of time that an individual is economically and emotionally dependent upon his or her family. In most pre-modern societies, adulthood came soon after the end of childhood, usually somewhere around the late teens. At this time an individual would get married and be considered a full adult member of society. In such a society, such age categories as "adolescence" and "youth," which we have come to take for granted, did not exist.

Several factors have led to a lengthening period of dependency and childhood. One factor is modern education. In pre-modern societies most people spent their lives doing what their mother or father had done. If a boy's father was a peasant farmer, he too would become a farmer; if a girl's mother looked after the home and the garden, she would do the same. Children learned to perform the work expected of them as adults by performing their tasks at home. By the end of childhood they were seen as soon ready to take on adult responsibilities.

Today, we learn most of what we need to know as adults, especially our future occupations, outside the home, in school. And because there is so much more to learn in a complex industrial society, we continue to attend school for many years. This means that many people are still students in their early twenties: still dependent financially on their families, often still living at home. This financial dependency prolongs the unequal relationship between parents and children past the point where young people willingly accept their parents' authority. It is difficult to attend college or university where you are expected to act responsibly, to think for yourself, and to succeed or fail by your own efforts, and then find yourself treated as a child at home.

In pre-modern societies, becoming an adult usually meant marriage and taking on the responsibility of raising your own children. Today, few couples get married until they are in their twenties. This prolongs the period of *emotional* dependence on the family. Young adults find that their parents' opinion of them continues to be an important part of their sense of self, just at the time when structural factors are likely to lower that opinion. Young people find themselves still locked into an intense emotional relationship with their parents at an age at which in another society they would be independent, responsible adults with a spouse and children of their own.

What makes this emotional dependence worse is that parents' expectations are usually undergoing a change. As their children grow up, most parents want to be freed of the arduous obligations of child care and expect their children to "start acting like adults." Unfortunately, the structural factors that prolong dependence mean that the home is the very last place where young people get to

There are no right or wrong answers to this "test," nor did the test-makers suggest a scoring scheme by which to decide whether the test-taker should have children. Instead, think of this test as a way of increasing your own sensitivity to the issues surrounding parenthood. Do you think you passed the test?

The NAOP (National Alliance For Optional Parenthood) "Am I Parent Material?" Test

Raising a child? What's there to know?

1. Do I like children? When I'm around children for a while, what do I think or feel about having one around all of the time?
2. Do I enjoy teaching others?
3. Is it easy for me to tell other people what I want, or need, or what I expect of them?
4. Do I want to give a child the love (s)he needs? Is loving easy for me?
5. Am I patient enough to deal with the noise and the confusion of the 24-hour-a-day responsibility? What kind of time and space do I need for myself?
6. What do I do when I get angry or upset? Would I take things out on a child if I lost my temper?
7. What does discipline mean to me? What does freedom, or setting limits, or giving space mean? What is being too strict, or not strict enough? Would I want a perfect child?
8. How do I get along with my parents? What will I do to avoid the mistakes my parents made?
9. How would I take care of my child's health and safety? How do I take care of my own?
10. What if I have a child and find out I made a wrong decision?

Have my partner and I really talked about becoming parents?

1. Does my partner want to have a child? Have we talked about our reasons?
2. Could we give a child a good home? Is our relationship a happy and strong one?
3. Are we both ready to give our time and energy to raising a child?
4. Could we share our love with a child without jealousy?
5. What would happen if we separated after having a child, or if one of us should die?
6. Do my partner and I understand each other's feelings about religion, work, family, child-raising, future goals? Do we feel pretty much the same way? Will children fit into these feelings, hopes, and plans?
7. Suppose one of us wants a child and the other doesn't. Who decides?
8. Which of the questions in this test do we need to *really* discuss before making a decision?

What's in it for me?

1. Do I like doing things with children? Do I enjoy activities that children can do?
2. Would I want a child to be "like me"?
3. Would I try to pass on to my child my ideas and values? What if my child's ideas and values turn out to be different from mine?
4. Would I want my child to achieve things that I wish I had, but didn't?
5. Would I expect my child to keep me from being lonely in my old age? Do I do that for my parents? Do my parents do that for my grandparents?
6. Do I want a boy or a girl child? What if I don't get what I want?

Continued

7. Would having a child show others how mature I am?
8. Will I prove I am a man or a woman by having a child?
9. Do I expect my child to make my life happy?

Does having and raising a child fit the lifestyle I want?

1. What do I want out of life for myself? What do I think is important?
2. Could I handle a child and a job at the same time? Would I have time and energy for both?
3. Would I be ready to give up the freedom to do what I want to do, when I want to do it?
4. Would I be willing to cut back my social life and spend more time at home? Would I miss my free time and privacy?
5. Can I afford to support a child? Do I know how much it takes to raise a child?
6. Do I want to raise a child in the neighbourhood where I live now? Would I be willing and able to move?
7. How would a child interfere with my growth and development?
8. Would a child change my educational plans? Do I have the energy to go to school and raise a child at the same time?
9. Am I willing to give a great part of my life—AT LEAST 18 YEARS—to being responsible for a child? And spend a large portion of my life being concerned about my child's well-being?

Source: National Alliance for Optional Parenthood

show not only that they can act like adults but that in fact they *are* adults. When parents think of acting "like an adult," they have a very idealized image of proper behaviour (one they probably could not live up to themselves). Since their children inevitably fail to meet these unrealistic expectations, they tend to think of their eighteen-, nineteen- or twenty-year-old sons and daughters as still being irresponsible children. In turn, young people rebel against this perception on the part of their parents, often trying to force their parents to treat them as adults. The resulting tension convinces each that the other is the problem. For many young people the only solution is to move out of the home.

Yet dependency can be a very seductive state. Having someone to cook for you, clean up, do your laundry, and pay your bills, can be attractive. Thus, even as many young people rail against their parents, they continue to take advantage of the more beneficial consequences of dependency. The result is something of a self-fulfilling prophecy, with young people taking advantage of the chance to be as irresponsible and immature as their parents consider them to be.

The result of this lengthened period of dependence is that adulthood is put off, and the historically recent age categories of adolescence and youth have emerged. These age categories, then, do not reflect a biological fact about age, but are social categories generated by specific structural features of our society. This does not mean that they are not "real," however. They are as real in our society as are ethnicity, race, or gender.

Family violence

Because the family has long been considered the most private institution in our society, there was little realization until recently how pervasive violence is as a part of family life. It was taken for granted that parents have a right to use physical force to discipline their children, and most parents had little hesitation in giving their child a slap in public. Violence between spouses was less acceptable, at least in public, but many men believed that they had as much right to hit their wives as to discipline their children. Still another form of violence we are beginning to learn about is elder abuse, mistreatment directed toward the elderly by their children and grandchildren. Clearly, resorting to physical violence or abuse was seen by some as a means of solving interpersonal problems. Far from being a safe haven in a difficult world, the family itself has been for many people a source of pain, humiliation, and anger.

The degree to which family violence was once seen as "normal" is indicated by the failure of physicians to report cases of child battering until fairly recently. Physicians typically ignored the suspicious broken bones, bruises, or lacerations they found on children. Some physicians were unwilling to get involved in what they considered to be private family matters; others considered the parents (rather than the child) to be their patients and were concerned to maintain confidentiality. It took an active and concerted campaign by the medical profession itself to alert physicians to the signs of child battering, to encourage them to investigate their suspicions, and to have them report cases of battering to the police (Conrad and Schneider, 1980).

Another example is the failure of the law to recognize marital rape as a crime until the Criminal Code was amended in 1983. That marital rape was not considered assault tells us both that it was taken for granted that wives should be sexually available at their husband's will and that the use of violence by men was considered acceptable when directed against their wives (Pettifer and Torge, 1987).

Although both people's attitudes and the laws have changed to some extent, family violence remains to a large extent unreported. The Canadian Urban Victimization Survey conducted in 1982 showed that only 44% of cases of wife abuse were reported to the police (Johnson, 1988). Half of those who did not seek help from the police indicated that they feared revenge by the offender, and about a third indicated that they "wanted to protect the offender" (Johnson, 1988: 19). Altogether 59% considered the abuse to be "a personal matter and of no concern to the police." There is good reason to believe that an even smaller proportion of cases of child or elder abuse are reported to authorities.

Because of the failure to report family violence, we do not have good statistics available on the prevalence of these types of violence. However, homicide statistics, which are usually quite complete, tell the same tale as surveys of sexual child abuse. People are at a greater risk of physical injury from a spouse or family member than from a stranger. Johnson and Chisholm (1989: 17) report that 40% of solved homicides between 1985 and 1987 were cases of domestic homicide, and in 37% of these cases men killed their wives or common-law partners.

There is no proof that wife battering and child abuse are increasing (or decreasing), but every indication that these forms of violence are widespread. A national survey conducted in 1986 (Lupri, 1989) of over 1800 men showed that 18% admitted to committing one or more acts of violence against their partners. The survey showed that younger men (aged 29 or younger), those with lower incomes (under $20 000 per year), and those with less education (less than a high school diploma) were the most likely to *admit* to violence. Men in British Columbia had the highest rate, 26%, while those in Quebec had the lowest, 13%.

The survey also suggests that incidents of male violence were the outcome of "stressful" life events, such as unemployment or having to work overtime. It is hard to see how anyone could claim that stress *caused* the violence. These men did not lash out in random violence directed at strangers or at those causing their stress; they beat their wives. The choice of the wife as the object of their violence means that they see their wives as suitable outlets for their aggression. The real cause of their aggression resides, then, in their perception of marriage as giving them a right to beat their wives, and of a wife as someone who can be safely beaten at their discretion.

THE FUTURE OF THE FAMILY

Economic aspects of family change

As the population grows, so do the number of households. What's more, some household types increase in number more quickly than others. While four out of five households are still made up of traditional families, non-family households grew nearly five times as fast as family households in the 1970s, and two-and-a-half times as fast in the 1980s. Traditional families continue to survive but their numbers are growing very slowly while non-traditional families—especially childless marriages, common-law marriages, and lone-parent households—are growing rapidly and show no sign of stopping.

In the case of well over half of all married couples, both spouses work for pay. The number of such *two-earner families* will continue to increase as more and more women enter the work force and stay in it for a larger part of their adult lives. Today, most women do not stop working when they get married. Of those who stop work to have a baby, most go back to work shortly after their child is born.

The rise of the two-earner family has caused many changes in the marketplace during the last decade. Since both spouses work, they have less time to spend on such tasks as cleaning, cooking, and taking care of the children. They look to outside services and hired help to do these tasks. Also, two incomes provide these couples with the extra money they need to buy conveniences. Their new demands account for a growth in the sales of frozen foods, restaurant foods, household care and child-care services. Two-earner couples have also contributed to the growth of the appliance industry (which makes items like microwave ovens and dishwashers) and the leisure goods industry (which makes VCRs and sports equipment, among other things).

Childless couples, in particular, have more *discretionary income*—more money to spend on things other than necessities like food and shelter—than families with children do; and this fact makes childless couples very important consumers. In fact, *two* factors explain their discretionary income: high earning power and low expenses. Most childless couples earn two incomes. In 1986, for example, 87% of childless couples under 35 were two-earner households. Childless couples also make about 20% more money than couples with children. In part, this is related to their high average education; the more education a woman gets, the more likely she is to avoid or delay bearing children. As a result, more highly educated, high-income people spend a larger portion of their lives without children, enjoying a high discretionary income.

Without child-care expenses to pay, these childless couples have a lot more money to spend on themselves. Economist Gary Becker (1981) has compared childbearing to the purchase of *consumer durables*—long-lasting, often expensive items like automobiles or dishwashers. This comparison has much to recommend it; but actually the lifetime expense of raising children—in energy and emotion, as well as money—far outdistances most consumer durables on the market. (The only durable that demands nearly as much time and money as a child is a home.)

It may be impossible today to talk about a typical family or typical marriage. Major trends in family life include declining family sizes, increasing numbers of lone-parent families, increasing numbers of families created by remarriage, more multiple-earner families, and more people living alone. The old-style "monolithic famly" model (Eichler, 1981)—with a single male breadwinner and stay-at-home wife who looks after two or three children—no longer describes the majority of Canadian adult lives.

By 1981, only 16% of families followed the traditional pattern with the husband as sole breadwinner, and this proportion is still falling. Data from the Canadian Survey of Consumer Finances (Wolfson, 1986) show a rise in the proportion of unattached individuals and of "empty nests." From 1965 to 1983, there was a one-quarter drop in the proportion of family units that were "traditional" husband-wife families with children, and a one-third increase in the proportion of single-parent families.

Rates of first marriage have fallen to an all-time low in Canada (Statistics Canada, 1987: 19). This falling national marriage rate has been led by large declines in Quebec which "has not only the lowest rate of all the provinces but one of the lowest rates in the world" (ibid). The trend of younger people toward opting for common-law unions over marriage partly explains this decline in marriages. There is evidence that people are merely delaying, not rejecting marriage, so that the average age at first marriage is increasing.

Late marriage has historically been associated with high proportions never marrying (Hajnal, 1965). Both are a common response to fear about economic conditions that make marrying and childbearing too risky for some tastes. People who delay marriage beyond a certain age appear to lose interest in ever marrying; they become accustomed to the single life and, for women, child-bearing often becomes riskier or impossible. So both increased common-law cohabitation and delayed marriage reflect a temporary (if not permanent) flight from marriage, and predict lower percentages of people ever marrying. Probably the family will survive as an institution, but not in the form we have grown up idealizing.

Only one type of marriage is growing much more common: remarriage. The number of marriages in which at least one of the spouses had previously been married has more than doubled since 1968, when divorces became easier to get. And, combined with fewer first marriages, remarriages have come to represent over twice as high a proportion of all marriages by 1985 as they were in 1968 (Statistics Canada, 1987: Table 5). Recently, three marriages in ten were remarriages for one or both partners. This tendency of the divorced to remarry is one main source of evidence that marriage remains a desired state.

CLOSING REMARKS

One way to summarize all this information about the family would be to suggest that more and more of us find our crucial sense of self and identity, our sense of accomplishment and worth, outside the family at work or school. As more families become two-earner families, this trend is likely to continue. It is reinforced by the large number of young people working part-time to earn extra money—and extra independence—while going to school. It is reinforced still further by the earlier and earlier removal of the child from the family during the day to attend daycare, pre-nursery and nursery school—many children are in daycare by the age of one. Finally, it is reinforced by the growing respectability of divorce, allowing couples, quite quickly, to decide they have made a mistake and should break up the marriage to try again with other partners.

What we may be witnessing, although it is too early to know for sure, is the decline of the ideal of romantic love and the emergence of a more instrumental conception of marriage and the family. Under these circumstances, the family hangs together as long as it remains instrumental and quickly falls apart if that ceases to be the case.

Will the family remain the most fundamental social institution? Yes, as long as it remains the main vehicle for primary socialization. Since most women are probably going to bear one or more children during their adulthood, that is not likely to change in the forseeable future. As an agent of socialization, the family, in a wide variety of forms, is likely to remain a basic institution in our society.

Discussion Questions

1. No one knows precisely why early societies in history, before industrialization, had patriarchal families. What explanation would you offer? Is there any evidence historians might gather to test the validity of your theory?

2. Does a division of labour between spouses have to lead to spousal inequality? Discuss how spousal inequalities might be avoided or reduced in modern marriages.

3. Has the mechanization of housework improved family relations? If so, how? What other kinds of mechanization might solve problems that remain today?

4. Under what conditions might the "flight from marriage and parenthood" stop or even reverse itself? What government policies, if any, might contribute to such a change?

5. What are some of the ways a two-income family might re-organize its use of time to reduce the tension and conflict parents (especially wives and mothers) commonly feel due to lack of time?

Data Collection Exercises

1. Conduct confidential interviews with at least six friends and acquaintances to measure their first-hand knowledge of, and thinking about, the sexual abuse of children: how it happens, why it happens, how common it is.

2. Collect historical data on one community or society to measure the proportion of women who worked for pay, the kinds of jobs they did, and the ways they integrated work and family responsibilities.

3. Make a time budget to measure how much time your father and mother spend doing different kinds of tasks—working for pay, domestic chores, child care, relaxing, and so on—on an average working day and on a Saturday or Sunday. (Normally, time budget researchers check people's activities—or ask them to record their own activities—every fifteen minutes from waking up until going to sleep for the night.)

4. Collect data from two couples you know who are roughly the same age where one is married and the other is cohabiting. What differences can you find in their satisfaction with the relationship, the ways they spend their time and money, and their feelings of commitment to their partner?

Writing Exercises

1. Write a brief (500-word) essay on the ways your own family life falls short of the *ideal* functions of family life (that is, regulation of sexual behaviour, continuation of the species, socialization of the young, and providing care and protection). If you wish, focus on *one* of these functions. Or you may want to recount a particular incident that illustrates your family reality particularly well.

2. Imagine you are a marriage counsellor who has completed an evaluation of a couple you know. Should that couple stay together or divorce? Write a brief (500-word) report to the couple advising them on what to do and explaining your reasons for thinking so.

3. The person you love has suggested you get married in the next six months. You are 19 years old, with two more years of school to go, and you only met this person four months ago; but you really love him/her. Write your love a letter (about 500 words) saying what you want to do about this situation, and why.

4. Briefly (500 words or less) explain—as though you were explaining to your parents—why a couple should (or should not) live together before marrying.

Glossary

cohabitation—a sexual union in which two people live together without marrying

equalitarian (or egalitarian) family—a family in which the husband and wife jointly make all the important decisions. This structure lies halfway between the patriarchal family, in which the father is the formal head of the household, and the matriarchal family, in which the mother is the formal head of the household.

family—a group of individuals who are related to one another through marriage, descent, or legal adoption

feminization of poverty—the growing tendency of poor people to be women, due to lone parenthood or impoverished old age

homogamy – a pattern of mating between people who are like each other, especially in their social characteristics. Conversely, **heterogamy** is marriage between people who differ in important respects.

marriage – a socially approved sexual and economic union between two or more people. Legal marriages can end in **divorce,** the legal and formal dissolution of marriage.

neolocal residence – a family household that is set up separate from the households of the spouses' parents

nuclear family – a family household consisting of two spouses and/or a parent and his/her children

polygamy – the union of a spouse to two or more spouses at the same time. Conversely, **monogamy** is marriage between only one woman and one man.

reconstituted family – a family to which one or both spouses bring children from a former union

serial (sequential) monogamy – the union of a spouse to two or more spouses in a lifetime, one after another

single-parent family – a family containing one parent (typically a mother) and his or her children (typically young and dependent)

Suggested Readings

Bernard, Jesse *The Future of Marriage*. New York: Bantam Books, 1973. This provocative book shows how the traditional marriage – in reality, an uneasy mix of "*his* marriage and *her* marriage" – is giving way to new thinking and new practices.

Burch, Thomas *Family History Survey: Preliminary Findings*. (Catalogue 99-955) Ottawa: Supply and Services, 1985. This is the first of a series of short books by Burch and others on the findings of the 1984 Family History Survey. These data tell us a lot about Canadians' real family experiences.

Eichler, Margrit *Families in Canada Today*, 2nd edition. Toronto: Gage, 1987. This classic work provides up-to-date family statistics, a review of the literature, and a sense of the current debates about family life in Canada.

Jones, Charles, Lorna Marsden, and Lorne Tepperman *Lives of their Own*. Toronto: Oxford University Press, 1990. This short book shows how women's lives have become more varied, fluid and unlike one another in the last 20 years, in response to changes in family and work life.

Mandell, Nancy and Ann Duffy (eds.) *Reconstructing the Canadian Family: Feminist Perspectives*. Toronto: Butterworths, 1988. An important collection of the work of feminist scholars, this book puts the modern family against a backdrop of women's "hidden history." The focus is on gender inequality in family life.

Wilson, S.J. *Women, the Family and the Economy*, 2nd edition. Toronto: McGraw-Hill Ryerson, 1986. This well-written book surveys a wide range of issues raised in this chapter and offers useful references for further reading and research.

References

Armstrong, P. and H. Armstrong (1978) *The Double Ghetto*. Toronto: McClelland and Stewart

Becker, G.S. (1981) *A Treatise on the Family*. Cambridge, Massachusetts: Harvard University Press

Bernard, J. (1973) *The Future of Marriage.* New York: Bantam Books

Burch, T. (1985) *Family History Survey: Preliminary Findings.* (Statistics Canada, Catalogue No. 99-955) Ottawa: Supply and Services

Campbell, A. (1980) *The Sense of Well-being in America: Recent Patterns and Trends.* New York: McGraw-Hill

Conrad, P. and J.W. Schneider (1980) *Deviance and Medicalization: From Badness to Sickness.* St. Louis, Missouri: C.V. Mosby

Eichler, M. (1990) "Gender and the value of time" pp. 396-405 in J. Curtis and L. Tepperman (eds.) *Images of Canada: The Sociological Tradition.* Toronto: Prentice-Hall Canada

_____ . (1981) "The inadequacy of the monolithic model of the family" *Canadian Journal of Sociology,* 6 (3), pp. 367-388

Fox, B. (1988) "Conceptualizing 'Patriarchy' " *Canadian Review of Sociology and Anthropology,* 25, 2 (May), pp. 163-182

Hajnal, J. (1965) "European marriage patterns in perspective" pp. 101-143 in D.V. Glass and D.E.C. Eversley (eds.) *Population in History.* London: Edward Arnold

Johnson, H. (1988) "Wife abuse" *Canadian Social Trends,* Spring, pp. 17-20

Johnson, H. and P. Chisholm (1989) "Family homicide" *Canadian Social Trends,* Autumn, pp. 17, 18

Leslie, G.R. and S.K. Korman (1985) *The Family in Social Context,* 6th edition. New York: Oxford University Press

Lupri, E. (1989) "Male violence in the home" *Canadian Social Trends,* Autumn, pp. 19-21

Lupri, E. and J. Frideres (1981) "The quality of marriage and the passage of time: Marital satisfaction over the family life cycle" *Canadian Journal of Sociology,* 6 (3), pp. 283-305

Mandell, N. (1987) "The family" pp. 145-196 in M.M. Rosenberg et al (eds.) *An Introduction to Sociology.* Toronto: Methuen

Marshall, K. (1987) "Women in male-dominated professions" *Canadian Social Trends,* Winter, pp. 7-11

Moore, M. (1989) "Female lone parenting over the life course" *Canadian Journal of Sociology,* 14 (3), pp. 335-352

Moynihan, D.P. (1965) *The Negro Family: The Case for National Action.* Washington, D.C.: U.S. Department of Labor

Parsons, T. and R.F. Bales (1955) *Family Socialization and Interaction Process.* New York: Free Press

Pettifer, S. and J. Torge (1987) *A Book About Sexual Assault.* Montreal: Health Press

Pool, I. and M. Moore (1986) *Lone Parenthood: Characteristics and Determinants (Results from the 1984 Family History Survey)* (Statistics Canada, Catalogue No. 99-961) Ottawa: Supply and Services

Statistics Canada, (1987) *Current Demographic Analysis: Report on the Demographic Situation in Canada, 1986* (Catalogue No. 91-209E) Ottawa: Supply and Services

Vaughan, D. (1987) *Uncoupling: How Relationships Come Apart*, New York: Vintage

Wolfson, M. (1986) "Stasis amid change−income inequality in Canada 1965-1983" *Canadian Statistical Review*, February, pp. 6-27

CHAPTER 8

Today's workplace is a miniature version of the modern world. It brings people together in places where they can interact with modern technology.

WORK AND THE ECONOMIC ORDER

THE ECONOMIC ORDER

Just about everyone works at something. Young people work at going to school and getting trained for a job. After getting out of school, most people work at a job or even a career. Some work in the home, keeping house or caring for children; normally, they get no cash payment for doing this. Others work at home and earn an income by selling some good or service outside the home. Most of us work in large organizations—in factories or offices—to earn an income. Working together in large numbers, we create goods and services, draw a salary or wage, and produce a profit for the boss.

We spend a very large proportion of all the waking hours of our lives preparing for work, then doing it—and in doing it, creating the **economic order** of our society. It should come as no surprise, then, if you find yourself wondering how this side of your life is going to turn out. So you may want to consider what sociology has to say about work and the economic order.

For this reason, we now turn to a more detailed examination of the **economic order**, the institutionalized system whereby material resources are produced, distributed, and consumed. The economic order is the system through which people create the goods (for example, food and shelter) and services (for example, medical care) they need to survive. It also provides the many other goods and services that most of us do not necessarily need, but very much want, such as automobiles, CD players, designer jeans, and junk food.

Because it is so fateful for our lives, the economic order is not merely an abstract system of economic institutions. People experience the economic order in myriad ways as they go about living their everyday lives. Few people probably use terms such as "the economic order" in everyday conversation, but most realize that there is a connection between what they receive in their paycheques every week and the nature and condition of the economic system within which they live. All of us are reminded of this connection when we go shopping for groceries or for an automobile, try to buy or sell a house, lose our jobs or get transferred to another city, pay our income taxes or fill up our car with gas. Neither our position in the economic order nor our life chances are really a matter of chance but are part of a system of economic relationships.

Most of us define our position in the economic order in terms of our jobs or occupations. Indeed, it is in the realm of work that we best see both the typical circumstances and the dramatic problems characterizing the economic order. This is not surprising. In a very real sense, work, like the family, forms one of the points where macrosociological processes and microsociological experiences meet for most of us. It is at work that we experience domination and participate in informal friendship or interest groups. It is at work that we form unions to look after our interests and develop a sense of ourselves as workers, managers, employers, or professionals. Our occupational identity, research has shown, is a key component of our social identity.

Yet the significance we, in our society, accord to work or occupation is a relatively new phenomenon. Not too long ago a person's position in the economic order was likely to be determined by who his or her parents were, by gender, or by other ascribed characteristics. Indeed, neither the forms of work which we have in our society nor the economic order with which we are familiar existed prior to the Industrial Revolution of the 18th century.

THE INDUSTRIAL REVOLUTION

The term **Industrial Revolution** refers to a number of large-scale economic and social changes that occurred in England during the 18th century and later spread to other parts of the world. Before the industrial revolution, the production of most goods took place in small shops or in people's homes, with simple tools the worker owned. The use of new sources of energy, such as water, steam, and later electrical energy, allowed the development of large-scale production, which proved more economical than the old handicraft method. The abundance of such inanimate energy made possible the development of machines and **mass production**. It increased the size, complexity, and cost of productive technology.

Mass production, as the name implies, is the production of goods in large quantities. It typically concentrates the process of production in a large self-contained area such as a factory. The work involved in producing some item is broken up into small, specialized steps, each performed by different individuals or machines in sequence. The use of machinery to perform routine tasks wherever possible at each stage of the production process is especially important in mass production.

The development of mass production transformed English society as a whole. The rise of factories gathered together large numbers—hundreds and even thousands of workers—under the same roof. First England, and then other western European nations, were transformed from essentially rural, agricultural communities into urban, industrial societies. These changes not only dislocated the population, they altered as well the ways in which people experienced society and their place in it.

Before the industrial revolution, societies had changed very slowly and few people thought about *why* society was organized as it was. Most people simply assumed that their form of social organization was "natural," or that God had so ordained it. The industrial revolution changed all that. Not only did the pace of social and economic change increase dramatically as industry and technology developed, it was obvious to everyone that these changes were a consequence of people's actions rather than the actions of either God or nature. The result was a new perspective on society: a recognition that society is created by human action and that society changes because of what we choose to do, or fail to do.

A new perspective on society

The development of a new perspective on society altered how people understood themselves and their relationship to one another; it was also the origin of sociology and of the other social sciences. As we shall see, the concern with the nature and future of social, economic, and political change—often called "modernization"—gave rise to various theories of society.

This new perspective affected all of the different groups found in society. For most workers, the factory was their first experience of power-driven machinery and highly specialized work. That experience began to create a group awareness of common problems that centred around work and relations with the employer. When combined with the new perspective, their experiences made it clear to the workers that their problems were an outcome of social relations and could be solved by changing those social relations. This set the stage for class conflict and, later, for the development of labour unions.

In the same way, the new perspective on society fostered what Karl Marx called *class consciousness* among the bourgeoisie, or capitalist class. Class consciousness refers to an awareness of class interests and a willingness to act to attain those interests.

Prior to the industrial revolution, the relationship between a master craftsman and his workers was one of mutual obligations. The workers were apprentices or journeymen entitled to a traditional level of payment, sometimes including room and board, and entitled to be taught the skills of the craftsman. Industrialization and the use of machinery led craftsmen to replace apprentices with untrained workers as cheap labour. The destruction of the traditional social relationship between the employer and the employee put an end to all notions of moral or social obligations of the employer to his employees. Unlike the craftsmen, who worked alongside the apprentices, the bourgeoisie felt comfortable with the idea of exploiting their workers and paying them the minimum wage possible.

Just as important was the fact that the bourgeoisie developed a set of attitudes—which included a sense of unlimited opportunity and inevitable progress—and a political ideology asserting that no one could or should place limits on either profits or production. In effect, they saw the whole world as ripe for the picking.

These bourgeois attitudes were legitimized by the social theories of the age. The new perspective on society spurred the development of social theory and, as noted above, eventually of sociology. The destruction of religious dogma and traditional beliefs meant that the world was now open for explanation as well as for exploitation. Since most of these theorists came from a bourgeois background, it is not surprising that their view of how society "works" fit in with and justified the attitudes of the bourgeoisie.

In 1776, the English philosopher Adam Smith published *The Wealth of Nations*. Many consider this book the essential work in what is now called classical economics. In it, Smith argued in favour of *laissez-faire* economic relationships—free markets in which everything could be bought and sold at the best price. The term **laissez-faire** refers to an economic policy that is free of government intervention; it is a synonym for the free enterprise system. Smith believed that such free markets would allow materials and products to fetch a just price and that the greatest number would receive the greatest benefits.

This was possible, Smith believed, because the market had its own logic. If there were free competition between buyers and sellers an "invisible hand" would produce the best of all possible outcomes. For this reason, classical economists argued against government controls on the market. For example, they opposed the protection of either labour or land, and argued against political interference in the market. Also, classical economists opposed all **cartels** and **monopolies** — whether organized by government or capitalists — that limited free competition in the marketplace (Friedman and Friedman, 1981).

Classical economists also favoured a new conception of social relations. They assumed that everyone was motivated by economic rationality — a desire to maximize one's own well-being in the marketplace. Ideally, people would cooperate and everyone could benefit equally. Rational exchanges were to be stripped of traditional elements that were not economically rational, such as racial, ethnic, or religious loyalties and beliefs. Social relations were to be based on what Karl Marx later called the "cash nexus" alone.

The idea that people can create the lives they want by choosing wisely in a competitive system is rooted in an outlook called *liberal democracy*, or the *liberal ideology*, which is derived from the philosophy of laissez-faire capitalism. **Liberal democracy** rests on free choice and free competition founded in a free market in labour, goods, and ideas (Macpherson, 1962).

These freedoms are usually found in societies with a capitalist economy, universal suffrage, and two or more political parties. But given social inequality — unequal starting points — freedom comes into conflict with fairness. That is because liberal democracy holds people responsible for protecting their own interests in exchange with others. It denies that any collective interests may be more important than individual interests: for example, environmental protection and world peace *versus* the unlimited use of resources or selling weapons. It also ignores the fact that some people are less able than others to protect their own interests.

Historically, Canada developed as a "hard frontier." Our vast resources, coupled with a harsh climate and terrain, helped to shape Canada's industrial development — a mix of dependency and prosperity.

Liberal democracy was not the only ideology to emerge from the industrial revolution. The destruction of the old economic and political order gave people new opportunities, new freedoms, and new rights, but it also produced an economic system characterized by terrible working conditions, unpredictable employment, poor pay, and – eventually – dramatic clashes between the working class and the capitalist class. It was in this climate of class conflict that Karl Marx developed his analysis and condemnation of capitalism.

Corporate capitalism

The term *capitalism* was introduced into economic and social theory by Karl Marx. Capitalism as an economic system began to develop around the 16th century. For Marx, capitalism is a system in which there is private ownership of the means of production; in which workers do not own what they produce; and in which profits are re-invested in the enterprise in order to generate ever more capital.

Marx described the form of capitalism common in his life-time, in which the means of production were owned by an individual entrepreneur who ran his business himself and who made all of the decisions affecting his enterprise. This form of capitalism enshrines the profit motive and the ideal of free competition motivated by personal gain. Greed is not only permitted under capitalism, it is encouraged. As a consequence, our culture sees the acquisition of enormous personal wealth as a central goal of life. Newspapers, magazines, television, and the other media typically glorify people who have achieved this goal.

Some of the fortunes people make in our society are gained by actions that help the economy grow: for example, by developing new technologies that produce goods more cheaply, or by finding new markets overseas. However, this is not usually the case. By and large, most people make their profits at other people's expense. This may be through stock market speculation, which adds nothing whatever to the economy's productivity, or by **exploitation** – hiring labour cheaply and selling the manufactured goods and services at the highest possible prices. Even allowing for the capitalist's right to a fair return on his investment, workers receive in wages only a small portion of profits made by their company. The surplus value of their work, or profit (after all costs are deducted), goes to the capitalist.

Today, capitalism has evolved away from the form described by Marx into corporate capitalism. Under **corporate capitalism**, the key players are not individual owners but large organizations or corporate groups. These corporate bodies make all the important decisions that affect economic activities. Individuals have influence only as officers in the corporate bodies to which they belong, especially as directors of the organization. This means that a separation has developed between the shareholders who "own" the corporations and those who control and run them on a daily basis.

Another important feature of modern corporate capitalism is the extensive developments of monopolies and oligopolies. When one company gets hold of 100% of the market, as Bell has done with telephone services in much of Canada, it holds a **monopoly**. When a company holds a monopoly, the consumer has no choice but to purchase the product that is available at the price that is asked, or do without. Those who control the monopoly wield an enormous amount of control over those who depend on it for goods or services. For this reason, the government tries to regulate the monopoly's actions in the interests of consumers.

An **oligopoly**, which is far more common, is a situation in which a few very large firms control an entire industry. We see oligopolies in banking, insurance, the oil industry, and (up until very recently) the auto industry—indeed, in most industries where competitors have each invested a large amount of money.

In principle, there could be vigorous competition among these firms. But ask yourself, when did a North American automobile company or cable television company offer consumers something new or better at a lower price? The answer is, never. There is virtually no competition among corporate giants—no innovation, no price competition, and no struggle to offer better products or service. On the contrary, there is often evidence of price-fixing—an illegal activity that is almost never prosecuted by government.

Canada has laws aimed at limiting monopolies and oligopolies. For example, the government can prohibit the merger of two companies if the resulting company will have a controlling share (that is, over 50%) of the market. In this way, government intervention tries to achieve the classical ideal of perfect competition, not thwart it (as critics of government interference are likely to claim).

Yet a great many monopolies and oligopolies remain—for example, in the mass media industry where a few industry leaders control the vast majority of newspapers, television, and radio stations. Everyone, including the government, which commissioned the (Kent) Royal Commission of inquiry into broadcasting, knows the problems this lack of competition creates. So far, the government has done little to change things.

The assumption that people can protect their own interest and that no one else—including government—needs to do so, is completely unfounded. Even during the heyday of laissez-faire capitalism (the 19th century), governments regularly interceded on behalf of business and hereditary wealth (Polanyi, 1944). Increasingly, governments also came to realize that widespread poverty endangered the social order. This problem called for more and more comprehensive poor laws and, eventually, social welfare legislation. **Poor laws** provided for public relief and support of the poor. Up through the first decades of the present century, this was the only public income assistance available to poor people.

Poor laws typically required a demonstration of poverty (what we would today call a "means test"), degraded the recipient of assistance, and required him or her to live and work in harsh, never-improving circumstances. English poor laws, whose effects were depicted so well in the novels of Charles Dickens, demonstrated clearly that middle-class people held the poor responsible for their troubles and felt a mixture of fear and contempt for them.

During the worldwide Depression of the 1930s, governments learned to intercede more effectively. British economist John Maynard Keynes showed that capitalism could not survive without large-scale government intervention in the economy. Government needed to "prime the pumps" and stabilize earning, spending, and saving.

Today, modern economies operate through an extremely complex mechanism of government legislation and assistance to both business and private citizens. Virtually no sphere of life goes unregulated today.

Some have argued that these changes mean that our economic system is no longer really capitalist at all but is now better described as industrial. Canada, they suggest, is an industrial society.

INDUSTRIAL SOCIETY

The term *industrial society* is used to refer not only to the prevalence of industry as a means of production, but to a whole packet of features taken to be essential to a modern society. The defining features of an **industrial society** are as follows:

(1) the disappearance of a subsistence economy;
(2) the commercialization of production;
(3) the dominance of large-scale mechanized production;
(4) the organization of production into large factories;
(5) an extensive social and technical division of labour;
(6) a decline in the proportion of the labour force engaged in agriculture;
(7) an increase in the proportion of the labour force working as wage-labourers;
(8) the urbanization of society;
(9) the growth of mass literacy;
(10) the application of scientific knowledge to all spheres of life, especially industrial production; and
(11) the rationalization of social life.

In this respect, the Soviet Union, which is not a capitalist society, would nevertheless be an industrial society. In effect, proponents of the theory of industrial society are arguing that, regardless of the political system in place or of economic ideologies, economic modernization requires every society to develop the features listed above.

Certainly, there is some merit to this argument and there are important similarities between industrial societies such as Canada and the Soviet Union. Indeed the similarity of experiences with industrialization around the world has produced what sociologists call the *convergence thesis*. The **convergence thesis** argues that as societies become industrialized, their cultures converge or become more similar to one another, regardless of differences that existed before industrialization.

This argument rests on the notion that industrialization requires certain patterns of social relations—for example, mass literacy, a nuclear family, and respect for rule of law—in order to function effectively. As these conditions are met, other changes occur, which have unintended consequences. For example, as people become literate, they become better informed, more politically active, and more eager to demand political liberties (see Inkeles and Smith, 1974).

The experience of the Third World has partly borne out the convergence thesis. Developing nations differ mainly in whether they incorporate new ("modern") elements into their existing culture—as Japan has done—or re-arrange their cultures around these elements—as in Singapore. Whichever way they do it, industrialization has everywhere been marked with certain common features.

The convergence thesis de-emphasizes capitalism as the crucial feature of the modern economic order in favour of the concept of an industrial society. If Canada, the Soviet Union, Japan, and Singapore are all essentially alike, then capitalism does not determine the form taken by the economy. But while there are similarities there are also important differences which the concept of capitalism helps clarify. The two concepts—industrialization and capitalism—are not necessarily contradictory but emphasize different aspects of complementary processes. In any case, industrialization in Western society occurred alongside, and in cooperation with, the growth of capitalism. The economic order we know today is, in many respects, an outgrowth of the one that developed two centuries ago during the Industrial Revolution.

The characteristics of industrial society

Understanding industrial society is crucial if we want to understand any other aspects of modern life. That is why the major paradigms—but especially the functionalist and conflict approaches—have a lot to say about industrial society; and what they have to say is sometimes contradictory. As the foremost conflict theorist, Karl Marx has emphasized the role of capitalism in making industrial society what it is today. On the other hand, Durkheim and Weber put forward functionalist explanations which emphasize the role played by the division of labour and bureacracy. The conflict theorists and functionalists agree that problems exist in industrial societies, but differ in their explanations of those problems and, accordingly, differ in the solutions they suggest for dealing with the problems.

The symbolic interactionists help us understand how ordinary people respond to, cope with, and make sense of the enormous structural changes taking place around them: how they "define the situation" and "negotiate" shared meanings. They have less to say about the origins of the problem: whether a result of capitalism, industry complexity, or bureaucracy, for example.

In his discussions of capitalism, Karl Marx developed a consistent and integrated theory of society linking both the means of production and the relations of production (such as class relations) to a model of society as organized around a mode of production. In contrast, the theory of industrial society has tended to provide a functionalist account of modern society. Put in crude terms, functionalists argue that a society must have certain characteristics if it is to modernize. Therefore it develops those characteristics. Even those sociologists who reject functionalism—as do many conflict theorists—take for granted that a modern society will have those characteristics, although they may be at a loss to explain how or why those characteristics developed.

However, both Emile Durkheim and Max Weber had explanations for how modernization had occurred and how a modern society is held together. For Durkheim (1965), modernization came about through a continuous growth in the division of labour, leading to specialization and what Durkheim called **organic solidarity**. For Weber (1958; 1961) it involved the increasing **rationalization** of social and economic behaviour and the growth of impersonal forms of domination such as the bureaucracy. We will examine each of these accounts in turn and see how well they fit the characteristics of modern society.

Specialization and the division of labour

A task has undergone a **division of labour** when it has been broken up into component subtasks, or steps, each of which is carried out separately by a sequence of different individuals. When this has been done, the tasks are said to be "specialized." With specialization, people become experts in performing a given task or step in the work process, whether it is drilling a hole in a strip of wood that will later become a coffee table, putting slices of pepperoni on dough that will become a frozen pizza, or sorting letters into appropriate slots for transportation to another city.

These two concepts, division of labour and specialization, are very important in the sociology of work and industry. Sociologists consider the extensive division of labour found in industrial society a key to our modern affluence. By breaking up one big job into smaller, easy to perform tasks, and by having many people perform each task repeatedly in a chain operation, the speed at which a task can be performed is greatly increased. This translates into a drastic reduction in the average cost of production per unit. More can be produced for less. Consumers benefit because producers sell their goods and services at a lower price, while maintaining a healthy profit margin.

But specialization has costs of its own. Specialization makes many jobs repetitive and uninteresting, causing workers to become bored and frustrated. Since people are not machines, most workers feel the effects of insufficient mental stimulation for eight hours each day. Specialization is dehumanizing and, as sociologist Harry Braverman (1974) wrote, it is also "de-skilling." It takes away skills people once had, making them less able to perform a wide variety of jobs and more dependent on their employers. Specialization turns work, a potentially creative and pride-inspiring activity, into something that is often mind-numbing and depressing.

Organic solidarity

Emile Durkheim was the first sociologist to see that extensive specialization would pose a serious challenge to social solidarity. The factories of early capitalism provided people with common experiences, common problems, and a sense of group interest. But the continuing growth of specialization and bureaucracy has fostered differences among people. Our jobs, our experiences, even our identities are different. Durkheim wondered what holds such a society together. Even if we all had a common religion or morality, that would not be sufficient. Different groups within the society, living different lives, need different codes of behaviour. Moreover, they also need some way of feeling, as well as being, part of the same social order. What is there to hold in check people's natural selfishness and egoism?

EXHIBIT 8.1

THE DIFFERENCE BETWEEN PEOPLE AND ROBOTS

The scientific management movement is most often associated with the work of Frederick W. Taylor, a manager and consultant to businesses in the early 20th century. Taylor's views were strongly influenced by the Protestant work ethic and found ready acceptance in North American businesses.

Under Taylor's philosophy, the role of management changed significantly from that of the past. His emphasis was on making management a science. To do this, management must plan, organize, and control every step of job performance. If the worker did exactly as he was told by a management specialist, he would gain through increased productivity and higher earnings. Taylor (1911: 46) illustrated his method in a "talk" with an imagined employee, Schmidt the pig-iron handler. Says Taylor to Schmidt, waving his hand toward the supervisor,

> If you are a high-priced man, you will do exactly as this man tells you tomorrow, from morning till night. When he tells you to pick up a pig and walk, you pick it up and walk, and when he tells you to sit down and rest, you sit down. You do that straight through the day. And what's more, no back talk. Now a high-priced man does just what he's told to do, and no back talk. Do you understand that? When this man tells you to walk, you walk. When he tells you to sit down, you sit down, and you don't talk back at him. Now you come on to work here tomorrow morning and I'll know before night whether you are really a high-priced man or not.

In this way, management began to take away worker autonomy, discretion, and skills. The result was, apparently, alienating. Later research by Elton Mayo and others showed that workers were not as motivated by the possibility of extra pay for extra work as Taylor had expected. In fact, they developed social norms for limiting productivity and enforced them consistently.

Taylor had forgotten that workers are social beings and, as such, they are motivated by other things besides pay. What are these other motivations?

Source: F.W. Taylor (1911), *Scientific Management*. New York: Harper and Row

In all periods of rapid social and economic change, as in the late 19th and early 20th century when Durkheim was writing, problems of disorganization—or *anomie*—are plainly evident.

Recall our earlier discussions of anomie: in Chapter One, of anomie causing suicide; in Chapter Four, of anomie causing criminal innovation. In all cases, it is the breakdown of moral order that leads to conflict and deviance, although their forms may differ from one situation to another. In this analysis of industrial change, labour-management conflict grows. People feel demoralized, even suicidal, because of the rapid swings in their social experience and their lack of ties to the rest of society. "What could solve these problems?" Durkheim asked himself.

In answering, Durkheim began by comparing modern society with earlier small homogeneous societies that had little division of labour. He investigated what held *that* kind of society together. Durkheim concluded that small homogeneous societies are held together by what he called *mechanical solidarity*. When the division of labour is minimal, based primarily on age and gender, most people make a living in the same manner, have roughly the same life experiences, share common beliefs, and have a sense of belonging to a common group. Members of the group feel a sense of solidarity based on these common experiences, sentiments, values and beliefs. It proves to be a very powerful form of social control.

Now, imagine all of these elements gone: the shared experiences based on geographic and social stability; the long acquaintanceship and intertwined kinship; even the common social norms and moral beliefs. What can pull together such a disparate collection of individuals? Durkheim's answer was **organic solidarity**. In this case, the source of solidarity is not moral sentiment but a sense of interdependence with others. The extensive division of labour means no one can live without someone else's cooperation. We all need the farmer and the grocer for food, the logger and construction worker for shelter, the doctor and nurse for health, and so on. We may not know these people we depend on, but we need them and know we do. In such a society, people learn to cultivate a "live and let live" philosophy.

It is almost as though an unwritten contract binds us all together. Without such a social contract, we cannot trust one another and live together in peace and safety. It is on this foundation—what Durkheim called the "non-contractual elements of contract"—that all social, political, and economic relations rest in a modern society.

Yet the new problems of social organization do not solve themselves. People need to make new rules to live by; and they still need sentimental attachments and intimate relations. They need to find ways of resolving disputes with the people and groups they rely on but may not know very well. Thus, the society with organic solidarity must develop new means of integrating people into a much more complex social order than existed before industrial times. This can be accomplished, Weber argued, through the bureaucracy.

MAX WEBER AND THE THEORY OF BUREAUCRACY

Before turning to a discussion of **bureaucracy**, it is important to understand the kinds of questions Max Weber's analysis of bureaucracy was designed to answer and the limitations he placed upon his concept of bureaucracy. Weber's interest in bureaucracy was not in forms of social organization *per se* but in how bureaucracies work as rational forms of *legitimate domination* (see Chapter Five).

Weber examined bureaucracies as forms of domination in two distinct ways. First, both the management of workers by a business enterprise and the administration of citizens by a government tends to take on a bureaucractic form in a modern society. Both the modern corporation and the modern state are characterized by a bureaucratic structure. Just as importantly, however, Weber also argued that a bureaucracy is as effective a means of controlling those who work within it as for controlling those who are dominated by it. The good bureaucrat never questions orders because both authority and responsibility belong to the bureaucracy itself rather than to the people who happen to work in it. Weber's view of the bureaucracy, as we shall see, is one-sided, but it is intended to describe forms of social domination, not forms of social organization.

Types of organizational control

In order to put the discussion of bureaucracy in a broader context than Weber does in his own work, let us first consider the issue of control in the workplace in general terms. The achievement of control in the workplace often occurs through combat over what economist Richard Edwards (1979) has called a "contested terrain." We often think of the workplace as a place where employees accept whatever rules and procedures are set down by employers. In fact, the workplace is like any other social arena: all participants fight for a say in how the workplace will be governed. Through collective action and individual resistance, workers get to play a part—sometimes larger and sometimes smaller—in determining how rules and procedures will be carried out in practice.

According to Edwards, attempts to control the workplace have fallen into three patterns corresponding to different types of productive process and technology. He calls these patterns *simple control*, *technical control*, and *bureaucractic control*.

Simple control uses very few formal rules and procedures. A boss tells the workers what they are to do that day; routines are established and tasks may even be assigned to particular workers day after day. But detailed management is lacking. The boss can see if someone is doing what he or she is supposed to, and can easily act to correct the situation if need be. This kind of control is most often found in small workplaces that lack a complex division of labour, especially if no union is present to limit the boss's authority: the kind of workplace most common up through the 19th century. Today, simple control at work can be seen in any small shop. Or think of a restaurant. The manager tells a waiter to serve Tables 8-15 on the patio during lunch, then help serve drinks inside, to Tables 40-58, during the evening. The waiter knows what he has to do. If he messes up—gets the customers angry, drops food or breaks dishes, fails to collect all the money owing—the manager will know it right away, or at least when accounts are tallied at the end of the day. If the waiter messes up a few days in a row, he will get fired. That's simple control.

Simple control is not well suited to complex mass production, where hundreds of employees are gathered together under a single roof, doing a large number of interrelated but different jobs. The boss cannot possibly watch everyone or even know what every worker is supposed to be doing. Another kind of control is needed: **technical control**.

Like simple control, technical control lacks elaborate rules and procedures, at least in the beginning. The technology of production actually controls the workers. Anyone who has worked in a factory, or seen Charlie Chaplin in the movie *Modern Times*, knows how this operates. Each worker has a very narrowly defined task to perform hundreds or thousands of times a day. An assembly line keeps the work rolling past the stationary worker who performs some operation on the product before it passes to the next worker in line. The rate of work is entirely determined by the rate at which the line is moving. Quality checks at various points can easily determine how well particular workers have done their job.

Technical control has changed in the past 50 years because it has created new problems that had to be solved in new ways, and because unions were unwilling to let working conditions go unchallenged. But technical control was also inappropriate to many modern work settings. It was particularly inappropriate where worker autonomy and strong motivation were essential, because machines could not do a job or monitor whether it was being done well, much less force it to be done quickly. Accordingly a new form of control over the workplace came into being: **bureaucratic control**.

This type of control combines two key elements: a great complexity of formal, written rules and procedures, and the promise of career rewards for conformity and effective performance—an internalized source of control over behaviour. A promised career functions as the carrot and written rules are the stick; together, they ensure conformity to organizational goals.

Bureaucratic control is most common in large, complex offices that manage production, provide services, or manipulate information. This work is too complex and the organization too large to respond to simple control, and since the work cannot be mechanized, technical control is impossible. Not only the work process but also the type of worker in this organization requires a different kind of control. The typical worker is more highly educated and, if not from a middle-class background, then at least the possessor of middle-class aspirations. Such a worker has been taught to follow rules, both by formal education (at least through secondary school) and a middle-class upbringing. He or she also desires upward mobility through personal effort; and these aspirations persuade the worker to trade present conformity for future rewards.

What, precisely, is this principle of bureaucracy upon which bureaucratic organization and bureaucratic control are founded?

Bureaucracy

Bureaucracy is one aspect of modern industrial society with which many of us are more familiar than we would like to be. A **bureaucracy** is a hierarchically organized type of formal organization found throughout industrial societies. Most of us think of the term "bureaucratic" as a synonym for wasteful, inefficient, rigid, or "red tape." But the bureaucracy seems to be the administrative form best suited to industrial society because it enables large groups of people to get large tasks done in a more or less efficient manner.

Max Weber saw the emergence of bureaucracy as important because he believed that rational and impersonal social relations characteristic of industrial society were fostered by bureaucracies. Moreover, because a bureaucracy *is* impersonal, Weber believed that it is the most effective means of decision-making in modern society. Not necessarily in the sense of making the best decisions, but in making sure that decisions are carried out as intended.

To better describe this form of organization, Weber (1958) constructed what he called an "ideal type" model of bureaucracy. According to this model, an ideal bureaucracy has the following characteristics:

(1) a high degree of specialization and a clearly defined division of labour, with tasks distributed as official duties;

(2) a hierarchical authority structure, with clearly defined areas of command and responsibility;

(3) a formal body of rules to govern the operation of the organization;

(4) administration that is based on written documents;

(5) work relations—among members of the organization and with clients—that are impersonal and are based on the status of the office-holder(s);

(6) recruitment of personnel on the basis of ability and technical knowledge—that is, on achieved as opposed to ascribed grounds; and

(7) freedom of personnel from arbitrary dismissal.

Weber recognized that the rationality and efficiency of a bureaucracy was relative. Bureaucracies are only efficient and rational when compared to the other forms of administrative organization that preceded them. A bureaucracy may make its decisions slowly and even badly, but it makes them carefully, impersonally and, for the most part, predictably. This last point is particularly important. Past forms of social organization made decisions on the basis of the personal whim of a ruler, the bribing of officials, or loyalty to members of one's own group. A modern economy and political administration, however, require predictability if planning is to be possible. Whatever its other disadvantages, a bureaucracy amply fulfils that requirement.

What is more, a bureaucracy may sometimes even work well. It reduces the chances for major errors and has all the merits (and faults) of large-scale production that we see in industrial mass production. The bureaucracy is very much like an assembly line for manufacturing and distributing information. Information goes in one end, gets processed, then comes out the other end as decisions and rules.

Bureaucratic decision-making is found in all the major organizations of our society: in big business, education, government, and military organizations. However, bureaucracy is not without its problems. Many are a consequence of the high degree of specialization within the organization.

Very few employees can see what the organization is trying to accomplish with its multitude of rules and positions. As office-holders bound by rules, they come to focus on those rules, not the intended outcomes; this is called **goal displacement**. They may even come to care more about the continued survival of the organization than about its success in achieving the goals for which it was created.

As well, an organization has no inherent morality. Although bureaucracies are rational structures, the behaviour of people within the bureaucracies is not rational. People working in a bureaucracy learn to follow orders or instructions without wondering why or thinking about the consequences of their actions. Its office-holders are expected to follow rules, not apply their own morality to their job. In any event, they rarely know enough about the organization's priorities and problems to do otherwise. For these reasons, large organizations are capable of producing very immoral behaviours—for example, dangerous environmental damage and political intrigue—with no one willing or able to take responsibility for them.

The bureaucracy is only one type of formal organization. A **formal organization** is a large social group that is engaged in specific activities for the purpose of achieving some specific goal. It is formal because it has an explicit structure, the purpose of which is to coordinate the activities of the members in the interests of the organization. A bureaucracy is an example of such a formal organization.

The structure itself is composed of a set of official *statuses*, such as president, vice president, and executive secretary. These various statuses are hierarchically arranged, with a line of communication and control usually running from the top down. Members are expected to behave toward one another in the impersonal way described by Weber in his model of the bureaucracy: that is, as holders of these statuses, not as individuals with distinct personalities. Who happens to sit in the seat of president, or has the job of sales clerk, is irrelevant. As they say in the military, you salute the uniform, not the person.

Obviously a formal organization is quite unlike an informal group—a group of family or friends. In an informal group, the personalities of the members largely determine how each relates to another. If one member leaves the group, he or she cannot be simply replaced by someone else. In a formal organization, the rights and responsibilities of an office remain unchanged, regardless of who occupies the job.

In general, this is how a formal organization works. Yet some organizations are more formal—more bureaucratic and hierarchical, for example—than others. Some have more levels of status than others from top officer to bottom, while others are more horizontal. Most have a "staff," or set of somewhat more autonomous, often expert advisors, as well as an administrative "line" that carries out decisions made higher up the hierarchy. To some degree, these variations in structure are determined by the goals of the organization: whether it is commercial, industrial, educational, or military, for example.

Yet formal organizations with different goals differ surprisingly little in their operation. There is less difference in the functioning of the Canadian Armed Forces, the Roman Catholic Church, and IBM than there is between any of these and your family. Size is the critical factor. With enormous size and complex goals comes an inevitable need for coordination and control over workers. Organizations differ most in the ways they achieve this control. Industrial history shows that strategies of control have varied for several reasons, chief among them changes in the mode of production.

Varieties of bureaucratic control

We typically think of bureaucracies as rigid and inflexible. But bureaucratic control in the workplace can take different forms. A hierarchical arrangement can also include both a horizontal and vertical division of labour, authority, and decision-making.

Polaroid was one of the first organizations to adopt this form of control. Employees were divided into a series of different categories and job slots, so that workers in film processing would have a different set of jobs from those in design or engineering activities. But jobs were not only divided functionally, or **horizontally**; they were also divided **vertically** into different levels. A series of divisions within each job family established job ladders within the organization. So for example, one might enter the organization as an engineer directly out of professional school; move up to a higher category containing engineers with some experience who therefore received higher pay; then join the engineers with some supervisory responsibilities; and so on up. Within a single job category, Polaroid had established a basis for grading and subdividing its workforce.

Among other aims, job stratification shows workers a ladder of upward mobility. An employee can see that by staying with Polaroid for some time, getting good evaluations, and pleasing the supervisors, he or she can advance up the hierarchy to ever better, more responsible, and higher-paying jobs. This leads the employee to think about the future consequences of his or her actions. In effect, the firm is telling the employee that a whole series of rewards will come to the worker who successfully fulfils the organization's expectations. Such inducements go well beyond what simple control and technical control can make available. Suddenly, a whole career, a pattern of lifetime mobility within the firm, becomes available to the employee who abides by the rules and meets the firm's expectations.

This form of control generates a strong sense of loyalty to the organization because the fates of the organization and the worker are so closely tied. Corporate loyalty bypasses the problem of worker motivation found under both simple and technical control. Workers who show insufficient loyalty or commitment to the organization are fired or discouraged from continuing. Those with enough loyalty are assumed to give their best efforts to their jobs and the organization: they are largely managing themselves. Such self-management is crucially important in work that cannot be closely or continuously supervised, a characteristic of professional and semi-professional work.

Like every other social arrangement, bureaucratic control has its short-comings. It produces "organization workers" whose loyalty may keep them from speaking out against policies that will actually harm the organization in the long run. It tends to reward conformity, seniority, and tradition, making the organization less flexible and less adaptable to new ideas and new strategies. Employees may find the stifling of their ideas hard to tolerate; the resulting alienation was a major theme of American literature in the 1950s and early 1960s, and continues to be a major interest of sociological research. We will examine the problem of alienation later in this chapter.

Bureaucratic control has begun to encounter new and different problems today. Intensified international competition and changing technology have made it very risky to guarantee lifetime careers. Large corporations have less need to hold on to workers for life and, if anything, need more freedom than ever before to hire and fire with changing market conditions. Think about some of the new high tech industries: they include software producers (who make up video games for Nintendo or data analysis packages for IBM), data base producers (who create mailing lists for advertisers, check your credit for banks, or keep up-to-date information on stock market listings), and hardware producers (who create computerized weaponry for the armed forces), for example. Writing about the new, fast-changing high-technology industries, Von Glinow (1988: 4) observes, "There is less formality and fewer layers of bureaucracy; financial risks are more often shared with employees." That is because of the high degree of uncertainty in these types of industry, caused by a dependence on outside capital, young and inexperienced management, foreign marketing and competition, a short product life, and the frequent introduction of innovations. Many believe that new forms of organization will be needed for firms to survive this uncertainty.

Perhaps most importantly, high-technology industries spend a high proportion of their earnings on research and development, since their new products and production methods grow out of this. This means they must employ and motivate a large number of highly educated "professionals," in this case engineers and scientists. This suggests not only the need, but also the possibility, for a new principle of organization: professionalization.

Professionalization

Perhaps the major alternative to bureaucracy in our society is professionalization. Whereas the bureaucracy is impersonal and monopolizes all authority for itself, professionalization assigns both high status and expertise to individuals. Professionals do high-status and high-paying specialized work typically requiring a long education and permitting a reasonable degree of autonomy in the workplace.

Access to high-paying jobs in industrial societies has increasingly required a "credential"—usually an educational degree—indicating that a person is qualified for the job. Degrees from medical schools are particularly valuable credentials: virtually no doctors are unemployed or poorly paid. Yet without a degree in medicine, no one is permitted to practise medicine. This limitation protects doctors by giving them a monopoly on medical practice, preventing competent nurses, paramedics, and other health professionals from practising medicine. Such a monopoly on what is, in effect, an essential service generates a high income for doctors.

Professional status provides an occupational group with higher income, control over access to the profession, and social honour and respect. For this reason we see lower-status educated groups—for example, social workers and psychologists—trying to **professionalize** themselves.

In some ways, we learn most about professionalization from the attempts that have failed. Mitford (1963) describes the attempts undertakers have made to upgrade their status. Not content with being viewed (and paid) as

The labour market is "segmented" so that certain kinds of people (with particular credentials) compete for certain kinds of jobs (with particular advantages and disadvantages).

TYPES OF WORK

technicians or businesspeople, undertakers seek greater credibility as "funeral directors" or "grief management consultants." So far their attempts have largely failed to persuade the public.

In some respects, professional associations are little different from trade unions: both aim to protect and promote the economic interests of their members. They do differ in two important respects. First, professional associations help middle-class people protect middle-class incomes, while unions help working-class people protect working-class incomes.

That, of course, is not how most people understand the tasks of professional associations. Because of the higher social origins of professionals, people more willingly believe that professional associations really act in the public interest rather than in the private interest of their members. Yet the public health movement in North America has not been championed by leaders of medical associations. The reduction of illness and mortality in our society has historically owed more to such factors as public works, sewage and garbage management, and clean water, than to the work of practising physicians. Even today, medical associations show little interest in workplace safety, environmental pollution, anti-smoking campaigns, or other fights against major causes of illness and death. Instead, North American medicine increasingly addresses itself to high-tech, high-cost remedies that benefit only the very few: for example, the recipients of organ transplants.

The second difference between professional associations and unions is that, as movements, they have used different means to protect their members. Unions typically threaten or use strikes to increase workers' incomes, employing collective means to pursue collective guarantees for their members. While professional associations occasionally do this, they tend rather to rely on political lobbying and the manipulation of public opinion through the mass media to control the public image of their members. Associations aim to protect their members from political interference and personal liability in dealings with the public. They also help their members earn whatever the market will bear in private dealings with customers. Professionalization does provide the public with some protection, but far from the amount they believe they are receiving.

In future, professionalization may provide the basis for organizing industrial work as well as personal services. It is too soon to tell how this will evolve. But one thing is certain: work itself will continue to evolve.

We noted at the beginning of this chapter that work forms one of the key points of contact between the macrosociological institutions which constrain our lives and the microsociological social processes whereby we organize our interactions and experiences. It is important to remember that work is not limited to what people do in their jobs or occupations. School work is as much work as is the part-time job many students take to cover their expenses. The previous chapter, on families, discussed another type of work, housework, at some length. This is fitting because housework is the most common kind of work in our society. Yet most people ignore housework when they speak of work: they focus mainly on *paid* work which, historically, has been men's work more often than women's.

This betrays a gender bias in our thinking about work and such things as the "labour force," which only includes the paid labour force (Marsden, 1985). The **labour force** is composed of all people over the age of fifteen who are employed for pay, or those who are not employed for pay but wish to be and are looking for paid employment.

Payment does not demonstrate the social value of work done, only the ability of the worker to convert his or her efforts into dollars. Even within the paid labour force, workers vary in this ability and the same effort expended in one sector of the economy or labour market will bring far more money than it will in another. Similarly, the same educational qualifications may bring twice as much money in one sector or market as they do in another. This means we must understand how these different parts of the economic order are structured, for they represent another set of limits on the supposed free competition for economic rewards.

Labour market segments

People compete for their jobs in a **labour market**. When you look in a newspaper you may notice that one section of the classified ads, the "Help Wanted" section, advertises for jobs in factories, as domestics, or in fast food outlets. A separate section of the newspaper advertises "Careers," such as management, accounting, or teaching positions, along with jobs for computer programmers or sales representatives. Clearly, there is not one big labour market in which every individual who is willing to work competes for the same jobs. Rather, there are many labour markets, and many segments within each of these. As the newspaper's ads show, some segments contain better-paying and higher-status jobs than others.

According to one model, called the "dual labour market" model, national labour markets comprise two (and perhaps more) subdivisions: a primary and secondary labour market. These are further subdivided by geography: by region, province, and size of community.

The **primary labour market** consists of jobs which offer high wages, good opportunities for advancement, and job security: positions like lawyer, plumber, and teacher. The **secondary (or marginal) labour market** consists of jobs paying low wages, offering little chance for advancement, and guaranteeing little job security: jobs like waitress, secretary, or bank teller.

Typically, people with different social characteristics, backgrounds, and skills are found in different labour market segments. For example, women and visible minorities are overrepresented in the secondary labour market, and white males are overrepresented in the primary labour market. Among white males, educational attainment typically determines in which market a person works. The more highly educated and highly skilled white males find work in the primary labour market.

The distinction between primary and secondary labour markets covers up important distinctions among different occupations and careers. Few teachers feel that they have the sort of advantages and opportunities that lawyers do; few bank tellers consider their work equivalent to that of waitresses. Nevertheless, it does provide us with a crude indicator of some of the differences in life chances which correspond to occupational differences.

Another major feature of any occupation is the sort of organization within

EXHIBIT 8.2

WAITRESSING

Every workplace—for example, a cocktail lounge—is a community, with a subculture of its own. In the cocktail lounge that Spradley and Mann studied, gender differences were made particularly distinct.

The two main work roles—bartender and server—were split along gender lines: males always tended the bar, females always took orders and served the drinks. Bartenders never took orders or served; waitresses were never permitted to mix drinks. The bartender was a high-status person in the lounge and the waitresses, low-status, and this status difference caused occasional difficulties, since bartender and waitresses had to work smoothly and cooperatively with one another. Usually conflict was reduced through joking—a common form of tension release.

Interestingly, this type of conflict is neither new nor limited to bars. An early study in the industrial relations literature (Whyte, 1947) was concerned with resolving the troublesome conflict between waitresses and chefs.

The conflict seems inevitable. Because they carry food orders from customers, waitresses (who have a low status because they have few skills and are usually female) must demand attention and service from chefs (who have a high status because they are highly skilled and usually male). The more pressure customers put on waitresses, the more pressure waitresses put on the chef. But if a waitress pushes too hard, the chef may respond by purposely delaying or ruining her order. Such conflict does no one any good: not the chef, the waitress, nor the customer.

Can you think of a way of solving this problem, so that conflict is at a minimum and customers always get what they ordered? Well, here's a hint: start with one of those revolving gadgets you can clip written orders on.

Sources: J.P. Spradley and B.J. Mann (1975) *The Cocktail Waitress: Woman's Work in a Man's World.* New York: John Wiley. Copyright © 1975 by Newbery Award Records, Inc. Reprinted by Permission of Random House Inc. W.F. Whyte (1947), *Human Problems of the Restaurant Industry.* New York: Harper and Row.

which a person works. Work organizations can be structured in many different ways, depending on the type of work being done or the ideologies in use about how work is best done. Schools are very different from automobile assembly plants in how work is organized. Even within one organization, different departments or divisions will be organized differently. The administration of a college or university will be much more bureaucratic in form than the teaching departments. Teachers have much more autonomy in their work than do most people working in the administration. But the people working in the administrative side of the school will have much more autonomy than do members of the maintenance staff.

Organizations also contain different labour market segments: some jobs that

EXHIBIT 8.3

HOW TO ORDER A DRINK

In the bar that Mann and Spradley studied, the highest-status customers were regular male patrons. They demonstrated their knowledge of the lounge subculture, and their status, in joking relations with the waitresses. Sexual innuendo was part of this display of membership, dominance, and subcultural mastery. All of these were evident when regulars purposely asked for the wrong drink.

> Consider the following example. Two young men enter the bar and take a table next to the wall in the lower section. The waitress approaches their table and places a napkin in front of each one. She waits in silence for their order. One of them looks up at her and says calmly: "Two double Sloe Screws on the rocks, uhhh, for Joe and Bill." The waitress turns quickly, goes to the bar, and in a moment returns with two, tall, dark bottles of Hamm's beer. . . . (She knew that) 1. The drink requested was not actually desired. 2. That another drink was actually being requested. 3. What that other drink was. (Spradley and Mann, 1975: 139)

Interestingly, female regulars and casual customers almost never order drinks in this way. Spradley and Mann note that, unlike male customers, female customers order separately, never in rounds; they ask many questions about drinks; they pay separately for drinks; they change their drinks frequently; and they *never* order at the same time, ask for the wrong drink, engage in drinking contests, or tip.

Source: J.P. Spradley and B.J. Mann (1975) *The Cocktail Waitress: Woman's Work in a Man's World*, New York: John Wiley, pp. 139, 142. Copyright © 1975 by Newbery Award Records, Inc. Reprinted by Permission of Random House Inc.

are well-paying and secure, and others that are not. Movement among segments within the organization is rare if not impossible. That is, a promotion from secretary to manager in business is just as rare as promotion from private to lieutenant in the military, or nurse to doctor in a hospital.

PROBLEMS OF INDUSTRIAL WORK: ANOMIE AND ALIENATION

We are far from having solved the societal problems caused by the changes that Marx, Weber, and Durkheim identified. Sociologists even disagree about the way to apply their insights in Canada's unique context.

Those who follow Marx's approach see modern problems of work as primarily a result of capitalism. These problems would disappear, or at least improve dramatically, if socialist economic organization replaced capitalism. Those who follow Durkheim's thinking see problems as primarily the result of an industrial division of labour: a faulty integration in the face of overspecialization, large numbers, and rapid change. Those who follow Weber's thinking see them as primarily the result of rationalization and bureaucratization—that is, the effects of outsized organizations and social relations based on positions, not people.

Canada's labour history is not among the most violent in the world, but it has not lacked in conflict. Compared to workers in other industrial countries, moderately large numbers of Canadian workers participate in a moderate number of strikes, but these strikes tend to last for a long time. (From Winnipeg General Strike)

Work satisfaction: its causes and effects

Many jobs are mindless and boring, yet survey evidence shows that most North Americans *say* they are satisfied with their jobs. In fact, four out of five workers say they are satisfied to some degree, and one in three describe themselves as "completely satisfied" (Campbell, 1980). Three out of four people even report they enjoy their work (Casale and Lerman, 1986: 117).

Yet we have good reason to doubt these findings. The majority of married people *say* they are very satisfied with their marriage, yet roughly four in ten will divorce at least once in the course of their lives. When asked their opinions in surveys, people tend to put a pleasant face on unpleasant situations. What is more, there is widespread evidence of dissatisfaction with work shown by high rates of absenteeism, indifference to what happens at work, the attitude that life begins when work ends, industrial sabotage, and attempts by workers to increase their control over the production process, through strikes and working to rule.

What causes people either to enjoy or to dislike their work, to be satisfied or dissatisfied with their job?

The bulk of research into causes of job satisfaction has focused on objective job characteristics. Locke (1976: 1342) suggests that job satisfaction results when work "is varied, allows autonomy, is not physically fatiguing, . . . is mentally challenging, . . . allows the individual to experience success, and . . . is personally interesting." He also suggests that satisfaction with rewards depends on "the fairness or equity with which they are administered and the degree to which they are congruent with the individual's personal aspirations" (ibid).

Sometimes people can learn to accept work conditions that are objectively unsatisfying to accommodate the frustrations of their job. In addition, sociological studies have found that people are able to commit to, and identify with, new job and career demands. So, for example, the factory worker promoted to supervisor gradually learns (and tries to adopt) the viewpoint of management, while the young academic leaves behind the viewpoint of student for that of teacher.

Similarly, people learn to replace goals which are unavailable with others that are available. For example, some work is less intrinsically satisfying — satisfying in and of itself — than other work. In less intrinsically satisfying work, workers seek satisfaction from other factors; for example, from pay, working hours, and working conditions. Such satisfactions are extrinsic rather than intrinsic.

However, even human adaptability has its limits. This is shown by the high rates of turnover and absenteeism even among well-paid automobile assembly-line workers. Feelings of work dissatisfaction are deep and their causes complicated. One of these causes is anomie.

The concept of anomie

To a large degree, people's job satisfaction reflects the degree to which their expectations are being met. Lower-status workers expect satisfactory extrinsic rewards, higher-status workers expect intrinsic ones. A century ago, Durkheim saw that satisfaction required a comfortable fit between wants and means. People are happiest when they want what they can get, rather than what they cannot get.

Human desires, Durkheim believed, are boundless. Without strong norms to control those desires, people are liable never to be satisfied with what they have and will always feel frustrated over what they cannot get. Strong norms and rules, by aligning what we can expect with what we can get, keep us satisfied (or at least prevent us from becoming overly dissatisfied).

By anomie, Durkheim meant a state in which an individual's wants are not being regulated by social norms, leaving that individual morally and socially adrift. Isolated individuals are more anomic than socially integrated ones. Rapid social change, social mobility, and overspecialization cut people off from other people. Without commitments to others, the anomic person is less likely either to feel safe or to act responsibly.

Industrial society induces anomie in other ways as well. One is by promoting cultural relativism, which calls into question all limits on our wants and achievements. Another is by bombarding people with information about the consumer goods we ought to want. No wonder that, in this churn of ideas, opportunities, and constraints, many people are not quite sure what they are doing, or why, or how they should proceed.

Anomic situations lead to low predictability in behaviour and a strong belief in luck. Anomie includes confusion about socially approved behaviours and lowered expectations that socially approved behaviours will bring desired goals. In fact, anomie may produce a strong expectancy that socially unapproved behaviours will be needed to achieve these goals. For example, a worker may see little connection between his work and the rest of his life, and between the effort expended and rewards obtained. There will also be a stronger tendency to resolve labour conflicts in violent and disorderly ways.

The concept of alienation

Durkheim and Marx are at odds when it comes to the explanation of worker dissatisfaction. Durkheim's theory of anomie suggests that the problem lies in an inadequate level of control by society over the individual. Marx saw the problem to be one of social relations among classes in capitalist society.

At the core of Marx's discussion of this issue is the concept of **alienation**. As described by Marx, **alienation** is composed of both objective and subjective dimensions. Marx viewed work as the most important medium for expressing and developing oneself—it is an activity in which people can develop their uniquely human qualities, from which both social and psychological consequences followed.

The objective dimension of alienation has several aspects: a separation of workers from the product of their labour; a lack of control by workers over the labour process itself; estrangement of workers from their own humanity; and estrangement of workers from each other (see Rinehart, 1987).

To get a better handle on this, try to imagine yourself selling sex for money. You're waiting on a street corner, or in a bar. Some stranger comes up and tells you what he wants you to do, and how. When you're finished having sex, all you have to show for it is some money. You haven't done anything you feel proud of—at best, you've lost a few never-to-return hours of your life making money. At worst, well, ... When you look around you and see how many other people are doing the same thing—selling their sex or their honesty and personal integrity for money—you lose a lot of respect for yourself and for the whole human race.

These are some of the "objective aspects" of alienation Marx had in mind. As you can see, they shade over into the more subjective aspects; they are "objective" only in the sense that they are inevitable consequences of social organization (and, in Marxist theory, inevitable consequences of capitalism). They are objective because they are real, not imaginary, troubles, rooted in real relations of power and production.

Subjective types of alienation vary more from one person to another; in that respect they look more like personal troubles. But like objective types of alienation, they can result from alienating work conditions. The subjective dimension of alienation includes feelings of powerlessness, meaninglessness, and self-estrangement. Workers experience these feelings as a direct result of being in control of neither the production process, nor their labour (Seeman, 1959). It is easy to see how a person selling sex (or personal integrity) for money might also feel powerless, meaningless, and self-estranged.

People who feel alienated or who feel they have little control over life, and people who harbour negative sentiments about neighbourhood, health, and general life course are less satisfied with their jobs. These signs of psychological alienation are as powerful predictors of job satisfaction as objective characteristics of the job itself (Rice et al, 1982; King et al, 1982).

People's feelings about their jobs arise out of an interaction between "individual expectations and traits" and the "objective characteristics of their experience" (King et al., 1982: 129). Feelings of alienation, distrust, and being victim of external control reduce job satisfaction. They also combine with objective job characteristics such as danger, unpredictability, long hours, excessive supervision, and low occupational prestige to magnify job dissatisfaction.

But alienation as Marx conceived it is not a personality disorder arising out of unique personal conditions. It grows out of the way society in general, and the economic order in particular, is organized. When it comes to work, choice and competition are always limited. True, a person can choose to work for the minimum wage rather than move his family halfway across the country in search of another job. But most workers weigh their social concerns—attachments to family, kinship, friends, and local culture—into their choices. Employers know they can often get workers for a low price precisely because we are social creatures. We may prefer to choose starvation over isolation, but neither option is really desirable or freely chosen.

Employers are always in a better position to accept and reject workers than workers are to accept and reject jobs, because there are usually more workers than jobs. What's more, workers are usually in immediate need of wages to survive. They may have to work at a job they do not want, or for a wage they cannot live on, simply to meet their basic expenses. They have no choice, and there is no real competition between the employer and employee here.

Nor is there free choice and competition in the consumer marketplace. Our dollar never commands the best possible brand of cookies or toothpaste at the best possible price, because often few brands are available, a number of different brands are owned by the same company, or so-called competitors have conspired to offer us the same-quality product at roughly the same price.

However, our mass media, churches, and even schools continue to promote the belief that people are free to make of their lives whatever they want: hard work and merit are rewarded; sloth and crime are punished. They also claim that government and other collective bodies—especially trade unions—interfere with people's right to choose. These kinds of ideas are trumpeted by leaders of business through the mass media they own or control.

Why is modern society alienating, then? Recall that alienation combines estrangement, powerlessness, and meaninglessness. People in our society may feel that life is meaningless because the values and experiences the mass media portray bear no relation to their everyday lives. They may feel like players in a drama without a script. Many Canadians feel powerless because they really are powerless. They cannot reasonably expect that their behaviour will produce the outcomes or rewards they seek. They are not competing as equals in a free competitive system, much less performing duties that guarantee rewards for a good effort. Finally, many feel estranged from their own lives. They cannot take real pleasure in the boring and meaningless activities that engage them every day.

Such conditions lead people to feel split between what they consider their real selves—creatures capable of thinking, feeling, and choosing—and their

EXHIBIT 8.4

HOW IT FEELS TO BE OUT OF A JOB

How people feel about being unemployed depends on many things: their gender, number of dependents, how long they have been unemployed, the amount of formal education they have completed, and previous life experiences (among others). Still, many experiences are common to unemployed people.

In the beginning, many unemployed people take letters of rejection very personally. They soon come to believe that they are unworthy of having a job and stop expecting to ever get one. Unfortunately this negative attitude gets reflected in their job interviews, and makes getting a job even harder. In turn, their repeated failure reinforces what they have come to believe: that they are incapable of getting hired.

Others become excessively worried about their future: about what will happen to them if they can't find a job in the next couple of months, where they will live, how they will live, and so on. This anxiety, and the insomnia that often accompanies it, soon becomes impatience and short temper with family and friends. In turn, this isolates the unemployed person from the people most able and willing to offer emotional support when it's needed.

Still others, though they become depressed and pessimistic about their future, recognize they are not to blame—they are only the victims of a system that is not functioning properly. However, this recognition of the facts does not make looking into the future and seeing the situation get progressively worse any easier to bear.

Finally, there are some who grow to resent people who are employed. They find themselves getting angry at people they have never met because these people have a job and, consequently, the money to eat in nice restaurants and buy nice clothes. Moreover, they worry about what is happening to them: they fear the violent jealousy and anger they feel toward strangers and wonder where these feelings will lead.

And, in fact, many people pass through *all* of these stages of confusion, depression, and anger as their period of unemployment grows longer and longer.

Source: Abridged by Sandra Badin from P. Burman (1988), *Killing Time, Losing Ground: Experiences of Unemployment*. Toronto: Wall and Thompson, pp. 195, 196, 203. Published with permission of the publisher, Thompson Educational Publishing, Inc., 11 Briarcroft Road, Toronto, Ontario M6S 1H3. Tel: (416) 766-2763, Fax: (416) 766-0398.

working selves. According to Sennett and Cobb (1973), people employ "dreams and defences" to heal these "hidden injuries." People who feel worthless dream of becoming worthwhile through their own (or their children's) upward mobility, by winning a lottery, or some other stroke of good fortune. Women's romance books and magazines are about Cinderellas who—as nurses, secretaries, or other male-helpers—meet and marry their Prince Charming through a combination of good luck, virtue, and wile.

Defenses against feelings of worthlessness include splitting the "real person" from the "performing person." People try to avoid feeling like they belong to the despised or menial role they play. They think, "In reality, I am someone else: not Clark Kent, but Superman. I possess enormous hidden powers that I will reveal at the right moment, winning deserved admiration." This theme of the dual, split, or hidden personality runs throughout mass entertainment because, for so many, it is a necessary escape from daily indignity. The process of splitting in this way is self-estrangement, a form of alienation.

This defense offers most people a (temporarily) constructive adaptation to a destructive social order: constructive because it allows people to continue functioning; temporary, because it fails to solve the problem. "It stills pain in the short run, but does not remove the conditions that made a defense necessary in the first place" (Sennett & Cobb, 1973: 219).

Cures for alienation

Alienation, then, is more than a lack of work satisfaction. It is easier to find satisfaction than it is to escape from feelings of alienation. People may make peace with their circumstances and teach themselves to feel satisfied with their lives, including their work. If asked, they will say they are satisfied and believe it. This is because they are comparing their objective conditions with ones which are even worse, and are feeling fortunate: like the one-legged person who is glad he is not completely legless.

We get nowhere by treating the symptoms of alienation if we leave the causes unchanged. The only way of curing the symptoms is by eliminating the causes of powerlessness, meaninglessness, and estrangement. This means giving people an opportunity—at work and elsewhere—to develop and express their creative selves: to make the workplace truly human.

Various ideas for doing this have been developed. They range from job rotation (for variety) and quality working circles (for cooperation and responsibility) to profit-sharing, career development plans, and worker representatives on boards of directors.

Under socialism and communism, these plans have gone further in the direction of government control and, to some degree, worker control over the labour process and societal profit-sharing. Yet as the recent spate of strikes and other forms of labour unrest in the Soviet Union and eastern Europe has shown, symptoms of deep alienation remain in these countries. Some believe this shows that Marxist theory was wrong and that the causes of alienation lie elsewhere: with specialization and bureaucratization as Weber argued, for example. Others believe Marxist theory has not yet been put into proper practice for long enough to allow workers to get accustomed to their new freedoms and responsibilities. Given the dramatic changes occurring in eastern Europe today, the next few years may well see a wide variety of different experiments both in political and economic organization.

EXHIBIT 8.5

JOBS OF THE (NEAR) FUTURE

Occupations contributing most to employment growth in North America in the foreseeable future are *not* glamorous, high tech jobs requiring a lot of education.

Occupations with the Largest Job Growth, 1986–2000.*

Occupation	Employment		Change in employment, 1986-2000		Percent of total job growth, 1986-2000
	1986	Projected, 2000	Number	Percent	
Salespersons, retail	3579	4780	1201	33.5	5.6
Waiters and waitresses	1702	2454	752	44.2	3.5
Registered nurses	1406	2018	612	43.6	2.9
Janitors and cleaners, including maids and housekeeping cleaners	2676	3280	604	22.6	2.8
General managers and top executives	2383	2965	582	24.4	2.7
Cashiers	2165	2740	575	26.5	2.7
Truck drivers, light and heavy	2211	2736	525	23.8	2.5
General office clerks	2361	2824	462	19.6	2.2
Food counter, fountain, and related workers	1500	1949	449	29.9	2.1
Nursing aides, orderlies, and attendants	1224	1658	433	35.4	2.0
Secretaries	3234	3658	424	13.1	2.0
Guards	794	1177	383	48.3	1.8
Accountants and auditors	945	1322	376	39.8	1.8
Computer programmers	479	813	335	69.9	1.6
Food preparation workers	949	1273	324	34.2	1.5
Teachers, kindergarten and elementary	1527	1826	299	19.6	1.4
Receptionists and information clerks	682	964	282	41.4	1.3
Computer systems analysts, electronic data processing	331	582	251	75.6	1.2
Cooks, restaurant	520	759	240	46.2	1.1
Licensed practical nurses	631	869	238	37.7	1.1
Gardeners and grounds-keepers, except farm	767	1005	238	31.1	1.1

Continued

Maintenance repairers, general utility	1039	1270	232	22.3	1.1
Stock clerks, sales floor	1087	1312	225	20.7	1.0
First-line supervisors and managers	956	1161	205	21.4	1.0
Dining room and cafeteria attendants and barroom helpers	433	631	197	45.6	.9
Electrical and electronics engineers	401	592	192	47.8	.9
Lawyers	527	718	191	36.3	.9

Source: U.S. Bureau of Labor Statistics, 1988: 57, Table 5.
*Numbers in thousands.

CLOSING REMARKS

The dramatic changes initiated by the industrial revolution continue unabated. Macrosociologically, capitalism, which transformed the economic order, has itself undergone significant changes. All sociologists, whether they prefer to view modern society as an industrial society, or whether they continue to make use of the concept of capitalism, recognize that the economic order continues to evolve and change. Even the bureaucracy, which has become the dominant organizational form both in capitalist and socialist countries, is being altered as new technologies such as the computer are transforming both workplace and the organizational forms used to control it.

These macrosociological changes are having significant microsociological effects. The industrial revolution made work into a central feature of people's lives and a crucial component of their social identity at the same time that it created the conditions which fostered alienation and anomie. The development of new forms of work organization and perhaps even new conceptions of what it means to work are changing our conception of work and of ourselves. How, for example, will the developments in computer-based "artificial intelligence" affect many of the high-status technical or professional jobs that have been impervious to automation until now? What happens to the status of the doctor when he or she—and one day we—are able to use a computer to diagnose and prescribe treatment? (Such computer programs already exist. They will get better and more accessible as time passes.) What will happen to the close link in our society between work and identity when people can look forward to having to change their job or career—perhaps several times—during the course of their working life? We will consider some of the changes which are transforming Canada in Chapter Ten, but the point is that the rapid and dramatic pace of change initiated by the industrial revolution has not abated, but is continuing still.

The economic order in a modern society such as Canada is an extraordinarily complex combination of macrosociological trends and microsociological actions. We still lack some of the tools needed to make sense of how class, status, and political power interconnect; of how organizations both dominate and facilitate; or of how operating a sewing machine in a factory and processing

Commercial, manufacturing, and financial power are shifting from North America to the Pacific basin and the European common market. In addition to large populations and cheap labour, these areas enjoy some other advantages—most notably, little investment in outdated technology and little military spending.

information on a computer can both equally be work.

What we do know for sure is that both macrosociological research on the economic order and microsociological research on work satisfaction (and identity) will continue to be a major preoccupation of Canadian sociologists for the foreseeable future. We can also expect it to continue to be some of the most exciting and important research undertaken by sociologists.

Discussion Questions

1. Weber argues that the elimination of tradition, intuition, and superstition from decision-making played an important part in the rise of modern economic and political life. On balance, did social life improve?

2. Durkheim recognized that anomie is a problem of modern societies that will not go away easily. New ways of attaching people to one another, and to new rules, are needed. Is the problem of anomie getting better or worse in Canada today?

3. Would people be alienated from their work in a non-capitalist society? Suppose you were studying a non-capitalist society—past, present, or future. What evidence would you look for to determine whether alienation was stronger or weaker than it is in Canada today?

4. Does the laissez-faire (or liberal) ideology increase or decrease people's sense of alienation from their work? From society as a whole?

5. Why would workers with the same amount of education who work equally hard make *less* money in the secondary labour market (for example, as waiters or taxi drivers) than in the primary labour market (as plumbers or lawyers)? And why would a highly educated, hard-working person be working in the secondary labour market?

6. Is it still appropriate for men and women to make very different kinds of educational and occupational (or career) plans in our society?

Data Collection Exercises

1. Collect statistical data on at least three countries that have industrialized or are industrializing today. With these data, show that as industrial production (for example, the proportion of people working in factories) increases, so does (1) the average person's annual income, (2) the percentage of people who can read and write, and (3) the percentage who live in cities.

2. Collect data from at least six working people to measure their jobs' objective characteristics *and* their degree of job satisfaction. Is there a close connection between the two? If not, why not?

3. Collect data from at least six recent graduates of the educational program you are currently enrolled in. What proportion is unemployed (or has been recently)? What proportion is *underemployed* (see definition in glossary for Chapter Five)?

4. Select a particular job that interests you. Find out what new technologies have been adopted for widespread use in that job in the last 20 years. Has their adoption resulted in people losing their jobs?

Writing Exercises

1. A group of people (funeral directors, sex therapists, pastry chefs, or child-care workers — you choose) wants to professionalize, in order to gain higher social status and better pay. You are asked to advise them on how to accomplish this. Write a 500-word memo suggesting what they should do. (Or, write a 500-word press release explaining to the public why they really *are* professionals.)

2. Ask a friend who is not in this sociology course to describe his or her feelings about school. Then write a 500-word essay demonstrating that your friend is (or is not) alienated.

3. A friend has written you from another city, despairing that he or she is unemployed and unable to find a job. Write your friend a 500-word letter suggesting what he or she should do about it.

4. BOWOOD INDUSTRIES is looking for a management trainee who will fit into their bureaucratically controlled organization. Write a brief (20-question) interview schedule, containing questions to ask applicants, that will determine who is the best candidate for the job.

Glossary

alienation — estrangement of workers from the product of their work, from the work process, from themselves and other workers

bureaucracy — a hierarchically organized type of formal organization found throughout industrial societies

cartel — an agreement among business organizations to limit production, pricing, and marketing of goods by its members. A **monopoly** is one group's exclusive control over the production and sales of a commodity or service. Both are limits to free competition.

division of labour — the breaking up of a job into a number of smaller jobs which are done by separate individuals

economic order — the institutionalized system whereby material resources are produced, distributed, and consumed

industrial society — a society characterized by large-scale mechanized production and an extensive division of labour

mass production – the production of goods in large quantities, by means of division of labour, mechanization, and large productive units (factories or offices)

organic solidarity – social cohesion that is based on differences between people and interdependence

price-fixing – a secret (and usually illegal) agreement between producers to charge the same price for a product or service they all offer, so that competition between them will not drive down the price they can get from consumers

rationalization – the process by which all human action – especially decision-making – becomes subject to calculation, measurement, and control

secondary labour market – contains all the jobs that are characterized by low wages, few opportunities for advancement, and little job security. Conversely, the **primary labour market** consists of jobs offering high wages, good opportunities for advancement, and job security.

specialization – expertise in doing one particular job which has previously been part of a larger job category

---

Suggested Readings

Bell, Daniel *The Coming of Post-industrial Society*. New York: Basic Books, 1973. This key work on the future of economic organization pulls together a great deal of earlier writing; it is also full of interesting ideas. The major debate about work started by this book has never ended.

Edwards, Richard *Contested Terrain: The Transformation of the Workplace in the Twentieth Century*. New York: Basic Books, 1979. This exciting book about the evolution of worker-employer relations in America explains how our own ambitions keep us doing what the boss wants us to do.

Krahn, Harvey J. and Graham S. Lowe *Work, Industry and Canadian Society*. Toronto: Nelson, 1988. An excellent introduction to work and industry in Canada, which includes up-to-date discussions of labour markets, women's work, and industrial conflict.

Inkeles, Alex and David H. Smith *Becoming Modern: Individual Change in Six Developing Countries*. London: Heinemann, 1974. This book shows how the industrialization of jobs also modernizes family relations, ideas about politics, and tolerance for different kinds of people.

Rinehart, James W. *The Tyranny of Work: Alienation and the Labour Process*, 2nd edition. Toronto: Harcourt Brace Jovanovich, 1987. Using Canadian data, the author explores the causes, consequences, and possible cures for alienation at work. He mixes statistics with accounts from illustrative case studies.

Smucker, J. *Industrialization in Canada*. Toronto: Prentice-Hall, 1980. This sophisticated book examines the ways Marx and Weber can help us understand why Canada industrialized the way it did. Particularly, it explores changing theories of management and changing responses of labour to management strategies.

References

Braverman, H. (1974) *Labor and Monopoly Capital*. New York: Monthly Review Press

Campbell, A. (1980) *The Sense of Well-being in America: Recent Patterns and Trends*. New York: McGraw-Hill

Casale, A. and P. Lerman (1986) *USA Today: Tracking Tomorrow's Trends*. Kansas City: Andrews, McNeel and Parker

Durkheim, E. (1965) *The Division of Labor in Society*. New York: Free Press

Edwards, R. (1979) *Contested Terrain: The Transformation of the Workplace in the Twentieth Century*. New York: Basic Books

Friedman, M. and R. Friedman (1981) *Free To Choose*. New York: Avon Books

Inkeles, A. and D.H. Smith (1974) *Becoming Modern: Individual Change in Six Developing Countries*. Cambridge, Mass.: Harvard University Press

King, M., M.A. Murray, and T. Atkinson (1982) "Background personality, job characteristics, and satisfaction with work in a national sample" *Human Relations*, 35 (2), pp. 119-133

Locke, E.A. (1976) "The nature and causes of job satisfaction" pp. 1297-1349 in M.D. Dunnette (ed.) *Handbook of Industrial and Organizational Psychology*. Chicago: Rand McNally

Macpherson, C.B. (1962) *The Political Theory of Possessive Individualism: Hobbes to Locke*. Oxford: Clarendon Press

Marsden, L.R. (1981) "The 'labour force' is an ideological structure" *Atlantis*, 7 (1) Fall, pp. 57-64

Mitford, J. (1963) *The American Way of Death*. New York: Fawcett, Crest Books

Polanyi, K. (1944) *The Great Transformation*. New York: Farrar and Rinehart

Rice, R.W., J.P. Near, and R.G. Hunt (1979) "Unique variance in job and life satisfaction associated with work-related and extra-workplace variables" *Human Relations*, 32 (7), pp. 605-623

Rinehart, J.W. (1987) *The Tyranny of Work: Alienation and the Labour Process* 2nd edition. Toronto: Harcourt Brace Jovanovich

Seeman, M. (1959) "On the meaning of alienation" *American Sociological Review*, 24 (December), pp. 783-791

Sennett, R. and J. Cobb (1973) *The Hidden Injuries of Social Class*. New York: Vintage

Von Glinow, M. (1988) *The New Professionals: Managing Today's High-Tech Employees*. Cambridge, Mass.: Ballinger Publishing Company

Weber, M. (1958) "Bureaucracy" section 8 in H. Gerth and C.W. Mills (eds.) *From Max Weber: Essays in Sociology*. New York: Oxford University Press

_____ . (1961) *General Economic History*. New York: Collier Books

CHAPTER 9

A large fraction of all the people who have ever lived a alive today. Not surprisingly, most of our waking hours a spent amidst large populations—at large workplaces, i large cities, within large nation-states. It is too soon know how we humans will adapt to this new reality.

POPULATION

POPULATION AND HUMAN SURVIVAL

In Chapter Eight we saw that the dramatic social upheavals that accompanied the Industrial Revolution led to a new perspective on society. The social world was no longer seen as the consequence of either natural "forces" or supernatural "design," but as a human creation. The implications of this change in attitude were dramatic. People realized that if *we* had made society the way it is, we can also remake it. We can reshape society to fit our needs. The development of theories about what form society could or should take ultimately led to the discipline of sociology, as well as the other social sciences.

It may be that we are in the midst of another revolution just as profound. We seem to be living in an era in which there is a fundamental redefinition of the social problems brought on by industrial development, and of the direction further development should take. Many of the classical problems associated with either industrial development or capitalism, such as exploitation, alienation, and bureaucratic rigidity, seem to have lessened, though are by no means solved. The rise of labour unions and social democratic political parties, the development of the welfare state, the active role taken by feminist movements—all of these have noticeably improved the lives of workers. We have also seen in the last few years an easing both of tensions and of political differences between Western capitalist nations and the state socialist governments of eastern Europe.

There are new concerns, however, about the course of industrialization and technological development. Most of these have to do with their impact on the environment and the ecology of the world. There seems little doubt that we are transforming the very planet on which we live in a dramatic fashion. We hear that the depletion of the ozone layer and the "greenhouse effect" are heating up the world and making it hazardous just to be out in the sun. The destruction of the Amazon rain forest and the emission of industrial pollutants threaten the quality of the air while oil spills and the dumping of industrial wastes threaten our rivers, lakes, and oceans. In the meantime, leaking containers of chemical toxins, the electromagnetic radiation from colour TVs, and the nitrites found in hot dogs are said to cause cancer.

These new social problems face us *all*, regardless of class or political system. The Soviet Union had its Chernobyl nuclear "mishap," just as the United States had its "accident" at Three Mile Island. The Third World suffers as much, or more, than does the developed world. Indeed, the Union Carbide accident in Bhopal, India showed that modern industry has placed the whole world at risk. Canada has so far been spared any major ecological disaster but there is no question that more and more Canadians today are concerned about our environment.

Today most of us have begun to realize that to a large extent the problem is "us," people. There are many other factors at work here, but many of our problems seem to be aggravated by the sheer volume of people in the world. There is no escaping the fact that the world has a population problem that we must solve during our lifetime. We must come to terms with this problem and understand it. The social science we look to for the materials to study the problem of population is demography.

The science of demography

Although sociology and demography are two separate disciplines, they are often intimately linked. Demographers are often found as members of university sociology departments and sociologists obtain much of the data with which they work from demographers. **Demography** is the scientific study of the size, structure, distribution, and development of the world's population. It is concerned with the implications of population for the organization of societies.

Demography has two branches. Formal or mathematical demography is concerned with making quantitative models of population growth and change. These models are useful in projecting changes in the size and structure of the population. The second branch, social demography, studies the historical, cultural, economic, and political conditions under which the size and structure of populations change. Social demography is more qualitative and somewhat more speculative than formal demography. It is closer to sociology in both style and substance.

Because demography is a separate social science discipline, we shall not be making specific reference to the three paradigms which we have regularly discussed in this text. All sociologists, whether they make use of a functionalist, conflict, or interactionist paradigm on demography, rely on demographic data for information and theories about the size, distribution and composition of the populations they study. For example, if sociologists want information on the social characteristics of the population, such as age, sex, marital status, ethnicity, religious affiliation, income, occupation, residence, household membership, citizenship status, and type of employment, they get it from demographers.

A key source for such data is the **Census**, a periodic national survey of the inhabitants of a country. It is more than an enumeration of the people: it is a way of taking inventory of the types of people who live in the country and their social characteristics. Demographers play a central role in collecting and analyzing Census data.

Sociologists also rely on demographers for information to help us understand population problems. Changes in population size or characteristics may not cause all of the world's problems, but they certainly make them worse. It is much harder to solve problems of poverty and inequality, intolerance and war, environmental damage and a falling quality of life, when the population is growing rapidly.

In this chapter we will focus on one central issue: population growth. The process of population growth illustrates well the premise of this book, that macro events and micro events are intertwined. Population analysis is typically macro in scope, because it looks at large numbers of people over long periods of time. Yet the actual patterns it uncovers are the result of millions of couples making personal choices, such as when to marry and how many children to have. As we shall see, the birth rate declined historically because millions of couples decided, quite separately, that it was in their best interest to have fewer children.

This combination of millions of micro-decisions yields the pattern we discern when we look at population through a macro lens. Demographers are very much like astronomers viewing the patterns among millions of stars and planets, each of which is moving in its own separate, though interdependent, orbit.

POPULATION GROWTH AND CHANGE

Changes in the size and structure of the population have important implications both for public policy and for the quality of our personal lives, because they have a direct impact on the demand for, and availability of, housing, education, health care, and employment (among other things). For example, a recent decision by the federal government to raise the ceiling on the number of immigrants allowed into Canada was informed by a prediction, based on current demographic trends, that unless more immigrants are allowed in, Canada's population by the year 2025 will be smaller than it is today.

Population growth and change take place within a cultural, political, economic, and social context. Certain cultural practices (for example, the use of birth control, the killing of female babies, or a low value placed on small or large families) all affect both the size and structure of the population.

Equally, the size and structure of a population affects cultural practices. For example, as the proportion of people who are over age 65 increases, tolerance for older people grows. There is a growing acceptance of aging as a natural and even desirable part of life. With the aging of the large baby boom generation, we are even likely to see a glorification of old age.

The idea that population growth constitutes a serious problem for the world is not a new one. It was first expressed by population theorist Thomas Malthus 200 years ago.

The Malthusian dilemma

Thomas Malthus (1766–1834) is considered to be the founder of demography. He was the first to take seriously the possibility that the earth would soon be "overpopulated." Malthus showed that population growth takes place *exponentially*. A population increasing exponentially (or geometrically) at a constant rate is adding more people every year than the year before.

Consider a population of 1000 women and 1000 men. Each woman marries and has four children. If all survive, in the next generation there will be roughly 2000 women and 2000 men. If all of these women also marry and have four children, in the next generation there will be roughly 4000 women and 4000 men; and in the generation after that, 8000 women and 8000 men. Thus, with a constant pattern of four births per woman, the population doubles every generation (roughly 30 years). In four generations, it has gone from 2000 people to 16 000 people. This is the power of exponential growth.

In contrast, increases in the food supply are only additive or *arithmetic*. The growth in the level of food supplies is limited by the amount of land available, the quality of the soil, and the given level of technological development a society has attained. Malthus believed that there is a very real potential for population growth to outstrip increases in the food supply. This possibility poses a continuous threat to the survival of the human species. Checks or limits on population growth have to be brought in, to ensure that growth is kept in balance with the existing food supply. Positive checks are checks against overpopulation which increase the death rate. They include war, famine, pestilence, and disease. Preventive checks are measures people take to limit the numbers of live births. They include delaying marriage, using contraceptives, abortion, infanticide, and sexual abstinence.

Malthus painted a grim picture of the world's future. Was he right? "Overpopulation" is a word that is often used but is hard to measure. An area is said to be overpopulated when the means available to the inhabitants to support themselves are not adequate. There are more mouths to feed than there is food. Still, sheer numbers alone do not determine whether an area is overpopulated. It is the relationship between the population and the environment in which it is located, as well as the type of technology available to exploit this environment, that determines whether an area is overpopulated.

For these reasons, it is virtually impossible to put absolute numbers on the world's carrying capacity, or the number of people who can be supported by the available resources at a given level of technological development. However, it is easy to see when a territory is far beyond its carrying capacity or ideal population. Then, scarcity starts to occur in dramatic ways, and the conflict over resources may increase.

What Malthus did not foresee was that technological advances in agriculture would make it possible to vastly increase the food supply, to the point where the great majority of the population in industrialized countries is able to live off the food produced by a small minority. Even in less-developed countries, most people have food to eat—though evidence indicates that a great many do not have enough and others do not eat the right kind for good health. Many of the famines that have plagued Africa in recent years are a consequence not of overpopulation but of improper use of land and even of civil wars and other political factors. For strategic reasons, a low priority is put on shipping food to particular regions of the country where rebel supporters are most numerous. The government may even intend to starve the rebels into submission. This procedure has a long history. Britain ignored the starving and troublesome Irish in 1843; the Soviet Union ignored the starving and troublesome Ukrainians in the 1930s; the USSR started actively to withhold resources from the Baltic states, as did the USA from Iraq, in 1990.

Some economists say that the reason for overpopulation is that Third World countries do not have enough resources (such as arable land or minerals) to exploit, or do not know how to exploit them. Yet this cannot be true. Industrialized countries rely heavily on Third World countries for many resources such as timber and zinc, iron and copper, oil and natural gas, that they cannot get in their own countries. They also rely on the Third World for food they cannot grow, for example, sugar, coffee, tea, and bananas. The less-developed countries *do* have valuable resources. However, control over these resources is often in the hands of the developed world, either directly through ownership of lands and mines, for example, or through the control of international prices.

It is in the interest of the industrialized nations to keep the prices of essential resources low. However, the amount paid for resources is often too low for Third World countries to re-invest in their own country, to develop manufacturing, and to attempt to break free from dependence on the industrial nations for capital and manufactured goods.

In poorer nations, then, the population problem is not just a matter of too many people, it is an economic problem too—a problem of poverty. Industrialized nations are preventing the Third World from gaining economic independence. With greater economic independence and development, these nations would not be overpopulated, even with the same number of people they have now.

In industrial countries the problem has shifted away from food scarcity to other types of scarcity. Industrialism requires energy and minerals. Unless we find new deposits, or a way of making synthetic copies, of these non-renewable resources, we in the industrial world may face life-threatening scarcity soon. This has already been made obvious in the case of petroleum, which is the source of plastics as well as oil and gasoline. The oil shortages of the 1970s showed us how dependent we are on petroleum in modern industrial society. Having escaped the food shortage Malthus predicted, we may soon be facing an identical shortage of needed raw materials. So, the Malthusian problem reasserts itself time and again: in the long run, how are humans going to support a population that is growing faster than the resources it needs to survive?

The dilemma is simply this: Any geographic area—whether Canada or the entire world—has a limited carrying capacity. The capacity of humans to reproduce is much greater than the Earth's carrying capacity. If we do not limit population growth, positive checks are inevitable. As Meadows and Meadows (1972) wrote in their book *The Limits to Growth*, we can choose to die from starvation, pollution, or the depletion of needed industrial resources. The specifics and timing of the disaster vary from one scenario to another, but the end of the story is always the same.

Faced with the risk of a worldwide disaster, many have come to advocate **zero population growth (zpg)** as a temporary solution, until a longer-term solution is found. **Zero population growth** occurs when the factors leading to population growth—especially births—are exactly balanced by the factors

EXHIBIT 9.1

THE WORLD POPULATION EXPLOSION

Most of the world's population increase has taken place in the past two centuries. It took hundreds of thousands of years for the human race to reach its 1960 total of about 3 billion people. But in the 30 years that followed, it grew by another 2 billion people, to its present total of over 5 billion.

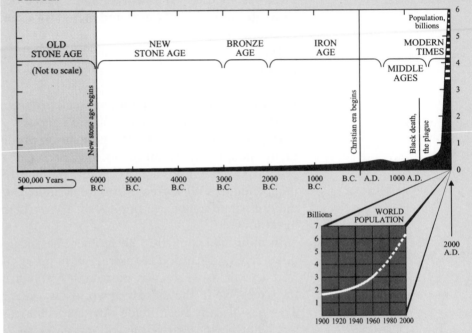

Source: G.T. Trewartha (1969) *A Geography of Population: World Patterns*. New York: Wiley, page 29

leading to population decline—especially deaths. Under conditions of ZPG, births and deaths are equal. Then the size of the population remains constant over time.

How realistic is such a goal? Quite realistic, if the demographic changes we are seeing in the industrialized world spread elsewhere. These changes are part of a process of **demographic transition**, which began in Europe about 200 years ago and profoundly altered the patterns of population growth.

Demographic transition theory	The term **demographic transition** refers to the transition a society undergoes, from *high* birth and death rates to *low* birth and death rates, that accompanies industrialization. This is the type of change that has taken place in Europe from the onset of the industrial revolution up to the present day. Currently, much of the Third World is in the middle of this transition process.

In its most general form, the transition is brought about by a package of changes called "modernization." As we shall see, modernization first causes a drop in mortality, then (after a time) a drop in fertility.

Dynamics of population change

What makes a population get larger or smaller is limited to a few possibilities. Within a closed system – a planet or an isolated island – only births and deaths affect the population. In an open system – like Canada as a whole or your own community – migration also affects the population size and composition. Leaving aside migration for the moment, we need to know a population's *fertility rate*, and its *mortality rate* in order to examine population growth.

A population's **fertility rate** is the average number of children a woman in a given society bears. For a society such as ours to replace itself – to stay the same size from one generation to the next – the fertility rate should be at least 2.1 children, or 1.05 daughters, per woman of childbearing age. Each woman who gives birth must reproduce not only for herself, but also for women in her generation who never reproduce (because they die before they reach reproductive age, choose not to have children, or are unable to do so).

Demographers have also invented a sophisticated way of measuring the risks of death in a population. What they do is calculate a **mortality rate** for people of each age. From this they can calculate life expectancies at each age. The most commonly used is life expectancy at birth. In Canada, a woman's life expectancy at birth is about 77 years. That is, the moment she is born, a woman can expect to live 77 years. (A man's life expectancy at birth is five or six years less.)

Pre-modern population growth

In pre-modern societies, births and deaths were pretty much in balance. Before the development of modern medicine and the spread of modern techniques of sanitation, death rates were very high, but so were birth rates. As a result, the rate of natural increase – the difference between births and deaths, expressed as a ratio of the total population – was quite low. The population was young and constantly changing through birth and death, but it was not growing very quickly.

Families would usually try to have as many children as possible. Children in non-industrial countries are an economic asset. In rural areas, they start to work at an early age as farm hands, doing chores in the home, or earning extra wage on other farms or in nearby factories. In parts of the world where old-age security, pension plans, and welfare assistance do not exist, children are the sole means of support for parents when they reach old age. The more children a couple has, the greater the likelihood they will be looked after in their "golden years." In societies that practise arranged marriages, children enable a family to form economic and social ties to other families for mutual assistance. The more children one has, the more ties one will have to other families.

In some cultures, having large families is a way for people to fulfil their perceived duty to God. People view many children, especially many sons, as a blessing or sign of good fortune. Some men even view the number of children they have fathered as a sign of virility. Often, women are accorded social prestige according to how many children they have been able to bear.

However, most of these reasons for having large families are traditional. Since they have not changed for centuries, they cannot, by themselves, account

In European history, first mortality rates fell, then fertility rates fell. In between, the population grew rapidly. To some degree, non-European societies are repeating this pattern. However, now in the developed world, fertility rates are continuing to fall, or levelling off, below replacement, leading some demographers to think we have entered a second demographic transition.

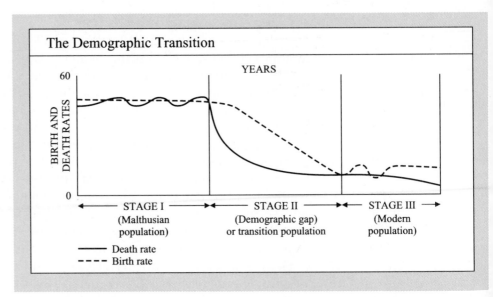

The Demographic Transition

for the rapid rise in world population during the last half-century or so. Therefore we must look elsewhere—to the change in death rates—for an explanation. Then we find that the population explosion occurred, not because people started to have more children than before, but because more children were surviving to adult, reproductive ages and having children of their own.

Just as birth rates have been very high for most of human history, so too have death rates. The lack of proper sanitation and curative medicine, poor nutrition, recurrent famines, and warfare kept the death rate high in pre-modern societies. The death rate was particularly high among newborn infants and young children. Childhood diseases, which we treat so easily now with antibiotics or which have nearly disappeared due to inoculation, were fearsome killers in the past. Being realistic, parents could not assume that even half their children would survive to adult age.

When European medicine, nutrition, and sanitation began to improve dramatically in the 18th century, the death rate began to fall. More children survived to reproductive age and had children of their own, many of which survived in turn to reproductive age. Women no longer had to bear ten children in the hopes that four would survive. They could be relatively confident that a majority of their children would survive. Then, they began having fewer children—only as many as they thought they could support.

During the transition period, a large growth in population occurs as a result of the temporary gap between fertility and mortality. For a while, people are still having as many children as always, but many more are surviving. Gradually, as happened in Europe and North America in the last two centuries, members of the population come to realize they do not have to have as many children as in the past.

The reasons for this are many: The burden of social security shifts from family to the government. As well, people become more rational about childbearing. Increased education, urbanization, and social and geographic mobility all reduce the economic value of children. So does the increased cost of raising a child. Finally, the changing role of women in society and the increase in female careers all reduce the willingness to bear children. So the birth rate begins to fall until, finally, it reaches approximately the same (low) level as the death rate.

Limitations of demographic transition theory

Demographic transition theory has enormous practical as well as theoretical implications. The theory describes what seems to be a universal process. It makes a very important contribution to our understanding of economic development and the relationship of population to that development. Indeed, this theory is the dominant way of thinking about population today and a part of every forecast of world and Third World populations. It rightly reminds us that a low-mortality/low-fertility population type is critical if people wish to maintain a high standard of living.

Yet research over the past 20 years has cast more and more doubt on the theory's validity (see Coale and Watkins, 1987). Newly discovered data show that the theory does not apply as well to European history, on which it was modelled, as people thought 20 years ago. It applies even worse to non-European, Third World countries. That is because of the theory's failure to consider many problems that are common in Third World countries today, such as the following:

(1) the permanent damage a long-term population explosion can do to a nation's economy or eco-system, which may make transition to the final stage impossible (or even restore a high-mortality/high-fertility balance). An example of this is Brazil's destruction of the Amazon rain forest, a result of both rapid population growth (and migration) and the Brazilian government's desire for a rapid increase in national revenues (through meat and lumber export).

(2) the inability of Third World countries to provide the socio-economic factors (social security, education, urbanization, social mobility, women's careers) that make fertility reduction attractive. Where, as in central Africa or the Indian subcontinent—or, for that matter, among teenagers in black urban America—people have very little opportunity to improve their lives by avoiding childbearing, they will have many children even if the benefit to be gained from having them is slight or short-lived.

(3) the need of Third World countries to choose among competing social investments—to spend money on social security *versus* education *versus* health care, for example. The theory gives no guidance as to which factors are most influential in the transition process and which should be considered top priority. China offers a classic example of this problem. China needs reforms of almost every kind: agricultural, industrial, educational, economic, and so on. Money could be usefully invested in any of thousands of different areas of activity; choosing, though inevitable, is almost impossible. Worse still, every year there are as many new Chinese

babies born as people alive in Canada—about 25 million. To planners, these new citizens represent new demands on the public purse.

Most Third World countries have to meet these pressures of a growing population and growing demands for economic improvement. Often, as in China, the result of so many conflicting demands is a political explosion.

Thus, demographic transition theory can more or less accurately describe Western demographic history in vague generalities. It can even describe the macrodynamics of current populations. However, it is unable to probe and illuminate details of demographic history in a given country. As such, it is scientifically unsatisfactory when dealing with details; for example, in contributing to forecasts and causal explanations.

The theory correctly describes many aspects of Canadian population history but it is not useful in projecting Canada's future. To understand why, we must examine the particulars of that history.

FERTILITY IN CANADA

As demographic transition theory would have predicted, Canadian *mortality* began to fall in the early 19th century and continued falling through the early 20th century, levelling off around mid-century. It did, however, continue to be high in certain subpopulations—in the North, on native reserves, and in isolated parts of the Maritimes, for example—well into the second half of this century.

Also as the theory would have predicted, by the end of the 19th century, *fertility* had already begun to decline. It has continued to decline—with two irregularities—until this decade. The two irregularities were the Depression of the 1930s, when many fewer than expected births occurred; and the 1950s, when many more than expected births occurred. Leaving aside these "blips," the Canadian transition to low fertility has gone pretty much as expected and, since about 1980, the birth rate has levelled off at a level just below zero population growth.

High fertility has played a critical part in Canadian population development. Contrary to what many believe, immigration has *not* played the decisive role in the 20th century in Canada. In fact, Beaujot (1988: 54) reports, "The net migration of 4.0 million persons from 1901 to 1981 comprised 21.2% of [Canada's] population growth over this period." The other nearly 80% was through natural increase by people within the country. The reason immigration had so slight an impact was, in large part, because in some periods as many people or more were leaving the country as were coming to it.

A dramatic example of the power of local reproduction is found in Quebec's history. The high birth rate among Canada's French population has rarely been equalled in the world (Bell and Tepperman, 1979). Between 1608 and 1760 roughly 10 000 colonists arrived in New France. Up until the 20th century, the francophone population doubled every 25 years. Almost all of the francophones living in Canada, and millions more who have assimilated into North America's anglophone population, are descended from these original colonists. This extraordinarily high level of population growth, referred to by francophone nationalists as "the revenge of the cradle," made up in some part for the failure to attract immigrants from France to Canada. It also helped prevent the assimilation of most francophones into an overwhelming anglophone majority.

The drop in fertility from high to low levels will mean an increased importance for mortality and migration in the population picture. We shall discuss these after completing our brief examination of fertility. In discussing Canada's particular case, we must consider some of the concepts and measures that demographers apply to the study of fertility.

Measuring fertility

As noted earlier, the fertility rate is the number of children the average woman of childbearing age bears in a given society. Not only is there a pattern in the number of children women bear—for example, religious, traditional-minded women are likely to bear more children than non-religious women—there is also a pattern in the age at which women are most likely to bear their offspring.

Age-specific fertility rates are annual fertility rates, or risks of childbearing, that are specific to women in particular age groups: ages 15 to 19, 20 to 24, 25 to 29, and so on. A **total fertility rate** is calculated from these rates. It estimates the average number of live births to a woman who lives through the age-specific fertility rates.

In societies that do not practise birth control, there is a correlation between a woman's age at her first birth and the total number of children she will bear. The younger a woman is when she has her first child, the longer she has left to bear more children, and the more children she is likely to have in total. Starting at age 15 and continuing to bear as many children as possible until menopause around age 45, a healthy woman could easily have ten or fifteen children.

However, in our own society, few women begin to bear children at so young an age; the average age at which a woman bears her first child is closer to 30 than it is to 15. What's more, few women continue to have children at the biologically possible maximum. This fact reflects an increasing emphasis on the role of women as individuals with career ambitions, which take them out of the home and into educational institutions and the workplace. So they have less reproductive time to bear many children. Also, the same cultural attitudes that make it possible for women to delay having children until they have completed their education and established themselves in a career make it socially acceptable for women to have fewer children overall.

However, even women who have their first child in their teens—more often than not, the result of an unwanted pregnancy—are unlikely to continue childbearing at a biologically maximum rate throughout their lives. Like women who begin their childbearing later, they are likely to have an ideal family size in mind that is closer to two or three children than to ten or fifteen. For this reason, age at first childbearing is a much poorer predictor of total fertility today than it was two centuries ago, or even two generations ago.

Not only are childbearing norms—the desired family size—lower today than in the past, but so are childbearing realities. Modern contraception allows most women to have the number of children they actually want, when they want to have them. They can space their childbearing, so that births occur almost exactly when they will be most convenient. This makes it possible, as never before, for women to have careers the way men do.

In recent years the biggest population change in Canada, as elsewhere, was caused by the **baby boom** of the 1950s. This was a sudden and considerable rise in the birth rate after the Second World War. The boom was a response to the lifting of long-term restraints on marriage and childbearing imposed by the Depression and then the war, as well as to the rapid rise of economic prosperity after the war. The birth rate reached its peak, then began to decline again around the end of the 1950s. It has since fallen to its lowest level ever.

However, the social changes caused by this burst of fertility will last well into the next century. The baby-boomers have had continuing problems with getting ahead, because of more than usually stiff competition for education, jobs, and marriage partners. At work, the trouble the baby-boom generation has had in career success is largely because of the surplus of inexperienced people compared to older, more experienced workers (Easterlin, 1980). Today, experience is in short supply, and older workers will be paid more. Teenagers are also in short supply, and are starting to receive more for their efforts.

In general, scarcity brings high rewards, and baby-boomers will never be scarce. Whether you were born in a small or large *birth cohort* has an enormous impact on your chances for success in a competitive society. A **cohort** is a group of people who share similar life experiences at the same point in time. For example, all the people who were born in the same year form a birth cohort. The people who got married in a given year form a marriage cohort. Cohorts are interesting because, although the people who make them up do not know one another, they go through many of the same life experiences at the same time, since they face the same constraints and compete for the same opportunities.

The larger your birth cohort—that is, the higher the birth rate at the time you were born—the more people you must compete with throughout life, and the more likely you are to fail.

Finding it harder to get jobs than in the past, members of the baby-boom generation are having smaller families. In the 1970s and '80s, Canadian women postponed marriage and childbearing and had fewer children. Dual-earner families are increasingly common, largely because most couples need two incomes to make ends meet in Canadian cities today. But difficulties in providing for themselves will not stop at age 65; baby-boomers will also have had more difficulty earning and saving for old age. Younger age groups supporting them through contributions to pension and social security funds will be too small to do the job. New solutions for supporting the aged will be needed early in the next century.

This illustrates an interesting turn-around in Canada's demographic outlook. During earlier periods of history, when birth rates were high, the dependency ratio—the ratio of (young) economically unproductive people to income producers—was high. As the birth rate has fallen, so (temporarily) has the dependency ratio; but now the dependency ratio is rising again. The ratio of (old) economically unproductive people to income producers is going to get

EXHIBIT 9.2

Population Growth And Economic Well-being

The consensus among those economists who have considered the question is that, within broad limits, population growth or sheer numbers of people is not a major factor in economic growth or economic well-being in modern economies that play an active role in world trade. Canada is such an economy. A study of economic growth and population growth for member countries of the Organization for Economic Cooperation and Development illustrates this absence of a correlation. Comparing the rate of change of economic growth and that of population growth for these 22 developed economies during the period 1960–85 shows no relationship between them.

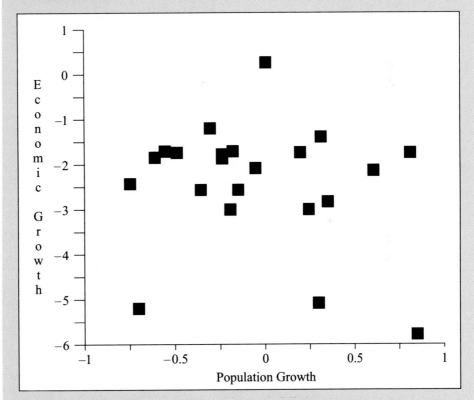

Source: *Charting Canada's Future: A Report of the Demographic Review.* (Supply and Services Catalogue No. H21-105/1-1989) Ottawa: Health and Welfare Canada, 1989, p. 9. Reproduced with the permission of the Minister of Supply and Services, 1990.

higher and higher as the baby-boomers pass into retirement. This problem of dependency will become a central concern of Canadian society in the next century.

Canada's dominant social and cultural concerns have continued to reflect the personal problems the baby-boomers were having as they passed through life. During the 1950s, parents and government were chiefly concerned with providing adequate primary schooling. In the 1960s and 1970s, concern focused on jobs and housing for the baby-boomers. In the early 21st century, old-age pensions, retirement rules, and nursing-home vacancies will probably be of great interest to most Canadians (see, for example, Foot, 1982).

In short, this unusual burst of high fertility has largely reshaped Canada's society and culture. The baby-boom generation has been most affected. Members of that generation will end up paying many of the social and psychological costs of their parents' high fertility—a fertility level that does not work well in modern industrial societies, where standards of living are high.

MORTALITY IN CANADA'S POPULATION

In Canada, mortality rates for both sexes have been steadily declining since 1921. However, a look at the data confirms that women continue to enjoy a lower rate at every age when compared to men.

Reasons for this are various. Males have a much larger mortality rate as infants and this, along with some other evidence, suggests that females are biologically more hardy than males. Tobacco and alcohol use also has an effect. Males make more use of these products and suffer the health consequences, which include earlier death. As well, men have typically died in large numbers as casualties of war, from automobile accidents, and from stress-related illnesses.

Cancer has become an increasingly important cause of death for all, and here too there are differences between the sexes. Females in 1900 had a much higher incidence of cancer than males, but now the roles are reversed. A reason for this is that the traditionally "female" cancers of the breast and uterus are today more treatable than in the past, and more treatable than traditionally "male" cancers of the digestive system and lung.

Socio-economic status is also a factor in mortality risks, although not as large a factor as in the past, having declined in importance since 1921. In most countries, people with high socio-economic status have the lowest mortality rates. The lower-status people are more likely to be exposed to occupational hazards. They have a generally lower standard of living—less (and poorer) food to eat and worse sanitation, for example. The poor also have less access to medical care. The importance of the latter is evidenced by the fact that, for illnesses that medicine has had little success in curing, there is no class difference in mortality rates; but for diseases that have witnessed substantial medical success, there are considerable class differences.

Ethnicity and race are other factors affecting mortality risks. Even today, Canadian native peoples have a lower life expectancy (because of higher age-specific mortality rates) than other Canadians, though the differences are not as great as in the past. French Canadians also have higher age-specific mortality rates than English Canadians. Reasons for these persisting differences are class-related: lower than average income, nutrition, and education among the non-dominant groups. They also reflect regional variations in environmental quality and standards of living.

Mortality data based on ethnic origin are almost non-existent in Canada. However, demographers have calculated that foreign-born people who immigrate to Canada have a lower mortality rate than native-born people, perhaps reflecting the highly selective nature of immigration.

Religious practices may also modify death rates, although these are sometimes difficult to separate from ethnic diversities. As well, their practices may include both positive and negative features, from a health standpoint. For example, Christian Scientists refuse medical aid, but their life expectancy is no different than anyone else's, because they also shun smoking and drinking. Mormons also shun smoking and drinking, and they have lower than average death rates.

What these data show is that mortality rates are a clear reflection of social inequalities. People live longer, healthier lives in rich regions of rich countries. Among people in these regions, the richest, best-educated people live longest of all. Race, ethnicity, and religion are important factors primarily in so far as they are associated with class position. They may also shape lifestyle, the health-related information people get, and the care they are encouraged to take.

EXHIBIT 9.3

THE HEALTH COSTS OF MODERNITY

Health planners around the world are asking, "Will today's developing countries repeat the history of the developed countries?"

A century ago, a person's life expectancy was only 35 years in France and about 40 years in the United Kingdom. Norway was even fighting a leprosy epidemic. Yet by 1930, better food, housing, and sanitation had driven down infant mortality, and life expectancy had risen to 60 years in many western European countries.

Within 30 years after that, the growth in life expectancy had started to level off. Replacing the old infectious diseases that had been major causes of death a century earlier were new causes of death. Increases in heart disease and cancer were largely due to "modern lifestyles" – specifically, to stress, smoking, high-fat diets, lack of exercise, and alcohol abuse.

Today, Third World countries are starting to succeed in driving down infant mortality due to infectious death-causing diseases such as diarrhea, tuberculosis, measles, and malaria. They still have a long way to go; because their economies continue to suffer due to chronic infectious diseases (such as sleeping sickness, river blindness, and leprosy), progress in public health is very slow.

As life expectancies grow and fertility drops in these countries, the population ages. More and more people in developing countries will enter the (older) age groups associated with high risks of heart disease and cancer. There are already strong signs that developing countries will have to fight the battle for good health on two fronts at the same time. They will have to continue their far-from-complete battle against infectious diseases and also keep "modern life" diseases from getting out of hand. Yet, says the World Health Organization, if present trends continue, cancer and heart diseases may be taking 24 million lives a year by the year 2000 – two-thirds of them in developing countries.

Adapted from John Maurice "Heart ills, cancer hit Third World 'survivors'" *The Globe and Mail*, Saturday, March 10, 1990, D4

Two non-class related influences are gender and marital status: the data strongly suggest that women continue to survive better than men, other things being equal. Marriage continues to contribute to people's well-being, especially for men (who register a larger increase in life expectancy through marriage than women do).

This being so, future mortality will largely be influenced to the degree to which social inequality is reduced, health information is diffused, and marriage as an institution is supported. It is this seeming simplicity of the problem that had led many to believe that we shall continue to make progress against death without significant social and cultural changes. However, there is no simple road to universal health and ever-increasing longevity.

The future of mortality

For a long time demographers have largely ignored mortality patterns. They have left the problem to actuaries, who work out risks of death at different ages for insurance companies. Demographers' readiness to ignore death as a factor in population change has several causes.

First, demographers may have felt that everything that needed to be said about death had been said. Malthus had said that preventive checks on population growth—measures that limited births—would largely avoid the play of positive checks, which increased deaths. Since Malthus, preventive checks have become more common and effective and positive checks have become somewhat less common in human history. Likewise, demographic transition theory argued that a declining death rate comes first, and a declining birth rate later. We are in the stage of declining or low birth rates now; the era of high death rates is long gone.

Second, demographers may have felt that all the major gains in the fight against mortality have been made. Fewer and fewer people are dying each year from infectious diseases—the traditional killer in high-mortality populations. (More and more are dying from **endogenous** causes: from deterioration of the heart or lungs, or cancer for example.) Conversely, for a long time there has been little increase in people's life expectancies in modern societies. We seem to have hit a plateau: at birth, Canadians cannot expect to live more than 70 to 80 years, and this fact has changed little for a generation or more.

As infectious causes of death have been beaten back by medicine, nutrition, and sanitation, more and more people living in developed countries have been dying from causes that can only be considered avoidable and often self-inflicted. Consider the main causes of death among Canadians in the prime years of their lives, ages 10 to 50. They include

(1) suicide,

(2) homicide, and

(3) accidents, especially motor vehicle accidents.

In some urban centres, deaths due to AIDS have joined this select group of causes as a prime killer. And periodically foreign wars, civil wars, and internal repression (for example, political executions and death camps) claim enormous numbers of young people, though the human costs of these to Canada have been much lighter, so far, than in other countries.

For the most part, these causes of death are uniquely human. To prevent them means understanding the uniquely human capacity for self-destruction and the destruction of others. So far, we know little about how to prevent any of these causes of death — probably less than we know about the ways to prevent death from cancer, though cancer is considered the most mysterious killer today. Part of our failure to address these uniquely human killers is because they have not been claimed as medical problems by the health establishment. As such, they receive less attention, respect, and funding than problems like cancer.

The medical establishment has failed to claim responsibility for avoidable deaths for a number of reasons. First, they are far from technologically (or chemically) fixable problems, in the way most medical problems are today. Second, they all have a strong and obvious social component. They are all hard to study, much less remedy, without running up against people's beliefs, politics, and vested interests. Finally, they call for preventive measures and, to a large degree, modern medicine is oriented to curing, not preventing, problems. Prevention may mean restructuring the society, not merely the person or persons at most immediate risk.

This lesson may be driven home to the health establishment as it tries to deal with other causes of death which lie more neatly within its definition of concerns: for example, cancer. Evidence is amassing that cancers are caused by dangerous substances all around us — in our water, our air, the foods we eat, and so on. Humans put those dangerous substances there: whether through auto emissions, factory smokestacks, toxic waste dumping, or badly tested manufacturing. Are they not responsible for causing this problem and paying to remedy it? Should they not be responsible for preventing it in future?

The AIDS epidemic tells a slightly different tale. For some, the epidemic is a morality play — a demonstration that drug addicts and sexual "perverts" get punished for their sins. So long as AIDS is limited to the drug-using and gay communities, this definition of the problem — unsound though it is — is likely to survive. Yet as Heilig and Wils (1989: 1) write, this conception is already outdated. Demographers and policy makers expect dramatic increases in the prevalence of this disease and its gradual spread through the rest of the population (see, for example, the Royal Society of Canada's 1988 report, *AIDS: A Perspective for Canadians*). Research in Switzerland, Austria, and the Federal Republic of Germany reveals that, already, AIDS is a problem of enormous scope.

Throughout history, new diseases have always arisen when old ones were beaten. This is why medicine has made no headway with the common cold, and little headway with cancer. It is why AIDS has emerged from nowhere — just like the Black (bubonic) Plague of the 14th century, which claimed something like a quarter of the population of Europe. For several centuries, the plague swept periodically through Europe, each time with somewhat less effect. Today, the disease is virtually unknown.

What history shows us is the futility of believing in progress towards perfect health. There will always be new killers to conquer, some of them (like suicide and war) because of avoidable social problems and others (like AIDS and cancer) a result of new or rapidly evolving life forms. Our failure to significantly decrease mortality (or increase life expectancy) in the latter half of the 20th century is because of too great a concern with high-tech medical cures, and not enough concern with preventive measures: social research and social reform.

New health strategies require a dedication to reducing the conflict between humans, in order to war more effectively on disease. They also require a confrontation with social-class inequality as the major non-genetic source of variations in how long, and how well, people get to live.

PATTERNS OF MIGRATION

There is one more factor relevant to population growth we must consider: migration. In and of itself, migration does not increase the world's population, it merely redistributes it. Yet such redistribution can have a profound impact. The enormous numbers of people moving into ecologically significant areas, such as the Amazon jungle in Brazil, threaten to alter the world's environment. In Canada, migration has played a particularly significant role in national development, and understanding the processes promoting or inhibiting migration is important for understanding much of Canada's current character.

As a country with a short history and extensive migration, Canada is particularly hard to analyze using demographic transition theory. That is not to say that demographic transition theory fails to apply to Canada. As we have seen, it has applied quite well in its general outline up to now. But the theory has nothing to say about migration and, when we come to consider Canadian history, immigration (movement into an area), emigration (movement out of an area), and internal migration play an important part. As noted earlier, migration will be playing an ever greater role, now that fertility is so low.

The **migration rate** is the number of people who enter or leave the population in a given year (per 1000 inhabitants at mid-year). The net migration rate is the number of immigrants, minus the number of emigrants, per year per thousand inhabitants.

Internal migration refers to people moving from one region of a country to another: that is, movement taking place within a country. Internal migration patterns are useful indexes of changing circumstances in various regions. As we shall see, they reflect changes in the job opportunities available to individuals of a particular region of the country, in a rising cost of living, in a lack of affordable housing, or in intense discrimination against a given ethnic group.

International migration refers to the number of people moving from one country to another, and these statistics also serve as useful indexes of changing circumstances in various countries.

All migration is affected by push and pull factors. **Pull factors** in migration are all those factors that encourage people to move to a particular area, or that make a particular location desirable. They include better job opportunities, more tolerance for ethnic or religious minorities, and greater freedom. Generally speaking, pull factors are those that promise people a better life. **Push factors** are all those factors that encourage people to leave an area: they

Like the U.S., Israel, Australia, and Argentina, Canada has always been a nation of immigrants, with enormous numbers entering (and often leaving) every decade. It is impossible to exaggerate the impact of so much population movement on our national identity.

include famine, a lack of job opportunities, discrimination, and fear of oppression.

Changes in the size of a given population are caused by variations in the birth rate, the death rate, and the net migration rate. The **growth rate** is the rate at which the number of people added to the population increases. (In the case of negative population growth, it is the rate at which population size declines.) The growth rate is calculated by subtracting the number of deaths and out-migrations from the number of births and in-migrations, and expressing the result as a proportion of the mid-year population.

Canada's population has shown enormous fluidity and mobility through migration; sociologist John Porter (1965) even compared the country to a great train station.

The growth of Canada's population to more than 25 000 000 has taken two centuries, thanks to a growth rate of about four percent in the century before Confederation and two percent in much of the century that followed. The national population grew because of high rates of childbearing and high rates of immigration.

Almost all Canadians are descended from immigrants, particularly immigrants who arrived in the last 50 to 100 years. But emigration was sometimes so common in Canada that it largely offset the effects of immigration. In 1982 alone, more than 45 000 people left Canada to live elsewhere. Demographers estimate that between 1851 and 1971, about 9 500 000 immigrants entered Canada while 6 500 000 left, for a net gain through immigration of about 3 000 000 people. Yet in this same period, 28 000 000 children were born and 11 500 000 people died, for a net gain through natural increase of about 16 500 000. Overall, fertility has influenced Canada's population history much more significantly than immigration (especially in French Canada).

However, the effects of immigration have fluctuated widely over time, while those of natural increase have not. Migration in and out of Canada has varied a great deal from one decade to another in response to various influences. Canadian economic development has proceeded rapidly from one resource-driven, economic boom-and-bust to another. With each resource discovery comes the opening of a new portion of the country. Willing workers extract the resource, whether it is fish, furs, timber, wheat, gold, or oil. Developing a resource industry creates new communities and new jobs in manufacturing, services, communications, and transportation. Often, more jobs are created than can be filled by native Canadians with the right skills. At these times, Canada opens its doors to immigrants, liberalizing legislation, increasing quotas, even searching out immigrants in preferred countries (Kalbach, 1970; Hawkins, 1972).

How long this need for workers lasts depends on the persistence of foreign demand for the resource at Canadian prices. When the demand dies down, as it usually does, the need for immigrant labour collapses. Immigration laws tighten up again and fewer immigrants are admitted. As opportunities evaporate, more people leave, chiefly for the United States.

A psychology of population instability results from (and in turn causes) the movement of migrants; its effect is out of all proportion to the number of migrants in the population (Porter, 1965). Particularly in the smaller communities of Canada—of which there are many—the influxes of immigrants are very noticeable. But immigration has profoundly affected the big cities as well. One of every six people counted by the 1981 Census was born outside Canada and immigrants tend to concentrate in the provinces of greatest economic activity. Within these provinces, they concentrate in the largest metropolitan areas: Toronto, Vancouver, Edmonton, Calgary, and Montreal.

In Canada's 25 largest cities, immigrants form a significant and growing proportion of the total population. By 1986, nearly 40% of Toronto's population, 30% of Vancouver's, and 20% of Edmonton's and Calgary's populations were foreign born, to cite a few important examples (Badets, 1989).

Up until very recently, postwar immigrants have been drawn to Canada primarily from southern Europe and the non-Western countries—Asia, Africa, the Caribbean, South America. These types of immigrants are particularly inclined to settle in large metropolitan centres. In this respect, they are not alone: more and more people are living near to large cities.

The churn

Canada's population is very mobile, with people often relocating themselves as their plans and opportunities change. Mobility and migration have a number of sources. Every separation and divorce brings someone a change of location: at least a change of households, and sometimes even a change of cities or regions. Likewise, every marriage brings one or both spouses a change of location. Beyond these, changes in location often result from increases in family size (through birth), decreases in family size (through death or children leaving home), and changes in family income and new job opportunities.

With so many economic and demographic events taking place, we would expect a large amount of movement within cities, and data from the 1981 Quality of Life survey bear us out. Over one-quarter of the survey respondents report having lived in their present dwelling only a year or less, and over half have lived there five years or less. Almost one person in five changed residences in the preceding year. Further, more than a quarter of the respondents think it unlikely they will still be living in the same dwelling two years from now.

Net population gainers from this inter-city movement are the already large cities and their surrounding suburbs. Metropolitan Toronto, Vancouver, and Ottawa-Hull, three of Canada's four largest cities, all increased their population by nine to ten percent between 1981 and 1986. According to the most recent Census, some smaller cities also posted large gains, among them Saskatoon (a 15% gain) and, in Ontario, Kitchener, Oshawa, and Windsor (with eight to nine percent gains).

But the fastest growing census subdivisions are the bedroom suburbs of Toronto like Vaughan (which increased by 119% between 1981 and 1986), and Markham and Ajax (which increased 40 to 50%). Suburbs of Ottawa and Halifax also made large gains during this period. Many businesses have recently moved to these rapidly growing communities, significantly increasing the white-collar and service jobs available there.

The amount of population movement is just as impressive if we shift our attention to larger units: to provinces and even regions. Statistics Canada has devised what they call a **churn rate**, which measures the total amount of migration in and out of a given province or territory each year.

The measure is most useful for comparing provinces. Data for 1982-3 (Statistics Canada, 1985: 12) show Quebec has the lowest churn rate: 16 people entering and/or leaving the province from any origin, per 1000 people in the province at mid-year. The Atlantic provinces display higher rates: 39 movers per 1000 population for Newfoundland, 48 to 49 movers for New Brunswick

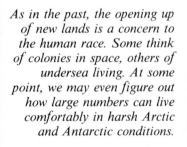

As in the past, the opening up of new lands is a concern to the human race. Some think of colonies in space, others of undersea living. At some point, we may even figure out how large numbers can live comfortably in harsh Arctic and Antarctic conditions.

and Nova Scotia, and 59 movers per 1000 for Prince Edward Island. These Atlantic coast rates are comparable to western Canadian rates of 49 to 51 movers per 1000 population for Manitoba, Saskatchewan, and British Columbia.

The meaning of these rates is clearer when we compare the remaining English-Canadian provinces and territories. After Quebec, Ontario has the lowest churn rate in Canada, with 29 movers per 1000 population. Alberta has the highest rate of all provinces, with 82 movers per 1000 population. The territories are higher still, with 151 movers and 239 movers per 1000 population for the Northwest Territories and the Yukon, respectively.

Several factors drive the churn rate up or down. One is the stable existence of long-standing communities and what we called in Chapter Six "institutional completeness." Another is the presence of strong regional cultures and, in the case of Quebec, a distinct language. Taken together, these stabilizing forces

During the first half of the century, immigrants to Canada came mostly from Europe, especially Great Britain, and from the United States. In each decade since 1961, the range of source countries has broadened and new countries have entered the list of top ten source countries, many of them Asian, Caribbean or Latin American.

Countries which formerly were major sources of immigrants have not ceased to send immigrants (Britain and the United States are still important sources) and certainly no new source country is playing the role that Britain once played as dominant source of immigration. Rather, immigration is far more diverse now than it was a quarter of a century ago in terms of the national, linguistic, religious and racial backgrounds of immigrants.

This is reflected in the spectacular growth in the **Other** *category, the category of countries sending too few immigrants to be counted among the top ten sources.*

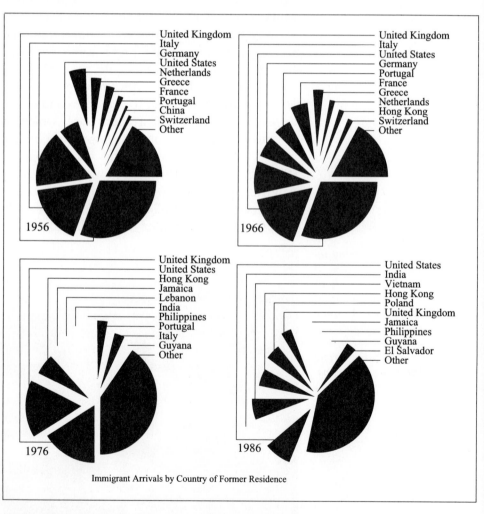

Immigrant Arrivals by Country of Former Residence

Source: *Charting Canada's Future: A Report of the Demographic Review (1989)* (Supply and Services Catalogue No. H21-105/1-1989) Ottawa: Health and Welfare, 1989, p. 32. Reproduced with permission of the Minister of Supply and Services, 1990.

largely account for the relatively low levels of churn in the Maritimes, Quebec, and certain western provinces. Economic instability—the development or collapse of "frontier," resource-based opportunities—works in the opposite direction, accounting for a high churn rate in Alberta and the Territories. Ontario has a relatively low churn rate because of relatively stable economic opportunities, well-developed institutional completeness, and a large base population.

Historically, the Canadian population has always been moving westward. The trend, though uneven, has been well established and the patterns witnessed in the 1970s are not new (Foot, 1982: 74). In this respect, Canada's population is not very different from that in the United States, which has also moved westward for the past century or so. American westward movement sped up dramatically after the Second World War. Demographers there also project a continuing westward movement rivalled in size only by strong southerly movement.

Though "population movements, both into and within Canada, have recently hit very low levels by historical standards . . . internal migration has returned to more traditional patterns following the slowdown in the oil boom in Western Canada" (Statistics Canada, 1987). Migrants are strongly attracted to Ontario once again; in- and out-migration are nearly balanced in Quebec; and the Atlantic provinces are back to losing more migrants than they take in. The overall trend may be westward, but countervailing economic, social, and cultural forces have slowed that movement dramatically.

Pulls and pushes

The process of mobility cannot be understood just by focusing on the personal characteristics of movers. Some communities are more likely to attract or lose people than others, depending on the opportunities they offer. Population churning is a joint result of two social processes. One is mobility resulting from changes in the quality of **human capital**: people's more common ability, via higher education, capital, or rare skills, to locate wherever they want to. A second is the changing relative attractiveness of different locations within Canada. Increasingly concerned with getting a high-quality lifestyle, more and more workers are drawn to communities with a pleasant environment and a wide variety of social, cultural, economic, and recreational opportunities.

The importance of geographic pushes and pulls is shown clearly in a study by Linda Gerber, who analyzed migration out of Canadian Indian reserves (Gerber, 1984). She reports, "Personal resource development (involvement in mainstream employment and education) stimulates out-migration, thereby increasing off-reserve residence levels" (Gerber, 1984: 158). But "distance from major urban centres and institutional completeness inhibit migration." Greater distance makes the move off-reserve more costly, since it makes frequent contact with the reserve community more difficult.

The native person leaving such a community must leave it behind for long periods, at a heavy psychic cost. Institutional completeness, on the other hand, makes out-migration less necessary, for it even allows people with more education and skills than usual (i.e., those with more "personal resource development") to continue living and working on the reserve.

The same can be said of ethnic and racial communities in large Canadian cities. Leaving such communities for other neighbourhoods and work settings dominated by other ethnic or racial groups is likelier the more education and job skills you possess and the higher your occupational aspirations. But, the greater the *social distance* between an ethnic group and the outside world, the less likely people are to make that "trip," especially if their own community is institutionally complete enough to allow them to stay.

CLOSING REMARKS

We began this chapter by referring to some rather grim prospects facing the world. It may be that industrial society has reached the limits of its development. Certainly many social scientists are making reference to the notion of post-industrial society. Just as the development of inanimate sources of energy led to the industrial revolution, it may be that the development of inanimate sources of *labour*—such as automation, computers, and robots—is leading to a new revolution.

Whether or not this is the case, it does seem that what is required of us now is

Population growth and the supporting economic growth have their most striking impacts on resources. The land is limited even in Canada, the high-quality agricultural land even more so. This graph explores the impact in 2036 of three population paths on Canada's forest inventory, assuming current rates of cutting and replanting. Forests are projected to decline overall in all three cases. In per person terms, the potential impact on this very Canadian resource becomes most striking. Canada will, at least in the medium term, have population growth and economic growth. The critical question is how effective we will be in ensuring that this growth is sustainable in terms of our environment.

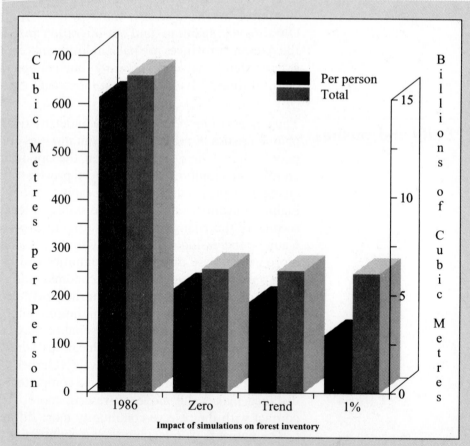

Source: *Charting Canada's Future: A Report of the Demographic Review* (Supply and Services) Catalogue Number H21-105/1-1989) Ottawa: Health and Welfare Canada, p. 13

EXHIBIT 9.4

POSSIBLE FUTURES D: DE-POPULATION

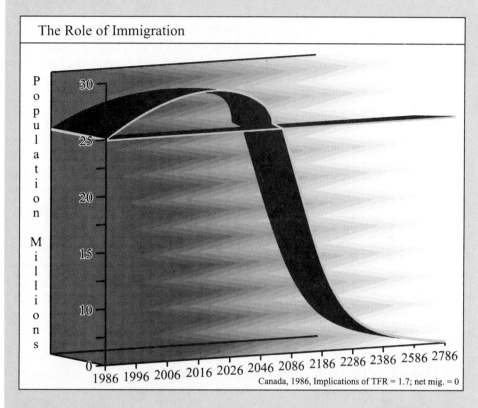

The Role of Immigration

Canada, 1986, Implications of TFR = 1.7; net mig. = 0

With Canadians bearing fewer children than are needed to replace their parents' generation, a disappearance of the Canadian population is entirely possible. Demographic projections show that, if all immigration were halted tomorrow and present rates of childbearing continued, the vanishing of Canada's population would take about 800 years—precisely, until the year 2786.

Similar projections show that, if immigration remains at its present level (about 80 000 net immigrants per year) and present rates of childbearing continue, Canada's population will *not* vanish but will level off at about the size it was (18 million) in 1950.

Similar trends are seen throughout the Western world. People who believe a large, young, and growing population is needed for economic and political well-being will increasingly argue that governments should encourage more childbearing *and* more immigration. What impact would such changes have on your family life? On your worklife? On ethnic politics in Canada?

Source: *Charting Canada's Future: A Report of the Demographic Review* (Supply and Services Catalogue No. H21-105/1-1989) Ottawa: Health and Welfare, 1989, p. 2. Reproduced with the permission of the Minister of Supply and Services, 1990.

a new vision of our world. We can no longer take inevitable progress for granted. We can no longer take for granted that things will somehow work out for the best. Cleaning up the world means changing our lifestyles and our expectations of one another. It means taking action to prevent war, famine, and pollution.

Is this being done? Are we moving in a direction that promises to change society for the better? If not, how do we go about getting started? The topic of *social change* to which we now turn addresses these issues.

Discussion Questions

1. If the world's population is doubling every 40 years and the population today is about 5 billion people, what will be the population of the world in 200 years? What will be the population density of the world? Will that be too many people?

2. What are reasons explaining why some countries pass through the entire demographic transition process very quickly and others take a much longer time?

3. Are future resource discoveries likely to have as great an impact on the Canadian population as past ones have? Why or why not?

4. If mortality rates are a clear indication of social (class) inequalities, and we are all in favour of people living, not dying, why is little action taken to eliminate these social inequalities in risks of death?

5. How is the changing age composition of Canada's population likely to change the industry that you are training to enter?

Data Collection Exercises

1. Examine a Census of Canada that is at least 50 years old. How do the questions it asks about some particular topic (for example, household composition, employment status, ethnic origin) and the ways it categorizes the answers differ from the most recent Census?

2. Collect data from published Canadian sources on the fertility (childbearing behaviour) of women 20-24 years and 30-34 years old from 60 years ago, from 30 years ago, and for today. What has changed?

3. Use published statistics to determine what proportion of people in your town or city have changed residences in the last five years. Does this proportion seem very high or very low, compared with your own experiences (for example, the mobility of the people you know)?

4. Collect statistics on the ages at which people typically leave (that is, die or retire from) the occupation you are training to enter. (If they are not available, what do you imagine they look like?) How would your career be affected if no one currently in the occupation was forced to retire at age 65?

Writing Exercises

1. Write a brief (500-word) speech to be delivered on the radio in a Third World country, explaining why people should limit themselves to two children (or fewer).

2. The year is 2027. The average surviving member of the baby-boom generation is 70 years old. Write a 500-word ad aimed at getting the (still enormous) baby-boom generation to drink PEPSI, not COKE.

3. Write a brief (500-word) biography of the most geographically mobile person you know, documenting the moves made—their timing and the reason behind them—and whether they had the desired result.

4. If you had the power to do so, what one law would you pass that would slow the spread of AIDS in the population? Write a brief (500-word) speech to Parliament explaining the way your law will work and the thinking behind it.

Glossary

carrying capacity—the number of people a geographic area can support, given the current level of available resources and technology

demographic transition—a fall in birth and death rates that accompanies industrialization, with the death rates falling first

demography—the scientific study of the size, composition (structure), distribution, and patterns of change in a human population

dependency ratio—the ratio of economically dependent people (aged 17 and under and 65 and over) to people of working age (ages 18 through 64).

endogenous—causes of death that are internal to the organism, not a result of externally induced trauma or infection. They illustrate the entropy principle as applied to humans.

growth rate—the rate at which the number of people added to a population increases. Negative growth rate is the rate at which population size declines.

migration (internal)—the movement of people from one part of a country to another

natural increase—the excess of births over deaths in a population

net migration rate—the number of immigrants to a certain area, minus the number of emigrants from that area, per year per thousand inhabitants

positive checks—occurrences (such as war, famine, pestilence, and disease) which have the effect of reducing the population or limiting its growth. **Preventive checks** reduce population growth by limiting the number of live births.

total fertility rate—an estimate of the average number of live children a woman will bear as she passes through the age-specific fertility rates of a society

zero population growth—this occurs when the factors leading to population growth are exactly balanced by the factors leading to population decline. It is also known as *replacement*, as the population size remains constant.

Suggested Readings

Beaujot, Roderic and Kevin McQuillan *Growth and Dualism: The Demographic Development of Canadian Society*. Toronto: Gage, 1982. An interesting and sociologically informed discussion of the history of Canada's population, with an eye on future directions and policies.

Easterlin, Richard *Birth and Fortune: The Impact of Numbers on Personal Welfare*. New York: Basic Books, 1980. Written by an economist, this book explains why it is best to be born at a time of low birth rates. It shows that the baby boom generation will have to fight hard for its rewards throughout life.

Laslett, Peter *The World We Have Lost*. London: Methuen, 1979. This classic work weaves dry statistics and historical documents into a fascinating picture of Europe (especially England) before the coming of industrialization. It asks whether we have lost more than we have gained from the change.

McEvedy, Colin and Richard Jones *Atlas of World Population History*. Harmondsworth: Penguin Books, 1978. A useful reference work that describes and maps all the important changes in the world population history.

McNeill, William H. *Plagues and Peoples*. Garden City, New York: Anchor Books, 1976. Written by a prize-winning author, this book shows how human history has been shaped by shifting "disease balances" and "disease pools." It will make you wonder whether people make their own history.

Petersen, William *Population*, 2nd edition. London: Macmillan Company, 1969. This well-written textbook covers all the major topics in population research from a sociological standpoint. Its survey of the literature is a good place to start any project of your own.

Pohlmann, Edward (ed.) *Population: A Clash of Prophets*. New York: New American Library, 1973. Are there too many people in the world? Too few births in North America? Will population growth destroy the natural environment? How does population growth affect the balance of world economic and political power? Read the debates on these issues here.

References

Badets, J. (1989) "Canada's immigrant population" *Canadian Social Trends*, Autumn, pp. 2-6

Beaujot, R. (1988) "Canada's demographic profile" pp. 39-70 in J. Curtis and L. Tepperman (eds.) *Understanding Canadian Society*. Toronto: McGraw-Hill Ryerson

Bell, D. and L. Tepperman (1979) *The Roots of Disunity*. Toronto: McClelland and Stewart

Coale, A.J. and S.C. Watkins (eds.) (1987) *The Decline of Fertility in Europe*. Princeton, NJ: Princeton University Press

Easterlin, R.A. (1980) *Birth and Fortune: The Impact of Numbers on Personal Welfare*. New York: Basic Books

Foot, D.K. (1982) *Canada's Population Outlook: Demographic Futures and Economic Challenges* The Canadian Institute for Economic Policy Series. Toronto: Lorimer

Gerber, L. (1984) "Community characteristics and out-migration from Canadian Indian reserves: path analyses" *Canadian Review of Sociology and Anthropology*, 21(2) May, pp. 145-165

Hawkins, F. (1972) *Canada and Immigration: Public Policy and Public Concern*. Montreal: McGill-Queen's University Press

Heilig, G.K. and A.E. Wills (1989) "AIDS costs more 'years of potential life' before age 65 than diabetes, TBC, or viral hepatitis" *Population Network Newsletter* (IIASA), No. 15, February, pp. 1-8

Kalbach, W.E. (1970) *The Impact of Immigration on Canada's Population*. Ottawa: Queen's Printer

Meadows, D.H. et al (1972) *The Limits to Growth*. New York: Universe Books

Porter, J. (1965) *The Vertical Mosaic*. Toronto: University of Toronto Press

Royal Society of Canada (1988) *AIDS: A Perspective for Canadians. Summary Report and Recommendations*. Ottawa.

Statistics Canada (1985) *Canada, The Provinces and the Territories: A Statistical Profile*, Small Area Data Program. (Catalogue No. 17-x-501) Ottawa: Supply and Services

_____ . (1987) *Current Demographic Analysis: Report on the Demographic Situation in Canada, (1986).* (Catalogue No. 91-209E) Ottawa: Supply and Services

CHAPTER 10

People make social change. Many factors contribute to the success of people's effort to bring about change; but, both Marx and Weber recognized (in their own ways), nothing is more important than ideas of power and the power of ideas.

SOCIAL MOVEMENTS AND SOCIAL CHANGE

UNDERSTANDING SOCIAL CHANGE

People have an incredible ability to consume experience, to adjust to surprises. What was *Wow!* today is going to seem *Hohum!* tomorrow. So it will be hard to impress on you just how very quickly the world is changing in important ways, because you have already started to take yesterday's changes for granted. But here's an example:

For most of human history, life was very quiet. Most of the time, people didn't hear many sounds. The sounds they heard were natural ones: animals, wind, and running water, for example. They didn't see many other people or very large buildings. People didn't travel long distances very often. That's why they didn't get to know people very different from themselves. They didn't know much about the world outside their own community, so they didn't spend much time thinking about things that didn't affect them directly. People just figured the world, the human race, God, and nature would go on forever, pretty much as they had done for centuries before.

Do you see how different life is today? We live in an era in which change is not only constant, it is programmed into the nature of our society. Elections every four years or so, new automobile models every year, television news every day, radio news every hour—our appetite for change and for news about change is ravenous. Whole industries are based on that appetite and seek not only to satisfy our desires but to inflame them and keep them constant.

Still, since change *is* so much a part of our life, most of us are quite sophisticated about dealing with change. New scientific achievements, new technologies, and new political crises are taken in stride. Because so much does happen around us and so many demands are made for our attention and on our pocketbooks, we have learned to be selective and pay attention to those matters that interest us or affect us directly. This practical interest in change is a part of the common-sense understanding of the world we discussed in Chapter One. It makes change both manageable and "sensible" for us in terms of everyday life.

Social scientists, of course, seek a fuller understanding of social change. Our interest is practical, too, but in a broader sense. If we are to make sense of the modern world and of modern society, if we are also to assure that the world is one in which we can all live a decent, healthy life—we cannot limit ourselves to understanding individual changes but must examine the *processes* of change that characterize our society and other societies. In this respect, understanding social change is not a specific area of study as is research on the family, on religion, or on population. Understanding social change is a key to understanding all aspects of society and reflects variations and transformations in all of them.

THE SOCIOLOGY OF SOCIAL CHANGE

From a sociological point of view, **social change** is the process by which any given aspect of social life or social organization is altered. Accordingly, the opposite of social change is **social persistence or continuity**. Sociologists have found considerable variations in the rate, nature, and direction of social changes among societies and over time. Change may start among the powerful and move downward, or it may have a humble origin and move upward.

Sociologists concerned with social movements and social change are usually macrosociological in their perspective. They see social change as *societal change*: the change of entire societies, or large portions of societies. Seen this way, social change is a large-scale, long-term process affecting large numbers of people.

Our discussion will partly focus on the large-scale, long-term side of social change. However, as you read this chapter, it is important to keep in mind that there is always a personal side to social change. The social impact of the telephone or the automobile, for example, was felt by millions of individual people who had to adapt to the changes brought about in their environment. These were people like you—people with personal tastes, personal feelings, and unique life histories. For social changes to occur, people must change their own lives—each in his or her own way. The impact of social change may first be apparent at either a macro or micro level, but careful examination will show effects at the other level.

On one hand consider the automation of manufacturing, a fast-moving macro-level change that has nevertheless had significant impact on the lives of thousands of individual workers and their families. On the other hand, decisions to postpone marriage or childbearing, to have no children or only one child, are micro-level choices made by individuals, choices whose impact builds up relatively slowly, over generations. Taken together, these individual choices have an enormous effect on the whole society. The distinction between micro and macro does not lie so much in the number of individuals affected or how important the change is, but in the point of origin of the change. Nevertheless, whether the change begins at the macro or micro level, understanding these changes as social processes usually requires a macro level of explanation.

Sociological theories of change may be divided into two types: theories of *evolution* and theories of *revolution*.

Evolutionary theories

Evolutionary theories see society as a social system that continually adapts to changes in its environment. Social change is viewed as essentially gradual, taking place over long periods of time. Thus, an evolutionary theorist can speak meaningfully of the Judeo-Christian tradition, or the influence of Athenian or Roman culture on modern language, arts, and thought.

Such thinkers often take a structural functionalist approach. They focus on

social statics, those social forces that maintain social stability or continuity. These include the institutions that protect, develop, and diffuse the cultural elements of a society—the family, churches, the educational system, and the mass media. They also include the institutions that slow down change and resolve conflicts within the social system, especially the legal system.

From the functionalist standpoint, change and conflict are inevitable, but so are continuity and the resolution of conflict. As we saw in the first chapter, functionalists see a social system as a set of interrelated and integrated structures that are organized in an orderly way to form a whole. Among structures that are *tightly* integrated, change in one part will provoke changes in the others. Some parts are more tightly integrated with others—for example, the political system with the legal system—while others are more loosely integrated—for example, the political system with the religious system.

For functionalists looking at social change, what is interesting is how the social system adjusts and re-adjusts to a continuing flow of new, often conflicting demands from its various subsystems.

Ralph Turner and Lewis Killian (1987) have developed a symbolic interactionist explanation of one type of social change: the development and persistence of **social movements**. In their version of the evolutionary approach they call *emergent norm theory*, Turner and Killian look to the microsociological processes whereby interacting individuals come to share a common understanding of the situation in which they find themselves. By constructing meaningful interpretations out of these situations they create norms that are appropriate for their circumstances and to which they can become committed. Although they argue that emergent norms are specific to a situation and differ from one situation to another, their approach is evolutionary: they see social change as the outcome of myriad instances of interaction and interpretation.

Revolutionary theories

By contrast, the second theoretical orientation sees social change as revolutionary, not evolutionary, in character; that is, the change from one type of social order to the next is abrupt, sometimes violent. The new social order is qualitatively different from the old one and breaks with the past in important ways.

A revolutionary theorist would emphasize the ways in which our civilization is *not* continuous with the Judeo-Christian tradition or Athenian and Roman thought. He or she would call attention to the revolutionary social changes brought about by the printing press, the Industrial Revolution, the French Revolution, atomic fission, genetic engineering, and informatics. The emphasis is on **social dynamics**—those social forces that promote social changes. These may include changes in population size and structure, technology, and the physical environment. Usually, conflict theorists, whether Marxian, Weberian, or other, would fall into this camp.

Varying importance of factors of social change

Social theorists also differ in the degree of importance they attach to various factors that cause social change. For example, some, like Malthus, believe the main cause of social change is change in the physical or demographic environment. Others, like Marx, see change arising out of class conflict and relations of production. Others still, like Weber, focus on new forms of religious and cultural symbols, on changes in formal organization, or technological innovation.

Unlike their 19th-century predecessors, most social theorists today realize the futility of trying to uncover a single, general law of social change they can apply to all types of social change. Instead, they emphasize the fact that social change is dependent on the context within which it takes place. Thus, they try to explain the change of a particular society or particular social institution within a society. As our knowledge increases, however, our understanding of that context becomes more complete and more complex. We begin to see that many interconnections among institutions are not limited to the borders of one nation or the actions of one society. A new approach developed recently, World Systems Theory, attempts to map out these interconnections.

But if change is so prevalent a feature of our society, how do we distinguish those changes that make a real difference in a society from those that merely reflect new fads or fashions? How do we know which changes are important? Should we pay as much attention to the development of digital audio tape technology as we do to political changes in eastern Europe?

The relations between fads, fashions, and change

As we shall see, most **fads** and **fashions** have no impact on social organization. Hula hoops, black lipstick, and heavy metal music sweep through the population like a plague, taking many victims; yet they are soon gone forever, unlamented, forgotten. What's more, they have changed no one's life permanently (except for the promoters, who have made a fortune from these fads). In general, fads and fashions have little long-term effect on social and cultural life.

Media images of "looking good" change all the time, and vary enormously from one society to another. Likely, in the next 30 years demographic shifts will bring some major changes in thinking about "who looks good."

Indeed, such collective behaviours are more likely to be effects, or symptoms, of social change, rather than its causes. A great many fads and fashions are reflections of teenage rebellion and teenage buying power, both of which have other sources.

Fashions and fads

A **fad** is a trivial, short-lived interest in and enthusiasm for something—for example, an activity like hula-hooping, a type of speech like rap, a dance like the Twist, or styles like the Mohawk, hot pants, or preppie clothing. Fads come and go, because we like the novelty of the fad at first but get bored and lose interest when the novelty wears off.

A **fashion** is something—whether a form of dress, or manner of speaking or behaving—that is considered admirable and is eagerly imitated in a particular time and place. Following a fad implies enthusiasm for some specific cultural object, activity, or event, whereas following the current fashion implies more abstract notions such as "good taste" and "style" as well as a willingness (and financial ability) to conform to social thinking. Fashions of these kinds include dress length preferences (short *versus* long), men's facial hair preferences (clean shaven *versus* bearded or mustached), and female body preferences (lean and boyish *versus* large-hipped and voluptuous).

Fashions are less trivial than fads. Some studies, for example, have attempted to link hemline lengths and fashion silhouettes with economic health (e.g., a shorter skirt means prosperous times ahead). One observer notes a shift in women's underwear back toward frills and sensuousness. He suggests women are displaying their underwear more publicly, to take full advantage of their attractiveness. But does this fashion signify anything more than the rise to popularity of miraculous new fabrics which are, at the same time, feminine and convenient to wear? For example, does it indicate more aggressive or egalitarian sexuality on women's part? Or more playfulness and ease where body display is concerned?

Fashions, not fads, lead us to ask these kinds of questions about cultural change. People who ignore or rebel against fashions are likely to be judged more harshly than people who ignore fads. Fashions embody current notions of beauty, good grooming, and up-to-dateness. On the other hand, following fads implies a somewhat more youthful or childish outlook that some may consider frivolous.

There is no absolute logic to any fashion or fad—no reason why it should occur at one given time and not some other. There is little predictability to the rise and fall of fads and fashions. Yet fashions and fads are usually engineered, not spontaneous, changes of thinking and acting—the result of advertisers spending huge amounts of money to promote a particular look or product.

Thus, fashions and fads are not only interesting for what they tell us about changes in popular ideas or behaviour. They are also sociologically interesting because they clearly illustrate the need people feel to conform to group rituals. In effect, fads and fashions are blank or neutral and draw their significance from people's willingness to invest them with meaning. For Durkheim, all religious ritual is of this character: the investment of *totemic objects*—usually plants or animals—with sacred meaning. What people are celebrating through religious ritual is not the totemic object but the group itself and the pleasure of belonging to it.

In a modern consumer society, some fashionable consumer goods may have a similar totemic meaning. The "Alligator" shirt, regimental necktie, Rolex watch, black tights, or leather jacket with gang insignia all convey an intention to belong to and identify with a particular subculture. The change of fashions within a subculture allow people to re-assess and re-assert their subcultural membership and cohesion: to celebrate their conformity in a secular (that is, not sacred) way.

PUBLICS AND PUBLIC OPINION

Publics

All collective actions, whether following fads and fashions or panics, rumours, riots, and mob actions, occur within a certain population we shall call the *public* and both shape and conform to the dominant *public opinion*. Thus, all collective action must be understood in the context of this public opinion.

Of course, there is no single public in modern industrial societies. A complex division of labour, a variety of ethnic groups and religious denominations, differences in age, gender, region of residence, social class, and personal experiences—all these make for a variety of publics, each with its own set of opinions, values, and interests. People who share a particular interest in, view on, preference for, or concern about something specific constitute a **public**.

The public is a rather amorphous body of individuals. The members of a public may not interact with one another, are often not aware of being part of a larger group, and are generally little influenced by other members of the public. Sometimes it is possible to reach the members of a public only through the mass media, since they are not connected socially in any other way. Thus, television shows, radio programs, magazines, newspapers, and advertising are all geared to reaching "the public" and, indeed, to reaching a variety of different publics.

Public opinion and propaganda

The goal of the media is not only to reach the public but also to shape public opinion. **Public opinion** is the opinion held by the members of a given public on a given issue, or the opinion held by the majority, or largest proportion, of people in a given population.

In principle, public opinion is central to the running of any democracy, since a "democracy" is by definition "government by the people." A Latin proverb says *Vox populi, vox dei*, which means "the voice of the people is the voice of God," and, in a democratic society, this proverb should be the guiding principle. From this standpoint, public opinion polling is the best way of listening to the voice of democracy's God.

Today these polls measure public opinion quite accurately. The complaint voiced against such polls is not that they are inaccurate, but rather that, by reporting their results to members of the population that was surveyed, such polls influence public opinion in undesirable ways.

The band-wagon effect is an example of how public opinion polls can influence public opinion. People seem attracted to being part of something that has succeeded: they want to "get on the band-wagon." One way the band-wagon effect is revealed is in post-election polls, when a much higher proportion of voters claim to have voted for the winning candidate than actually did so. What is worrisome about the band-wagon effect is the tendency for people to adopt opinions they perceive as popular and, specifically, to support a politician who seems likely to win simply because they want to back a winner.

While political and other public opinion polls contribute to this illusion-making, a far larger role is played by journalists who report propaganda under the guise of news. A fine line divides social facts from social fantasies, news reporting from propaganda. **Propaganda** is information, ideas, or doctrines disseminated for the purpose of influencing the opinions and actions of others. Sunday-school lessons, advertising, and election campaigns are all propaganda in this sense. Propaganda is all attempts to influence others' thoughts and opinions. It implies nothing about the truth of the information or about the validity of the ideas or doctrines that are being spread. What is irksome about propaganda is not that it is partly or largely deception, but that it masquerades as disinterested, objective truth.

Propaganda can be viewed as the active, or recruiting, side of *ideology*. Recall from earlier chapters that ideology incorporates conceptions of right and wrong, good and bad, desirable and undesirable. Ideologies are held by entire groups of people, and are used to guide their interpretations of, and reactions to, external events.

In an age of increasing concentration of the news media in fewer hands, the best protection against blind acceptance of propaganda is education, an openness to new information, and a tolerance for ambiguity: the willingness to consider varied interpretations of a single issue.

One realm in which public opinion and social change regularly connect is in the formation of social movements. Unlike other collective behaviours, social movements form as a conscious reaction to social change, and for the purpose of bringing about social change. That is why social movements are particularly important but, from the standpoint of social change, relatively rare.

SOCIAL MOVEMENTS

The term **social movement** refers to any form of collective action that is aimed at promoting or resisting change in a given society. Such movements will usually engage in both political action and in media campaigns in order to get their views across and to ensure that they achieve their goals. The recent formation of English-rights political groups in Ontario and of western-rights political groups in Alberta are two examples of social movements that have engaged in political action.

The visibility of social movements varies. For example, government legislation against discrimination on the basis of gender or ethnicity (or any other irrelevant consideration in the workplace) will bring about social change. *Behind* this decision to legislate against discrimination one is likely to find a history of efforts made by social movements—for example, continued vocal lobbying by women's groups and groups representing minority rights—to get this legislation passed.

Not all lobbies that influence legislation are social movements. For example, the free-trade deal will cause both expected and unexpected social changes, and negotiations over the deal were much influenced by powerful business leaders. Well-organized and coordinated, these powerful people worked behind the scenes to support the legislation they wanted passed. However, we do not normally consider these people a social movement. Usually the term "social movement" is reserved for people who mobilize publicly in large numbers to exercise some influence on the society.

There are many aspects of society with which social movements may be concerned: the economy, polity, organized religion, education, values, beliefs and morals, or the definition of human rights, for example. Normally a social movement will focus its attention on a particular issue: abortion on demand, an end to the storage of toxic waste in a community, a nuclear-weapon-free Canada, prohibition of seal hunting, opposition to free trade, and so on. Regardless of the specific concern, all social movements are guided by a particular ideology and generate propaganda that explains and glamourizes their cause.

Sources of discontent

Social movements generally arise out of discontent—a feeling that society is not functioning properly and needs changing. One important theory of social movement formation—*relative deprivation theory*—argues that movements arise out of feelings of deprivation on the part of a significant number of individuals. An alternative approach to analyzing social movements, *resource mobilization theory*, assumes that there is validity to the movements' goals and, instead, addresses the methods they use to put forward their views.

Relative deprivation

As **relative deprivation theory** explains, people may find a discrepancy between the social rewards they are getting and those to which they feel entitled. They then experience feelings of deprivation when they compare their own situation to that of others. Under this condition, people have a strong incentive to launch or join a social movement whose goal it is to bring about a change in the distribution of social rewards.

There is some debate about the nature of discontent that fuels social movements. Social scientists generally agree that *absolute* deprivation—a serious, objectively valid, and prolonged lack of social rewards—is less likely to cause social movements to form than *relative* deprivation, which is largely subjective, may be temporary, and may even be trivial.

Indeed some have argued that social movements are most likely to receive their greatest surge of support when there is a "revolution of rising expectations" (Runciman, 1966). They argue that it is under conditions of improvement, even rapid improvement—not grinding, desperate poverty—that people are most likely to mobilize for protest. This is because people's expectations for change and improvement leap ahead of the rate at which change can take place.

In general, relative deprivation theory draws our attention away from objective factors in social movement formation to subjective ones. It raises doubts about the validity of a social movement: doubts about whether the movement has appropriate goals and whether its members are comparing their lives with those of appropriate reference groups. After all, the higher the group with which they compare themselves, the less satisfied (and more rebellious) they are likely to feel.

The feelings of frustration and discontent caused by a sense of deprivation are *necessary* for the emergence of a social movement: that is, you cannot have a movement forming without them. However, they are not *sufficient*, which is to say they are not enough—by themselves—to get a movement going. A great many people feel discontented for some or much of their lives, yet do not join social movements. Thus, another condition we shall discuss—resource mobilization—is needed before a movement forms.

Resource mobilization

Resource mobilization theory does not look at *why* people want to promote or resist social change, but rather *how* people launch social movements. Social movements are not seen as the result of a group's grievances, but as the ability of a discontented group to get organized. Important elements in "getting organized" include gathering together and making use of a variety of resources such as effective leadership, public support, money, legal aid, connections to influential officials and public personalities, and access to the mass media. In some instances, it may also include the acquisition of, and training in, the use of weapons.

Without discontent, there would be no social movements. Yet we can assume that discontent is a constant of human life: it is always lurking somewhere, waiting to express itself. Without resource mobilization, it can never express itself in a social movement. Instead discontent remains hidden or comes out in the forms of non-political, individual pathology: random violence, mental illness, heavy drinking, and so on.

Without access to key resources, discontented people cannot hope to bring about change, or resist the powerful, and are unlikely to make the attempt. Thus, it is valid to see the rise and fall of social movements as evidence of a changing access to key resources, not of changing levels of contentment or discontent. The absence of social movements does not prove that contentment reigns in a population: rather, it indicates the presence of official power to suppress protest and of an inequality in the resources needed for movement formation.

TYPES OF SOCIAL MOVEMENTS

It would be possible to classify social movements in any number of ways. For example, we could classify them according to their size and level of resources, or according to members' reasons for discontent. Or we could classify them according to the institution with which they are most concerned—health, education, religion, law, and so on.

One classification of social movements includes the following six types:

(1) religious movements—social movements with religious goals. We shall discuss these further shortly.

(2) regressive movements—social movements that aim to steer change in the direction of the past, back to the "good old days"

(3) reform movements—social movements that seek to change certain aspects of a society while retaining its general character intact

(4) revolutionary movements—social movements that seek a complete change in people's conditions, ways of thinking and ways of acting

(5) resistance or conservative movements—social movements that resist change in general, aiming to maintain the status quo

(6) counter movements—social movements that directly oppose already existing social movements (For example, the "right to life" movement is a counter-movement to the "pro-choice" movement.)

All such classifications have merit; but from a sociological point of view they miss the features that best describe their *social* organization. Weber made exhaustive studies of both religious and political social movements and found interesting similarities among them, whatever their institutional focus, reasons for discontent, or level of resources. Religious movements have been much studied by sociologists because they are similar in many respects to other kinds of movement and they can therefore be used as a model for understanding all social movements.

Religious movements

All social movements, whether religious or political, are likely to begin with a charismatic phase during which the movement is led by an inspiring leader. Leaders are charismatic when they are able to inspire devotion and enthusiasm among followers regardless of the cost to these followers. Almost by definition, charismatic social movements operate at a fever pitch and are, for this reason, rather unpredictable: they can be loving one minute and extremely violent the next.

Few movements and even fewer individuals can operate at such a fever pitch for long periods of time. At the very least, ordinary, everyday concerns of making a living, raising children, and conducting relations with non-members of the movement are bound to interrupt the flow of passionate involvement.

Once the charismatic leader of a social movement dies or retires, the movement either disbands or undergoes a process of **routinization**. During this process, a bureaucratic structure emerges, institutional roles and patterns of authority are established, and day-to-day administrative duties replace the original goals of the movement to fill the time of the most dedicated.

The institutions that are created capitalize on people's faith in the original inspiration. These institutions—increasingly rational and rationalized—are able to withstand the tests of faith that people experience in everyday life and even the periodic, quite dramatic trials of faith—the major disappointments—they encounter.

Movements that can achieve institutional completeness are able to insulate their members from such interruptions, thereby prolonging the period of passionate involvement. This is exactly what Reverend Jim Jones tried to achieve in Jonestown, which he and his followers built in a remote area of Guyana. However, the very process of creating and maintaining such institutional completeness is likely to routinize the movement—move it toward greater predictability and concern with everyday matters of conformity and bookkeeping. In a word, religious movements—sometimes called *sects*—are likely to become routinized churches. This did not happen in Jonestown because the decision to move from the United States to Guyana created new problems and imposed severe hardships, which retarded the routinization of the movement.

From time to time, people renew their faith by fundamentally re-assessing it and the lives they have built on it. These periods of history are marked by charismatic upheavals: dramatic renewals of religious faith and a fundamental questioning of other institutions. Other periods seem to coast on the routinized institutions established by the passion of earlier generations.

Today, religious life is, for the most part, rarely charismatic. It is organized into churches and denominations. Some religious groups display higher levels of **religiosity** than others: that is, stronger and more diverse involvement by the membership in the church's or sect's affairs, and more profound personal commitment to the values of the religion. Sociologists today find that people's behaviour varies little by religious denomination. Whether you are Protestant, Catholic, or Jewish, for example, has relatively little impact on your behaviour, even in areas of life (like birth control or dietary habits) where a religious doctrine has been stated.

However, religiosity continues to make a difference to people's behaviour. People who are very pious, whatever their religion, are in many respects very similar to one another and very different from people who are not pious. They tend, for example, to embrace more conservative social, ethical, and political values; to value tradition over modernity; and to feel a strong allegiance to their own group and distance from other groups.

Religiosity varies considerably across the country, as surveys of religious values and behaviour reveal. Reginald Bibby (1987: 108) writes that Atlantic Canada "is the nation's true Bible Belt." (The *Bible Belt* refers to the sections of the U.S., especially in the south and midwest, where Protestant fundamentalism historically prevailed.) Yet the more striking reality found in most regions, social categories, and religious groups is what Bibby calls the pervasiveness of "fragment adoption." People use the parts, or fragments, of a religion they want to—whether a practice, belief, or service—and ignore the rest. In this respect, for most people religion has become like any other consumer item. What's more, Bibby suggests that religious organizations have become "fragment outlets" which "have made it possible for Canadians to move with relative ease from religious commitment to religious consumption" (Bibby, 1987: 110).

This response, according to Bibby, has simply reinforced in people's minds the notion—already put there by science generally and social science particularly—that religion is a cultural product or artifact. Like any cultural artifact—art or music or ways of speaking, for example—religion changes to suit its times. However, the ready acceptance of this principle by religious bodies themselves has robbed religion of its central defining feature: its traditional concern with the sacred and holy.

It was Durkheim (1915) who pointed out that religious life, by its nature, is set off from the everyday world: that's why it so often uses special language and texts, special clothing, music, sounds, and smells. It demands special self-sacrifices of its ministers or priests, and special behaviour and deference from its congregation. To eliminate these unworldly (sacred) features from religion is to eliminate the barrier that separates religion from, say, pop psychology or dinner-time conversation.

It is in reaction to this secularization and, as Durkheim would say, "profanation" of religion that new religious movements have grown up and gained enormous popularity in the last two decades. Some of these are *millenarian* movements; others are called *fundamentalist* religions because they call for a return to religious fundamentals. In particular, they seek to reawaken charismatic passion in believers, to distinguish the sacred from the profane, or even to have religious (sacred) beliefs dominate social, political, and economic (secular or profane) ones.

Millenarian movements

Millenarian movements, which combine religious and political movements, have existed throughout history. A **millenarian movement** prophesies that a radical change in the social order will occur in the very near future by miraculous or supernatural means. In modern times, millenarian movements have been particularly common in countries that have been subjected to colonial rule. They have been described as a pre-political response of oppressed peoples to the frustration of colonial rule.

Members of these movements envision radical social change either as a return to the glorious past (the good old days), or the imminent end of the world. Both visions reflect a desire by the oppressed to end their oppression, either by re-establishing control over their own destiny, or by punishing their oppressors. Although they sometimes believe the end of the world is near, members also believe that those who subscribe to the given new faith will be saved.

Fundamentalism

Fundamentalist religious groups (sometimes called *sects* or *cults*) are politico-religious movements that preach a strict, literal interpretation of the holy scriptures and the maintenance of traditional religious beliefs and practices. They are also characterized by a tendency to see everything and everyone as either right or wrong, good or evil, with no grey areas in between.

Fundamentalist movements tend to form around strong, vocal, and politically active charismatic leaders. Such movements are found in increasing numbers in North America, especially the United States among "born-again" Christians, but they are certainly not limited to the United States. Fundamentalists are found almost everywhere today. In the Islamic world they have played a significant role in revitalizing religious faith and in taking political power.

Spontaneous expressions of public sentiment are often associated with a particular secular or religious leader. This is one way of measuring the leader's charisma.

A key fundamentalist figure in Iran was the recently deceased Ayatollah Khomeini, who controlled both the Iranian state and the Iranian Islamic religious hierarchy. His movement displayed the classic features of millenarian movements: a belief that the end of the world was near (unrest in the Middle East was taken to be the start of a *jihad*, or holy war, that came just before the end); a strong reaction against colonial rule (that is, American imperialism via the overthrown Shah of Iran), and a desire to punish the imperialist powers.

Because fundamentalist movements rely heavily on charismatic leaders, the personal preaching or teaching of charismatic leaders–in North America people like Oral Roberts, Jerry Falwell, Jimmy Swaggart, and Ernest Angley–has been very important to the spread of such movements, especially in rural areas. Today, however, much of the fundamentalist message is spread through the mass media.

Television evangelism has become an enormously influential and well-funded religious enterprise. **Evangelism** is the art or practice of preaching to a large audience. Evangelists are preachers of the Gospel who travel–in person or through the air-waves–to many different parts of the country and even to distant lands, holding religious meetings whenever and wherever possible. They preach to any who are willing to listen and attempt to convert as many as possible to their version of religious truth.

An old-time image of the travelling evangelist is nicely captured in Sinclair Lewis' American novel (later made into a movie) *Elmer Gantry*. Today, television evangelism reaches far larger numbers of people than the travelling preacher could ever hope to do. Television evangelism uses all the modern techniques of mass persuasion, mixing religious ritual (prayer, for example) with newscasting, current events debates, music, and inspirational philosophy.

As a result, fundamentalist Christianity has become an enormously prosperous business. According to American Gallup polls, one-third of all American adults claim to be "born-again"—people who have experienced a turning point in their lives and have made a personal commitment to Jesus Christ. To churches and church-run bookstores, they represent 59 million people who are ready to spend for their faith.

According to *American Demographics* magazine (Edmonson, 1988: 31), a market research journal, Christian-book buyers represent the religious, highly motivated end of the evangelical movement. Total sales in 1985 on books, music, curriculum materials, Bibles, church supplies, gifts, toys, computer software, and various publications totaled $2.3 billion. This figure pales before estimates of the donations television evangelists raise every year. Such figures are informative because they indicate the numbers of people who are heavily involved in fundamentalist religion today and their enormous buying (and potential political) power in North America.

OTHER SOURCES OF SOCIAL CHANGE

Social movements, religious and otherwise, are only one important source of social change in the modern world. We have already discussed the significance of population pressure as a force for social change, in the last chapter.

Other important sources of social change include fears for the physical environment, new ideas (for example, commitment to racial equality or increased concerns about health and wellness), technological innovation, and the globalization of world markets. We shall discuss each of these briefly in turn.

The changing physical environment

As we noted in the last chapter, we have seen a dramatic and justifiable growth in environmental concern around the world within the last ten years. More and more people feel strongly about the need for improvements in water purity, air quality, and waste disposal standards (including landfills, recycling, the impact of unnecessary packaging, and the handling of toxic chemicals). People want assurance that consumer products are environmentally safe, and more and more people support energy conservation, the reduction of acid rain, and pesticide safety.

Environmental concern is as economically significant as it is socially significant. To a very large degree, protecting the environment requires not only changes in consumer behaviour and the price of consumer products; it also calls for more government regulation of the marketplace, more expensive production costs, and therefore the risk of job losses in certain sectors. A company that cannot afford to make the changes the government demands may decide to relocate to another region or country with lower environmental standards.

Yet these costs, risks, and changes are inevitable. In recent decades, humans have dramatically transformed the environment. The entire global ecology is affected, particularly the equilibrium of the biosphere: the interdependence between living systems. This raises issues related to humankind's very survival. The ultimate source of concern for environmental change is its potential effect

EXHIBIT 10.1

Possible Futures: Environmentalism

"I believe we are living on a rare hinge of history. The present is the future that futurists foresaw in the early 1960s. We are at the end of industrial society and the beginning of post-industrial societies. The experiences of the past ten years offer little insight into the nature of the next ten years. The next 40 years will be little like the past 40. And neither the processes and institutions of the past 200 years of industrialism nor the past 2000 years of Western Civilization have much relevance (at least as they are presently mythologized and taught) over the next two hundred to two thousand years. . . .

"One of the reasons I feel so is because of the massive attention and resources we shall soon have to devote to impending environmental problems which will occur on a macroscale but will have devastating and presently uncertain local impacts and consequences. The conclusions of countless national and international studies is that the survival of huge numbers of species and habitats is at stake; that tropical forests are vanishing; that underground water tables are falling far faster than they can ever be replenished while the remaining water is contaminated with pesticides and industrial wastes; that billions of tons of topsoil are being lost annually; and, most dramatically, that the mean temperature of the atmosphere is projected to rise significantly, climate and weather patterns expected to alter, the level of the oceans to rise, the protective ozone layer to thin and perhaps vanish, and other heretofore "abnormal" occurrences to become common—including a possible slide into the next ice age—and all as a consequence of the accumulation in the atmosphere and earth of gases released primarily by human industrial and agricultural activities over the last 200, and especially 50-odd years.

"Assuming that these probabilities become realities, or that, in anticipation and response to them, human priorities and actions change, it is ludicrous I believe to assume that the future will be "business as usual." Earning a living and acquiring more products will cease to be the primary concern and activity of people in the so-called "developed" parts of the world. Sheer survival will—or at least attempting to prevent, forestall or prepare for Mother Nature's dramatic revenge."

Source: Jim Dator (1989) "Which Pacific Century?" pp. 1, 6. By permission of Jim Dator, Social Sciences, University of Hawaii

on the "livability" of the globe and its ability to support the variety and complexity of on-going human activity.

Throughout the world, international bodies (like UNESCO), governments at every level, and even local movements are developing plans for research, education, legislation, and regulation of the environment. The failure to take preventive and preparatory steps will lead to the positive checks Malthus associated with overpopulation—massive death and dislocation. Society will change very dramatically if the Earth is unable to support our current standards of human life.

New ideas and inventions

Like the biophysical environment around us, new ideas, too, can be a powerful force for social change. We have already seen this in relation to social movements, whether religious or political. Every movement starts with an *idea*. Likewise, environmental protection, population control, and world peace all start with *ideas*.

No one can doubt the power of ideas to bring about social change. Consider the importance of the following ideas (and ideals) in world history: liberty, equality, justice, beauty, God, truth. People have given up their lives in support of all of these, at one time or another. They are still doing so.

Even Karl Marx, who viewed ideas as the result of social conditions—not their cause—devoted his life to writing down his ideas about class relations and capitalism. He knew that without these ideas and the class awareness they might provoke the chances of a class revolution and communist society were slight or non-existent.

Yet ideas are neither necessary nor sufficient for social change to occur. The sudden onset of AIDS as a disease, first noted in significant numbers in 1983, seemingly from nowhere, resulted in a series of significant changes in our society. These were changes not only in our sexual habits but even in our understanding of appropriate medical practices and priorities, in our definition of the civil liberties of people who are ill, and in our faith in the inevitable progress of science and medicine. The response to AIDS shows that social changes can occur without any necessary connection to previously changing ideas. Of course, such changes will lead to new ideas, but ideas are not *necessary* to initiate social change.

Likewise, ideas are not *sufficient* for social change. Throughout history, a great many ideas—beliefs, discoveries, and so on—have been forgotten or lost. For ideas to be spread or disseminated they must be backed by people who have the power to support them. Ideas are more likely to be disseminated when they arise among the powerful than among the powerless. This is one reason why there was so little known or preserved artistic or literary production by women in Western culture before this century. As well, ideas that go against popular or ruling ideologies are likely to be ignored or suppressed. Those who support such ideas must be willing to fight for them.

Ideas that cannot be used, given current technology or economic means, are also likely to be lost. Like popular discontent, new ideas depend on resource mobilization for their survival. To survive and spread, new ideas must have a social infrastructure: a social movement or institution that adopts them. Thus, when we see ideas survive in the form of innovations, discoveries, or inventions, these are the few ideas (of a great many) whose "time has come."

Innovations are new material objects or methods of doing something that are introduced into a culture. There are two forms of cultural innovation: discovery and invention. A **discovery** involves finding out about and making known the existence of something that was always there, but whose existence was not known (for example, the discovery of radium by Marie Curie and her husband).

Discoveries do not come out of nowhere. They are usually the result of patient research, which itself has an institutional basis: a societal commitment to finding out and making use of new knowledge. In turn, this commitment to

EXHIBIT 10.2

POSSIBLE FUTURES F: POST-INDUSTRIALISM

	Pre-industrial	Industrial	Post-industrial	
Mode of Production	Extractive	Fabrication	Processing; Recycling Services	
Economic sector	**Primary** Agriculture Mining Fishing Timber Oil and gas	**Secondary** Goods-producing Manufacturing Durables Nondurables Heavy construction	**Tertiary** Transportation Utilities **Quinary** Health, education Research, government, Recreation	**Quarternary** Trade Finance Insurance Real estate
Transforming resource	**Natural power** Wind, water, draft animal, human muscle	**Created energy** Electricity—oil, gas, coal, nuclear power	**Information** Computer and data-transmission systems	
Strategic resource	Raw materials	Financial capital	Knowledge	
Technology	Craft	Machine technology	Intellectual technology	
Skill base	Artisan, manual worker, farmer	Engineer, semiskilled worker	Scientist, technical and professional occupations	
Methodology	Commonsense, trial and error; experience	Empiricism, experimentation	Abstract theory, models, simulations, decision theory, systems analysis	
Time perspective	Orientation to the past	Ad hoc adaptiveness, experimentation	Future orientation: forecasting and planning	
Design	Game against nature	Game against fabricated future	Game between persons	
Axial principle	Traditionalism	Economic growth	Codification of theoretical knowledge	

According to Daniel Bell, the coming post-industrial society will differ on a number of dimensions from any society that has existed before. In that new society, all wealth, progress, and productivity will depend on knowledge—especially theoretical knowledge gained through formal education. New information technology will play a central role in making that knowledge useful.

Source: D. Bell "The social framework of the information society" pp. 163-211 in M.L. Dertouzos and J. Moses (eds.) *The Computer Age: A Twenty-Year View*. Cambridge, MA: MIT Press, pp. 166, 167

science, research, and technology has particular cultural roots. In Western societies, it has flourished as a value only in the last 300 years, alongside Protestantism and capitalism. It has required funding but also a commitment to ideas like "efficiency" and "productivity".

Invention also relies on such a cultural and social basis. It is the creation or design of something that did not previously exist (for example, the bow and arrow, automobile, television, or Nintendo game). The growing rate of invention demonstrates the result of a continued and growing commitment to research and development in modern societies, and an ever-better funded infrastructure.

Diffusion is the process by which ideas spread from their point of origin to other points or areas—for example, from group to group within society, and from one society to another. The rapid growth of innovation through invention and discovery has relied on one of the dominant values of scientific work: public dissemination of the results of research. Thus diffusion increases as the media mechanisms for diffusing ideas increase. Improvements in communication technology since Gutenberg invented the printing press have increased the rate of cultural and scientific diffusion of ideas. As ideas and innovations spread more rapidly, new discoveries and inventions develop more quickly.

Canadian inventions

The Canadian case shows the importance of cultural values and economic infrastructure for innovation. The paradox of Canadian history is that Canada is a great producer of ideas and inventions, but has virtually no national technical industries to show for it.

Canada has indeed produced some remarkable inventors and inventions, among them Alexander Graham Bell and the telephone, Charles Saunders and the short-growing-season Marquis wheat strain, Ted Rogers and the batteryless radio, and Sir Frederick Banting and insulin. Yet Canada has let many opportunities for exploiting inventions slip away. This problem ultimately has both cultural and financial origins. The public attitude toward anything new in Canada has often been one of distrust or avoidance. In theory, institutions such as universities should be at the leading edge of technology; but in practice, most Canadian educational institutions handle innovations quite badly. Business corporations do the same, feeling threatened by new ideas, especially if they attack or question prevailing ways of doing things.

In many cases, Canada has had a genuine head start over all other nations in a particular innovation, but we have been unable to make these pay off. Waiting for the risk capital to get industry going takes too long, and by then the advantage has been lost. This happened with the variable-pitch propeller, the hydrofoil boat, the jetliner, and the electronic organ.

A major problem is our banks. They have succeeded in guarding the savings of ordinary people, but they have stressed conservative investment practices at the expense of imagination. For years, Canadian industry has suffered from a lack of risk capital. Indeed, it is this basic reluctance of Canadian banks to help finance Canadian industry that many sociologists believe is at the root of Canada's reliance on foreign investment, which has led to a high degree of domination of the Canadian economy by multinational (especially American) corporations.

If we can overcome this disabling lack of imagination and capital, two benefits will occur: Canada's balance of trade will improve and the "brain drain" of scientists out of the country will reverse itself. Some see the new "Canadarm" as an encouraging example of Canada's increasing ability to innovate. But examples are too few to allow for complacency. Strong measures to encourage innovation in Canada will be needed. We cannot expect the multinational corporations to undertake research and development here in Canada. Typically, they carry these activities out at their head offices, or in educational institutions, in the home country. Developing the capability for Canadian invention will also require more investment of private and public resources in Canadian universities, which have been drained of operating resources for nearly two decades.

Technological innovation

Much social change today results from technological innovation. Genetic engineering and informatics (the combination of computing and communication technologies) are among two of the youngest yet most influential forces in our society today, and they are both forms of technological innovation. Yet we must be careful to avoid the pitfalls of technological determinism.

Technological determinism is a perspective that holds that a given society's social structure, its culture, and its historical development are the direct result of particular technological changes. It is easy to overstate this position: to believe that technology does, or can do, more than is really possible. Without denying the importance of technology in shaping a society's structure, culture, and historical development, it is too simplistic to claim that these are all *determined* by technology. Like any other kind of single-minded determinism, this argument supposes that a given type of technology necessarily produces the same results regardless of culture, place, or socio-historical setting.

However, societies are more complex than this model assumes. In fact, the same technology may be used quite differently—in some cases, not at all—in different types of organization, society, or culture. The precise effect the introduction of a technological innovation will have depends not only on the nature of the innovation, but on the context into which it is introduced: on the motives and attitudes of the people who control the new technology, and on the culture (including belief systems, cultural practices, and existing technology) of the given society.

This is the reason why many ideas and inventions in the past have been ignored and forgotten. There can be no doubt that much of folk medicine around the world, of Alexandrian science, of Greek philosophy, and of Arab mathematics is lost to us because no social institutions existed to preserve, develop, and disseminate this knowledge. Science and technology were unable to create the social acceptance they needed for their own survival. Even today, we see a vast variation in the uses made of computing technology from one society to another, and from one organization to another within the same society.

EXHIBIT 10.3

Possible Futures: Crime

New Kinds of Crime

By 2040, crimes against property will be organized in even more business-like ways. Like all businesses, crime business will become larger in scope, more capital-intensive and technologically sophisticated, and more subtle in the use of persuasion (although violence will continue to distinguish organized crime from legitimate business). Multinational crime organizations will be the norm.

Crime will also be more closely linked with "legitimate" business, both by owning legitimate businesses and helping legitimate businesses get what they want. It will be more closely linked with politics. Politicians will rely on big crime to help keep the public order, control lower level criminals, maintain control over the quality of their goods and services (for example, drugs, prostitution), and help them get re-elected.

Crime will be more professional, as professional expertise in both business (for example, commerce, management, international trade) and criminal skills (for example, drug testing) will continue to grow. Criminal organizations will continue to use juvenile delinquents and semi-professionals as freelance help (a farm team), while discouraging uncontrolled, independent initiatives.

New Kinds of Criminals

For demographic reasons, Canadian society will contain a different mix of living creatures, human and non-human, than it does today. Age and gender barriers will fall in crime as in everything else. For these reasons criminal groups will include more women, more aged criminals and fewer young ones, highly intelligent robots, extraterrestrials, and possibly intelligent animals and plants (due to genetic engineering).

The latter three types of new criminal raise questions of whether a non-human being can be considered to have committed a crime? Can we establish *mens rea* in a dog or Alpha Centauran?

New Problems of Policing

The greater effectiveness of crime and variety of criminals will demand more professional, scientific policing. New policing techniques will run into conflict with constitutional rights to privacy and rules of evidence. New legislation will be needed to get around these obstacles. The tight link between crime, business, and politics will make law enforcement a very "political" activity. At the same time, the internationalization of crime will make law enforcement depend on effective international diplomacy (as it has with drug dealing in Central and South America). Police will have to decide whether enforcing the law in a given case will upset working relations with the crime bosses.

Of course, many human problems and concerns (for example, love, friendship, belief, peace, artistry) lie entirely outside the domain of technological improvement, at least for the time being. Some human problems

This microchip circuit can sit on your fingertip and replace 100s of larger components in a "thinking" machine.

This microcomputer can sit on your desk and replace dozens of clerical workers in an office.

This robotic factory can sit on the outskirts of your city and replace 1000s of manual workers.

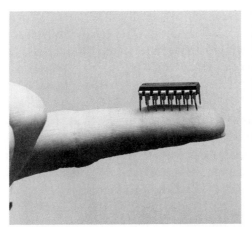

are just not readily "technifiable," especially where complex emotions and ideas are involved. As well, many people are not receptive to technological innovation: to having their problems "technified," even when it is possible. They want to talk to a human psychiatrist, for example, not a machine programmed to respond like a psychiatrist. They want to learn from a human teacher, not instructional software. They would rather talk to a bank teller than use an automated money machine.

New technologies will have the most impact where they are dealing with problems that *are* readily technifiable: that is, where they are addressing a problem that is specific and instrumental (for example, how to get money out of your bank account), where the consumer-population is looking for a technical innovation in that area, and where the technology is easy to use (for example, where it requires little information from the user to do a great deal for him or her).

Having said all this, there can be no doubt we are in the midst of a wide-ranging microelectronics revolution which is transforming many aspects of our society.

An example of technological change: microelectronics

At the root of this technological revolution is a tiny silicon chip with printed circuitry that is capable of carrying electrical impulses. The flow of electrons through these circuits is really the flow of information and, because the chips are tiny, a great deal of circuitry (thus information) can be combined in a small space. Computers make a lot of use of microelectronic components, providing a great deal of flexible "thinking" power at low cost. Thus the essential feature of microelectronics is that they perform tasks involving logic very quickly and cheaply.

In industry, microelectronics are used in control systems for manufacturing. Computers control such manufacturing process variables as temperature and pressure, making possible very complex cycles or routines. They also operate precise cutting tools and provide automatic sampling and inspection—or "quality control"—of the product.

Many factors have influenced the widespread adoption of microelectronics. Historically, the main reason for mechanical innovation has been **automation**, the replacement of people in the production process with machines. Machines accept worse working conditions, are easier to control, do not go on strike, and in the long run may be cheaper to run than human workers. However, a desire to replace workers may *not* be the prime motive for the microelectronic revolution; rather it may be the need to expand output rapidly, increase quality, and improve safety.

As well, microelectronically controlled production allows for easy and cheap custom production: the production of (nearly) as many customized, unique products as there are customers.

There is much concern, and some evidence to justify it, that microprocessors will reduce employment for humans. Robot technology is becoming more common in industries around the world, and has proved itself more reliable and accurate than humans in precise and repetitive jobs. Even some management personnel are being replaced, as computers can work out cash flow strategies and monitor work patterns better than people can.

Replacing workers with machines is bound to cause some unemployment and the need to retrain workers to use the computerized machinery. Some argue that, despite the loss of jobs during the initial introduction of microelectronics, some areas of industry will benefit through increased demand for their products. So far, there has not been much displacement of clerical labour; as some tasks are eliminated, often others are created by computerization. However, in due course, larger numbers of clerical workers may well be displaced, through rapid reductions in the costs of computing and improvements in their reliability and flexibility.

Massive job turnover will require some massive planning and re-organization, coupled with encouraging older workers to learn about the new technology. New employment opportunities will be in the knowledge industries. The biggest problem facing us is knowing how to transfer labour from manufacturing industries (where jobs are becoming fewer) to knowledge and service industries, which are less easily "technified" and where job displacement is less likely.

The most logical way to do this is through expansion of the educational system. As well as training new workers and retraining older ones, this expanded system would also provide a base for research and development into new technologies, creating (potentially) millions of new jobs.

We are now in the midst of what many have called the "information revolution," similar in scope to the industrial revolution of the past century. It includes rapid, significant changes in computing, and also in communication media: in radio, TV, and telephone, to name a few. We are only beginning to learn the potential of the computer, and incredible possibilities remain to be tapped in the area of artificial intelligence. Since computers can only do what they are programmed to do, what they will accomplish in future will depend almost entirely on human imagination. Already, computers are playing a major role in architecture, biotechnology, space exploration, and of course business.

Computers provide a path towards higher productivity in an industrial context. At work, they do not seem to increase or decrease job satisfaction, nor, indeed, to change the nature of work in any fundamental ways. They do, however, affect the communication structure of organizations by making possible both more *centralization* and *decentralization* of decision-making.

In organizations with centralized decision-making, orders (or decisions) flow from the top down and information flows from the bottom up. In principle, people at the same level are not supposed to communicate and cooperate (though, in practice, they do so all the time). All important decisions are made at the top (or "centre") of the structure. Proponents believe that this kind of decision-making increases corporate responsibility, expertise, and consistency.

In organizations with decentralized decision-making, more people share information, communicate, and cooperate. Important decisions are made at lower levels in the organization than in centralized organizations. Proponents believe that decentralization increases initiative and allows staff with the most practical experience (i.e., knowledge of marketing problems, client wishes, etc.) to make decisions affecting their own work. In general, giving staff more decision-making power is said to motivate them to work harder.

Many consider decentralization a good thing, likely to increase autonomy and self-determination. They equate centralization to bureaucracy and authoritarian rule. Computers tend to make centralized operation easier and more effective, by enhancing our ability to address an entire complex problem at one time. Likewise, computers allow the correlation of large bodies of information within central computer memories.

However, neither capability will necessarily increase centralization. They just as easily allow decision-makers to take actions independently in acccessing the central memory. Decentralization, then, is just as likely an outcome as centralization. It is not the computer that will make this decision.

In government, for example, the trend towards centralization began long before computers were invented; computers cannot be considered the cause of centralization, should that occur. It remains up to us whether we use computers to centralize or decentralize decision-making.

The same is true with privacy: the decision is up to us whether or not the computer will invade our privacy. Computerization allows the central assembly of information from many sources and its easy accessibility for many uses. It also facilitates auditing and control: it is easy to spy on other people with computers, so legal rules must be applied to the use of such information. If these rules are followed, the automation of information will be a major improvement in our society. If we fail to make and enforce such rules, the fault will be ours—not that of the computers. In the past, there have always been ways to get information about people, with or without computers. Privacy is not a new problem in our society. It remains up to us whether we let computers invade our privacy or not.

The most heated opposition to computers, outside the concern over job loss, is because some people compare themselves with machines. Then, computers may hurt people's self-esteem, because they can do many of the things people can do, and indeed, some things people cannot do. With the development of artificial intelligence, the number of computer accomplishments will likely grow.

But is it necessary for us to believe we are unique in our thought capabilities? Other scientific breakthroughs associated with Galileo, Darwin, and Freud have had the same injurious effects on people's self-esteem, reminding us that we are part of nature and subject to physical and natural laws—not outside or above nature. Perhaps this realization is all the more valuable today, in the face of imminent environmental disaster.

Questions surrounding computerization today include "How much can human behaviour be simulated by computers?" "In what areas can (and should) computers replace human beings?" and "How far should we explore the human mind with computer simulation?" These questions will likely be answered in the future, by people and not computers. With the proper use, computers can become instruments of human betterment. With wrong use, they can become instruments of terror and subjugation.

GLOBAL CHANGE
Social evolution

The central idea behind most evolutionary theories of social change is that social organization tends towards increasing complexity. As the world becomes what Marshall MacLuhan called a "global village" through the shrinking of distances by faster travel and communication, the entire world is becoming a single, complex social order.

Within this context, we continue to see the operation of two main processes of social evolution: differentiation and integration. **Differentiation** is the process whereby various sets of activities previously performed by one institution are divided up, then performed by a number of separate institutions.

A good example, as we saw in Chapter Seven, is the family. In the past, families had the major responsibility for production, consumption, and education. Today, the family remains only a unit of consumption. Educational institutions outside the home have the main responsibility for educating family members, while workplaces outside the home are the main centres for production, providing members with a means of making a living.

Integration, a complementary process of social evolution, combines the various parts or elements of a society to form a unified whole. The more tightly integrated the various elements of a society are, the more likely a change in one element will have repercussions for the others. In a highly evolved system, the parts will be highly differentiated, with a lot of slack between them. They will also be highly integrated in a way that allows the parts maximum autonomy and flexibility, yet ensures the maximum opportunity for resolving conflict through peaceful means.

In the past, large parts of the world were isolated from one another. As they came into contact through colonialism, they began to differentiate and some areas industrialized rapidly while others did not. They were tied together in relationships of dominance and submission, not autonomous and flexible integration.

We have now entered a new stage of global history in which economic and social differentiation is being matched by mechanisms of multinational integration such as the United Nations, the World Bank and International Monetary Fund, the Red Cross and Amnesty International, military alliances (NATO and the Warsaw Pact, for example); and multinational corporations. However, this process of integration is far from complete, because it is an integration of unequal, rather than equal, partners. It is marked by uneven development and conflict throughout the world.

World System Theory explains the uneven pace of development in the various countries of the world, by looking at the nature of the relationships among these countries. This theory is based on the premise that we can understand the internal conditions of a given nation-state only by under-standing its relation to other nation-states. The theory argues that the world's nation-states are all integrated into a world system; therefore, changes in one will provoke changes in the others. This integration of all the various nation-states in a world economic system began in the 15th century, with the expansion of capitalism in western Europe. The process, however, is far from finished.

Although they are all integrated, nation-states do not relate to one another as equals. Some nation-states dominate others politically and economically. Dominant regions are called the *core*, while subordinate regions form the *periphery*.

Core regions are industrialized and get the raw materials and cheap labour they need for manufacturing from the peripheral regions. Because they are economically and politically dominant, core nations have the power to extract an economic surplus (usually in the form of cheap materials and labour) from the periphery, helping them to develop and prosper at an ever faster rate. At the same time, the periphery—ever more depleted of materials, labour, and capital—becomes more and more dependent on core nations for manufactured goods.

Foreign firms and investors (from the core countries) control the economies of peripheral countries. As a result, profits made in the periphery are drained out of the local economy and flow back to the core. Moreover, foreigners decide what types of economic activities should take place, and what resources should be exploited in the periphery. They make these decisions with their own interests, not the interests of the local economy, in mind. It is in their interest to keep the periphery dependent on the core because this ensures they will have a continued source of cheap raw materials and labour, and a market for their manufactured goods.

EXHIBIT 10.4

TIED TO THE FUTURE

In 1950, sociological research on modernization in the Middle East required interviews with people in Turkey. Several interviews were conducted in Balgat, a tiny Turkish village eight kilometres from the capital city, Ankara. The interviewer, named Tosun, described Balgat as follows:

> I have seen quite a lot of villages in the barren mountainous East, but never such a colorless, shapeless dump. This was the reason I chose the village. It could have been half an hour to Ankara by car if it had a road, yet it is about two hours to the capital without almost any road and is just forgotten, forsaken, right under our noses.

An agricultural community, Balgat was led by a hereditary Chief who, as much as possible, controlled the flow of information and ideas. For example, the Chief possessed the only radio in Balgat and chose who would be permitted, of an evening, to visit and listen to the radio. Though the Chief gave Tosun an interview he let it be known he didn't want anyone else giving interviews. In talks with Tosun, the Chief expressed a preference for the old ways (including old style-clothing), for village life over city life, and for Turkish life over any other.

However, the town's Grocer—its only non-farming person—eluded the Chief's control on thinking and expressed a very clear preference for new ways over old ones, for city life over village life, and for Westernization. He thought, talked, and dressed just as he wished to, though it earned him contempt and ridicule from many in the village. About the Grocer, Tosun wrote,

> The respondent is comparatively the most city-like dressed man in the village. He even wore some sort of a necktie. . . . He most evidently wanted to feel that he is closer to me than he is to them and was curiously careful with his accent all during the interview. . . . Although he presented to take the interview naturally, he was nervous and also was proud to be interviewed although he tried to hide it.

By 1954, a mere four years later, a great deal had changed. A road (and bus service) now joined Balgat to Ankara, and the town population had grown greatly. Many households now owned radios. The Grocer was dead, and the Chief's son had taken over from his father. However the new Chief had little interest in preserving old ways of life. Like many others now, he wore a necktie.

Source: D. Lerner (1964) *The Passing of Traditional Society*. New York: Free Press, pp. 20, 22. Copyright © 1958 by The Free Press, a Division of Macmillan, Inc.; copyright renewed 1986.

Core nations engage in a policy of *imperialism*, and for peripheral nations, the result is *underdevelopment*. **Imperialism** is the exercise of political and economic control by one state over the territory of another, often by military means. Its purpose is to exploit the indigenous population and extract economic and political advantages. Traditionally, imperialism occurred

Unfortunately, an atomic war would not kill everyone. Survivors would face genetic destruction, environmental damage, a crippled economy, shattered lives, contaminated food and water, social disorder, and many lost friends and relatives.

through the acquisition of colonies—the settlement and administration of foreign lands. Some argue that a new and more subtle form of imperialism has become more common in the 20th century: neocolonialism. Under neocolonialism, core nations exercise economic control over a country that is (formally) politically independent.

Underdevelopment is the effect on the periphery of such unequal conditions of exchange between the core and the periphery. It is characterized by a dependence on the export of raw materials and on manufactured imports; little or no domestic control over the economy; a small industrial base; little economic diversification; a high proportion of the population in rural areas; high rates of unemployment; a lack of social programs to provide for basic necessities of life, such as health care; a high illiteracy rate; and a very low standard of living for the majority of the population.

Underdeveloped nations vary in the number and combination of underdeveloped characteristics they display. However, they are similar in one important way: the reasons for their condition. International economic disparities are a product of exploitive relationships among nation-states. The underdevelopment of the periphery is not due to a lack of resources, illiteracy, or a traditional or backward mentality. It results from subordination to, and dependence on, the core.

Similar problems can be seen in semi-peripheral countries like Canada, which are not quite as dominant as the core countries and not as dependent on the core as peripheral countries. They suffer many of the same difficulties gaining economic independence as peripheral countries do (though to a lesser extent) and inflict much of the same harm on peripheral countries as the core countries do.

World System Theory is a useful corrective to social evolutionary theories—the most common of which are theories of "modernization"—which see differentiation and integration taking place smoothly and fairly. It helps to explain why some parts of the world develop more rapidly and fully than others.

World System Theory fails to take into account factors for social change that are internal to the nation-state—for example, the role of social classes within the respective core and peripheral nations. As a result, it cannot explain why Canada, a former colony and major exporter of raw materials, is not underdeveloped today to the same degree as Peru or Uganda.

Still, World System Theory reminds us that all significant social change is likely to produce conflict. No change, even change that evolves out of an earlier stage of development, can escape these forces.

Will further integration or technological developments such as computerization lead to a reduction of inequalities among the nation-states? Again, that is up to us. Some nations, such as South Korea, have taken advantage of new economic and technological opportunities to develop rapidly; others seem to fall further and further behind the core nations. Still, predicting the future in a time of such momentous changes as we are undergoing on a routine basis is a very difficult task. Often we must be satisfied with no more than the sheer exhilaration of living through it.

CLOSING REMARKS

This chapter has been successful if it has suggested some of the many ways in which the different aspects of society we have examined in this text — such as the family, population, the economic order, culture, ethnicity, and even deviance — are interrelated. Understanding the implications of these interrelationships for societal change, and for our individual lives, is the challenge of the sociological imagination.

We have also noted the complex interrelationships between evolution and revolution — the two master patterns of world history. We have observed that no event or change process has only one cause; more often than not, there are a great many related causes which we must struggle to pick apart. These often include political, economic, technological, cultural, and environmental factors. More than that, we have noted repeatedly the power of ideas to influence human actions, and the unexpected power of our actions to shape people's ideas.

By now, you will have realized that doing research on social change — indeed, in any area of sociology — is a complicated matter. Such research requires imagination but also requires care and a systematic way of proceeding. It is time, then, to talk about methods of sociological research: the way sociologists find out what they need to know in order to make theories and test theories about social life.

Discussion Questions

1. "There is no logic to any fashion or fad — no reason why it must occur at a given time and not some other." Can you think of any exceptions to this rule?

2. Is public opinion usually ahead of, or behind, the views of political leaders? An example of where it is behind leaders' opinions is on the re-instatement of capital punishment: a majority of the public want it, leaders do not. Can you think of an example of where it is ahead of leaders' opinion?

3. Why are charismatic leaders more likely to emerge in some periods of history than in others?

4. Ideas are a powerful force for social change, but they must come from somewhere. Why are certain kinds of ideas — for example, gender equality — more likely to arise and find acceptance at some times and not others?

5. Computers are capable of doing great good and great harm. What factors will determine which use is made of them in your lifetime?

6. What are some other trends — besides those mentioned in the chapter — that are likely to continue gaining importance into the next century? Make a prediction about how they are likely to develop, and with what social consequences.

Data Collection Exercises

1. Collect some information about religious camp meetings (or other crowd behaviours) in the 19th century and compare it with a similar crowd in this century. How has people's crowd behaviour changed, if at all?

2. Select a particular social movement — current or historical — for closer study. Find out what resources members needed in order to become an effective voice of protest.

3. Study the science or technology of an ancient or medieval society to find out what discoveries they had made in a particular area—for example, in medicine, sanitation, bridgebuilding, or weaponry. Were their discoveries built upon by later civilizations, or lost and "rediscovered"?

4. Study a small group you know well—your family, for example—to find out whether change within a group is characterized by contradiction and conflict. Is change discontinuous and marked by "leaps" from one stage to another?

Writing Exercises

1. Write a 500-word essay arguing that a recent change in fashion (e.g., clothing), recreation (e.g., a new leisure activity) or lifestyle (e.g., aerobic exercise) is likely to last beyond the next ten years.

2. Invent an imaginary social movement to protest something you consider unjust. Now write a 500-word manifesto, outlining the goals of your movement and why they are justified.

3. Write a brief questionnaire (20 questions or less) you can use to examine the religious values and practices of six classmates, so you can tell which ones are closest to fundamentalism in their views.

4. Write a 500-word essay explaining why one particular social change some people support—you choose the one you want to write about—is unlikely to happen during your lifetime.

Glossary

charisma—an exceptional capacity to inspire devotion and enthusiasm among followers

differentiation—the process whereby various sets of activities are divided up and performed by a number of separate institutions. A complementary process is **integration** whereby various elements of a society are combined to form a unified whole.

evangelism—the art or practice of preaching to a large audience, particularly on religious matters, with the aim of persuading and converting followers

fad—a trivial, short-lived preference or enthusiasm for some activity, type of speech, dance, style, etc. A fad is more trivial than a **fashion**, which is something considered admirable and is eagerly imitated in a particular time and place.

propaganda—information, ideas, or doctrines disseminated for the purpose of influencing the opinions and actions of others

resource mobilization—the ability of a group to gather, organize, and use necessary resources (such as money, leadership, support, and connections) to promote its views

routinization—a process by which a bureaucratic structure emerges in a (formerly) charismatic social movement, to better administer the day-to-day goals of the movement

social movements—forms of collective action that is aimed at promoting or resisting change in a given society

Suggested Readings

Chirot, Daniel *Social Change in the Twentieth Century*. New York: Harcourt Brace Jovanovich, 1977. A brilliant and ambitious attempt to understand all social change since 1913 in the context of the "world system." Read how Canada managed, in only 80 years, to move from the periphery to the semi-periphery of world events.

Clark, S., J.P. Grayson, and L.M. Grayson (eds.) *Prophecy and Protest: Social Movements in Twentieth Century Canada*. Toronto: Gage, 1975. An excellent collection of articles on a wide variety of Canadian social movements, both political and religious. The introductory sections, written by the editors, are particularly valuable for understanding the field.

Hobsbawm, E.J. *Primitive Rebels*. New York: Norton, 1959. This is a classic set of essays on "archaic forms of social movements in the 19th and 20th centuries." It includes fascinating chapters on bandits (like Robin Hood), the mafia, city mobs, and rural anarchists, and demonstrates why social change is more likely to come about if protest is highly regimented.

Marsden, L. and E. Harvey, *Fragile Federation: Social Change in Canada*. Toronto: McGraw-Hill Ryerson, 1979. Though slender in size, this book examines the connections among most major sources of social change in Canada—particularly technological, demographic, and economic change—and the role social movements and elites play in mobilizing and shaping social responses.

Posgate, D. and K. McRoberts *Quebec: Social Change and Political Crisis*, 2nd edition. Toronto: McClelland and Stewart, 1984. This is a much-respected analysis of the connection between social, political, and economic changes in Quebec over the province's long history and, especially, since the Quiet Revolution.

Skocpol, T. *States and Social Revolutions*. Cambridge: Cambridge University Press, 1979. A masterful comparison of the revolutions that occurred in France, Russia, and China. It attempts to explain why revolutions occur when and where they do, and the reasons they turn out differently.

References

Bibby, R.W. (1987) *Fragmented Gods: The Poverty and Potential of Religion in Canada*. Toronto: Irwin

Durkheim, E. (1915) *The Elementary Forms of the Religious Life*. London: George Allen and Unwin

Edmonson, B. (1988) "Bringing in the Sheaves" *American Demographics* 10 (8) August, pp. 28-32, 57-58

Runciman, W.G. (1966) *Relative Deprivation and Social Justice*. London: Routledge and Kegan Paul

Turner, R. and L.M. Killian (1987) *Collective Behaviour*, 3rd edition. Englewood Cliffs, NJ: Prentice Hall

Weber, M. (1964) "The types of authority and imperative coordination" section 3 in T. Parsons (ed.) *The Theory of Social and Economic Organization*. New York: Free Press

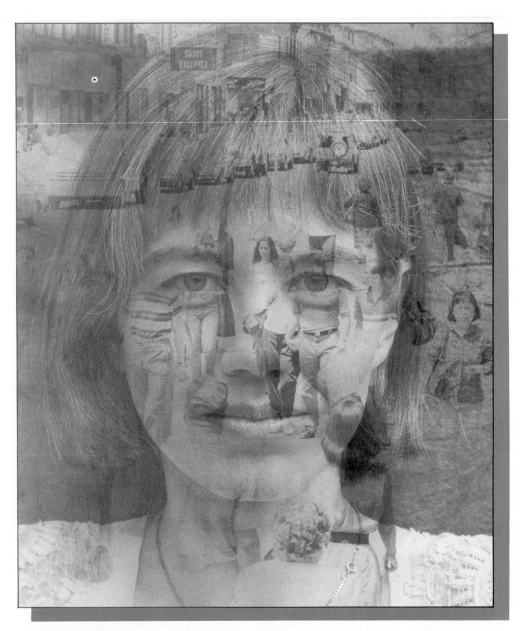

CHAPTER 11

Ultimately, all science is about causes and effects.

METHODS OF RESEARCH

SCIENTIFIC RESEARCH IS RIGOROUS AND OBJECTIVE

We began this book by noting that everyone is a sociologist of a kind. All of us make use of common sense to understand the social world in which we live, the behaviour of other people, and the events which take place around us. For this reason, much of what we have discussed in this book may have seemed familiar to you.

Almost certainly, you will have already discovered for yourself some of what we are saying about family life, culture, conformity, work, inequality, and so on. More likely than not, you will have made your "discoveries" when experiencing personal troubles. You may have even discovered for yourself what we are saying throughout the book: namely, personal troubles are the other side of public issues.

Personal experiences help to persuade us of the truth of many sociological findings; but they are no substitute for research. We cannot create sociology simply by living. That is because much of what goes on around us is neither obvious nor easily explained. What's more, personal experiences and emotions may hide as much from us as they reveal, because we are so intimately wrapped up in certain ways of seeing things.

So, understanding social life requires more than experience in living. It requires careful research; and fortunately, everyone is used to doing research in their own lives. Think about how we go about finding the lowest price on a new car or read magazine reviews before buying a CD player. Research is nothing more than the careful asking and answering of questions. Because of this, a lot of what we shall discuss in this, the last chapter of the book, is familiar to you from your own experience. But be warned, much of it is not.

Scientific research differs in many ways from the everyday research with which we are all familiar, but one particularly important difference has to do with standards. If you are trying to find an inexpensive motel in Florida you might check newspaper ads, make phone calls, perhaps contact a travel agent, until you are satisfied that you have made the best choice. You set your own criteria for deciding what the best choice is, for deciding when you have done enough research, and for deciding that your research has been done as thoroughly and as well as possible. You have no one to please but yourself. In scientific research, in contrast, the standards are set by others, the scientific community. This means that we must make use of accepted and tested methods—or make a convincing case to others why we should not. It also means that our research must be as objective and as rigorous as possible if others are to accept its findings as valid.

As we discuss the research process and the methods that are used by sociologists it may sometimes seem as if we are dressing simple things up in complex words to make them more confusing. That is not the case. Scientists expect even the simplest research project to be carefully planned and done in a rigorous manner. If you are to engage in sociological research you need to learn the concepts and vocabulary of social research: the words with which sociologists speak about what they are doing.

Even if you never plan to do any scientific research of your own, learning how such research is done will allow you to better understand and evaluate the many reports, studies and polls to which we are constantly exposed.

BASIC IDEAS OF SOCIAL RESEARCH

Cause and effect

Most social research tries to answer the question "Why?". Why are some people poorer than others? Why do racial groups come into conflict? Why do so many people from small towns move to large cities? Why has the Canadian divorce rate risen in the last twenty years? Why are some societies more democratic than others?

To answer the question "Why?" is to find the cause of some effect. We can restate the first question above as follows: What causes some people to be poorer than others? Restated this way, each question asks about an "effect"—poverty, racial conflict, migration, divorce, and democracy, respectively. An **effect** is something brought about by a cause or agency. In sociology, the sort of agency or force we examine that produced the result, consequence, or outcome is usually a social process.

Explanation and prediction

In trying to find the causes of observed effects, social research aims at explanation. Formally defined, an **explanation** is something that gives the meaning of, gives reasons for, accounts for, or interprets, something else. Take the question about poverty: Why are some people poorer than other people? The process of explanation will require us to venture informed guesses or probable explanations, called *hypotheses*, which we will then test with data. You will recall from Chapter One that a **hypothesis** is a proposition or statement about the relationship between some tentative cause X and its effect Y that we can test through research.

Many sociological researchers (for example, Blau and Duncan, 1967; Boyd et al, 1985; and others) have shown that some people are poorer than others because they have not received enough formal education to get a well-paying job. Then, X is the level of education a person has received and Y is that person's income. If our hypothesis is correct, the higher the level of education a person gets, the higher his or her income should be. We can now examine the data to verify the hypothesis—that is, test it with facts. If the data show that people with a higher level of education always earn a higher income than people with less education, then we have come part of the way towards an explanation.

Explanation, however, does not end merely by showing a connection between X and Y. We must also understand the reasons for that connection: *why* more education leads to higher earnings. Without understanding the process, we have only gained an ability to predict Y from X. **Prediction** is the

Correlation is not causation. Indeed, sociologists and policy-makers often wonder about the connection between them. For example, should insurance companies deny driver's insurance to people attitudinal data reveal to be accident-prone?

Profile Of The Accident-Prone Driver (percent)

	Number Of Accidents In Past Five Years	
	Two or More	None
Risk Taker		
I don't like to take chances (disagree).	42	31
I am the kind of person who will try anything once.	64	53
Restless		
I would probably be content to live in the same town the rest of my life (disagree).	40	28
We will probably move at least once in the next five years.	50	32
Pressured		
I work under a great deal of pressure most of the time.	69	57
Impulse Buyer		
I am an impulse buyer.	47	35
When I see a brand somewhat different from the usual, I investigate it.	73	63
Money Problems		
Our family is too heavily in debt today.	36	25
Worrying about money.	52	30
Optimistic		
My greatest achievements are ahead of me.	78	61
Five years from now our family income will probably be a lot higher than it is now.	81	60

Continued

Cosmopolitan
I like to think I am a bit of a swinger.	46	28
I would like to spend a year in London or Paris.	41	30

Interested in Movies
I like to watch disaster movies.	47	32
Attended an x-rated movie.	19	9

Less Conservative
Communism is the greatest peril in the world today.	48	59
U.S. would be better off if there were no hippies.	46	60
Unions have too much power in America today.	67	77
Most big companies are just out for themselves.	77	67

Source: Reprinted by permission of the publisher from "Psychographic and buyer behavior: theory and recent empirical findings" by S. Mehrota and W.D. Wells, in A. Woodside, J. Sheth, and P. Bennett (eds.) *Consumer and Industrial Buying Behavior.* Copyright © 1977 by Elsevier Science Publishing Co., Inc.

act or process of forecasting an outcome. It requires us to infer the outcome of an event or series of events from scientific—especially statistical—analyses of known events. You ask me to guess whether Frank earns more money than Alexander. I ask how much education each has received. You tell me Frank completed Grade 12 and Alexander only completed Grade 9. Remembering my (imaginary) discovery that higher education usually means higher earnings, I hypothesize that Frank earns more. If the hypothesis is valid, my prediction will be right.

Unfortunately for sociologists, the real world is more complicated than that. In social research, we almost never find an X that always causes Y or a Y that always results from X. Most of the processes sociologists study are multi-causal and conditional. By **multi-causal**, we mean that many Xs combine in complicated ways to produce a single Y. By **conditional**, we mean that a particular X will cause Y under some conditions but not others.

The relationship between education and earning power is a case in point. Education is not the only factor that can influence earnings. There are many others—gender, race, region of the country, even physical appearance—that also affect how much money a person makes. In addition, education has more influence on earnings in some kinds of work than others. Consider two people making hamburgers at a fast food outlet. One has a grade 9 education, the other a grade 12 education. They are doing the same job and earning exactly the same amount of money, so education has no effect on earnings in this case. The effect of higher education is greatest when it allows a person to enter a restricted line of work—such as a skilled trade, a profession, or a managerial position—that pays higher-than-average wages. The "returns to education"—the amount of income an additional year's education will bring—vary from one industry or sector of the economy to another.

For these reasons, it is not at all easy to predict even something as simple as how much money a person will earn. It is even harder to *explain* an observed result. To explain something well means understanding the entire process that ties X and Y together.

Variables and units of analysis

Researchers speak about Xs and Ys in a particular way, so it is worthwhile defining some terms before going further. Xs and Ys are **variables**. A **variable** is any trait, quality, or social characteristic that can vary in size over time, across individual cases, or among different groups. Sociologists typically measure the variation in terms of **deviation**, a statistical measure of the degree to which a score varies from the mean, or group average.

Frank, Alexander, Sarah, and Monica – the people we study – are **units of analysis**: the units under investigation in a given piece of research.

The Y variable we are trying to explain and predict is the dependent variable. A **dependent variable**, such as income in the example above, is influenced, changed, or caused by the effect of other variables. An X variable, or **independent variable**, causes a change or variation in the dependent variable. The independent variable is the causal or explanatory variable. As already noted, a dependent variable can be influenced by many independent variables. As well, any independent variable can influence many dependent variables. So when we come to research a particular relationship – the relationship between education and earnings, say – we are isolating one particular relationship in a vast network of possible Xs and Ys.

Qualitative and quantitative data

Data on education and earnings are usually quantitative data. They are based on precise measurement in recognizable units. We can say exactly, in dollars and cents, how much a person earns. We can say exactly, in years, grades, or degrees and diplomas, how much education a person has completed. What is more, everyone knows what dollars and grades are, so we can easily share and discuss our findings. With quantitative data, it is easy to *replicate* a study someone else has done – that is, do it the very same way, to see if we get the same results. We know exactly what the earlier researcher was measuring, and how.

What's more, such precise and clearcut measurement allows us to evaluate the results with powerful statistical methods. These methods permit us to judge whether our finding could have occurred by chance alone. They help us to compare the relative importance of different Xs in their effect on Y. Quantitative measurement also allows researchers to create mathematical models for their theory. In short, quantitative measurement allows sociology to produce findings that are more like those of economics and the physical sciences.

Much of what sociologists study cannot be quantified, however. Take love, for example. Consider how difficult it would be to measure precisely how much in love two people are. If you wanted to attach numbers to their "degree of loving," what questions would you ask them? How would you combine the

EXHIBIT 11.1

The Qualitative And Quantitative Pardigms Compared

Qualitative Paradigm	Quantitative Paradigm
Advocates the use of qualitative methods.	Advocates the use of quantitative methods.
Naturalistic and uncontrolled observation.	Obtrusive and controlled measurement.
Subjective.	Objective.
Close to the data: the "insider" perspective.	Removed from the data: the "outsider" perspective.
Grounded, discovery-oriented, exploratory, expansionist, descriptive and inductive.	Ungrounded, verification-oriented, confirmatory, reductionist, inferential and hypothetico-deductive.
Process-oriented.	Outcome-oriented.
Valid: "real," "rich," and "deep" data.	Reliable: "hard" and replicable data.
Ungeneralizable: single case studies.	Generalizable: multiple case studies.
Holistic.	Particularistic.
Assumes a dynamic reality.	Assumes a stable reality.

Source: Charles S. Reichardt and Thomas D. Cook "Beyond qualitative versus quantitative methods" in T.D. Cook and C.S. Reichardt (eds.) *Qualitative and Quantitative Methods in Evaluation Research*. Beverly Hills: Sage Publications, 1979

answers to get an overall evaluation? What are your measurement units? We must turn to qualitative data in order to do research on love.

Unlike quantitative data, **qualitative data** do not require, or easily lend themselves to, precise measurement. It would be relatively easy to form a judgment about how much in love two people are. This is possible because being in love constitutes a social relationship. People will typically display or indicate to one another—and to others—that they are in love. Qualitative research requires clear, detailed description of people's behaviour, combined with some information from them about their own feelings. This usually involves observing people, talking to them, trying to understand them and their point of view. We get a subtler, more complex picture of the relationship when we do *not* try to compress their feelings into a simple measurement. All research needs this sensitivity of understanding; some research simply cannot be done without it.

DESIGNING A STUDY

Types of research design

Planning and carrying out research requires the preparation of a research design. A **research design** is an orderly plan for collecting, analyzing, and interpreting data. The design chosen will depend on the nature of the problem that is being studied. It will also depend on the time, money, and skill that are available.

We can do research on any question in a number of different ways: there is no one "right" way to do research. The best research design will match an interesting question with the skills and resources we actually have available (that is, with *feasibility*). However, sometimes interest and feasibility do not match up very well. Consider the following example.

Some researchers suggest that migrants are more dynamic and ambitious than the people they leave behind. This hypothesis makes some sense: after all, emigration does carry risks, and taking risks requires courage, energy, and ambition. So we have a theory that explains the hypothesis; now we need some data to test whether the hypothesis is valid. How should we measure whether immigrants really are more ambitious and dynamic than average; and whom should we measure? We shall consider questions of measurement a little later. For now, let us consider the second question: *whom* to measure.

The researcher realizes that in the time available it will be impossible to study all immigrants. She decides to study immigrants from Portugal who live in Montreal. She makes her decision on the grounds of convenience: it happens that she speaks Portuguese and lives in Montreal. That's fine for her, but do *we* have any reason to suppose that Portuguese immigrants in Montreal represent all immigrants living everywhere? Unless she can give us a satisfactory answer to that question, the researcher should not go any further with this project.

Suppose the researcher does go on. She has a test that measures, on a scale from 1 to 10, how dynamic and ambitious a person is. She tests 50 Portuguese immigrants in Montreal and finds they score an average 6.5 out of 10. Is this score high or low? Does it prove her hypothesis right or not? To answer this, she must compare their score with another group's. But which group is appropriate: (a) Canadian-born people of non-Portuguese ancestry; (b) Canadian-born people of Portuguese ancestry; or (c) people born and continuing to live in Portugal?

The answer is (c). The researcher needs to compare these Portuguese non-immigrants with Portuguese immigrants, to see whether they differ in their average dynamism and ambition. If the immigrants score significantly higher, she has supported or validated her hypothesis. If they score the same or lower than the non-immigrants, the data have defeated her hypothesis. The important point to note is that any data she may have collected from groups (a) and (b) are simply irrelevant. These data cannot answer the question the researcher has posed.

The example shows that we should not try to answer this particular question unless we can go to Portugal to collect the data we need. If we cannot go to Portugal, we should study something else about immigrants or something else entirely. There is no way to complete this project with data only collected in Canada. This is the kind of problem a researcher can, and should, anticipate when designing research.

Ultimately, all research tests theories about causes and effects. The research cycle is the sequence of stages through which all research must pass.

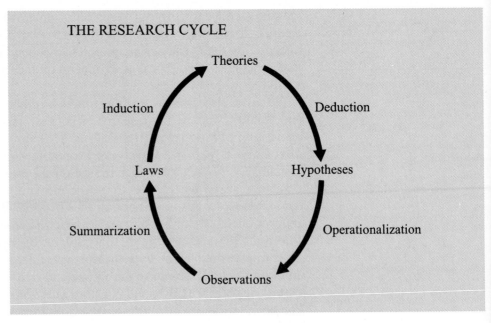

THE RESEARCH CYCLE

Source: "The research cycle," from Peter Li "Methods of sociological research" chapter 2 in L. Tepperman and R.J. Richardson (eds.) *The Social World: An Introduction to Sociology,* 1st edition. Toronto: McGraw-Hill Ryerson, 1986, p. 39

Experiments and quasi-experiments

Most scientists mean something more specific by the term "research design." Typically, they mean the decision to test a hypothesis with an experiment, quasi-experiment, correlational analysis, or single-case analysis. We shall consider each of these designs in turn, and show that each can bring particular insights to our research.

An **experiment** is a research method designed to investigate the effect of one variable on another. The experiment takes place under well-controlled, carefully regulated conditions, in an artificial setting, usually a laboratory. In brief, the experimenter introduces the independent variable, then observes and measures its effect on the dependent variable.

The experimental method allows the researcher to control any factors that might influence the phenomenon under study. One of the ways of controlling variables is by assigning subjects to two groups—an experimental group and a control group—in an unbiased way: either by random assignment or careful matching. The **experimental group** is exposed to the effects of the independent variable introduced by the researcher. The **control group** may be closely matched to the experimental group, and contain the same mix of ages, genders, educational levels, and so on. The experimenter does not expose control subjects to the independent variable whose effects he or she is studying.

Some sociologists argue that the experimental method is artificial: it is hard to imagine a real-life situation similar to the experimental ones research subjects usually find themselves in. For this reason, some prefer a research design that is more natural: for example, a quasi-experiment. A **quasi-experiment** modifies the experimental design, to study a problem that does not lend itself very readily or naturally to an experiment. Like an experiment, the quasi-experiment uses experimental and control groups, and compares people's behaviours before and after the experimental group receives their special treatment. However, the quasi-experiment does not randomly select or match experimental and control group subjects. Nor can it control other changes in the environment.

Consider the following example. Research has shown that delinquent behaviour often accompanies stress within a child's family. This has led to a number of quasi-experiments—sometimes called demonstration projects—that test the effects of direct state intervention in the families of juvenile delinquents. The experimental treatment is family-focused and the counselling programs are designed to treat youngsters as parts of their family units, rather than as isolated individuals. Services provided usually include family therapy, crisis intervention, and intensive counselling for the young offender and the family.

The results of these studies vary. For example, Baron and Feeney (1977) examined a Court Diversion Program in Sacramento (California) and reported that the program did help to reduce rates of recidivism. On the other hand, Urban and Rural Systems Associates (1978) found that the family-oriented program they studied did reduce the number of minor offenses (for example, curfew and liquor-law violations), but did not reduce the number of more serious offenses (for example, running away from home and drug offenses.)

Substitutes for experiments

Neither the experiment nor the quasi-experiment is very common in sociological research. Far more common is **correlational analysis**, a type of research design that measures the association between two phenomena—cross-sectional analysis—or associated changes in two phenomena—longitudinal analysis.

In general, a **longitudinal study** involves gathering data from the same sample at intervals over time. It is a very useful method for studying trends and the effects of particular changes. One form of longitudinal analysis, called a **panel study**, is the basis for Statistics Canada's monthly Labour Force Survey. Each month Statistics Canada surveys a new batch of respondents and some of the respondents it had surveyed the month before. In this way it can keep a running record of employment changes over time.

However, even panel studies are relatively rare in sociology. There are problems with the initial selection of people, because most people do not want to commit themselves to repeated study. The group, or panel, may undergo changes as a result of being on the panel, and therefore becomes less representative of the general population. Most important, it costs a great deal of money to re-interview people after a lapse of time, especially if many of the original sample have died, moved away, or lost interest in the project.

More common is the **retrospective survey**, where respondents are asked to report what has happened to them in the last month, year, or other period. This method is used to collect valuable data about family life—as, for example, in the Family History Survey—and about work life—as in the Annual Work Pattern Survey.

Such research has produced some interesting results that could not have been gained in another way. For example,

(1) At any given moment, the proportion of people who are living common-law, or are single parents, is small. However, during a lifetime, a large proportion of the adult population passes through these statuses. Cohabitation and single parenthood prove to be brief but common experiences, not—as many believed—rare and semi-permanent ones. (See Burch, 1985; Moore, 1989.)

(2) At any given moment, the proportion of people who are unemployed is large. However, for most, unemployment is a brief and common experience. For a minority—the chronically unemployed—frequent and long-term unemployment occurs whenever the economy worsens. It is they who are pushed into poverty when jobs become scarce. What's more, we can identify who these high-risk people are (Shaw, 1985).

The most common research design in sociology is cross-sectional analysis. A **cross-sectional study** gathers evidence on subjects at just one point in time. The researcher tries to discover and explain the pattern of associations among variables. However, it is difficult to sort out causes from effects, because the data give no clue about the time sequence. The researcher cannot know which variable changed first—presumably, it is the cause—and which changed next (and is therefore the effect). Moreover, a problem of "spuriousness" may arise: in cross-sectional analysis, it is more difficult to determine whether both the (supposed) cause and effect are both the result of a third factor researchers are failing to measure.

This research design remains attractive because of low cost and easy execution. The researcher has to collect data only once, which means he or she can afford to collect a lot of data at one time, rather than thinner data on several occasions. Consider the following example of a cross-sectional survey.

Common sense says that it is better to be rich than poor, famous than unknown, and powerful than powerless. But are high-income people really more satisfied with life, as lay-wisdom tells us? Canadian research by Atkinson (1980) says "No; your income makes only a small difference in overall life satisfaction." Income does influence people's satisfaction with their financial situation. Not surprisingly, people with high incomes are more satisfied financially (with income, standard of living, and savings). However, it does not necessarily make people happier in other areas such as interpersonal relationships and self-development (Campbell, 1980).

Most surveys find only a modest relationship between levels of income and overall life satisfaction. The belief that money can buy you happiness is, for the most part, a myth. After reviewing hundreds of cross-sectional surveys from around the world, Dutch sociologist Ruut Veenhoven (1984: 397) reports that "current beliefs on happiness are based on presupposition rather than on accumulated experience." Veenhoven's efforts remind us that no single cross-sectional study can be conclusive. Testing a theory with cross-sectional data means finding support in many bodies of data and many past studies. Even so, at least four problems remain once we have established the lack of a correlation between income and happiness. They have to do with non-findings, the sequence of causation, spuriousness, and meaning.

Non-findings

In general, finding little or no relationship between variables tells us less than finding the presence of a relationship. A non-finding always allows for the possibility that we have failed to measure one or more of the variables in an appropriate way. For example, "satisfaction" or "happiness" may not mean what we thought it did.

Sequence

Does our finding prove what we think it does: namely that income has little or no effect on happiness? Or does it really prove that happiness has little or no effect on income—a much easier result to believe in.

EXHIBIT 11.2

RESEARCH AND IMAGINATION

C. Wright Mills (1959: 211) wrote that the sociological imagination requires an ability to shift playfully from one perspective to another. "It is this imagination . . . that sets off the social scientist from the mere technician."

You can stimulate your sociological imagination

by deliberately inverting your sense of proportion. If something seems very minute, imagine it to be simply enormous, and ask yourself: What difference might that make? And vice versa, for gigantic phenomena. What would preliterate villages look like with populations of 30 millions?

Try some of the following exercises to develop your own sociological imagination. For example, ask yourself how Canadian society would change if . . .

(a) nobody ever died, (or, instead, if no one lived more than twenty years), or
(b) people could transport themselves instantly from any place on earth to any other, or
(c) everyone changed their gender once a month, or
(d) people had to live on the income their next-door neighbour earned, or
(e) parents-to-be could select precisely the characteristics their child(ren) would have, or
(f) at age ten, children could choose who they wanted to live with, or
(g) all government leaders were chosen by lottery, or
(h) employees were paid the highest salaries for the most disagreeable, disgusting, or dangerous work, or
(i) no one could inherit savings, property, or wealth, or
(j) no one could live with their spouse for more than one year, or
(k) intelligent robots were granted full citizenship status

Source: C.W. Mills *The Sociological Imagination.* New York: Oxford University Press, 1959, p. 211

Spuriousness

Is there a missing third factor that obscures the real relationship between income and happiness? Consider the interview situation. People are telling interviewers about their lives and, as in any conversation, they are likely to want to put a pleasant face on things. Perhaps people do not want to look (or feel) like losers in the eyes of the interviewer. Our culture says people should be happy – they should think positively – and should avoid looking like losers. So, whatever they really feel, some people will emphasize how happy they are.

Meaning

Whatever our conclusion about the statistical relationship, we gain little insight into the processes of becoming and remaining happy from a cross-sectional survey. What does happiness really mean to these respondents? How do they stay happy under difficult circumstances? We learn nothing about these important questions from this design.

Single case analysis

The study of a single case – whether a single person, a group or a society – has a great deal of appeal. **Single case analysis** is a type of research design that involves a detailed, in-depth examination of a single example of a class of phenomena. By getting to know a lot about that single case, we learn not only about the "why" of something, but also about the "how." That is, we learn more about the process by which a cause creates an effect.

Single case analysis is reasonably common in sociology, although less common than in certain applied fields like clinical psychology, social work, and management studies. The reason sociologists shy away from it is because you cannot be certain that the case you have studied truly represents all of the cases you might have studied. So you run a great risk when you try to generalize from these findings to other cases.

The problem is simple to understand. Suppose you are a visitor from outer space. Your spacecraft crashes just outside 243 Fourteenth Avenue in Sometown, Canada and while you wait for the repair ship to arrive, you decide to study earthlings. Disguising yourself in the shape of a retired gentleman, you spend the day watching and talking to the first human being you meet. You learn quite a lot about that person; but are you justified in telling your fellow space-creatures about humans in general? Not really. No one person you could have studied could stand in for the whole human race, because people vary in a great many ways.

One solution is simply to make a smaller claim for the truth value of what you have discovered. Instead of calling your work an explanatory, or theory-testing, project, you might be wiser to call it an exploratory, or theory-building, project.

Another is to test the observed data – especially data as they vary over time – against two or more competing theories. Robert Yin (1984) calls this process "pattern matching." One theory will predict a certain sequence of changes over time; another theory, a different sequence. The theory that matches the observed sequence best is the (more) valid explanation. Yin (1984:

111) cites research by Donald Campbell (1969) as one example of this strategy.

Campbell examined the effect of the 1955 reduction in Connecticut's speed limit. There were claims that the reduction had led to a decline in the number of fatalities and, in fact, there was a decline in the year following the change in speed limit. But Campbell's research showed that over a ten-year period, this decline was within the range of normal fluctuations in fatalities.

If the theory that a lowered speed limit lowered fatalities was valid, it would have produced a large, one-time only decline immediately after the speed limit came into effect. This did not happen: therefore, the theory was not supported *by this single case*. However, we have no licence to generalize from Connecticut to all jurisdictions, or from speed limits to other kinds of legislation (for example, seat-belt or gun laws).

We are in a slightly stronger position if we conduct a type of single case analysis called deviant case analysis. **Deviant case analysis** is a research design that studies a single case that fails to conform to an expected pattern. By failing to support a given hypothesis, the case forces us to revise and enrich the original hypothesis.

We start a deviant case analysis by conceding that there is some truth to the theory we are testing. For example, recall our findings about the non-relationship between income and happiness. For reasons already stated, we feel we need more insight into this finding: particularly, to determine sequence, eliminate spuriousness, and understand its human meaning. To do this, we select a deviant case for study.

We could start with a study that focused on a particular subpopulation, such as the very rich or the very poor. For example, Diener, Horowitz, and Emmons (1985) sampled people from *Forbes* business magazine's list of the wealthiest Americans, and compared them with people selected randomly from telephone directories. Those agreeing to participate completed a questionnaire about life concerns and life satisfaction.

In this survey, wealthy respondents prove to be happy a higher percentage of the time, score significantly higher on two different life-satisfaction scales, and report significantly lower levels of "negative affect" – that is, unhappiness. Not all the wealthy are happy, of course; in fact, some are just as unhappy as the unhappiest ordinary person sampled. Further, few respondents, whether wealthy or ordinary, believe that money is a major source of happiness.

This research found that wealthy and ordinary people also differ in what satisfies them. Wealthy respondents more often mention self-esteem and self-actualization as sources of their satisfaction, while ordinary people more often mention food, shelter, and other basic human needs and safety concerns as sources of satisfaction.

In sum, this research has challenged the conventional wisdom and shown that very rich people really are happier than everyone else. Perhaps that is because they never have to worry about the things the rest of us worry most about. Perhaps it is because they can afford to concentrate their attentions on self-esteem and self-actualization much more than the rest of us. Still, we have little sense of the process of becoming and being happy.

Here, the single case method of study would help. It encourages closely detailed work and a deep understanding. Consider, for example, historian Michael Bliss' long biography of Canada's first millionaire, Sir Joseph Wesley Flavelle (Bliss, 1985). Flavelle rose from humble origins to become exceptionally rich and powerful. What we learn from his biography is the great importance of Methodist religion in his life. No Ebenezer Scrooge, Flavelle was actively involved in the life of his church and carried his religious beliefs into all his secular activities. His religion not only encouraged him to participate in social and political activity, it congratulated him on his good works and success.

Armed with this insight, we can consider a new theory for testing. The theory might run as follows: for most people, income has little effect on happiness. For people with a high income, money has a positive effect on happiness if they (a) see their income as a heavenly reward or proof of their merit, and (b) use their income to engage in socially gratifying (and religiously meaningful) activities. Stated otherwise, Scrooge was miserable not because he was rich but because he was socially isolated and irreligious (just as Dickens suggested!).

Note how much richer our understanding of the relationship between income and happiness becomes when we move from multiple case to single case analysis. People are no longer treated as "units of analysis" whose "variables" are manipulated: instead, they are complex systems of thought and action. Having said that, we have no more right to generalize our results from data on Flavelle than does the space creature we mentioned earlier. With deviant case analysis, we have enriched our theory and found some new variables. We must study them more systematically with experimental, quasi-experimental, or correlational methods. With single case analysis we have only explored, not explained, happiness in a general sense.

MEASUREMENT

Measurement scales

Measurement is a process of finding the extent, size, or degree of something. Quantitative sociological research depends on its ability to measure things: the rate of suicide, the degree of integration of people into society, the level of satisfaction with life, and so on. Unfortunately, measurement is often very difficult, especially when the variables to be measured are abstract concepts such as satisfaction, alienation, segregation, and inequality.

Measuring concepts well means, first, developing an operational definition of those concepts. An **operational definition** links the meaning of a concept to procedures for measuring it. An operational definition of intelligence, for example, would be the score obtained on a set of specific questions answered in specific ways. The IQ score reflects the method used to measure intelligence. There may be something else we mean by intelligence that is independent of the means we use to measure it but, without a specific measure, the concept cannot be used for quantitative research.

In order to measure particular traits and characteristics, we need to identify variables which can be scaled. Scales are systems of units arranged in steps or degrees, allowing the researcher to assign numbers to observed events or responses. After reducing them to number scores, the researcher can manipulate response patterns to bring out whatever relationships exist among

There are many sources of information, or data, about popular values and sentiments that permit sociologists to study causes and effects unobtrusively.

them. There are a number of ways in which this can be done.

One of the most common types of scales developed by sociologists to arrange variables is a **nominal** or **categorical scale**. A nominal scale is used to arrange a set of categories that we cannot order from high to low, large to small. For example, to the question "What language do you speak at home?", people may answer English, French, German, Polish, Italian, Greek, and so on. A score on a nominal scale simply indicates the category into which an individual falls. We would not say that speaking English gives one a higher or lower score than speaking Greek. The numbers we would assign to these scores would simply identify them and allow us to correlate language spoken with other social characteristics.

An **ordinal scale** contains categories that do range from high to low, so that movement along the scale indicates an increasing or decreasing size on some dimension. For example, eligible answers to the question "How often do you telephone your grandmother?" may include "very often," "occasionally," and "rarely." We know that "very often" is more often than "occasionally" and that "occasionally" is more often than "rarely." This ordering, from high to low, is what characterizes an ordinal scale.

Like an ordinal scale, an **interval scale** contains categories that range from high to low. In the ordinal scale we cannot be certain of the distance between categories. We do not know if the person phoning his grandmother "very often" does so eight times as often as the person who phones his grandmother "occasionally," or if the person phoning his grandmother "occasionally" does so only twice as often as the person who phones "rarely." In an interval scale, the distances or intervals between neighbouring categories are the same.

Finally, a **ratio scale** has both characteristics of an interval scale—hierarchical ordering and equal distances between categories—and one more as well: an absolute zero point.

On an interval scale, respondents cannot indicate a complete absence of something: of work satisfaction or telephone calls to grandmother, for

EXHIBIT 11.3

GOOD DESCRIPTION: A FIRST STEP

Explanation is the main job of pure research, but good description is often the job of applied research. The importance of good description is illustrated by a research project a sociologist conducted on behalf of a Canadian school board.

Each year that school board distributes millions of dollars of special aid to "inner-city" schools. Inner-city schools have more problems than other schools: they are often old and under-equipped. They often have more trouble getting the equipment or repairs they need and recruiting high-quality teachers.

Compared to the average, inner-city students tend to come from poorer economic backgrounds and typically have more trouble doing well at school. They often live in crowded housing. Often they are recent immigrants or members of visible minorities. Their parents may have received little formal education. Sometimes the family has broken up by separation or divorce, and only one parent is living at home. Inner-city children may grow up experiencing high rates of family instability, frequent parental unemployment, economic and social discrimination, and a general sense of hopelessness.

The sociologist's job was to analyze data on all the students of all the primary and secondary schools in the city and measure the "inner-cityness" of each school population. A ranking of all schools, from most to least "inner-citylike," resulted. On the basis of this ranking millions of dollars were distributed among the city's schools. No wonder accurate description was needed. What would you have measured if you were advising the school board on how to divide up the money?

example. For some variables, no absolute zero exists. For example, no one has absolutely no intelligence, energy, or physical attractiveness. Judgments on these issues are always bound to be relative. However, in a great many cases, absolute zero does exist. Perhaps you earned absolutely no dollars last month and telephoned your grandmother zero times last week. Maybe no one among the people you know will name you as their "best friend." Where an absolute zero does exist, it is better to use a ratio scale than any other.

Unobtrusive measures

Remember that research is a social enterprise. Even physicists, who study inanimate objects, realize that the act of measurement itself can disturb the thing being measured. As a result, researchers may never be able to get a truly accurate measure of something in its natural state. If this is true of atoms and molecules, imagine how serious the problem is when studying people. For this reason it is often important that the measurement process itself be unobtrusive. An **unobtrusive measure** is one in which there is no interaction between the investigator and the people being studied. Because it does not require interaction, the responses of the people studied are not likely to be "reactive."

EXHIBIT 11.4

DESCRIBING "TYPES OF PEOPLE"

Market researchers have long studied teenage lifestyles to figure out what types of teenagers buy what kinds of things. Doing so means first distinguishing different "types of teenagers." Townsend (1985) came up with the following groups. Are you on this list?

GREASEBALLS—The boys wear brown jackets and tractor caps. The girls sport heavy makeup and tight sweaters. Also in the Greaseball segment are Headbangers, who wear chains and black concert shirts that say "Twisted Sister."

RAH-RAHS—This segment includes jocks, their boy- or girl-friends, and people who wish they were jocks. Rah-Rahs are popular conformists with few intellectual or political interests. They used to include Preppies, a disappearing teenage segment.

NEW WAVERS—Also popular, but more involved in current events, New-wavers are fashion-conscious in an attention-getting way: all their clothes carry an Esprit label. They are emulated by Pseudo-wavers who don't quite make it.

BRAINS—These are the smart kids, arrogantly articulate and fiercely competitive for high grade-point averages. They are the driving force behind the student newspaper and known to outsiders as Encyclopedias.

ZOBOS—Mostly female, Zobos are distinguished by their high political consciousness and studied bag-lady fashion look. You may see one in a long skirt made from an Indian bedspread and high laced-up hiking boots. Zobos spend a lot of time demonstrating solidarity with the Third World.

RESISTORS—They defy classification or fashion identification, evident in their uniform of T-shirts, sweatshirts, and chinos. Their message is that they are totally unaware of image, being above such trivia.

Source: Adapted from Bickley Townsend "Psychographic glitter and gold" © *American Demographics*, November 1985. Used with permission.

People are not only objects of sociological study, they are students of their own lives. People know when researchers are studying them. They judge the purpose and meaning of questions they are asked, and answer in ways that relate to the researcher's goals. In short, people play a role when they are aware of being studied. Sometimes they give the researcher answers they think the researcher is looking for; sometimes they give the researcher the exact opposite, to shake the researcher up a bit. Sometimes they think about things they have never considered before, and are transformed by the research process. In none of these cases is the respondent a passive object of study.

It is very difficult for researchers to do much to avoid or minimize such reactions from the people they study. It is far better to avoid the problem than to have to remedy it. That is where unobtrusive measures come in. Sociologists look for unobtrusive measures and often find them. They already exist in nature, if we are willing to look.

In their classic work on the topic, *Unobtrusive Measures*, Webb et al (1966) discuss the strengths and weaknesses of several types of unobtrusive measure. One type is the "physical trace," the proof of erosion or accretion. A pathway worn through grass, over a carpet, or even on wood or stone shows where a great many people have been heading. By definition, the best-worn path is most popular; sociologists might want to find out why. Likewise, the largest line-up, the most graffiti or pennies in a wishing well—these accretions show where the most people (or the most active people) are spending their time. Again, sociologists might want to find out why.

A second type of unobtrusive measure is the archival record, particularly any running record officially collected for public use. This includes records of births, deaths, and marriages; tax records, Census forms, court records, and records of Parliamentary debate. It also includes the mass media—television, newspapers, and books—and the arts. The problem with such data is that they were created for a reason other than research, at another time: their meaning is by no means always certain.

A third type of unobtrusive measure is offered by data that are usually not part of the public record, such as sales records, institutional records, and personal documents (such as diaries, letters sent and received). Such data have often been used in inventive ways. However, they provide only partial evidence and need to be pieced together with a critical eye, if used at all. For example, it is not at all certain that what a person says in a suicide note really explains the suicide. It is likely but not certain that a rise in the sales of weight-reducing or smoke-ending products proves a growing popular concern with health.

Other forms of unobtrusive research include the observation of external physical signs (beards, tattoos, clothing, expressive movements), physical locations (for example, clustering *versus* segregation), and the sampling of overheard conversation.

SAMPLING

Surveys and sampling

As we have seen, there are many ways to measure things in sociological research, yet no matter how you choose to measure something, you cannot expect to measure it for everyone. The population of Canada, let alone the population of the world, is simply too large. This is why researchers study samples of people, not entire populations.

A **population** is the set of all individuals who share some specific characteristic of interest to the researcher: for example, they may all be Canadians or merely people who are over 45, speak Chinese at home, play bridge for recreation, or drive sports cars. We define a population in relation to the specific research question we want to answer. Every research project may imply a different population.

A **sample** is a relatively small number of people drawn from the population of interest. Almost all research studies samples, not total populations. Pure research by academic sociologists, market research, political polls, labour market surveys by government—all use samples which may represent no more than one percent of the population under study, or even less.

Even with a sample that comprises only a small percentage of the total population, great accuracy is possible. Estimates of the total population characteristics from a small sample are no more than few percentage points off in 19 times out of 20, if the sample is drawn correctly. Thus, samples are accurate enough for most purposes, as well as being convenient and relatively cheap.

The only time that sampling is *not* used in social research is when perfect accuracy is necessary and cost is no consideration. In practice, this is possible in only one case: a national Census of Canada, carried out on the total population once every ten years. However, for reasons of cost, the Census asks each household member only a few questions. A 20% sample of the population that is questioned at the same time yields more complete and sociologically interesting information.

Yet even when Statistics Canada tries to survey the whole population of Canada, as in the Census, many people are missed: possibly five or ten percent of the population. The Census is most likely to miss fugitives, transients, illiterates, and people living in someone else's household. In short, a Census is likely to miss the poorest, youngest, and least educated portion of the Canadian population.

Another reason to sample rather than study an entire population is to avoid "contaminating" the pool of respondents. Every time we study a person, we risk changing his or her thoughts and behaviour. For many reasons, it is better to study people who have not been studied previously. However, the more surveys researchers conduct, and the more people they study, the harder it becomes to find people to study who have been untouched by research.

Types of samples

Of the many ways to draw a sample of the population, some are better than others. The question to be answered will define a suitable sample. Cost and the time available determine the feasibility of using one sampling method rather than another.

The simplest type of sample is a **convenience (or availability) sample**. People who are accessible or willing to participate in the survey make up the sample. Interviewers station themselves in a public place—a busy street-corner, an airport waiting room, a museum lobby or large shopping centre, for example—and ask everyone who passes to answer a few questions. A convenience sample is likely to represent the population that passes through that public place fairly well.

For this reason, a convenience sample is good for generating new ideas, trying out measurements, and getting very preliminary research findings: for exploring the problem. It is never good enough to test a theory.

Another easy but imperfect method is to use a **snowball sample**. A **snowball sample** is made up of individuals referred to the researcher by others already in the sample. Think of a snowball rolling downhill, getting bigger as it goes; that is how a snowball sample grows.

The obvious advantage of a snowball sample is its ease and low cost. A less obvious advantage is its usefulness in finding rare or hidden subjects. Imagine trying to put together a sample of cocaine users, chess players, Gypsies, or parents of children with leukemia. It would be much easier to sample them through networks of similar people than by advertising in the newspaper, stopping people on a street corner, or telephoning names drawn at random from a phone book. Where researchers are studying illegal or deviant behaviour, an introduction to the potential subject by an existing subject may make all the difference between cooperation and a refusal.

However, as with the convenience sample, we cannot be sure a snowball sample really represents all members of the population. Sociologists will use a snowball sample cautiously and for purposes of exploration, not explanation.

A third type of sample is the quota sample. A **quota sample** begins by defining categories that are in the same proportion as one finds in the population, then draws a certain number of respondents within each category. Suppose we want to study attitudes toward a more traditional school curriculum. We know that the population of the school district is 51% male, 49% female; 25% Catholic and 75% Protestant; 90% native-born and 10% immigrant; and so on. To get our sample of 100 adult respondents, we will continue selecting available people until we have 100 with the same "statistical profile" as the population.

In some ways, this sampling method is much better than the pure convenience sample. For example, it is more likely than the convenience sample to yield a variety of characteristics and opinions. However, we have no guarantee that people sampled in this way accurately represent the opinions of the whole population.

To avoid unwanted biases, good surveys use randomly selected samples. Researchers draw **random samples** from the population so that every member has an equal chance of being selected for the survey. To draw a **simple random sample** at your college, we would start with a complete list of all the students. Blindfolded, we would draw names out of a hat until we had the number of names we needed. Or we would assign an identification number to every name and use a table of random numbers, or a computerized random number generator, to select the sample.

A **systematic sample** is just as good. If we need a sample of 100 people and there are 5000 students at your college, we would select our first respondent on the list randomly, then select every 50th name after that. Like the simple random sample, the systematic sample avoids introducing a bias into the selection process. Everyone has the same chance for an interview. However, in both cases pure chance may fail to give us enough cases of a kind we need: enough graduating students, handicapped students, or students in a particular field of study, for example. To prevent this from happening, we would use a stratified sample procedure.

Stratified sampling divides the population into categories (or strata) according to a characteristic of interest—in this case, let's say field of study. In general, the stratifying variable should be a major independent variable in your study. Then the researcher samples randomly within each category, using either the simple random or systematic sampling method. Doing this ensures we will get no fewer (or more) respondents in a given category than are to be found in the population; and we will have chosen them without bias. In effect, a stratified sample is an unbiased version of the quota sample we discussed earlier.

Finally, there is the **cluster sample**, which divides the population into geographic locales, then samples randomly within each locale. The cluster sample is like a stratified sample in which the stratifying characteristic is location. Like the stratified sample, it is relatively unbiased. However, once a researcher chooses locales for sampling, people outside those locales have no chance of being studied. Like the convenience sample, the cluster sample reduces the costs associated with distance and travel. It is particularly useful, then, if distances are large, as in a national survey. Smaller distances do not require cluster sampling or justify it.

DATA COLLECTION STRATEGIES

Sociologists collect many different kinds of data and collect them in a variety of different ways. This section will briefly touch on five particular data collection strategies: secondary data analysis, participant observation, content analysis, interviewing, and questionnaires.

Secondary data analysis

Sociologists often collect data first-hand to answer a question they are posing. However, they often also use data other researchers have collected to answer other questions. **Secondary data analysis** examines and interprets data that have been gathered by another researcher or by the federal government. For a small cost, researchers can buy computer-readable tapes of data from the 1986 mini-Census or the monthly Labour Force Survey, for example. Statistics Canada currently makes available scores and perhaps hundreds of high quality data tapes for both academic research and market research. Indeed, scholars outside government probably analyze government-collected data more thoroughly than anyone else.

Secondary analysis of data collected by other academics is also common. Archives such as the one at York University (Toronto) enable scholars to share with one another the data they have collected. Given the enormous costs of collecting survey data, sometimes in the millions of dollars, such data sharing is sensible and desirable.

The disadvantage of secondary data analysis is that these data were not collected with the researcher's goals in mind. For example, government-collected data rarely contain many of the variables that interest sociologists. Government data usually measure economic and demographic variables but shy away from data on people's feelings and attitudes. Government researchers avoid asking sensitive or intimate questions that might embarrass the Government if a Member of Parliament attacked a Statistics Canada survey in Parliament.

Participant observation

Observation has a longer history than any other form of social research. Since all of us can observe, it is also the easiest and least expensive form of research. But observation by itself can and usually does lead to distortions. We tend to "read into" a situation more than might be there, or else we fail to note subtle cues, gestures, or meanings we do not know enough to catch. Because observation has so many limitations, sociologists make use of a particular variation known as participant observation to gain first-hand information on

Advertisements in magazines and newspapers provide sociologists with good evidence of changing attitudes and values; they also promote social change.

Mature executive, not quite bald, seeks female of any shape or size who enjoys game shows and platonic sympathy sessions. Send photo with reply.

Submissive, super-thin young man seeking well-fed woman for tumultuous encounters.
Please call, 555-5555.

Widower in quest of second spring. Chooses not to take control or be controlled. Genteel female 30+, please call 555-5555.

Compassionate, feminist man seeks an intelligent woman unencumbered with outmoded attitudes or a barndoor-sized behind. Reply in writing, Box 0000.

In search of harmony. Decent guy seeks decent girl.
Call 666-6666.

FEMALE Sleek, sultry, blonde, seeks down-to-earth, muscular male for lasting relationship. Send colour photo with reply. Bambi, 555-5555.

Interesting, open-minded couple, thirtysomething, wish to meet same to research the effects of French wine in an uncontrolled environment. Please reply to Box 0000.

Well established, handsome, married male executive, 65, is searching for a sweet young thing, early 20s, to share occasional weekends at chalet. Reply to Box 000 with photo.

Outgoing, professional woman with love of tennis, skiing, music and theatre seeks male professional in 40s with similar outlook. Call after 6. 555-5555.

forms of social interaction and social processes.

Participant observation is a method of gathering data that requires the sociologist to become a participant in the social group being studied. Because the researcher takes part in the activities of the group, he or she gains an insight into the subjective understandings of the group members.

The people being studied are usually unaware of being studied, and so they are more likely to behave in a typical, non-reactive manner. The participant observer might hang out with hustlers in bars (Prus and Sharper, 1977), go to synagogue with orthodox Jews (Shaffir, 1974), smoke marijuana with jazz musicians (Becker, 1963), befriend slum kids (Whyte, 1961), or work in a mental hospital (Goffman, 1961).

This research method assumes that researchers cannot understand something fully without intimately experiencing it first-hand. The method relies heavily on the skills, feelings, insights, and intuition of the researcher. Since his or her subjective understanding of the situation is critical, the results are findings that one cannot easily generalize to other groups or the population at large. Still, participant observation provides a useful alternative or supplement to survey research—which rarely includes observation of actual behaviour—and to experimental research—which observes behaviour in an artificial setting.

In participant observation, the sociologist acts as both object (i.e., participant) and subject (i.e., observer) of the research process. This double role causes conflict and confusion for the new researcher. It also runs a double risk of distorting the research. On one hand, by participating in the group, a researcher risks taking on the world-view of that group and losing an objective sense of what the group is doing. On the other hand, by observing the group while participating in it, the researcher risks changing the very processes he or she has set out to study.

Like all activities—law, medicine, social work, journalism, and the ministry, for example—that require an intimate knowledge of people's lives, participant observation raises many ethical questions. How should the sociologist treat illegal behaviour, whether confessed or observed? How should the sociologist respond to vicious and immoral behaviour? How should the researcher deal with conflicts and coalitions within the group, and whose side should he or she take? There are no simple answers to these questions. That is why participant observation is much harder to learn and teach than any other type of research method.

Nevertheless, while participant observation is difficult, it has produced a large legacy of excellent research. This particular research style was popularized among sociologists at the University of Chicago in the 1920s and came to be the method of choice for microsociologists such as symbolic interactionists. One microsociologist, Erving Goffman, produced such provocative and insightful research reports from his observations that his books are among the best-selling sociology books to date (see, for example, Goffman 1959, 1961).

Content analysis

Content analysis involves analyzing the content of communications. They may include private letters, books, speeches and conversations, scripts of TV shows, comic books, magazine articles, and popular songs. The researcher picks out the main themes and classifies them according to a predetermined set of categories.

The researcher chooses particular categories for classifying the data to illuminate the issues under study. For example, a researcher (Wilson, 1977) may study how women are stereotyped in magazine articles. Are they portrayed as less intelligent and more vain than men, or as sexual toys "created" for the pleasure of men? Answering these questions will mean classifying and analyzing the content of many articles in a consistent, systematic way.

Content analysis requires researchers to make judgments, both when drawing up lists of categories and when classifying the data according to those categories. Sometimes people classifying or *coding* the content will judge the material differently. For example, in analyzing the content of children's television programs, different coders may use different criteria for deciding what constitutes a "display of violence or aggression." They may also differ in the way they measure the intensity of the supposed display of violent behaviour.

The ways around this problem are, as always, preventive and remedial. To prevent the problem, the researcher must train the data coders thoroughly in how to use the coding scheme that has been devised. To remedy the problem, the researcher will check the consistency of the coded material: whether it seems to shift over time, and whether some coders are providing results that vary a great deal from the other coders' results. Some badly flawed codework will have to be discarded and redone.

Interviews

Interviews are another important method of gathering data in sociology. In an **interview**, an interviewer asks subjects questions in a face-to-face encounter or over the telephone. An interview may collect qualitative or quantitative data, and it may ask structured or unstructured questions.

A **structured interview** asks each respondent a standard set of questions in the same form and the same order. This type of interview often forces the respondent to choose from among predetermined choices. Some questions may also be open-ended, allowing the respondent to answer in his or her own preferred way. An **unstructured interview** is more flexible than that. There are more open-ended questions the interviewee can answer freely. The interviewer often follows up on answers, to gain more insight into the interviewee's views and feelings.

Structured interviews permit the researcher to easily tabulate and analyze responses on a computer. Unstructured interviews provide data that are harder to compare across respondents. As well, unstructured interviews are particularly liable to errors resulting from poor interviewing skills. As with content analysis, these problems are more easily prevented than remedied afterwards. To prevent them, researchers must carefully select and train their interviewers and evalute the material they are collecting as the research goes on.

Questionnaires

Researchers often use **questionnaires** in surveys, too. They are sets of questions given to respondents and designed to collect answers to the research question. Usually questionnaires are sent by mail and filled out by the respondent without the assistance of an interviewer.

A questionnaire can be short—a few questions—or very long—running to dozens or even hundreds of questions. The longer a questionnaire is, the less likely a respondent is to complete it or even begin filling it out. This fact encourages the researcher to make a questionnaire as short and appealing as possible, and to offer the respondent incentives for completing the questionnaire.

The researcher must avoid asking questions that are ambiguous or offensive, or that fail to permit a wide variety of responses. Ambiguous questions on a political attitude questionnaire might include "How much do you prefer

Mulroney over Broadbent because he is more charismatic?", or "Would you vote for the Liberals if they supported free trade but opposed the Meech Lake accord?" Unambiguous questions will use familiar words and ask the respondent to make only one judgment at a time.

Questionnaires can offend respondents very easily. Since getting and keeping their cooperation is always a problem, the researcher must avoid offending them at all costs. Questions about personal income, intimate behaviour, religious beliefs, and relations with close relatives risk offending respondents most. However, such questions are less likely to offend people in a face-to-face interview.

Questions offering too narrow a range of answers are hard to avoid, since it is difficult to anticipate how widely people's views will vary. One way around this is by using open-ended questions. However, the answers to these questions must then be coded for analysis—a costly and error-prone procedure. Open-ended questions also slow down the rate at which respondents can answer, and therefore reduce their willingness to cooperate. The best way to prevent such problems is by pre-testing the questionnaire on people who are not part of your sample and re-writing troublesome questions.

Some people are less likely to fill out a questionnaire than others. Even in a well-planned questionnaire survey, the response rate may fall well below 50%, meaning that half of the sample or more are failing to provide the data requested. This forces us to ask whether the non-response is random or systematic. Response bias can seriously mar a study's validity.

Suppose you are using a questionnaire to study attitudes towards the Conservative Party. Only half the questionnaires are completed and returned. Of these, 90% of the respondents indicate they voted for a Conservative candidate in the last election. With such results you will be unable to learn much about the views of Liberal and NDP supporters. People who responded may even be the strongest supporters of the Conservative party and you will have learned little about moderate Conservatives. You know that your respondents do not represent the entire voting population but you cannot tell precisely how the non-response of Liberals, NDPers, and moderate Conservatives has biased your data. Such studies are almost impossible to salvage.

The great advantage of collecting data by questionnaire is the low cost. In this way, a careful researcher can collect a lot of good-quality information for much less than an interview study would cost. It is for this reason that sociologists have thought, learned, and written a great deal about questionnaire construction.

CLOSING REMARKS

In this chapter we have really only scratched the surface as far as sociological research is concerned. Even so, we have presented what may seem to be a bewildering number of methods for doing research and a large inventory of issues to keep in mind in order to assure that it is good research. Why this largesse? Why do sociologists not agree on a common set of methods they can apply to all research problems? The reason is that sociologists study such a wide variety of social phenomena that no one set of methods and no simple set of guidelines are appropriate for all of them. As you have already seen in earlier chapters, sociology's field is extraordinarily wide and the issues with which it deals are both diverse and complex. Sociologists have made good use of all these methods to uncover a wide variety of facts about social life.

Few of you reading this book will become practising sociologists. But, as we noted at the beginning of this book, you are all sociologists of a kind. If we have accomplished nothing else we hope that we have helped you to understand some of what is going on around you and have helped to stretch your sociological imagination.

This is an extraordinary time in human history. We have, quite literally, the ability to blow ourselves to bits. Or, failing that, to poison the air and the water, and ourselves. All of us have a responsibility to understand what is going on around us. Sociologists have an important role to play in this "information revolution," a revolution not only in the means of information but also in the content. It is this which makes sociology such an exciting area of study, no matter what specific area one specializes in. Understanding the world we live in, seeing the interrelations among the different segments of society, remaining true to the sociological imagination—this is what sociologists try to do. Combining all of these goals is a difficult task. It is also an exciting one.

Discussion Questions

1. You are likely to learn more by studying a small problem in depth than a large problem superficially. Show this in respect to a particular example: for example, how the presence of a child with leukemia may affect relations between family members *versus* the social effects of illness in Canadian society.

2. Discuss the arguments for and against experimenting on human beings. What useful information could we gain about social relationships only by experimenting? To what practical uses could we put this information?

3. Discuss how you might measure students' satisfaction with a college course they are taking. Should this measure be used to award promotions and cash bonuses for good teaching?

4. How would you select a sample of AIDS victims for study? That is, what type of sampling method would be most likely to produce the required number of cases? Then, what would be your preferred method of collecting data? Why?

5. (This one assumes fluency in English.) What difficulty would an extraterrestrial have content-analyzing this year's best-selling books and most-watched television programs? What would the being find out about North Americans by doing this?

6. Suppose a researcher has found that many juvenile delinquents have a very low opinion of themselves: especially their intelligence and appearance. Give two interpretations of this finding and devise research that would prove only one was right.

Data Collection Exercises

1. Collect published statistics on the average income and average education of people in (at least) ten different occupations. Which occupations seem to most closely follow the rule that education and income vary together? Which occupations seem to deviate most from that rule? Can you explain your findings?

2. Think of a sociological generalization—e.g., high education and high income go together—that you feel pretty certain is valid. After you figure out what the two deviant cases would be, select one for study. Find and interview a "deviant case" and come back prepared to explain your results.

3. Select a sociological question that interests you. Decide what data you would collect to answer that question if you had $1 million to do it. Now, imagine that you have to answer that same question using only the data published by Statistics Canada and available in your college library. What difficulties will you run into?

4. By observing your classmates, figure out which pairs of students are best friends, which are mere acquaintances, and which ones are enemies. Are your classmates generally friends of their friends' friends and enemies of their enemies' friends? Check your conclusions three months later. Has anything changed?

Writing Exercises

1. Write a 500-word letter to the sociological researcher we discussed earlier (p. 00) that explains why she will have to go to Portugal and interview Portuguese non-immigrants if she wants to prove that Portuguese immigrants are more dynamic and ambitious. Tell her, also, why Canadian-born people of Portuguese ancestry are irrelevant to her research.

2. See if you can make statistics lie. Collect some statistical data on a sociological problem that interests you (for example, some data on unemployment, or crime, or intermarriage). Now, see if you can interpret those data in two directly opposite ways. For example, in 500 words try to show that, viewed one way, the crime rate is rising but viewed another way, the crime rate is falling.

3. Design a short questionnaire to examine the extent and reasons for heavy drinking among college students.

4. Design an experiment to find out if teachers are more likely to give working-class students failing grades than they are to fail middle-class students. Describe how you are going to select subjects for the control and experimental groups. Generally, describe experimental procedure from start to finish.

Glossary

experiment—a research method designed to investigate the effect of one variable on another under well-controlled and regulated conditions. A control and experimental group are compared before and after the experimental treatment.

explanation—something that gives the meaning of, gives reasons for, accounts for, or interprets, something else

participant observation—a research technique in which the sociologist becomes a member of a group in order to observe and study it first-hand

population—the set of all individuals who share some specific characteristic of interest to the researcher. A **sample** is a relatively small number of people drawn from the population of interest.

prediction—the process of forecasting by inference from scientific, especially statistical, analysis of past events

quantitative data—data that are based on precise measurement and to which rigorous statistical methods can be applied. Conversely, **qualitative data** do not require, or do not lend themselves to, precise measurement.

research design—an orderly plan for collecting, analyzing, and interpreting data scale—a system of units arranged in steps or degrees. Measurement scales include nominal, ordinal, interval, and ratio.

snowball sample—a sample of individuals, most of whom have been referred to the researcher by others in the sample

variable—any trait, quality, or characteristic which can vary in size over time or across individuals or groups

Suggested Readings

Babbie, Earl *Observing Ourselves*. Belmont, California: Wadsworth, 1988. This author has written a number of enjoyable textbooks on sociology and social research. This one focuses on the methods of qualitative research and does so very well.

Converse, Jean M. and Howard Schuman *Conversations at Random: Survey Research as Interviewers See It*. New York: John Wiley, 1974. In this witty and entertaining book, the vignettes, anecdotes, and reflections of interviewers point out the dangers and challenges of data collection by interviewing.

Hammond, Philip *Sociologists at Work: Essays on the Craft of Social Research*. New York: Basic Books, 1964. This highly readable account of some important sociological research projects includes information that rarely comes to the attention of average readers.

Majchrzak, Ann *Methods of Policy Research*. Beverly Hills: Sage Publications, 1984. This easy-to-read book discusses the problems of doing social research for a client in an organizational setting. Identifying points of conflict and "stakeholders" is critical for the research to succeed.

Northey, Margot and Lorne Tepperman *Making Sense in Social Science*. Toronto: Oxford University Press, 1986. This short, friendly book aims at making students better essay-writers. Along with discussions of research design, theory making, measurement, and argument are general principles of style, usage, and grammar.

Whyte, William Foote *Street Corner Society: The Social Structure of an Italian Slum*. Chicago: University of Chicago Press, 1955. Whyte studied youth in an Italian slum of Boston during the 1930s. This is a classic study using participant observation and shows the strength and weakness of the method.

Yin, Robert K. *Case Study Research: Design and Methods*. Beverly Hills, California: 1984. This author develops the notion of "pattern-matching" to test competing theories on only one case—a single person or organization. The writing is energetic, the research advice offered practical and thorough.

References

Atkinson, T.H. (1980) "Public perceptions on the quality of life" in Statistics Canada *Perspectives Canada III*. (Catalogue No. 11-511E) Ottawa: Supply and Services, pp. 275-291

Baron, R. and F. Feeney (1977) "Juvenile diversion through family counseling — A program for the diversion of status offenders in Sacramento County" unpublished

Becker, H.S. (1963) *Outsiders: Studies in the Sociology of Deviance*. New York: Free Press

Bliss, M. (1985) *Canada's First Millionaire*. Toronto: McClelland and Stewart

Burch, T. (1985) *Family History Survey: Preliminary Findings.* (Statistics Canada, Catalogue No. 99-955) Ottawa: Supply and Services

Campbell, A. (1980) *The Sense of Well-being in America: Recent Patterns and Trends.* New York: McGraw-Hill Ryerson

Campbell, D. (1969) "Reforms as experiments" *American Psychologist,* 24, pp. 409-429

Diener, E., J. Horowitz, and R.A. Emmons (1985) "Happiness of the very wealthy" *Social Indicators Research,* 16, pp. 263-274

DiMaggio, P. and J. Mohr (1985) "Cultural capital, educational attainment and mate selection" *American Journal of Sociology,* 90 (6), pp. 1231-1261

Goffman, E. (1959) *Presentation of Self in Everyday Life.* Garden City, NY: Doubleday

_____ . *Asylums: Essays on the Social Situation of Mental Patients and Other Inmates.* Garden City: Anchor

Hunter, A. (1989) "Formal education and initial employment" *American Sociological Review*

Moore, M. (1989) "Female lone parenting over the life course" *Canadian Journal of Sociology* 14 (3), pp. 335-352

Prus, R.C. and C.R.D. Sharper (1977) *Road Hustler.* Toronto: Gage

Shaffir, W. (1974) *Life in a Religious Community: The Lubavitcher Chassidim in Montreal.* Toronto: Holt Rinehart Winston

Shaw, R.P. (1985) "The burden of unemployment in Canada" *Canadian Public Policy* XI:2, pp. 143-160

Urban and Rural Systems Associates (1975) *Juvenile Diversion Demonstration Program — Final Report Evaluation* Comprehensive Offender Program Effort (COPE)

Veenhoven, R. (1984) *Conditions of Happiness.* Dordrecht, Holland: Reidel Publishing

Webb, E.J. et al (1966) *Unobtrusive Measures: Nonreactive Research in the Social Sciences.* Chicago: Rand McNally

Whyte, W.F. (1961) *Street Corner Society.* Chicago: University of Chicago Press

Wilson, S.J. (1977) "The changing image of women in Canadian mass circulating magazines" *Atlantis* 2 (2), pp. 33-44

Yin, R.K. (1984) *Case Study Research: Design and Methods.* Beverly Hills, CA: Sage Publications

Visual Credits

The Bettman Archive (p. 21)
Ruth Bradley-St-Cyr (p. 159)
Jamie Bush (p. 356)
Canadian Pacific Railway (p. 242)
Canapress Photo Service (pp. 9, 27, 45, 268, 302, 315)
Canapress Photo Service/Bill Becker (p. 64)
Canapress Photo Service/G. Harvey (p. 132)
Canapress Photo Service/Bill Herriot (p. 337)
Canapress Photo Service/M. Van Manen (p. 112)
Canapress Photo Service/Ward Perrin (p. 202)
The Confederation Life Gallery of Canadian History (p. 172)
Kelly Dickson (p. 356)
Ford of Canada (p. 306)
General Motors of Canada (p. 323)
Lyn Hancock/Economic Development and Tourism (p. 293)
Health and Welfare Canada (p. 59)
Dick Hemingway (pp. 2, 68, 86, 127, 148, 164, 174, 182, 217, 323, 334, 349)
Tony Honeywood, De Havilland Aircraft Photographic Department
    (p. 238)
Little Apple Studios (Kathleen Bellesiles) (p. 323)
Elizabeth Long (p. 356)
Amy Lui-Ma (p. 356)
Maria Mascioli (p. 92)
National Archives of Canada/PA48697 (p. 291)
Orion Pictures Corporation (p.121)
Photo Researchers (p. 74)
Prentice-Hall Canada (p. 256)
Prentice-Hall Canada (p. 260)
Robin Rich (p. 92)
Sharon Sawyer (p. 356)
Alexander Tepperman (p. 224)
Tissot, James, *The Convalescent*, 1872, Art Gallery of Ontario, Toronto,
    Gift of R.B.F. Barr, Esq., Q.C., 1966 (p. 63)
Marta Tomins (p. 36)
Toronto Disarmament Network (p. 156)
Toronto Telegram Collection, York University Archives (p. 188)
UPI/The Bettmann Archive (p. 126)
Cover photo courtesy of Peter Van Rhijn / Super Stock / Four By Five

NAME INDEX

A

Aries, Philippe, 91
Armstrong, Hugh and Pat, 223
Atkinson, T.H., 63, 344
Adler, Freda, 117-18
Adorno, T.W., 190

B

Badets, J., 292
Baer, D., 63
Bailey, F.G., 103
Baldus, Bernd, 78
Baron, R., 343
Beaujot, R., 282
Becker, Gary, 232
Becker, H.S., 114, 356
Bell, D., 282, 319
Bennett, P., 338
Berger, Carl, 173
Berger, John, 53, 54
Bernard, Jesse, 222
Berry, J.W., 169
Bibby, R.W., 45, 87-88, 313
Blishen, B.R., 63
Bliss, Michael, 348
Bogardus, E.S., 189
Bourdieu, Pierre, 55
Braverman, Harry, 247
Breton, Raymond, 178
Brym, R., 181
Burman, P., 264
Burch, T., 217

C

Campbell, A., 224, 260, 344
Campbell, Donald, 347
Casale, A., 260
Chandler, D.B., 131
Chaplin, Charlie, 250
Chisholm, P., 230
Clement, Wallace, 153
Coale, A.J., 281
Cobb, J., 264-65
Conrad, P., 230
Cook, Thomas D., 340
Cooley, Charles, 79-80
Coser, Louis A., 28
Creese, G., 148

D

Dator, Jim, 317
Davis, Kingsley, 93, 140
Diener, E., 347
DiMaggio, P., 54
Durkheim, Emile, 17, 114, 246
    anomie, 261
    deviance, 104
    as founder of sociology, 16
    legal sanctions, 123
    moral density, 78
    organic solidarity, 247-49
    religious life, 314
    on social facts, 12-13
    totemic objects, 307-308
Dychwald, K., 90

E

Edmonson, B., 316
Edwards, Richard, 250
Eichler, Margrit, 207-208, 224, 232
Emmons, R.A., 347
Erikson, Erik, 77

F

Feeney, F., 343
Flavelle, Sir Joseph Wesley, 348
Flower, J., 90
Foot, D.K., 286, 295
Fox, B., 181, 223
Francis, Diane, 154
Freud, Sigmund, 76-77, 93
Frideres, J., 171, 224
Friedman, M. and R., 242
Friedson, E., 22

G

Garreau, Joel, 63
Gerber, Linda, 295
Ginzberg, E., 192-93
Glazer, Nathan, 168
Gleiter, Karen, 218
Goff, C.H., 117
Goffman, Erving, 94, 140, 356, 357
    impression management, 122-23
Grabb, E., 63
Gracey, H.L., 87
Gray, John, 43, 152
Guindon, H., 170
Guppy, N., 148
Gusfield, Joseph, 125, 141
Gwyn, Richard, 62, 63

H

Haas, J., 89
Hagan, John, 113, 121, 122
Hajnal, J., 232
Hawkins, F., 272

Heath, A., 147, 149
Heilig, G.K., 289
Henry, F., 192-93
Hirsch, E.D., 56
Hogan, Denis, 90
Hogarth, John, 127
Horowitz, J., 347

I

Inkeles, A., 245
Innis, Harold, 51

J

Johnson, H., 230
Johnson, T., 22
Johnston, W., 63
Jones, C.L., 23, 91
Jones, Jim, 135, 312-13

K

Kalbach, W.E., 292
Kett, Joseph, 92
Keynes, John Maynard, 244
Khomeini, Ayatollah, 315
Killian, Lewis, 305
King, M., 262
Korman, S.K., 220

L

Lachapelle, R., 181
Lerman, P., 260
Lerner, D., 328
Leslie, G.R., 220
Letkemann, Peter, 94
Lewis, Oscar, 57
Lewis, Sinclair, 315
Leyton, Elliot, 118-20
Li, Peter, 175, 184, 194, 342
Lipset, S.M., 62
Locke, E.A., 260
Lupri, Eugen, 116, 224, 231
Luther, Martin, 45

M

Mackie, M., 189, 191
Maclennan, Hugh, 170
McCormick, E., 136
MacLuhan, Marshall, 51, 326
Macpherson, C.B., 242
Malthus, Thomas, 275-78
Mandell, Nancy, 204, 205-206
Mann, B.J., 258, 259
Mann, M., 151
Marsden, L., 23, 91, 257

Marshall, K., 149, 223, 226
Martin, Wilfred, 85
Marx, Karl, 241, 246, 318
    alienation, 262-63
    capitalism, 243
    cash nexus, 242
    economic determinism, 138-39
    as founder of sociology, 15
    means of production, ownership of, 138,
        140
Matza, D., 121
Maurice, John, 287
Mead, George Herbert, 80-82, 95
Meadows, D.H., 277
Mehrota, S., 338
Meissner, M., 148
Merton, Robert, 18-19, 108-109
Methot, S., 157
Mills, C. Wright, 5, 345
    elite domination, 150
    sociological imagination, 5
Mitford, J., 255
Mohr, J., 54
Moore, M., 220, 222
Moore, Wilbert, 140
Moynihan, D.P., 168, 211
Murdock, George, 39

N

Newman, Katherine, 154, 155
Niosi, Jorge, 154

O

Oliver, Thomas, 29
Ornstein, Michael, 142, 158
Orwell, George, 137

P

Parker, Tom, 7
Parsons, Talcott, 166
    doctor-patient relationship, 14
    family functions, 204-205
Pavlov, Ivan, 73
Pearson, Lester, 61
Pettifer, S., 230
Piaget, Jean, 75, 95
    collective monologue, 80-81
    moral development, 77-78
Polanyi, K., 244
Pool, I., 220
Porter, John, 61, 154, 176, 292
    vertical mosaic, 165, 180-81, 182
Posterski, D.C., 45, 87-88
Prus, R.C., 356

R

Rainville, R.E., 136
Reasons, C.H., 117
Reichardt, Charles S., 340
Reitz, Jeffrey, 182, 192
Rice, R.W., 262
Richardson, Jack, 146, 154
Riesman, David, 28
Rinehart, J.W., 262
Rogers, J.W., 111
Runciman, W.G., 310
Runkle, Nancy D., 218
Rushton, Philippe, 70-71

S

Sapir, E., 49
Schlozman, K.L., 21
Schneider, J.W., 230
Scott, John F., 212
Seeman, M., 262
Sennett, R., 264-65
Simmel, George, 60
Shaffir, W., 89, 166, 356
Sharper, C.R.D., 356
Sheth, J., 338
Slater, Philip, 6
Smith, Adam, 241-42
Smith, D.H., 245
Spradley, J.P., 258, 259
Stone, Gregory, 140
Sumner, Graham, 46
Sutherland, Edwin, 109
Sykes, G., 121

T

Taylor, F.W., 248
Tepperman, L., 23, 91, 282
Thomas, D.S., 24
Thomas, W.I., 24, 167
Thrasher, F.M., 114
Toffler, Alvin, 59
Torge, J., 230
Townsend, Bickley, 351
Trewartha, G.T., 278

Tribe, Verna, 78
Trudeau, Pierre, E., 61, 113
Turner, Ralph, 305

U

Udry, J.R., 218

V

Vaughan, Diane, 206
Veenhoven, Ruut, 8, 344
Verba, S., 21
Von Glinow, M., 255

W

Watkins, S.C., 281
Webb, E.J., 352
Weber, Max, 246, 312
    authority, 136
    capitalism and values, 45-46
    charisma, 134-35
    class system, 139, 140
    conflict, 21
    as founder of sociology, 16-17
    rationalization, 247
    status, 143
    theory of bureaucracy, 249-50, 251
    verstehen, 24
Wells, W.D., 338
Westhuis, Kenneth, 13
White, C.A., 54
White, H.C., 54
Whyte, S.F., 356
    gangs, 114
Witts, A.E., 289
Wilson, S.J., 357
Wolfson, M., 232
Woodcock, George, 63
Woodside, A., 338
Wright, Erik Olin, 141-42
Wrong, D., 80, 95

Y

Yin, Robert, 346

SUBJECT INDEX

A

Acculturation, 177
Achieved status, 143
Adolescence, 92-93
Affirmative action, 150, 154
Agents of socialization
  defined, 84
  families, 84
  mass media, 87-88
  peers, 86-87
  schools, 85
AIDS, 288, 289, 318
Alienation, 262-65
  cures for, 265
Amalgamation, 177
Anomie, 248, 261
  adaptations to, 108-109
  defined, 16
  innovation, 109
  theory, 108-109
Anthropology, 11-12
Anti-Semitism, 188-89, 190
Apartheid, 166, 177
Artifacts, defined, 10
Ascribed status, 143
Assimilation, 177
Authoritarian personality, 190
Authority, 135-36
  legitimate, 135
Automation, 324
Aveyron, Wild Boy of, 72-73

B

Baby boom, 176, 284
Band, 170
Behaviour
  and learning, 73-74
  sexual, 113
Bilateral society, 214
Bilingualism, federal policies, 61
Biological determinists, 70
Blacks, 179-80
Bourgeoisie, 138
Bride-price, 209
British North America Act, 59-60, 61
Bureaucratic control
  horizontal vs. vertical jobs, 254
  varieties of, 254-55
Bureaucracy
  goal displacement, 252
  ideal, 252
  nature of, 251-53
  organizational control, 250-51
  vs. professionalization, 255-56
  Weber's theory of, 249-50

C

Calvinism, and rise of capitalism, 44-45
Canada, and U.S. compared, 62
Capital punishment, 124
Capitalism
  corporate, 243-45
  and religious values, 44-45
  Weber's view of, 17
Cartel, 242
Census, 274
Chain migration, 178
Charisma, 134-35
Childhood, 91-92
Children
  abuse of, 230, 231
  care and raising of, 224-26
Class, 15
  and juvenile delinquency, 120-23
  Marxist definition of, 21
  and social inequality, 134, 138-43
Class consciousness, 241
Cognitive development, 74-76
Cohabitation, 217-18
Cohort, 284
Collective monologue, 80-81
Colonization, internal, 171-72
Comprador elites, 150-51
Conditioning, 73
Conflict theory
  deviance, 105
  dominant ideology, 20
  primary socialization, 69-70
  as sociological paradigm, 19-21
Conjugal family, 215
Consanguine family, 215
Content analysis, 357-58
Control group, 342
Convergence thesis, 245-46
Correlational analysis, 343
Counterculture, defined, 52
Cricket, cultural basis of, 43
Crime
  causes of, 108-10
  defined, 110
  future, 322
  judgment, 127-28
  organized, 111
  leaving, 118, 120
  prosecution for, 126-27
  repressive vs. restitutive laws, 123-24
  responses to, 123-28
  victimless, 110

white-collar, 110, 117
who commits, 115-17
Criminals, female, 117-18
Cross-sectional study, 344
Cultural capital, 55-56
Cultural determinism, 71-72
Cultural diffusion, 58
Cultural innovation, 58
Cultural integration, 41, 50-51
  ethnocentrism, 51
  mass media, 50-51
Cultural literacy, 55, 56
Cultural pluralism, 59, 61
Cultural universals, 39-40
Cultural variation, 52-57
Culture(s)
  Canadian, 59-64
  defined, 37
  and ethnic survival, 182-84
  how they change, 58-59
  and human nature, 38-40
  ideal, 40-41
  importance of values, 44-46
  language, 49-50
  material, 41-42
  non-material, 41-42
  norms/folkways, mores, 46-48
  of poverty, 56-57
  real, 40-41
  shared symbols and meanings, 43-44
Culture shock, 58

D

Data collection, 355-59
  content analysis, 357-58
  interviews, 358
  participant observation, 355-57
  questionnaires, 358-59
Definition of the situation, 24
Demographic transition theory, 278
  fertility/mortality rates, 279
  limitations to, 281-82
  pre-modern population growth, 279-81
Demography, defined, 274-75
Dependency ratio, 284-85
Dependent variable, 339
Deviance
  benefits to society, 104
  causes, 108-110
  conflict theories, 105
  defined, 101
  functionalist approach, 103-104
  labelling perspective, 105-106, 108
  nature of, 101-103
  responses to, 123-28
  and social control, 102-103

and social resources, 122
Deviant behaviour
  crime, 110-12
  norm violations, 112
  social variations, 113
Deviation, 339
Differential association theory, 109
Diffusion, 320
Discovery, 318, 320
Discrimination, 191-93
  defined, 187
  index of, 193
  systemic, 193
Division of labour, 247
Divorce, 219-21
Dominant ideology, and cultural variation, 54-55
Domination
  charisma, 134-35
  patterns of, 134-36
  power/authority, 135-36
  and social inequality, 134
  symbols of, 136-38
Dowry, 209
Dyad, 14

E

Economic determinism, 138-39
Economic order, 239-40
Economics, 12
Ego, 76, 77
Egocentric, 75
Elite(s)
  comprador, 150-51, 153
  corporate, 152-53, 154
  defined, 150
  domination, 150-55
  mobility into, 152-55
  power, 150-51
Elmer Gantry, 315
Emergent norm theory, 305
Endogamy, 209-210
English Canadians, 169-70
Environmentalism, 316-17
Equalitarian family, 210-11
Equality of condition, 145
Equality of opportunity, 145
Ethnic groups
  boundary maintenance survival, 182-87
  in Canada, 168-76
  Charter Groups, 168, 169-70, 173
  defined, 167
  discrimination, 191-93
  distinctive symbols and concerns, 184-85
  European, 173-75
  institutional completeness, 178-80

institutional self-segregation, 170
language retention, 181
native peoples, 170-72
visible minorities, 175-76
Ethnic politics, 185-87
Ethnic relations, patterns of, 176-82
Ethnic stratification, 180-82
Ethnicity
defined, 167
reasons for survival, 168
Ethnocentrism, 51, 195
Eskimo, 169, 170
Evangelism, 315-16
Exchanges, expressive vs. instrumental,
212-13
Exogamy, 210
Experiment, 342-43
Experimental group, 342
Exploitation, 243
Extended family, 215

F
Fad, 307-308
False consciousness, 20-21
Family
as agent of socialization, 84
Canadian, 217
child care/raising, 224-26
conflict theory of, 205
as context for social life, 203-204
defined, 206
economic aspects of change in, 231-33
functionalist theory, 204-205
generation gap, 227, 229
modern, problems of, 222-31
patterns, 208-16
reconstituted, 222
single-parent, 221-22
spousal inequalities, 222-24
symbolic interactionist theory of, 205-206
types, 210,11, 215
violence in, 230-31
Family household, 208
Fashion, 307-308
Feral children, 72-73
Fertility
age-specific rates, 283
Canadian, 282-83
measuring, 283-86
total rate of, 283
Fertility rate, 279
Folkways, defined, 46
Folk wisdom, 7
Formal organization, 253
French Canada, BNA Act provisions,
59-60

French Canadians, 169-70
Functionalism, see Structural
functionalism
Fundamentalism, 314-315

G
Gender inequality, 137-38
and status, 143
Gender roles, 83
blurring of, 83-84
Gender socialization, 82-84
masculine/feminine ideals, 83
Generalized other, 81-82
Generation gap, 227, 229
Genocide, 177-78
Global change, 326-29
Groups, 4

H
Heterogamy, 213-14
High culture, defined, 53
Homogamy, 213
Human capital, 295
Humanities, 11
Hypothesis, 7, 8, 336

I
I vs. Me, 82
Id, 76
Ideology, 20, 54
Immigration to Canada, 173-75, 176
Imperialism, 328-29
Impression management, 122-23
Incest taboo, 47
Independent variable, 339
Indians
non-status, 171
registered (status), 170-71
Industrial Revolution, 240, 241-43
Industrial society, 245-47
Information revolution, 325
Innovations, 318
Institutional completeness, 178-80
parallelism, 185
Interaction, 22
Intermarriage, attitudes to, 186
Internalization, 80-82
game phase, 81
generalized other, 81-82
I vs. Me, 82
play phase, 80
preliminary phase, 80
Interviews, structured vs. unstructured, 358
Invention, 320
Canadian, 320-21

J

Juvenile delinquents, 116-17
  neutralization theory, 121-22
  and social class, 120-23

K

Kin group, 214
Kinship relationship, 214-16

L

Labelling theory, 105-106, 108
  primary vs. secondary deviation, 106
  stigma, 106
  recidivism, 123
Labour force, defined, 257
Labour market segments, 257-59
Laissez-faire, 241-42
Language
  and cultural determinism, 71-72
  defined, 49
  developmental approach to, 75
  and ethnic survival, 181, 182-84
  idioms, 75
  sexist, 49-50
Latent functions, 18-19
Laws, repressive vs. restitutive, 123-24
Learning
  and behaviour, 73-74
  developmental approach, 74
Legitimate domination, 249-50
Liberal democracy, 242
Life cycle, defined, 90
Life cycle squeeze, 225
Literacy, 50
Longitudinal study, 343
Low Income Cut-off Point, 156-57

M

Macrosociology, 4-5
Manifest functions, 18
Marital rape, 230
Marriage
  breakdown, 220
  defined, 209
  mate selection, 213-14
  and romantic love, 211-13
  steps of, 218
  types of, 209-11
Mass media, 50-51, 87-88
Mass murderers, profiles of, 118-20
Mass production, 240
Mate selection, 213-14
Matriarchal family, 211
Matrilineal society, 214
Matrilocal marriage, 210
Meaning, 346

Measurement, 348-52
  unobtrusive, 350-52
Measurement scales, 348-50
  interval, 349
  nominal, 349
  ordinal, 349
  ratio, 349
Mechanical solidarity, 249
Melting pot, 177, 180
Meritocracy, 154
Métis, 169, 170
Microelectronics, 323-36
Microsociology, 4-5
Migration
  churn rate, 292-95
  internal, 290
  international, 290
  patterns, 290-96
  pull factors, 290, 295-96
  push factors, 290-91, 295-96
  rate, 290
Modern Times, 250
Modes of production, 15
Monogamy, 209
Monopoly, 242, 243-44
Moral density, 78
Moral development, 76-78. See also
  Personality development.
Moral enterprise, 124-25
Moral entrepreneurs, 124-25
Morality
  autonomous, 77-78
  heteronomous, 77
Mores, 46
Mortality
  Canadian, 286-88
  endogenous causes, 288
  future patterns of, 288-90
Mortality rate, 279
Mosaic, 165
Multiculturalism, 59, 61

N

Native peoples, 170-72
  internal colonization, 171-72
Nativist groups, 173
Nature vs. nurture, 70-73
Negativism, 80
Neolocal marriage, 210
Net migration rate, 290
Neutralization theory, 121-22
Non-finding, 345
Norms, 46
Norm violations, 112
Nuclear family, 215

O

Objectivity, 8
Oligopoly, 244
Operational definition, 348
Organic solidarity, 247-49
Organizational control
  bureaucratic, 251
  simple, 250
  technical, 250
Overpopulation, 276-77
Oversocialized view of individual, 80

P

Panel study, 343
Paradigm(s)
  compared, 25-26
  conflict theory, 19-21
  defined, 17
  structural functionalism, 17-19
  symbolic interactionism, 22, 24-25
Parallelism, 185
Parent-child relationship, 214-16
Participant observation, 355-57
Patriarchal family, 210
Patriarchy, 223
Patrilineal society, 214
Patrilocal marriage, 210
Peer group, 86-87
Personality development
  internalization, 80-82
  looking-glass self, 79-80
  psychoanalysis, 76-77
  self, defined, 78-79
Plea bargaining, 126-27
Pluralism, 176-77
Political science, 12
Polling, political, 29-30
Polyandry, 209
Polygamy, 209
Polygyny, 209
Poor laws, 244
Popular culture, 53-54
Population growth
  carrying capacity, 276
  demographic transition theory, 278-82
  Malthusian dilemma, 275-78
  modernization, 278
  positive/preventive checks on, 276
  rate, 291
  zero, 277-78
Poverty, 156-59
  absolute vs. relative, 156
  causes of, 158
  culture of, 56-57
  feminization of, 157, 222
  public attitudes to, 158-59

Power, 135
Power elite, 150-51
Prejudice, 187
  social distance, 189-91
Prestige, 144
Price-fixing, 244
Primary labour market, 257
Primary socialization, 63
Professionalization, 255-56
Prohibition, 125
Proletariat, 138
Propaganda, 309
Protestant ethic, 17, 45
Protestantism, and rise of capitalism, 44-45
Psychoanalysis, 76-77
Psychology, 12
Public, defined, 308
Public opinion, 308-309

Q

Quasi-experiment, 342-43
Quebec, maintaining culture, 60-61
Questionnaires, 358-59
Quiet Revolution, 60

R

Race, defined, 167
Race relations, patterns of, 176-82
Racial groups
  in Canada, 168-76
  visible minorities, 168, 175-76
Racism, 195-96
  confirmation bias, 196
  personality type, 190
Recidivism, 123
Reference group, 86
Relative deprivation theory, 310-11
Religion
  as cultural universal, 39-40
  and ethnic survival, 183, 184-85
Religious movements
  evangelism, 315-16
  fundamentalism, 314-15
  millenarian, 314
  religiosity, 313
  routinization, 312
Remarriage, 221
Research
  applied, 29-30
  defined, 7
  market, 29
  political polling, 29-30
  program planning and evaluation, 30
  value-free, 10-11
Research design, 341-48
  deviant case analysis, 347

experiment/quasi-experiment, 342-43
experiment substitutes, 343-46
pattern matching, 346
single case analysis, 346-48
Reserve, 170
Resocialization, 94-95
Resource mobilization theory, 311
Retrospective theory survey, 343-44
Role expectations, 27
Roles, defined, 27
Romantic love, 211-13
Royal Commission on Bilingualism and
Biculturalism, 61
Rules of Thumb, 7

S

Sample
cluster, 355
convenience, 353
quota, 354
random, 354
simple random, 354
snowball, 353-54
stratified, 354
systematic, 354
types, 353-55
Sampling, 352-55
Sanctions, social, 47
Scales, 348
Scapegoats, 104
School, as agent of socialization, 85
Science, defined, 7
Scientific management, 248
Scientific method, defined, 7
Scientific research, 335-36
Secondary (marginal) labour market, 257
Segregation, 177
Self-segregation, 177
ethnic, elements of, 178-80
institutional, 170
Sequence, 345
Serial monogamy, 209
Sex, and assembly line, 6
Significant other, 79
Signs, defined, 43
Single-parent family, 211
Social change
evolutionary theories, 304-305
fads and fashions, 306, 307-308
microelectronics, 323-36
nature of, 303-304
new ideas and inventions, 318, 320-21
physical environment, 316-17
propaganda, 309
public opinion, 308-309
publics, 308

revolutionary theories, 305
sociology of, 304-308
technological innovation, 321-26
Social continuity (persistence), 304
Social control
defined, 102
and deviance, 102-103
formal/informal, 102
gossip, 103
Social determinism, 71-72
Social deviations, 112
Social distance, 189-91
Social diversions, 113
Social dynamics, 305
Social evolution, 326-29
differentiation, 326
integration, 326-27
Social facts, 12-13
Social inequality, 133
caste system, 140
and class, 138-43
conditions/opportunities, 145
conflict theory of, 138-40
pragmatic acceptance of, 151
structural functionalist theory of, 140
symbolic interactionist theory of, 140-41
types of, 133-34
Social institutions, defined, 26-27
Social interactionism, 24-25
Socialization
agents, *see* Agents of socialization
anticipatory, 88
cognitive development, 74-76
defined, 69
development of self, 78-82
gender, *see* Gender socialization
learning and behaviour, 73-74
over life cycle, 90-93
moral development, 76-78
nature vs. nurture, 70-73
secondary, 70
into student role, 87
workplace, 89
Social marginality, 89
Social mobility, 146-50
in Canada, 147-48
exchange, 147
horizontal, 147
intergenerational, 147
intragenerational, 147
structural, 147
vertical, 147
women's vs. men's, 148-49
Social movements, 305
defined, 309
relative deprivation, 310-11

religious, *see* Religious movements
resource mobilization, 311
sources of discontent, 310-11
types of, 311-16
Social relationship, 26-27
Social research
  cause and effect, 336
  conditional processes, 338
  data collection, 355-59
  description, 350, 351
  explanation and prediction, 336, 338-39
  measurement, 348-52
  multi-causal processes, 338
  population, 352
  qualitative/quantitative, 339-40
  sample, 352
  sampling, 352-55
  secondary data analysis, 355
  single case analysis, 346-48
  study design, 341-48
  variables, 339
Social resources, 122
Social sciences, 11-12
Social statics, 305
Social stratification. *See also* Social
  inequality.
  class system in Canada, 141-43
  education, importance of, 149-50
  elite domination, 150-55
  mobility within, 146-50
  poverty, 156-59
Social structure, 14
Sociological imagination, 5, 345
Sociology
  applied research, 29-30
  basic concepts, 26-27
  defined, 4
  differences from other social sciences,
    13-15
  history of, 15-17
  pure, 28
  as science, 10-11
Solidarity, 123
Specialization, 247
Spuriousness, 346
Status
  achieved vs. ascribed, 143-45
  defined, 143
  and racist/sexist prejudices, 136-38
  and social inequality, 134
  socioeconomic, 144
  and symbolic resources, 143-45
Status inconsistency, 144
Status politics, 125
Statuses, defined, 27
Stereotypes, 187-88

Stratification system, 133, 134
Structural functionalism
  and deviance, 103-104
  manifest vs. latent functions, 18-19
  primary socialization, 69
  as sociological paradigm, 17-19
Street crimes, 117
Subculture, 37
  deviant, 113, 114
Subeconomy, ethnic, 192
Subjectivity, 8
Submission, 134
  patterns of, 134-36
  symbols of, 136-38
Suicide, Durkheim's view of, 16
Suite crimes, 117
Superego, 76-77
Symbol, 22, 43-44
Symbolic interactionism, 22
  labelling theory of deviance, 105-106, 108
  primary socialization, 70
  as sociological paradigm, 22, 24-25

T
Taboo, 47
Technological determinism, 321
Technology, 50-51
Theory, 8
Total institution, 94

U
Underdevelopment, 329
Underemployment, 150
Units of analysis, 339

V
Values, importance of, 44-46
Variable, 339
Verstehen, 24, 25
Violence, domestic, 115
Violent predators, 117, 118
Visible minorities, 168, 175-76

W
Waitressing, 258
Wealth of Nations, The, 241-42
Work satisfaction, 260-61
Work, types of, 256-59
World System Theory, 327-29
Women
  abuse of, 230-31
  double ghetto, 223-24
  social mobility, 148-49

Z
Zero population growth, 277-78